**EUROPEAN HISTORICAL DICTIONARIES**
**Edited by Jon Woronoff**

1. *Portugal,* by Douglas L. Wheeler. 1993
2. *Turkey,* by Metin Heper. 1994
3. *Poland,* by George Sanford and Adriana Gozdecka-Sanford. 1994
4. *Germany,* by Wayne C. Thompson, Susan L. Thompson, and Juliet S. Thompson. 1994
5. *Greece,* by Thanos M. Veremis and Mark Dragoumis. 1995
6. *Cyprus,* by Stavros Panteli. 1995
7. *Sweden,* by Irene Scobbie. 1995
8. *Finland,* by George Maude. 1995
9. *Croatia,* by Robert Stallaerts and Jeannine Laurens. 1995
10. *Malta,* by Warren G. Berg. 1995
11. *Spain,* by Angel Smith. 1996
12. *Albania,* by Raymond Hutchings. 1996
13. *Slovenia,* by Leopoldina Plut-Pregelj and Carole Rogel. 1996
14. *Luxembourg,* by Harry C. Barteau. 1996
15. *Romania,* by Kurt W. Treptow and Marcel Popa. 1996
16. *Bulgaria,* by Raymond Detrez. 1997
17. *United Kingdom: Volume 1, England and the United Kingdom; Volume 2, Scotland, Wales, and Northern Ireland,* by Kenneth J. Panton and Keith A. Cowlard. 1997; 1998
18. *Hungary,* by Steven Béla Várdy. 1997
19. *Latvia,* by Andrejs Plakans. 1997
20. *Ireland,* by Colin Thomas and Avril Thomas. 1997
21. *Lithuania*, by Saulius Suziedelis. 1997
22. *Macedonia,* by Valentina Georgieva and Sasha Konechni. 1998
23. *The Czech State,* by Jiri Hochman. 1998
24. *Iceland,* by Guðmundur Hálfdanarson. 1997
25. *Bosnia and Herzegovina,* by Ante Čuvalo. 1997
26. *Russia*, by Boris Raymond and Paul Duffy. 1998
27. *Gypsies (Romanies),* by Donald Kenrick. 1998
28. *Belarus*, by Jan Zaprudnik. 1998
29. *Federal Republic of Yugoslavia,* by Zeljan Suster. 1999
30. *France,* by Gino Raymond. 1998
31. *Slovakia*, by Stanislav J. Kirschbaum. 1998
32. *Netherlands*, by Arend H. Huussen Jr. 1998
33. *Denmark*, by Alastair H. Thomas and Stewart P. Oakley. 1998
34. *Modern Italy*, by Mark F. Gilbert and K. Robert Nilsson. 1998
35. *Belgium*, by Robert Stallaerts. 1999
36. *Austria,* by Paula Sutter Fichtner. 1999

# Historical Dictionary of Belgium

Robert Stallaerts

*European Historical Dictionaries, No. 35*

The Scarecrow Press, Inc.
Lanham, Maryland, and London
1999

SCARECROW PRESS, INC.

Published in the United States of America
by Scarecrow Press, Inc.
4720 Boston Way
Lanham, Maryland 20706

4 Pleydell Gardens, Folkestone
Kent CT20 2DN, England



British Library Cataloguing in Publication Information Available

**Library of Congress Cataloging-in-Publication Data**

Stallaerts, Robert.
Historical dictionary of Belgium / Robert Stallaerts.
p. cm. — (European historical dictionaries ; no. 35)
Includes bibliographical references.
ISBN 0-8108-3603-3 (alk. paper)
1. Belgium—History—Dictionaries. I. Title. II. Series.
DH511.S73 1999
949.3'003—dc21 98-49221

∞™ The paper used in this publication meets the minimum requirements of American National Standard for Information Sciences—Permanence of Paper for Printed Library Materials, ANSI Z39.48–1984.
Manufactured in the United States of America.

ALLAERTS, ROBERT. ORDER NO: 000802BNZ
ORDER DATE: 02AUG2000

STORICAL DICTIONARY OF BELGIUM / ROBERT
ALLAERTS.

ROPEAN HISTORICAL

MAN & LITTLEFIELD P 1999 1 VOLS
59.50 CLOTH
108-3603-3 98-49221
135361
QTY ORDERED: 001
QTY SHIPPED: 001
730409/0036
CKWELL BOOK SERVICES

ALESTER COLLEGE 200610007 CUMC

F
I
R
M
O
R
D
E
R

# CONTENTS

# EDITOR'S FOREWORD

With an identity dating to Roman days, Belgium is an ancient country. At the same time, independent only since 1830, Belgium is a young state. Occupying northwestern Europe's linguistic, cultural, and commercial crossroads, Belgium is a nation whose history encapsulates much of Western social, political, and economic life. The great "isms" that have shaped so much of that life—Catholicism, Protestantism, clericalism, secularism, capitalism, socialism, centralism, federalism—have all swirled through Belgium. The country has endured centuries of foreign rule and suffered repeated invasions. As such, it is a land that has been rocked by conflict. Language divisions continue to engender discord. Yet in spite of—or because of—its history, Belgium is today a nation whose citizens esteem values of freedom, tolerance, and nonviolence. It is a leading participant in the drive toward European integration and close transatlantic cooperation. Its capital, Brussels, has become the center of regional and global organizations large and small. History has made modern Belgium a complex country, a paradoxical place at once both insular and cosmopolitan. Having recently redefined itself in adopting a regional structure of government, it is a nation that, as it becomes less national, becomes more international with each succeeding decade.

This *Historical Dictionary of Belgium* provides an overview of the history and current events of this remarkable country with an extensive chronology, a broad introduction, and entries that highlight many of the most significant people, parties, and organizations; describe the political and social institutions; and touch on the economy and culture of Belgium. This information is supported by a very comprehensive bibliography the readers should consult to learn more about the topics that interest them.

This volume was written by Robert Stallaerts, who was born and grew up in Belgium. His fields of study are moral science and economics and the way these issues affect each other in political participation and self-management. He worked at the Center of Ethics of the University of Antwerp for eight years. Now, he is engaged in a research project on health structures in Bosnia at the University of Ghent and a member of the Mercator Hogeschool in the same town. His earlier research in Yugoslavia resulted in another volume for this series, the *Historical Dictionary of the Republic of Croatia* (1995). We are very glad to present his expertise again in this, his home country.

Jon Woronoff
Series Editor

## ABBREVIATIONS AND ACRONYMS

| | |
|---|---|
| ABVV | Algemeen Belgisch Vakverbond—General Federation of Belgian Trade Unions |
| ACLV | Algemene Centrale van Liberale Vakbonden—Federation of Liberal Trade Unions |
| AGALEV | Anders Gaan Leven—Flemish Ecologists |
| BBI | Bijzondere Belastingsinspectie—Special Tax Inpectorate |
| BBC | Benoemings- en Bevorderingscollege—College for Appointments and Promotions |
| BDBH | Belgische Dienst voor Buitenlandse Handel—Belgian Service for International Trade |
| BEF | Belgische Frank/Belgian Franc |
| BENELUX | Economische Unie tussen België, Nederland en Luxemburg—Economic Union between Belgium, the Netherlands and Luxembourg |
| BLEU | Belgium-Luxembourg Economic Union |
| BSP/PSB | Belgische Socialistische Partij—Parti Socialiste Belge—Belgian Socialist Party |
| BRTN | Belgische Radio en Televisie - Nederlandstalige uitzendingen—Belgian Radio and Television - Dutch-speaking programs |
| BWP | Belgische Werklieden Partij—Belgian Workers' Party |
| CBF | Commissie voor Bank en Financiewezen—Commission for Banking and Finance |
| CBR | Conseil de Région Bruxelles Capitale—Raad van het Brusselse Hoofdstedelijke Gewest—Council of the Brussels Region |
| CCF | Conseil de la Communauté Française—French Community Council |

| | |
|---|---|
| CEPIC | Centre Politique des Indépendents et Cadres Chrétiens—Political Center of Independents and Christian Cadres |
| CGSLB | Confédération Générale des Syndicats Libéraux de Belgique—General Confederation of Liberal Trade Unions of Belgium |
| COCOF | Commission de la Communauté Française—French Community Commission |
| COCON | Commissie van de Nederlandse Gemeenschap—Flemish Community Commission |
| CRB | Centrale Raad voor het Bedrijfsleven—Central Economic Council |
| CRISP | Centre de Recherche Industrielle, Sociale et Politique—Center for Industrial, Social and Political Research |
| CRW | Conseil Régional de Wallonie—Walloon Regional Council |
| CSC | Confédération des Syndicats Chrétiens et Libres de Belgique—Confederation of Christian Trade Unions of Belgium |
| CVP | Christelijke Volkspartij—Christian People's Party |
| DM | Deutsche Mark—German Mark |
| EC | European Community |
| ECOLO | Walloon Ecologists |
| ECSC | European Coal and Steel Community |
| ECU | European Currency Unit |
| EEC | European Economic Community |
| EMS | European Monetary System |
| EMU | European Monetary Union |
| EURATOM | European Atomic Energy Community |
| EU | European Union |
| FDF | Front Démocratique des Francophones—Democratic Front of Francophones |
| FEB | Fédération des Entreprises Belges—Federation of Belgian Enterprises |
| FGTB | Fédération Générale du Travail de Belgique—General Federation of Belgian Trade Unions |
| FN | Front National—National Front |
| GATT | General Agreement on Tariffs and Trade |
| GIMB | Gewestelijke Investeringsmaatschappij voor Brus- |

| | |
|---|---|
| | sel—Regional Investment Company of Brussels |
| GIMV | Gewestelijke Investeringsmaatschappij voor Vlaanderen—Regional Investment Company of Flanders |
| KPB/PCB | Kommunistische Partij van België/Parti Communiste Belge—Belgian Communist Party |
| MIC | Mouvement Chrétien des Indépendents—Christian Movement of Independents |
| MOC | Mouvement Ouvrier Chrétien—Christian Workers' Movement |
| MPW | Mouvement Populaire Wallon—Walloon Popular Movement |
| NA | Nationale Arbeidsraad—National Labor Council |
| NATO | North Atlantic Treaty Organization |
| OECD | Organization for Economic Development |
| PL | Parti Libéral—Liberal Party (Brussels) |
| PLP | Parti de la Liberté et du Progrès—Party for Freedom and Progress |
| PMV | Participatie Maatschappij Vlaanderen—Flemish Participation Society |
| PNP | Partij voor Nieuwe Politiek—Party for New Politics |
| POB | Parti Ouvrier Belge—Belgian Workers' Party |
| PRL | Parti Réformateur Libéral—Liberal Reformist Party |
| PS | Parti Socialiste—Socialist Party |
| PSC | Parti Social Chrétien—Social Christian Party |
| PVV | Partij voor Vrijheid en Vooruitgang—Party for Freedom and Progress |
| RAD/UDRT | Respect voor Arbeid en Tijd/Union Démocrate pour le Respect du Travail—Respect for Labor |
| RDG | Rat der Deutschsprachigen Gemeinschaft—Council of the German Community |
| RTBF | Radio-Télévision Belge Francophone |
| RW | Rassemblement Wallon—Walloon Union |
| SERV | Sociaal-Economische Raad voor Vlaanderen—Social and Economic Council of Flanders |
| SHAPE | Supreme Headquarters for Allied Powers in Europe |
| SP | Socialistische Partij—Socialist Party |
| SRIW | Société Régionale d'Investissement de Wallonie—Regional Investment Company of Wallonia |
| TAK | Taal Aktie Komitee—Flemish Language Action Committee |

| | |
|---|---|
| ULB | Université Libre de Bruxelles—Free University of Brussels |
| UWE | Union Wallonne des Entreprises—Walloon Association of Enterprises |
| VBO | Verbond van de Belgische Ondernemingen—Association of Belgian Enterprises |
| VERDINASO | Verbond van Dietse Nationaal Solidaristen—League of Supporters of Dutch National Solidarity |
| VESOC | Vlaams Economisch en Sociaal Overleg Comité—Flemish Economic and Social Consultation Committee |
| VEV | Vlaams Economisch Verbond—Flemish Economic Association |
| VL BLOK | Vlaams Blok—Flemish Bloc |
| VLD | Vlaamse Liberalen en Democraten (1992- )—Flemish Liberals and Democrats |
| VNV | Vlaams Nationaal Verbond—Flemish National Union |
| VR | Vlaamse Raad—Flemish Council/Parliament |
| VTM | Vlaamse Televisie Maatschappij—Flemish Television Society |
| VU | Volksunie—People's Union |
| VOB | Verbond van Ondernemingen te Brussel—Association of Enterprises of Brussels |
| VUB | Vrije Universiteit Brussel—Free University of Brussels |
| VVOB | Vlaamse Vereniging voor Opleiding en Technische Bijstand in het Buitenland—Flemish Association for Training and Technical Assistance Abroad |

# CHRONOLOGY

| | |
|---|---|
| 58-51 B.C. | Julius Caesar subjects the Gallic tribes; among them are the Belgae |
| A.D. 406 | Germanic tribes cross the Rhine and conquer Gallia Belgica (Belgian Gaul) |
| 843 | The Treaty of Verdun divides the Carolingian Empire in three parts |
| 876 | Baldwin with the Iron Arm, Count of Flanders, builds a fortification in Ghent against the Vikings |
| 1012 | Emperor Henry II of the Holy Roman Empire grants Lotharinga to Duke Godefrey I |
| 1099 | In the First Crusade, Godfrey of Bouillon captures Jerusalem and is elected king |
| 1180 | Count Philip of Alsace builds the Count's Castle at Ghent |
| 1196 | Bishop Albert de Cuyck of Liège grants a charter proclaiming freedom of the individual and the right to a court trial |
| 1288 | Jean I of Brabant defeats the Archbishop of Cologne in the battle of Woeringen and gains control of Luxembourg |

| | |
|---|---|
| 1302<br>11 July | In the Battle of the Golden Spurs near Courtrai, the Flemish towns defeat the French army |
| 1312 | Charter of Kortenberg (Brabant) |
| 1316 | Peace of Fexhe (Liège) |
| 1356 | Charter of the Joyful Entrance (Joyeuse Entrée, Brabant) |
| 1357 | Treaty of Ath. Flanders gains Antwerp and Mechelen |
| 1369 | The Burgundian Duke Philip the Bold marries Margaret of Male, daughter of the count of Flanders |
| 1382 | In the Battle of Beverhout near Bruges, Philip van Artevelde of Ghent defeats the count of Flanders |
| | Charles VI of France triumphs over the Flemings under Van Artevelde's leadership in the battle of West Rozebeke |
| 1384 | In the person of Philip the Bold, the Burgundian dynasty commences its reign over Flanders |
| 1404/5 | John the Fearless succeeds Philip the Bold and Margaret of Male |
| 1419 | Philip the Good succeeds to John the Fearless |
| 1425 | Philip acquires Namur by purchase |
| 1428 | Reconciliation of Delft. Jacoba of Beieren cedes the hereditary rights to Holland-Zeeland and Hainault to Philip the Good |
| 1429 | Philip the Good acquires Namur |
| 1430 | Philip the Good marries Isabella of Portugal and institutes the Order of the Golden Fleece |

| | |
|---|---|
| 1430 | Joyful Entrance of Philip the Good into Brabant |
| 1433 | Jacqueline, countess of Holland, cedes Hainault to Philip the Good |
| 1441 | Philip the Good buys the Duchy of Luxembourg |
| 1453 | Philip the Good acquires Ghent through the battle and the Peace of Gavere |
| 1467 | Charles the Bold succeeds Philip the Good |
| | Six hundred Franchimonteses attack the camp of Charles the Bold and the king of France |
| 1473 | Charles the Bold establishes the highest Burgundian Court, the Parliament of Mechelen |
| 1477 | Charles the Bold, Duke of Burgundy, dies at the Battle of Nancy; his daughter, Mary of Burgundy, succeeds him |
| | The towns of Flanders force the "Great Privilege" on Mary of Burgundy |
| 1482 | Mary of Burgundy marries Maximilian of Habsburg and brings the Habsburg dynasty into the Low Countries |
| 1483 | At the death of Mary of Burgundy, Maximilian becomes regent of the Low Countries |
| 1493 | The Treaty of Senlis guarantees the neutrality of the prince-bishopric of Liège |
| 1494 | By the Peace of Cadzand, the Flemish towns lose their privileges |

| | |
|---|---|
| 1500 | Charles V, born at Ghent, will become king of the Netherlands, Spain and its colonies and German emperor |
| 1507 | Margaret of Austria assumes the regency of the Netherlands |
| 1522 | Adriaan Floris Boeyens crowned as Pope Adrian VI |
| 1529 | By the Treaty of Cambrai, France gives up its suzerainty over Flanders and Artois in favor of Charles V |
| 1530 | Mary of Hungary becomes regent of the Netherlands |
| 1540 | Charles V takes over the government of Ghent by the Concessio Carolina |
| 1548 | The Imperial Diet adopts the Augsburg Transaction. The Low Countries become independent within the Empire |
| 1549 | The Pragmatic Sanction unifies the inheritance of the Seventeen Provinces under one prince |
| 1555 | Charles V abdicates in favor of Philip II. His absolutist policy will provoke war and the secession of the northern provinces from the Low Countries |
| 1559 | Philip II promotes the town of Mechelen to an archbishopric |
| 1566 | The Iconoclastic Movement spreads throughout Flanders |

| | |
|---|---|
| 1567 | Armed Calvinist resistance is crushed at the battle of Oosterweel |
| 1568 | Revolt in the Netherlands; its prominent leaders Counts Egmond and Hoorne are beheaded in the Great Market of Brussels |
| 1572 | Plantin publishes his *Biblia Polyglotta* in Antwerp |
| 1576 | Pacification of Ghent |
| | Spanish Fury at Antwerp |
| 1577 | Installation of the Calvinist Republic in Ghent |
| 1578 | Battle of Gembloux, won by Don Juan of Austria, appointed governor of the Low Countries by Philip II |
| 1579 | Union of Arras in the south and Union of Utrecht of the northern provinces |
| 1581 | Plakkaat van Verlatinghe (Edict of Abjuration). Separation of the seven northern provinces |
| 1584 | Murder of William of Nassau |
| 1585 | Spanish troops under Alexander Farnese conquer Antwerp; the northern provinces close the Scheldt estuary |
| 1598 | Rule of Archduke Albrecht and Archduchess Isabella |
| 1609-1621 | Twelve Years' Truce |
| 1648 | By the Treaty of Munster, Spain recognizes the independence of the United Provinces |
| 1688 | War of the League of Augsburg. Louis XIV of France invades the Spanish Netherlands |

| | |
|---|---|
| 1695 | Bombardment of Brussels |
| 1701 | Beginning of the War of the Spanish Succession |
| 1713 | Treaty of Utrecht. France acquires maritime Flanders (Dunkerque), Gallician Flanders (Valenciennes), Philippeville and Thionville. The Spanish Netherlands come under the rule of the Austrian House of Habsburg |
| 1714 | Treaty of Rastadt and Baden. The Spanish Netherlands are surrendered to the Republic of Holland pending their transfer to Austria |
| 1715 | Barrier Treaty of Antwerp. The Spanish Netherlands are ceded to Austria |
| 1719 | Revolt led by Anneessens |
| 1740 | Maria Theresa succeeds Charles VI of Austria |
| 1745<br>11 May | Battle of Fontenoy. French begin the conquest of the Austrian Netherlands in the War of the Austrian Succession |
| 1748 | Peace of Aix-La-Chapelle<br>Austrian Netherlands restored to Habsburgs |
| 1780 | Joseph II of Austria succeeds Maria Theresa |
| 1789 | Brabant Revolution led by Vonck and Vandernoot |
| 1790 | Leopold II of Austria succeeds Joseph II |
| 1794<br>26 June | The French general Jourdan defeats the Austrians at the battle of Fleurus |
| 1795<br>1 October | The National Convention in Paris decrees the annexation to France of Liège and the former Austrian Netherlands |

| | |
|---|---|
| 1798-1799 | Peasants' Revolt in Flanders against the French revolutionary regime |
| 1799 | Napoleon Bonaparte becomes first consul of the French Republic |
| 1801 | Concordat between Pope Pius VII and Napoleon Bonaparte |
| 1804 | Napoleon Bonaparte proclaims himself emperor |
| 1814 | The Great Powers secretly agree in London to unite the Low Countries into the Kingdom of the Netherlands |
| 1814-1815 | The Vienna Congress grants official recognition to the United Kingdom of the Netherlands |
| 1815 | Second Treaty of Paris |
| | William I becomes king of the United Kingdom of the Netherlands |
| 1830 | The Belgian Revolution deposes William I. The Provisional Government proclaims Belgian independence on 4 October |
| 1831 21 July | Leopold I of Saxe-Coburg takes an oath to the constitution as the first king of Belgium |
| 1838 | The Flemish writer Hendrik Conscience publishes "The Lion of Flanders" |
| 1839 | William I recognizes the independence of Belgium |
| 1865 17 December | Leopold II accedes to power as second king of Belgium |

| | |
|---|---|
| 1873<br>17 August | Law on the use of the Flemish language in the courts of Flanders |
| 1884 | Formation of a homogeneous Catholic government |
| 1893 | Introduction of universal plural-vote male suffrage. |
| 1898 | The Equality Law recognizes the Dutch language as one of the two official languages of Belgium |
| 1909<br>23 December | Albert I becomes the third king of Belgium |
| 1912 | Letter to the king by the Walloon politician Jules Destrée, saying "there are no Belgians" |
| 1914-1918 | Belgium, with the exception of the IJzer area, is occupied by the Germans during World War I |
| 1918<br>11 November | Armistice; the day becomes an annual national holiday |
| 1919 | Universal single-vote male suffrage is introduced |
| 1920 | Belgium signs a military convention with France |
| 1930 | The State University of Ghent adopts Dutch as its language of instruction |
| 1932 | Dutch becomes the exclusive language of administration and of instruction in primary and secondary education in Flanders |
| 1934<br>23 February | Leopold III ascends the throne as the fourth king of Belgium |
| 1936 | Belgium renounces military pact with France |

| | |
|---|---|
| 1940-1945 | Occupation by the Germans in World War II |
| 1944<br>20 September | Prince Charles takes up the regency of Belgium during the absence of and the period of controversy following the return of Leopold III |
| 1947 | The Benelux Treaty is signed by Belgium, the Netherlands and Luxembourg |
| 1949 | Women gain the right to vote |
| | Belgium joins NATO |
| 1950<br>20 July | End of the regency and return of Leopold III to the throne |
| 1 August | Leopold III abdicates in favor of his son Prince Baudouin |
| 1951<br>17 July | Baudouin takes the oath to the Constitution as king of Belgium |
| 1957 | Treaty of Rome. Belgium becomes one of the six founding members of the European Economic Community (EEC) |
| 1960<br>30 June | Independence of Belgian Congo (Zaire) |
| 20 December | Strike against the Unity Law |
| 1961-1962 | Flemish nationalist marches on Brussels |
| 1962<br>8 November | Law on the language frontier and the statute of the communes Voeren (Les Fourons) and Komen (Comines) |
| 1968 | Language riots focusing on Flemish demands for a linguistic division of the University of Leuven |

| | |
|---|---|
| 1970 | The First Constitutional Reform redefines the position of Flanders, Wallonia and Brussels |
| 1973 | The Cultural Council of the Dutch-language Community issues a decree stipulating Dutch is the only language to be used in employer-employee relations in Flanders |
| 1980 | Second Constitutional reform<br>Signing of Dutch Language Union Treaty between the Netherlands and Belgium |
| 1987<br>15 October | The government of the Flemish Christian Democrat Wilfried Martens falls over the problem of Voeren |
| 1988 | Third Constitutional reform |
| 1990 | |
| 4 April | The government announces the king will not sign the new law on abortion and declares that he will step down from the throne for a short transitional period |
| 15 May | French-speaking teachers demonstrate in Brussels; unrest in French education lasts until November |
| 5 June | Prime Minister Martens exposes the proposed governmental measures based on the report of the "Gang" (Bende) commission |
| 28 October | Elections take place for the Council of the German Community |
| 30 November | Minister of Education Coens presents his reform of the universities |
| 1991 | |
| 9 January | The Flemish Council approves the Plan on the Sanitation of the Flemish soil |

| | |
|---|---|
| 12 January | Minister of Environment Kelchtermans signs the contract with Aquafin for the environmental cleanup of the waters in Flanders |
| 6 February | The French-speaking Socialists (PS) approve at their congress a strengthening of the Walloon Region |
| 16 February | The Flemish government approves a sum of 5.7 billion BEF for the recycling of Limburg |
| 19 March | The Flemish Council approves the new decree on the Flemish-speaking Radio and Television |
| 6 June | The Senate approves a law granting Belgian nationality to all immigrant children of the third generation under 18 |
| 12 June | Parliament accepts a constitutional reform giving female ascendants the right to accede to the throne |
| 20 June | Nurses manifest their "white anger" in the streets of Brussels |
| 24 November | Black Sunday: in the national elections the extreme right-wing party of the Flemish Bloc wins seats in Parliament |
| 1992 | |
| 28 February | Jean-Luc Dehaene reaches an agreement between Christian Democrat and Socialist parties to form a new government; the government program foresees further fundamental constitutional reform of the state |
| 30 September | St. Michael's Agreement on constitutional reform |
| 1993 | |
| 14 July | Fourth Constitutional reform agreed on in Parliament |
| 31 July | Unexpected death of King Baudouin who is suc- |

| | |
|---|---|
| | ceeded by Albert II |
| 1996 | |
| 20 June | The Chamber approves changing the law on parliamentary immunity |
| 28 June | The government approves an action plan against organized crime |
| 13 August | Marc Dutroux is arrested for kidnapping of minors; this opens revelations and sparks public debate on the Dutroux case and the functioning of justice |
| 25 August | Flemish radicals provoke irregularities during the 69th Pilgrimage to the IJzer memorial near Diksmuide |
| 30 August | The ministerial council agrees to adapt the Law Lejeune on the conditional release of prisoners |
| 10 September | King Albert asks in an unusual press declaration that the cases of Dutroux and Cools should be thoroughly investigated and that controls on justice should be introduced |
| 20 October | Massive crowds parading in the White March in the streets of Brussels express their solidarity with the parents of missing children |
| 5 November | The central social deliberation on a new interprofessional agreement breaks down |
| 2 December | The president of the Chamber, Langendries, proposes to call together party-presidents in a States-General to reform the institutional system |
| 6 December | The Government presents the so-called St. Nicholas plan to reform justice |

| | |
|---|---|
| 1997<br>23 January | Two leaders of the Socialist Party, Merry Hermanus and François Pirot, are arrested on charges of corruption in the Dassault case |
| 2 February | More than 35,000 demonstrate in Tubeke for government intervention to save the Forges de Clabecq declared bankrupt |
| 26 February | Spitaels resigns as president of the Walloon Assembly |
| 27 February | The director of Renault unexpectedly announces that the Vilvoorde factory will be closed and 3,100 will be unemployed on 31 July |
| 15 April | Marc Verwilghen, president of a Parliamentary Commission, presents the report on the Dutroux Case in the Chamber of Representatives |
| 18 April | Parliament approves the report of the Dutroux Commission |
| 7 October | The Flemish minister Peeters declares that the law for the provision of linguistic facilities will be more stringently applied |
| 14 October | The Court of Cassation withdraws by the so-called "Spaghetti"-arrest the Dutroux case from investigating judge Jean-Marc Connerotte |
| 31 October | Federal Agriculture Minister Karel Pinxten confirms the rumors of the country's first case of mad cow disease |
| 20 November | Vic Anciaux of the People's Union resigns as state secretary from the Brussels' government |
| 1977<br>5 December | Ex-Socialist Party (PS) president Guy Spitaels confesses he gave his secretary permission to open an |

| | |
|---|---|
| | account in Luxembourg in which Dassault money was received |
| 1998 | |
| 14 January | Paul Marchal presents his Party for New Politics |
| 7 March | Former PSC-president Detrez launches a new party |
| 23 April | Dutroux escapes; Minister of Justice St. De Clerck and Interior Minister J. Vande Lanotte resign |
| 24 April | T. Van Parys and L. Tobback replace the resigning ministers |
| 28 April | Prime Minister Dehaene reads the new government declaration on the reform of police and justice before Parliament |
| 2 May | Belgium is officially accepted as a member of the European Monetary Union (EMU) along with 10 other European countries |
| 24 May | Eight parties conclude the Octopus agreement on the reform of justice and the police forces |
| 25 May | Philippe Maystadt accepts the presidency of the PSC |

Base 800030 (A01911) 6-85

# INTRODUCTION

In 1830, the inhabitants of the southern part of the United Kingdom of the Netherlands revolted against King William I. The National Congress declared independence and proclaimed the installation of a parliamentary monarchy. The European powers placed Leopold I of Saxony-Coburg on the throne of Belgium. The monarch took an oath of loyalty to the new Constitution on 26 July 1831. The new country, Belgium, united the Dutch-speaking people of Flanders and the French-speaking people of Wallonia around its bilingual capital, Brussels.

Belgium lies along the North Sea in northwestern Europe, surrounded by France, Luxembourg, Germany and the Netherlands. Its area covers 56,538 sq. km. The frontier along the North Sea is 66 km. long. Belgium's total frontier length amounts to 1,445 km. The average temperature in 1997 was moderate at 10.8 degrees, and there were also the usual 180 days of rain. The north of the country enjoys a sea climate, the south a very moderate land climate.

In 1997, 10,170,000 residents were recorded in the state registers. Of these 951,000 lived in the region of Brussels, 5,899,000 in the Flemish region and 3,321,000 in the Walloon region. This last region also counts 70,000 members of the German community. There are 912,000 foreigners registered in the country, more or less evenly distributed over the three regions. They are more concentrated in the capital, as this region stretches out over only 162 sq. km.

Administratively, the parliamentary monarchy of Belgium comprises three economic regions, three linguistic communities and 10 provinces. The economic regions, which enjoy large competences and have their own government and council or parliament, are the Region of Flanders, the Region of Brussels and the Walloon Region. The linguistic communities are the Flemish, the Walloon and the German Community. In Flanders, the competences of community and region were brought together in one body. The small German-language community has been appended to the Walloon Economic Region.

Physically and geographically, Belgium can be divided into two large regions. The north of Belgium was partly reclaimed from the sea and a broad low-lying coastal plain still extends behind a belt of dunes. The plain gradually rises to the south into the hills of the Ardennes, where a maximum height of 694 meters is reached at Botrange. In detail, the following geographic zones can be distinguished: the Anglo-Belgian Basin comprising the Central (Bas) plateaus, the plain of Flanders and the Campine (Kempenland); Belgian Lorraine, a part of the Paris Basin in the west and southwest; and the Ardennes, a part of the Hercyninan Belt.

The Ardennes is a plateau with dense forests and is deeply cut by the Meuse River and its affluents. The higher points contain peat bogs and swamps. East of the Meuse lies a large depression called Famenne, east of it the Fagne. South of the Sambre-Meuse Valley lies the Condroz plateau. Still further south of the Ardennes lies a series of hills, the Belgian Lorraine. The sandy and clay soils of the Central plateaus cover the north of Hainaut, the south of Brabant and the Hesbaye plateau of Liège. The lowest part of the country, the plain of Flanders, comprises maritime Flanders, bordering the sea and the dunes, and the interior part of West and East Flanders. In the northeast lies the Campine in the provinces of Antwerp and Limburg.

Belgium's economy is a classic model of a highly developed and export-oriented market economy. The gross national product (in market prices) amounted to 8,428 billion Belgian francs (BEF), and national income to 6,732 billion BEF in 1996. In the same year, Belgium's imports (CIF) reached 4,994 billion BEF, exports (FOB) were 5,247 billion BEF. Thus, Belgium, is a small open-market country that is clearly highly export- oriented.

On 30 June 1994, employment in the primary sector (agriculture) amounted to 92,000, in the secondary sector (industry) to 991, 000 and in the tertiary sector (trade, services and administration) to 2,594,000 persons. Around 500,000 full-time unemployed were registered that year and 48,000 more were part-time unemployed. As in all highly developed countries, the tertiary sector is predominant. In 1995, the various sectors contributed as follows to gross domestic product: agriculture, forestry and fishing, 1.5 percent; manufacturing and mining, 23.9 percent; construction, 5.4 percent; electricity, gas and water, 2.7 percent; distribution, 13.2 percent; finance and insurance, 6.2; transport and communications, 8.4; public administration and defense, 8; education and health, 8.9 percent; other services, 16.8 percent.

In 1993, the gross national product was regionally distributed as follows: Flanders, 58.6 percent; Wallonia, 25.6 percent; and Brussels, 15.8 percent. Thus, the industrial center of the country shows a marked shift from Wallonia to Flanders and Brussels.

## History

### The Roman Period (58 B.C.-A.D. 481)

A much debated question centers on the origin and ethnic nature of the Belgians. Archeologists did considerable work, but it remains difficult to create a reliable picture of the early situation of the territory that later comprised the Kingdom of Belgium. The coastal land was regularly inundated by the sea and was full of swamps and rivers. The population in the last centuries before the Christian era were described as Celtic tribes.

In *De Bello Gallico* (The Gallic Wars) of Julius Caesar, the Celtic tribes are enumerated by name. Caesar wrote that of all tribes, the Belgians were the bravest. Of course, this description tends toward myth-making, as his writing serves as a glorification of his own war campaign.

By the conquest of Caesar (58-51 B.C.), Gallia Belgica (Belgian Gaul) was established. It was divided into *civitates*, administrative units that conformed to the earlier territories of the different tribes. On the great crossroads, Roman fortifications and towns appeared, such as Tournai, Arlon, Tongeren, Maastricht and Nijmegen.

For some time, the Romans tried to defend their eastern frontier along the Rhine. From the third century on, Germanic tribes invaded the Roman Empire and assimilated the Celtic tribes, as well as the fewer Romanized elements. Out of this melting pot developed the Flemish or Dutch language.

Most Romans withdrew south of the main road Bavai-Cologne. The southern part of the present territory of Belgium therefore became much more Romanized. The road grew into an early forerunner of the present language frontier, as French developed from the language of the Romanized population.

As a consequence of these historical developments, on the later Belgian territory, there were always at least two language groups; such a thing as a common Belgian language never existed.

## The Merovingian and Carolingian Kingdoms (481-843)

At the beginning of the sixth century, the already weakened grip of the Romans on their Gallic territories ended. A Frankish dynasty from the region of Tournai, the Merovingians, built up a new kingdom with its center south of the present Low Countries. Merovée and especially his son Clovis are considered to be the fathers of modern France. During his military and diplomatic campaign, Clovis adopted Christianity. However, central administration was guaranteed largely by personal allegiances. The territory slowly disintegrated under the later Merovingians. In the developing feudal system, the lands in possession of local leaders could easily tear apart, and in fact regularly did so.

A new dynasty, the Carolingians, gave a new impetus to centralization and the restoration of Romanized culture. Charlemagne, born in 768 near Liège, managed to revive the Holy Roman Empire on Western European soil. He subdued the Frisians and the Saxons among other Frankish tribes and unified the whole territory of the ancient Frankish Kingdom. He renewed the efforts at Christianization and had himself crowned by the pope of Rome. He encouraged arts and literature and founded court schools. This Carolingian renaissance was, however, short-lived.

## The Early Middle Ages (843-1012)

The reign of Charlemagne's son, Louis the Pious (Louis le Pieux, 814-840) ended with the division of the empire into three kingdoms. The frontiers were laid down by the Treaty of Verdun (843). The treaty determined the basic political configuration of Western Europe up until modern times and influenced centuries of political and military action, including many wars. The western part of the empire, including Flanders, would become France, the eastern part developed into the Holy (Germanic) Empire. The middle part would be further split into an Italian Kingdom and Provence in the south, Burgundy and Lotharinga in the center and the area between the Rhine and the Meuse in the north. In 959, this last area was divided again and the territory entitled Lower Lotharinga comprised present-day Wallonia. Lotharinga and Flanders were buffeted by constant pressure from France and the Empire and subject to feudal or imperial ties. This also affected the division of modern-day Belgian territory as for ages Flanders would be linked by ties of suzerainty to France, and the eastern lands to the Holy (Germanic) Empire. Nonetheless, drives towards unification of the Low Countries, sometimes backed by the great rivals, were present as well.

## The High Middle Ages (1012-1384)

During the Middle Ages, an image of separation and loose internal ties prevailed. Lotharinga was given in 1012 by Emperor Henry II to Duk Godefroi I. He made an unsuccessful attempt to unify additional territory in the Low Countries and to throw off the ties of suzerainty. After 1100, central authority weakened further and local dukedoms flourished in Brabant, the counties of Hainaut, Luxembourg and Limburg and the independent bishopric of Liège. Flanders strove for autonomy within the Frankish kingdom under its counts Baldwin I and II.

Some counts of Flanders played an important role in the Crusades. The effects produced at home, however, were devastating. Local lords took the occasion to strengthen their power and anarchy and arbitrariness reigned.

Moreover, regional forces—the towns—developed and fought for their autonomy and privileges. Due to the cloth industry and trade, Ypres, Bruges and Ghent grew into autonomous power centers. More often than not, they fought the count of Flanders and their suzerain, the king of France. In 1302, the Flemish leaders Pieter de Coninck and Jan Breydel defeated a French army at Courtrai in the battle of the Golden Spurs.

Economic ties with England through the wool industry led to strategic alliances. Jacob van Artevelde of Ghent led the struggle of the Flemish towns against the count and his suzerain, the king of France. This opposition between the towns and the state authorities was to remain a central feature in the Burgundian period.

## The Burgundian Dynasty (1384-1482)

The integration of the territories that now comprise Belgium, Luxembourg and the Netherlands was achieved mainly under the Burgundian dynasty. In 1369, Margaret of Male, daughter of the count of Flanders, was married to the youngest son of the king of France, the Burgundian Duke Philip the Bold (Philippe le Hardi). Flanders, Artois, Franche-Comté, Nevers and Burgundy became united under this ruler. He reigned from 1384 to 1404 and initiated the administrative integration of the regions under his personal rule. In Flanders, the duke established a Chamber of Accounts (Rekenkamer) for financial matters and a central court as general Court of Appeal; a prosecutor general was installed in order to curb the power of the town courts in favor of those of the count.

Philip the Bold was succeeded by John the Fearless (Jean sans Peur, 1404-1419), who directed much of his attention to conquering the French throne and was finally murdered by a rival.

His son Philip the Good (Philippe le Bon, 1419-1967) extended considerably the possessions of the Burgundians in the Low Countries. In 1428, by the reconciliation of Delft, Jacoba of Beieren ceded to Philip the Good the hereditary rights to Holland-Zeeland and Hainault. He also incorporated Namur (1429) and Brabant (1430). He was able to buy the Duchy of Luxembourg in 1441; almost all the territories of the Low Countries were now under one ruler and only the dioceses of Utrecht and Liège remained more difficult to control. They were under church protection. However, Philip managed to put his bastard son on the throne as bishop in Utrecht. Liège remained under French influence. Next, Philip was able to loosen the feudal ties of Flanders with France and, by the Treaty of Arras in 1435, Philip was recognized as a European sovereign. He was thus freed from his obligations as vassal of the French king.

Philip wished to further the centralization of his territories and created the following institutions: one Great Council (Grand Conseil) for legislation and justice, two Council Chambers (Chambres du Conseil) for financial matters, one at Lille and the other at The Hague. Within each province Philip set up a Ducal Court, a Chamber of Accounts and the Estates for Political Consultation. In 1430, Philip the Good founded the Order of the Golden Fleece with the intention of binding unconditionally to him his fellow noblemen. In 1433-1434, Philip introduced a common monetary unit for Flanders, Brabant,

Holland-Zeeland and Hainaut. The latter part of Philip's reign from 1440 to 1467 constituted a period of peace, stability, low taxes and a luxurious court life.

Times changed rapidly. Even before his Joyful Entrance into Flanders in 1467, Philip's son Charles the Bold (Charles le Téméraire, 1467-1477) secured by military force his recognition as the hereditary regent of Liège. In 1465, Charles fought the army of the French king at Montlhéry in Picardy with such force that he won his nickname "Le Téméraire" (The Bold). But his Joyful Entrance into Ghent and Mechelen would be disturbed by protests against increases in taxes. Charles vigorously continued the effort to centralize the Burgundian territories. He established two central Accounting Chambers, a High Appeals Court for all the provinces, the so-called Parliament of Mechelen, and a State Council for drafting laws. He imposed French as the sole administrative language of his territories. In 1473, he also succeeded in imposing his power in Gelre, one of the last autonomous regions in the Low Countries. Then, he went to war in order to connect the Low Countries with his possessions in Burgundy. He conquered the Duchy of Alsace and Lorraine. This proved fatal as Charles fell near Nancy in a battle against the Lotharingians and their Swiss allies in 1477. Along with the revolt of the territories just conquered by Charles, the defeat at once meant the loss to France of Franche-Comté, Picardy, Artois and Burgundy itself. Moreover, the heiress of the Low Countries, Mary of Burgundy, was forced to grant the Great Privilege in order to obtain the support of her subjects. This temporarily reversed the trend toward unification and centralization under the Burgundian dynasty.

The lifestyle at the court of the Burgundian dukes, copying the French example, was luxurious and exceptionally stimulating for the arts. By ducal commissions, the arts of sculpture, tapestry, music, literature and especially painting developed into unprecedented heights. The so-called Flemish Primitives are still acknowledged as the creators of some of the finest masterpieces ever made. Rogier Van der Weyden, Jan Van Eyck, Hans Memling and others all worked in the service of the Burgundian dynasty.

**The Habsburg Dynasty (1482-1794)**

In 1477, Mary of Burgundy succeeded her father Charles the Bold. Yielding to the resistance raised by the union of the Flemish towns

(Membres de Flanders: Ghent, Bruges and Ypres), she granted the Great Privilege and acquiesced in supervision by a newly established Great Council. Thus was the central power of the duchess curtailed and a new unifying impulse was generated through the creation of a constitution and common political institutions for the whole of the Netherlands. Under permanent threats, not in the least from France, Mary engaged in a dynastic marriage with Maximilian of Habsburg. This brought the Austrian dynasty to Flanders: at Mary's death in 1482, Maximilian of Austria assumed the regency over the Low Countries. He was staunchly determined to bring the towns back under his control. Nevertheless, he had to contend with their resistance and once even fell prisoner to Bruges. Finally, in 1494, the towns surrendered and lost all their privileges in the Peace of Cadzand. In 1493, Maximilian became Holy Roman Emperor and, the next year, he delegated the rule of the Netherlands to his son Philip of Clève. This Philip entered into a dynastic marriage with Joan of Aragon. Their son Charles of Luxembourg became heir to both the Spanish Crown and the Austrian Habsburg lands.

## Spanish Rule (1506-1713)

The Spanish rule was to bring further integration of the Low Countries in the first part of the sixteenth century and final separation into two parts in the second part of that century.

In 1500, Charles V was born at Ghent. He came of age in 1515 and, in 1517 with the death of the Spanish king, he inherited the Spanish lands. In 1542, he became Holy Roman Emperor as well. This brought the Netherlands under the rule of Spain. The integration of the Low Countries was achieved during the reign of Charles V, who completed the territorial unity of the region. In 1521, the emperor conquered Tournai (Doornik) from the French. Then, he succeeded in reimposing his temporal power over the dioceses of Liège and Utrecht and, finally, he acquired Gelre. In addition, Charles V ruled the provinces as an autonomous and hereditary unit. By the Treaty of Cambrai of 1529, France renounced its suzerainty over Flanders. Moreover, in 1548, the Imperial Diet adopted the Augsburg Transaction, which granted the Low Countries independence within the Habsburg Empire. And the Pragmatic Sanction of 1549 united under one prince the inheritance of the territory of the Low Countries, from then on called "The Seventeen Provinces."

In 1555, Charles V abdicated the throne in favor of his son Philip II. The new monarch ruled the Low Countries from Spain and showed himself to be an irreconcilable Catholic absolutist. The religious struggle between Catholics and Protestants finally led to the division of the Low Countries.

The Pacification of Ghent (1576), a treaty among the provinces, maintained the federation of the Seventeen Provinces and acknowledged religious tolerance. The provinces of Holland and Zeeland were accorded the right to remain Protestant. This compromise went much too far for some Catholics in the Low Countries and for the monarchy in Spain. In 1577, the Estates voted the First Union of Brussels, which prescribed Catholicism as the sole religion for all of the Seventeen Provinces. Similarly Artois, Hainaut and Gallician Flanders signed the Confederation of Arras, imposing the Catholic religion. In January 1579, the Seven Provinces of the north (Holland, Zealand, Utrecht, Gelderland, Overyssel, Friesland and Groningen) reacted by signing the Union of Utrecht. It united the territory that was to become the future Netherlands. Thus, the division of the Low Countries into the Protestant north and the Catholic south grew into an irreversible reality. The "Plakkaat van Verlatinghe" of 1581 codified the separation of the seven northern provinces from the Catholic south. The assassination in 1584 of the relatively moderate William of Nassau put a definitive end to the chances for any further reconciliation.

The Spanish under Farnese began the reconquest of the rebellious southern provinces. Calvinist towns fell one by one: Dunquerque, Ypres, Bruges (1584), Brussels (1585) and finally Antwerp in August 1585. In 1595, the French king Henry IV invaded the Spanish Low Countries. By the peace of Verviers (1598), Calais and much of Picardy were ceded to France. Philip II died in 1598 and the Spanish Low Countries were inherited by his daughter Isabella and her husband Albert. A 12-year truce (1609-21) stabilized the situation in the Low Countries. After the death of Isabella, a Franco-Dutch coalition marched into the Spanish Netherlands. In 1648, by the peace of Munster, Spain finally recognized the independence of the United Provinces and conceded the loss of the territory near Breda and Maastricht and part of northern Flanders (Axel and Hulst). This brought both the beginning of the blockade of the mouth of the Scheldt River and the ruin of the port of Antwerp. Artois and the fortresses in the Sambre-Meuse valley were surrendered to France.

At the end of the seventeenth and the beginning of the eighteenth century, war raged once more in the Low Countries. Again and again France invaded the southern provinces. Once more Flanders lost territory to France. The Treaty of Utrecht in 1713 transferred to France parts of maritime Flanders around Dunquerque and Gallician Flanders around Valenciennes. Under the terms of the Treaty of Restatt and Baden in 1714, the Spanish Netherlands came into Austrian hands.

**Austrian Rule (1715-1794)**

With Austrian rule, a period of relative stability set in. However, the reforms imposed by the foreign Austrian rulers seldom enjoyed the support of their Flemish subjects. Emperor Charles VI (1715-1740) founded a Supreme Council for the Low Countries in Vienna. Maria Theresa (1740-1780) and even more Joseph II (1780-1787) imposed institutional, religious, educational and economic reforms. Agrarian, Catholic and conservative forces stood up against the Austrian rulers. In 1789, the aristocratic and clerical Hendrik Van der Noot united with the more progressive Frans Vonck to provoke a successful revolt. In 1790, the revolutionaries proclaimed the independence of the "Confederation of the Belgian States" (Confédération des Etats Belges Unis). Due to the lack of unity between the factions of the revolting forces, Austrian rule was temporarily restored. France then invaded the territory and defeated the Austrians in the battles of Jemappes (1792) and Fleurus (1794). The Austrian Netherlands, Liège and the Duchy of Bouillon were annexed to France.

**The French Period (1794-1815)**

Occupied by France, the southern Netherlands took part in the dramatic history of the republic and the Napoleonic wars. Internally, administration, justice, religious institutions and education were subject to statist and modernizing reforms. The hegemony of the French language and culture was imposed. Flemish Catholic and conservative protests were ignored. The country had to play its part in the French military adventures. Finally, when Napoleon was defeated at Waterloo, the allied forces decided to lend their support to the creation of a

United Kingdom of the Netherlands. It again united the Seventeen Provinces of the Netherlands and present-day Belgium.

**The Holland Period (1815-1830)**

At the Congress of Vienna, the European great powers created the United Kingdom of the Netherlands. But resistance against the Dutch King William I was provoked mainly by two major features of his policy. First, his insistence on the neutrality of the state and educational institutions was interpreted as anti-Catholic in Flanders. It was strongly contested by the clergy and the bishops. Second, his language policy ran into protests from the French speakers in the south. William I promulgated Dutch as the official language. This greatly irritated the population of Wallonia and the French-speaking bourgeoisie of Brussels, who were traditionally oriented toward France and French culture. These opponents did not limit themselves to the language question, but were also opposed to accepting Holland as the new economic and cultural center of the new kingdom.

The Belgian revolution started with a social revolt. In 1830, the proletariat of the Brussels periphery revolted against the introduction of new technology and the new taxes of William I. The bourgeoisie armed itself against this threat, but then directed its arms against William I of Holland. On 23 September, William I tried to restore order. But, after an armed clash in the Park of Brussels, the troops of William I retreated. In October, a Provisional Government was formed and it proclaimed the independence of Belgium. It remains a matter of controversy whether the nation of Belgium preexisted in the mind of the Belgian revolutionaries, or whether that consciousness was provoked by the events of 1830 and after.

**The Kingdom of Belgium**

The European great powers confirmed the new power balance created by the Belgian revolution. They fully recognized the newly founded Belgian state. It defined itself as a liberal parliamentary monarchy with French as the official language. Prince Leopold of Saxe-Coburg, who was related to the British royal family, was put on the throne. A property-related electoral system clearly promoted the interests of a Belgian bourgeoisie in the wake of a nascent industrial revolution. Despite the liberal undertones of the Constitution, the majority of the population and rulers were still conservative and Catholic. This was exemplified by the long period of homogeneous Catholic governments after independence.

As a reaction, in 1846, a liberal congress was held and a Liberal Party founded. From 1847 until 1884 Belgium was ruled predominantly by the Liberals, led at first by Charles Rogier, who had been one of the leaders of the 1830 revolution, and subsequently by H. J. W. Frère-Orban. Belgian Socialism remained fragmented until the foundation of the Belgian Workers' Party in 1885.

Leopold II succeeded his father in 1865. He was able to maintain the neutrality of Belgium in the Franco-Prussian war that broke out in 1870. His major achievement was the acquisition of the Congo as a personal possession in 1885. In 1908, a year before Leopold's death, it was annexed by the Belgian state.

Surprisingly, despite the early industrialization of Belgium, trade unions did not really gain major influence until the third quarter of the nineteenth century, when socialist and Christian unions were established. Universal suffrage was adopted for men over 21 in 1893. Real social progress was achieved only through the traumas of both world wars.

During World War I, the Flemish movement was given an opportunity to popularize its nationalistic goals at the IJzer Front. After the war, the first social security measures were introduced during the reign of King Albert I, the "knight-king" who returned as a war hero from World War I. Under his command, the Belgian army had been able to resist the Germans for four years at the Ijzer Front in West Flanders. Similarly, a new social concertation system was established after World War II as a result of an agreement between trade unions and employers made in exile, in London during the war. Though both wars had a massive devastating effect on the economy and the population of the country, they laid as well the foundations for social reconciliation and economic recovery after the wars. This was less so on the political level, as the royal controversy divided the country after World War II on the question of whether Leopold III—accused of passive collaboration with the Germans during the war—should return. Belgium had capitulated after a 16-day campaign following the German invasion in May 1940 and the king as commander in chief of the army refused to leave the country for exile in Britain. After the war, Leopold was temporarily replaced by his brother, Prince Charles, as regent. The king finally abdicated in favor of his son, Prince Baudouin, in 1950.

Much of the history of the 150 years since the establishment of the Belgian kingdom could be summarized as a struggle to attain power by three distinct forces. First, the liberal bourgeoisie fought Catholic hegemony. Second, the socialist movement organized itself to represent and secure the interests of the workers. Third, the Flemish movement gradually expanded its interests from a struggle for cultural and linguistic rights into a social and political movement. All three movements had successes and setbacks, but by the middle of the twentieth century, they succeeded in producing a diversified society. The picture then became even more fragmented with the advent of single-issue parties. The Green Movement entered the scene in the 1970s and the rightist nationalist movement in the 1980s. This latter movement threatened to destroy the political system that had been built by compromise and reform since World War II.

## The Federalization of Belgium

The constitutional reforms over the period from 1970 to 1993 turned the unitary system of Belgium into a nearly total federation of three economic regions and three language communities. Regions and communities now all have their own councils, governments and/or parliaments with considerable independent competences.

In 1970, the first articles on the constitutional reform for the federalization of Belgium were voted. The reform introduced for the first time explicitly recognized institutions based on the linguistic identities of the regions, though their powers were still restricted and controlled by national institutions. The first step was to grant the French and the Flemish Cultural Communities their own Cultural Councils. They took over the legislative powers from the federal parliament on cultural affairs and had the right to issue decrees in this field. However, execution and control of the decrees were still maintained by the ministers of the national government. From 1970 to 1980, the Cultural Councils approved numerous decrees and also worked on the creation of separate Flemish and Walloon cultural policies, along with the preservation of monuments and historic buildings on their territories. Both Councils were also responsible for their respective language institutions in the bilingual region of Brussels. In 1973, the

German Community Council of the German Community was installed in a small eastern border zone of Belgium.

The second constitutional reform, laid down in the Constitutional Amendment of 1980, considerably expanded the powers of the communities. First, welfare policy was included in the competence package of the Councils of the Cultural Communities. Second, the regions of Flanders and Wallonia and their Councils—the Flemish Regional Council and the Walloon Regional Council—were established and entrusted with some new powers on "territory-related" matters, such as the economy, town and country-planning and the environment. Under the new regulations, the councils had the right to install their own government or executive. The German Community, a very small economic entity, was not granted its own regional council and had to act under the Walloon Region. The Cultural Councils continued to be responsible for the language policy in Brussels, but the Regional Councils had no legal authority with respect to Brussels, as its own executive was formed there. In fact, Brussels did not secure all the competences of a full region. In contrast to the French-speaking Community and the Walloon Region, Flanders preferred to merge its two Councils into one Flemish Parliament. Given this complex configuration, the Belgian case has been described as an asymmetrical federation.

The Constitutional Amendments of 1988 and 1993 further increased the autonomy and the legal and economic powers of the regions. Until 21 May 1995, the members of the parliaments and councils—with the exception of the German Council—were indirectly elected. They were still elected as members of the National Parliament and delegated to their community organs. The double mandate of these members was perceived as a hindrance to the optimal functioning of the autonomous regional organs; in fact, it was a last conservative check on the new federalist tendencies. The Constitutional Amendment of 1993 reversed this situation and since then members of the regional parliament and councils are chosen directly. They are no longer entrusted with dual national and regional mandates. Following the St. Michael's Agreement and the Constitutional Amendment of 1993, politicians expected a communal truce until 1999, when the financial regulations of the communities were to be reconsidered.

In fact, Flemish demands regarding the federalization of social security funds revived the debate much earlier. Walloon Minister-

President Collignon asked the federal prime minister to clarify and moderate the Flemish demands. Some French-speaking academics devised a French counterstrategy, even including a threat of total independence of the French-speaking Community and an association with France. However, the debate on the autonomy and financing of the communities was silenced by the outbreak of the political and juridical scandals that shook Belgium from the middle of 1996. Now fundamental reform of the national juridical and political systems took priority. This provoked a new turning point in Belgian politics and society. The massive protest reaction of the population—the so-called White Movement as everyone dressed in white or carried with them white objects, such as white flowers or white balloons—brought into the open the sudden awareness of the big gap between the ordinary citizen and the upper echelons of the political and juridical systems. The destabilizing events went back some years: the unsolved hold-ups and murders of the gang of Nivelles (Bende van Nijvel); the corruption of high politicians in the Agusta case, including Willy Claes, secretary-general of NATO; the unsolved hired assassination of the former president of the Socialist Party André Cools; the slowness and inefficiency of the juridical machinery in the Dutroux case.

Along with other questions of political corruption, this contributed to the mistrust of the Belgian citizens in the political and juridical system. Especially the cases of pedophilia and murder of kidnapped children, where immediate identification was evidently easy, mobilized the average citizens. The politicians of the traditional parties, already shaken by the growing influence of the so-called anti-political parties of the far right, hurriedly tried to counter this movement by immediate reforms of the political and juridical systems. However, it is still not clear whether governmental and opposition parties can and will master their traditional divisions and whether the new reforms will satisfy the general public. Even if the "White Movement" is now seeking its second breath, it still seems to weigh heavily on Belgian political life.

It remains to be seen whether the integration of Belgium within the European Union will stabilize the internal relations between the communities. In foreign affairs, the federal government continues to pursue policies that promote strong European and Atlantic links in following positions set immediately after World War II, when under Paul-Henri Spaak, Belgium played a leading role in establishing the new Europe, with the creation of Benelux, the European Coal and

Steel Community, NATO EEC, EC and finally the EU. The headquarters of the EU and NATO are in Brussels. The federal government still plays its expected role and contributes to ensuring the national economic conditions necessary to securring Belgium's inclusion in the European monetary union and the replacement of the franc with the euro. But regional politicians are now more and more promoting the idea of the Europe of regions to replace the idea of a unitary Belgium. Both Flanders and Wallonia would easily find their place, but what about the capital of Europe, Brussels?

## THE DICTIONARY

- A -

ABORTION ACT. In 1990, a coalition of Liberals, Socialists (qq.v.) and Greens passed in Parliament an abortion law, called the Michielsen-Lallemand Bill which stated that abortion should in some defined circumstances no longer come under criminal law. King Baudouin (q.v.), who objected to abortion on religious grounds but wished to respect the will of parliament, wrote the prime minister that he should not sign the bill, a necessary procedural step of every law to become valid. On the other hand, he wanted to respect the will of parliament. Consequently, Article 82 of the Constitution (q.v.) was cited by the prime minister and on 3 April 1990 the king was declared to be unable to reign for 36 hours. The cabinet took over his functions and signed the bill. Parliament then used Article 82 to declare the king's inability to reign at an end.

Of course, the legal procedure of declaring the inability to reign was initially intended to apply only in occurrence of war or serious illness of the king. This had in fact happened on 28 May 1940, during World War II (q.v.). The application of the same article now indicates how Belgian politicians used creativity to resolve a difficult situation.

ABSIL, JEAN (1893-1974). Composer of chamber music. He won the Grand Prix de Rome award in 1922.

ADRIAN VI (1459-1523). He has the honor of having been the only pope from the Netherlands (1522-1523). He was born Adriaan Floris Boeyens in Utrecht and studied at the theological faculty of the University of Louvain, where he became professor and dean.

He was the tutor of Emperor Charles V (q.v.). When he was cardinal in the Spanish Tortosa, he was elected pope.

AGALEV. Agalev (Anders GAan LEVen) is the green party of the Flemish ecologists in the Dutch-speaking part of Belgium. Its counterpart in the French-speaking part of the country is Ecolo (q.v.).

AGRICULTURE. As a small and highly industrialized and urbanized country, the role of agriculture in gross domestic product and employment is rather small, in fact less than 2 percent. However, farming is very intensive and highly productive. Farming supplies about four-fifths of the food requirements of Belgium. About two-thirds of the farms are intensively cultivated units of less than 10 hectares. As of the late 1980s the leading crops were wheat, potatoes, sugar beets, and barley. Most cereal production is located in Wallonia, while the flood plain areas of Flanders are flat and fertile and lend themselves to intensive cultivation, especially horticulture (fruits, lettuce, tomatoes, chicory, etc.). One-third of this production is exported. Livestock and dairy farming are major agricultural industries: Belgium produces about 95 percent of its meat requirements and is totally self-sufficient in butter, eggs, and milk. In the late 1980s the livestock population of Belgium numbered some 6 million pigs, 3 million cattle, 130,000 sheep, and 23,000 horses.

Initially, the European Union's (EU) (q.v.) Common Agricultural Policy, which guaranteed prices, encouraged increased output of livestock products. Now quotas on milk production, decreases of livestock and environmental constraints put the farmers under pressure to reduce production. For example, the number of milk cows fell by some 20 percent since 1984. Notwithstanding the growing competition, fishing is still very important in the coastal zone of West Flanders. *See also* ECONOMY.

AGUSTA CASE. Scandal in which the Socialist Parties (PS, SP) (q.v.) were involved in the late 1980s. An Italian helicopter manufacturer, Agusta, paid bribes in order to win a large army contract. Guy Spitaels (q.v.), president of the Walloon regional government, resigned from this function on 21 January 1994 as a consequence of the so-called affair of the three Guy's (Spitaels, Coëme and Mathot).

According to General Prosecutor Eliane Liekendael, the Agusta case was linked to the Dassault (q.v.) case. However, a parliamentary prosecution commission of the Walloon regional government did not follow this interpretation. It charged Spitaels in the Dassault, but not in the Agusta case. Many other public personalities were involved in both cases, for example Willy Claes, Guy Coëme (qq.v.), Etienne Mangé, Luc Wallyn, Johan Delanghe, Alfons Pulinckx, Merry Hermanus, François Pirot, André Bastien and Jean-Louis Mazy.

ALARM-BELL PROCEDURE. Articles 38 and 38 bis of the Constitution (q.v.) grant the right to two-thirds of a linguistic group to suspend the adoption of language laws.

ALBERT I, KING (1875-1934). King Albert I reigned from 23 December 1909 to 17 February 1934. He stood at the head of his troops at the IJzer Front during World War I (q.v.), defending his country against the German invaders. At the end of the war, the "knight-king" was immensely popular. The country recovered slowly and, during his reign, the first measures furthering social progress were introduced. On 17 February 1934, the king tragically fell from a rock at Marche-les-Dames (q.v.). The king being a good climber, some historians expressed doubts about the official version of his decease.

ALBERT II, KING (1934- ). King of Belgium, prince of Liège (q.v.). Son of Leopold III (q.v.) and younger brother of Baudouin (q.v.). He acceded to the throne upon Baudouin's unexpected death on 31 July 1993. While there was speculation that Albert's son Philippe should accede to the throne at Baudouin's death, the choice was made during a secret night meeting of Prime Minister Jean-Luc Dehaene (q.v.), Interior Minister Louis Tobback, and the three vice premiers Willy Claes (q.v.), Melchior Warthelet and Guy Coëme (q.v.). Socialist Louis Tobback (q.v.) seems especially to have insisted that Albert should accede to the throne. Prime Minister Dehaene flew straight to Spain to invite Albert to become king and he promptly accepted. His earlier somewhat frivolous image—considered by some a reason to pass the crown immediately to his son Philippe—soon changed into that of a serious and concerned king. In the reaction to the Dutroux case (q.v.), he assumed more than just a formal role.

ALECHINSKY, PIERRE (1927-1956). Avant-garde painter who belonged to the Cobra (q.v.) Group.

ALVA, DUKE OF (1507-1582). Fernando Alvarez de Toledo. Spanish regent sent by King Philip II in 1567 to pacify the rebellious Dutch provinces. He exercised personal rule through a Council of Troubles—soon called the Council of Blood by the rebels—and ruthlessly suppressed resistance, countenancing atrocities in campaigns against the rebels in 1572 and 1573 and executing thousands. Leaders of the revolt whom he had put to death included Count Egmont and Count van Hoorne, who were executed at Brussels (q.v.) in 1568. His imposition in 1569 of a 10 percent tax on all goods sold—the notorious 10th penny—stiffened popular resistance. He was recalled to Spain in 1573.

AMNESTY. Following the liberation of Belgium in World War II (q.v.), more than 50,000 citizens were convicted of collaboration with the enemy. Most lost their political rights and their right to a state pension. Flemish political parties such as the People's Union (Volksunie, VU) (q.v.) in the 1950s and later the Flemish Bloc (Vlaams Blok) (q.v.) made complete amnesty one of their major demands. This claim has always been rejected by Walloon socialists and patriotic organizations. *See also* COLLABORATION; WAFFEN SS.

ANNEESSENS, FRANS (1660-1719). Deacon of Brussels (q.v.). He led a revolt against the Austrians in 1719 in defense of the freedom of artisanry. The revolt failed and Anneessens was decapitated. After independence, a statue was erected in Brussels to his memory.

ANTWERP. Antwerp (Antwerpen) is both the largest agglomeration in Flanders (q.v.) and the largest port of Belgium.

At the end of the Middle Ages following the decline of Bruges, Ypres and Ghent (qq.v.) in Flanders, Antwerp in Brabant (q.v.) assumed the role of major town of the Low Countries. Antwerp developed into a rich commercial and intellectual center in the first half of the 16th century. This came to a sudden end with the wars of religion. Due to the Spanish repression of Protestantism, the commercial and intellectual elite fled to the north. The reconquest of Antwerp by the Spanish troops and its plundering during the so-called "Spanish Fury" in 1576 destroyed most of its material and human splendor. The secession of the northern provinces resulted in the blockade of the Scheldt (q.v.) mouth and the near ruin of Antwerp. After a long period of inactivity, the port revived during the French and the Dutch period when new docks were built. Freedom of navigation problems reappeared with the secession of Belgium from the United Kingdom of the Netherlands in 1830. Only in 1863 could King Leopold I (q.v.) buy back the toll rights on the Scheldt. From then on, the port of Antwerp continually expanded. It is now one of the biggest ports in the world and the administrative capital of the province of the same name.

Antwerp has preserved only a minor part of the monuments from its rich past. The building of the Cathedral of Our Lady started in 1352 and continued until the first decades of the sixteenth century. Its north spire is said to be the highest in the Low Countries. The church contains monumental baroque paintings by Peter Paul Rubens (q.v.). The tomb of this Antwerp painter can be visited in St James Cathedral. Along with the public buildings and guild houses of the Grand Market, the beautiful house and workshop of the printer Christoffel Plantijn (q.v.) has been preserved. The Rubens's House was turned into a museum. *See also* BRABO; LANGE WAPPER; SCHELDT.

ARBITRATION COURT. This high court arbitrates on disputes between the linguistic communities and the federal government. It is composed of judges and ex-politicians.

A case in point was the following. The Arbitration Court decided to declare illegal the decision to subsidize the magazine *Carrefour* for the budget year 1995. This magazine was to be subsidized by the French Community Council (Conseil de la Communauté Française, CCF) and distributed in communities along the Flemish border around Brussels. To this the Flemish Parliament objected and its opposition was sustained by the Arbitration Court. *See also* CONSTITUTIONAL REFORM; FEDERALISM.

ARDENNES. The Ardennes is a large wooded plateau located in the south of Belgium and in Luxembourg and northeastern France. The name is believed to be of Celtic origin. Two alternative explanations are given. *Ar-Den* was the Celtic word for oak. *Ardu* meant high. The Ardennes could thus have been the high lands with oaks (now replaced by firtrees). It was the site of heavy fighting in World War I (q.v.) during the invasion of the Germans in 1914. In World War II (q.v.), a late offensive of the Germans under Marshal von Rundstedt resulted in the battle of the Bulge (q.v.) from December 1944 to January 1945. The Belgian part of the Ardennes is now incorporated in the Walloon region, which promotes its natural riches through well-directed tourism, both in summer and in winter. The highest points of the Ardennes—also the highest points of Belgium—are Botrange, Baraque de Fraiture and Baraque Michel at about 700 meters each. *See also* BASTOGNE; WALLONIA.

ARLON. Main locality of the province of Belgian Luxembourg (q.v.). The city dates back to Roman times. In the first century, a center was erected at the crossing of the routes from Trier to Reims and from Tongeren to Metz. Preserved today are remnants of a thermal bath, a city wall of the third century and a big tower with a fragment of an antique relief. The space around the tower contains a plan showing the city walls and epigraphs. Finds of the Roman sites can be seen in the local Musée Luxembourgeois.

ARRAS (ATRECHT). Main town of Artois (q.v.), now in the extreme northeast of France. In the early Middle Ages, it was famous for its tapestries and under the influence of the counts of Flanders (q.v.).

ARRAS (PEACE OF, 1435). By the Peace of Arras (Atrecht) (q.v.) of 1435, France and the Burgundian Duke Philip the Good (q.v.) came to an agreement. By ceding some territory, Philip the Good secured temporarily freedom of the century-old feudal ties of Flanders to France.

ARRAS (UNION OF, 1579). League formed in 1579 by the largely Catholic southern provinces of the Spanish Netherlands. The league proclaimed its loyalty to the Spanish crown. The league was formed in opposition to the Union of Utrecht (1579) of the seven northern provinces, which continued the revolt against Spain. At the time of the league formation a number of cities now in Belgium, including Brussels, Antwerp, Ghent and Bruges, were held by rebel forces. They were reconquered in the 1580s under the military and diplomatic efforts of Alexander Farnese, the Duke of Parma.

ARTOIS. Artois and its main town Arras (Atrecht) (q.v.) now lie in the extreme northeast of France. In the early Middle Ages, the region fell under the influence of the counts of Flanders (q.v.), as it belonged to the dowry of Margaret of Male (q.v.), and it came by her marriage into the possession of the Burgundians and Habsburgs. It was frequently claimed by the French and also finally united to France in 1659.

ASSOCIATION OF BELGIAN ENTERPRISES. The Association of Belgian Enterprises (Verbond van Belgische Ondernemingen, VBO) is the social partner that represents corporate management in interprofessional consultations. Its president is Karel Boone, its official spokesman Tony Vandeputte.

ASSOCIATION OF ENTERPRISES OF BRUSSELS. The Association of Enterprises of Brussels (Verbond van Ondernemingen te Brussel, VOB) is the regional employers organization of Brussels (q.v.).

ATOMIUM. National symbol of Belgium. It was erected at the 1958 Brussels World Exhibition. The nine solidly bound balls of the metallic structure symbolize the then nine (now 10) provinces and the unity of Belgium. At the occasion of the designation of Brussels as European cultural capital of 2000, the atomium will be restored and modernized.

ATRECHT. *See* ARRAS.

AUDIT OFFICE (REKENHOF). The Audit Office is an institution of the federal Parliament (q.v.). Its task is to control all financial transactions of all executive organs and institutions of all parliaments in Belgium, i.e., the federal Parliament and the parliaments of the regions and communities. It publishes its findings in the so-called "Blunderbooks."

AUSTRIAN RULE (1713-1795). At the end of the War of the Spanish Succession, Holy Roman Emperor Charles VI (q.v.) acquired the former Spanish Netherlands by the Treaty of Utrecht (1713) (q.v.). By the Pragmatic Sanction (1713) (q.v.), his daughter Maria Theresa (q.v.) was recognized as his successor. She introduced a period of peace and stability in the Low Countries (q.v.). She was succeeded by her son Joseph II (q.v.). His progressive reforms were rejected by the clergy and other proponents of the Ancien Regime. The Austrians retained power following the Brabant Revolution (q.v.) of 1789 with the accession to the throne of Leopold II in 1790. Austrian rule ended following the battle of Fleurus (q.v.) on 26 June 1794, where the French general Jourdan defeated the Austrians. In 1795, the Austrian Low Countries were annexed to France.

## - B -

BALDWIN I, COUNT OF FLANDERS (?-879). The first known Flemish count was Baldwin I "with the Iron Arm," who ruled over the region of Ghent (q.v.) from 862. He was the son of Audoacer, whose family probably ruled three *pagi* or regions between the Scheldt (q.v.) and Lys Rivers. Baldwin made his name and fortune by eloping with Judith, the oldest child of Charles II the Bald (823-877), Holy Roman Emperor (875-877) and king of West Francia (843-877). Judith was already the widow of two West Saxon kings and of a stepson of Alfred the Great. The marriage was legalized in 863 and Baldwin received the *pagus Flandrensis*. He ruled the region until his death in 879. His son and heir, Baldwin II (q.v.), subsequently expanded the territory.

BALDWIN II, COUNT OF FLANDERS (?-918). He was the son and heir of Baldwin I (q.v.) and Judith, daughter of Charles the

Bald. He assumed rule over Flanders (q.v.) at the death of his father in 879. He married Elftrude, the daughter of Alfred the Great. The beginning of the reign of Baldwin II was characterized by the numerous invasions of the Norsemen (Vikings) and Baldwin took refuge in the marshes of the newly acquired *pagus Flandrensis*. He was known as a good defender of his territory against the Viking incursions. When the Norsemen left, Baldwin began a series of successful expeditions to expand his territory to the south and the west.

BANKING. The National Bank of Belgium, Belgium's central bank, has had the exclusive authority to issue bank notes for Belgium since 1873. It deals primarily with technical management of the currency and safeguarding of monetary stability by regulating the supply of money and the country's external reserves. It also sets exemplary reference interest rates. In recent years, it has followed a successful policy of aligning short-term interest rates to those of Germany and of pegging the Belgian franc to the D-Mark. The practices of the commercial banks are further supervised by a Bank Commission. Commercial banks must meet some liquidity and solvability requirements. The banks are also asked to lend a certain proportion of their capital to the government for the financing of the national debt. Beginning in 1934, the commercial banks were forbidden by the van Zeeland government to hold shares in enterprises. While commercial banks lend to industry and deal with institutional clients, the savings banks are set up to serve the individual citizens. In answer to the projected harmonization of the banking sector in Europe and in reaction to growing competition, banks in Belgium sought partners with which to merge, including banks from abroad. So far, however, real transformations have not been spectacular, apart from some proposals to rationalize the extended network of local bank services. On the other hand, there is some progress in the long announced privatization of the banking sector. For example, the traditional official state bank, the ASLK, has been privatized.

BARRIER TREATY (1715). Treaty signed on 15 November 1715 by which the Austrian Habsburg dynasty ceded to the Dutch a number of fortifications in the Austrian Netherlands along the French frontier as security against an attack by France.

BASTOGNE. Village in the Ardennes (q.v.). During World War II (q.v.) in December 1944 German troups made a major breakthrough in the Ardennes in an attempt to repeat their surpise encirclement of 1940. American forces found themselves surrounded in the town and, when asked to surrender, General Anthony McAuliffe, the American commander, gave the famous one-word reply "Nuts!" *See also* BATTLE OF THE BULGE.

BATTLE OF THE BULGE (1944). American name for a World War II (q.v.) battle known to the Germans as the Rundstedt Offensive. On 16 December 1944 German divisions launched a surprise counteroffensive through the Ardennes (q.v.). The Germans hoped to repeat their surprise tactic of 1940 and directed their drive at Antwerp (q.v.) to cut off the supplies flowing into the port and so deprive the Allies of material needed for their final push into Germany. The Germans scored some initial victories but Allied counterattacks together with a failure by the Germans to capture enough fuel doomed the drive. This was the last major German attack in Western Europe in World War II. *See also* BASTOGNE; MALMEDY.

BATTLE OF THE GOLDEN SPURS (1302). In addition to their role as regional power centers, the towns developed and fought for their privileges. Due to the cloth industry and trade, Bruges, Ghent and Ypres (qq.v.) developed into autonomous centers of power. More often than not, they fought the counts of Flanders (q.v.) and their suzerain, the king of France. In 1302, the Flemish leaders Pieter de Coninck (q.v.) and Jan Breydel defeated a French army at Courtrai (q.v.) at the battle of the Golden Spurs. The event was glorified by the romantic writers of the 19th century Flemish movement (q.v.). The date of the battle—11th of July—was adopted as the national holiday of the Flemish Community (q.v.).

BAUDOUIN, KING (1930-1993). Duke of Brabant, former king of Belgium (1951-1993). He succeeded his father Leopold III (q.v.) after a six-year period of regency held by his uncle, Prince Charles (q.v.). Leopold III abdicated in favor of his son after a mathematically inconclusive but politically explosive plebiscite on the so-called royal controversy (q.v.).

During Baudouin's reign, the new impetus for industrialization in Flanders sparked by export industries financed by foreign capital led to economic growth superceding that of Wallonia (qq.v.). Social progress boomed in the golden 1960s. The oil crisis in the early 1970s marked the beginning of structural difficulties. Especially the old industries of Wallonia withered away. After Baudouin's sudden death on 31 July 1993, his brother, Albert II (q.v.), assumed the throne, as Baudouin's marriage to Fabiola di Aragon remained childless.

BEAUCARNE, JULOS (1936- ). French-speaking actor and popular singer.

BELGIAN COMMUNIST PARTY. The Belgian Communist Party (Kommunistische Partij van België/Parti Communiste Belge, KPB/PCB) was established in 1925 by fusion of two earlier local Communist parties.

In 1935, the Belgian Communist Party embraced the popular front line of cooperation with non-Communist left-wing parties. In 1937, a Flemish wing (KPB) was founded. The Communist Party engaged actively in the Resistance movement against the Germans in World War II (q.v.). The relatively modest electoral results obtained before the war were reversed by a major success with the party winning a 12.7 percent vote and 23 seats in parliament in 1946. The Communists participated in three cabinets during the postwar years between 1944 and 1946. As a consequence of the cold war, they were dropped from power and their support fell steadily. Limited influence was exerted through infiltration in the trade unions.

The party succeeded in regaining some interest in intellectual circles during the period of Euro-communism, but it finally collapsed in a last internal critique of Stalinism. Some minor dissident Communist groups such as Maoists and Trotskyists survived the traditional Communist Party.

BELGIAN DYNASTY (1831- ). The Provisional Government (q.v.) of 1830 opted for a constitutional monarchy. The king was required to take an oath to the Constitution (q.v.). Until the Constitutional Amendment of 1996 succession was regulated by the rule of male primogeniture.

The following monarchs have governed the Kingdom of Belgium: Leopold I (1831-1865); Leopold II (1865-1909); Albert I (1909-1934); Leopold III (1934-1951); Baudouin (1951-1993); Albert II (1993- ) (qq.v.).

A recent constitutional amendment approved female accession to the throne.

BELGIAN REVOLUTION (1830-1831). The resistance of the Belgians against the Dutch King William I was provoked mainly by two major features of his policy. First, his insistence on the neutrality of the state and its educational institutions was constantly interpreted as anti-Catholic by the Flemish clergy and Catholic politicians. Second, King William's language policy encountered persistent protest from French-speaking circles. William I had promulgated Dutch as the official language except in the French-speaking southern provinces, but this aroused indignation among the population of Wallonia (q.v.) and the French-speaking bourgeoisie of Brussels (q.v.), who were traditionally oriented toward France and French culture. Moreover, their resentments were not confined to the language question as they were also not eager to accept Holland as the economic and cultural center of the new kingdom. The Belgians disliked the Dutch tariff system, which gave insufficient protection to Belgian industry. Belgium was given only equal representation in the lower chamber of the states-general or assembly, although her population was larger than that of Holland. The public debt was equally divided, although the Dutch share was many times larger than the Belgian. Walloon papers in Liège under the Catholic De Gerlache and the Liberal Charles Rogier displayed a strong anti-royalist attitude. At the same time, there existed in upper circles some justified antipathy to the person of the king, whose authoritarian actions were resented.

Nevertheless, the Belgian revolution started as a social revolt. In 1830, the proletariat in the Brussels area revolted against the introduction of new technology and new taxes by William I. The bourgeoisie armed itself against this threat, but then directed their arms against William I of Holland. The actual outburst of nationalistic feelings was sparked by a cultural event.

The national theater of Brussels had staged an opera of French composer Daniel Aubier, *La Muette de Portici*. The opera contains a song lyrically exalting the striving for freedom and independence and fueling the revolt against the foreign occupier. It stirred the enthusiasm of the people. In a spontaneous revolt, the masses flocked into the streets of Brussels and occupied the Brussels Park. On 7 September, volunteers from Liège joined the revolutionaries. On 23 September, William I tried to restore order, but following a violent armed clash in the Brussels Park, his troops retreated and evacuated the city. The rebels lost 400 men, the king's army 750. Then, the bourgeoisie recovered leadership of the revolt.

On 25 September, a Provisional Government was formed with Rogier as leader. The bombardment of Antwerp by the Dutch on 27 October hardened Belgian resistance. It proclaimed the independence of Belgium on 4 October. On 3 November 1830, the 30,000 citizens entitled to vote chose a National Congress, the first Parliament of Belgium. As its first act, the Congress determined that Belgium would be a parliamentary monarchy. A Constitution was drafted on the British pattern. Also, from the very beginning, the new ruling class expressed its preferences for the French nation and culture. The only official language in administration and justice would be French. The government gazette would be published exclusively in French. The first Belgian minister of national defense would be a French general. The vice president of the National Congress proposed offering the Belgian throne to the French royal family. Members of Parliament even proposed union with France. All these French-inclined proposals were of course more firmly supported by the Walloon representatives. They represented a response to the simmering resentment of French-speakers to the measures of King William I, who had promoted Dutch language and culture during the preceding 15 years.

In choosing a king, the more radical elements favored the candidacy of one of Napoleon's relatives while moderates supported selection of the Duke of Nemours, the second son of King Louis Philippe of France. On 3 February 1831, the Congress voted in favor of the King's son, but vigorous opposition from Lord Palmerston, the head of the British foreign office, compelled the French to reject the offer. The throne was subsequently offered to and accepted by Prince Leopold of Saxe-Coburg-Saalfeld, uncle to the future Queen Victoria of Britain. Walloon discontent was tempered by the fact that the new king of Belgium was married to Louise-Marie, the daughter of the French king. He took the oath to the Constitution as Leopold I on 21 July 1831—Belgium's National Independence Day.

The New Constitution (q.v.) provided for a parliamentary monarchy with ministerial responsibility and contained provisions providing for freedom of religion, assembly, and the press. The separation of church and state permitted the Roman Catholic Church to expand its school system.

William I did not accept his defeat until 1839, when under pressure from the European powers, he recognized the new state and ceded a part of Luxembourg and Limburg to the Kingdom of Belgium. *See also* PROVISIONAL GOVERNMENT.

BELGIAN SERVICE FOR INTERNATIONAL TRADE. The Belgian Service for International Trade (Belgische Dienst voor Buitenlandse Handel, BDBH) promotes Belgian industry and encourages contacts with foreign partners.

BELGIAN SOCIALIST PARTY. *See* SOCIALIST PARTY.

BELGIAN WORKERS' PARTY (1885-1940). The Belgian Workers' Party (Parti Ouvrier Belge, POB/ Belgische Werklieden Partij, BWP) was the first official Belgian socialist party. It was founded in 1885 by a fusion of regional workers' organizations.

Its ideological basis became the "Charter of Quaregnon," a revolutionary document. In reality, the party followed a far more reformist and pragmatic course. In 1912, it even entered into a temporary alliance with the Liberals against the Catholics (qq.v.). After World War I (q.v.) and with the introduction of the general franchise for men, the POB became the second party after the Catholics and before the Liberals. In the years immediately before World War II (q.v.), the party was strongly influenced by the nationalistic fervor of its new chairman, Hendrik De Man. Following his corporatist ideas, he dissolved the party in 1940 and began to collaborate with the German occupier. The Resistance (q.v.) organized a new Belgian Socialist Party (Parti Socialiste Belge, PSB/Belgische Socialistische Partij, BSP) under Paul-

Henri Spaak (q.v.). After World War II, the Socialists remained the second party, reaching their highest electoral result in 1961 with 36.7 percent of the vote. From then on, the party's electorial success declined due to linguistic polarization of the escalating community problem. Moreover, in 1967, the Flemish- and French-speaking wings held separate congresses and the party had to split definitively in 1978 into two autonomous socialist parties for both parts of the country, the Socialistische Partij (SP) and the Parti Socialiste (PS). *See also* SOCIALIST PARTY.

BENELUX. In 1921, Luxembourg signed a convention with Belgium, creating the Belgium-Luxembourg Union: the two countries agreed to apply the same customs tariffs. Under the impulse of Paul-Henri Spaak (q.v.), minister of foreign affairs of the Belgian government-in-exile, the Benelux Treaty of London of 5 September 1944, was signed. It established a customs union between Belgium, Luxembourg and the Netherlands. The Benelux Customs Union became a reality on 1 January 1948. All tariffs on trade between the three countries were abolished, a common external tariff for third countries was established and all quantitative restrictions to trade inside the Benelux were lifted. A new step was taken by a treaty of 3 February 1958, when an economic union was agreed on.

Since 1 July 1960, there is free movement of persons between the three countries. This arrangement constituted a forerunner to the establishment of an external frontier and the abolition of internal control on the movement of persons of the European Union (q.v.). *See also* CUSTOMS AND MONETARY UNION WITH LUXEMBOURG.

BERGEN. *See* MONS.

BERNISSART (IGUANODONS OF). On 1 April 1878, the skeletons of several iguanodons—a genus of herbivorous dinosaurs—were found by the miner Jules Creteur. They were reconstructed by the paleontologist Louis Dollo and are exhibited in the Museum for Natural Sciences in Brussels (q.v.).

BINCHE. Little town in Wallonia (q.v.) that is world famous for its carnival staged by the so-called Gilles. These are men dressed with feathers on their head who dance to a fascinating rhythm and at times throw oranges to the public.

BLACK SUNDAY. It refers to the election of Sunday, 21 November 1996, in which the extreme right-wing parties of the Flemish Bloc and Front National (qq.v.) won significant gains.

BOESMANS, PHILIPPE (1936- ). Avant-garde composer of serial music. He won the Italia Prize in 1971 and the UNESCO Award of the International Tribune of Composers in 1980. With Henry Pousseur (q.v.) and Pierre Bartolomée, he belongs to the so-called "Liège (q.v.) musical phenomenon." All three have strong ties with the Center for Music Research of Wallonia (q.v.).

BOON, LOUIS PAUL (1912-1979). Journalist and writer of socialist inclination. He wrote historical novels on ordinary people in a neo-realist vein such as *De Kapellekensbaan, Priester Daens and Het Geuzenboek* (Chapel Road, Priest Daens (q.v.), The Berggar's Book). On the other hand, he was a thorough moralist defending pacifism and respect for basic human values as in *Mijn Kleine Oorlog* (My Little War). Boon experimented with literary structures in *De Vrieskelders* (The Freeze Cellars), and he was a cynical humorist as well. He was proposed several times as a Nobel Prize candidate for literature, but without success.

BOSCH, JEROME (c.1450-1516). Hieronymus Bosch is perhaps the best, and certainly the most enigmatic, painter of the late Flemish Primitives. Little is known with certainty about his private and intellectual life. His paintings contain much appreciated apocalyptical scenes in brilliant colors and magnificent compositions. Endowed with an uncanny mastery of detail, he filled his paintings with strange plants and animals and weird, funny, and frightening figures believed to have been inspired by folk legends, religious literature and elements of late Gothic art. The symbolism in such works as the *Garden of Earthly Delights* is open to wide interpretation. Some earlier interpreters believed Bosch belonged to a Dutch sect, possibly the Broeders van het Gemene Leven (Brothers of the Common Life), but recent research defends a more orthodox interpretation of his grotesque and symbolical scenes.

BOUILLON, GODFREY DE (c.1060-1100). Godefroi IV de Boulogne. Leader of the First Crusade. He was elected the ruler of the Latin Kingdom of Jerusalem after its capture from the Saracens in 1099. He was depicted in later writings as the ideal Christian knight.

BOURLET, MICHEL. Prosecutor at Neufchâteau investigating the Dutroux case (q.v.). He declared that he would bring the investigation to a good end "si on me laisse faire," meaning if they will let me proceed without interfering. This expression fed distrust of Belgian justice and contributed to the success of the White March (q.v.). Later, before the parliamentary Dutroux commission, Bourlet declared that he had made the remark because he faced having to arrest a member of the judicial police, George Zicot, and feared resistance from the juridical authorities or politicians.

BOUTS, DIRK (c.1415-1475). Painter belonging to the so-called second generation of the Flemish Primitives. His Hypolite altar piece hangs in the St. Salvador Cathedral in Bruges (q.v.). His Last Supper and the Torturing of St. Erasmus are in St. Peter's Church at Louvain (q.v.).

BRABANÇONNE, LA. National anthem of Belgium. The music and lyrics were devised by the French actor Jenneval during the Belgian revolution in 1830. The lyrics were rewritten in 1860. The anthem begins: "After centuries of Slavery, The Belgian, rising from the grave..."

BRABANT (DUKEDOM). In 1288, Jean I of Brabant defeated the Archbishop of Cologne in the battle of Woeringen. He gained Luxembourg (q.v.). In 1312, the Charter of Kortenberg guaranteed rights for the citizens and established a council of four nobles and 10 burgers to supervise its application. Jean III attempted to discard the charter, but failed and two new charters (the Chartes Romanes) were imposed on the duke, confirming and even extending the earlier rights. In 1356, the Joyous Entry (Joyeuse Entrée) (q.v.) codified the earlier customary rights and charters. They remained in force until the French Revolution.

Brabant came under the control of the Burgundian Duke Philip the Good (q.v.) in 1430. From then on, it gradually became integrated with the Low Countries (q.v.). Under the Habsburg dynasty (q.v.), it took over the leading economic and cultural role from Flanders (q.v.).

BRABANT (PROVINCE). Brabant was constituted as one of the nine provinces of the Kingdom of Belgium. Due to its bilingual character, it was split in 1995 into a Walloon and a Flemish Brabant. It has two provincial councils, but only one governor and vice governor. The provincial powers in Brussels (q.v.) were assigned to the regional and community councils.

BRABANT REVOLUTION (1789-1790). The Brabant Revolution (Brabantse Omwenteling/Révolution Brabançonne) was a revolt against the Ancien Regime and the enlightened despotism of Joseph II (q.v.). In 1789, the aristocratic and clerical Hendrik Van der Noot (1731-1827) united with the more progressive Frans Vonck (1735-1791) to provoke a successful revolt. In 1790, the revolutionaries proclaimed the independence of the Confederation of the United Belgian States (Confédération des Etats Belges Unis). However, due to the lack of unity between the factions of the revolting forces, Austrian rule (q.v.) was restored.

BRABO. Massive statue at the Grand Place of Antwerp (q.v.). It represents a Roman soldier who cut off the hand of a giant and threw it away. It refers to the mythical explanation for the name of the town: *werpen* means to throw away.

BREL, JACQUES (1929-1978). Flemish French-speaking singer. He presented sensitive songs about the land and people of the seaside. In Flanders (q.v.) he was both admired for his songs and disliked for some Francophone utterances.

BREUGHEL, PETER THE ELDER (?-1569). Pieter Brueghel de Oude painted exquisite portraits of the lives of ordinary people during the Spanish period in the 16th century. He became a master painter in Antwerp (q.v.) in 1551 and visited Italy. In 1563, he married in Brussels (q.v.) and died there six year later.

BREYDEL, JAN (12?-13?). With his companion Pieter De Coninck (q.v.) and an army of 20,000 men from the Flemish towns, he defeated the French army at the Battle of the Golden Spurs near Courtrai (qq.v.) on 11 July 1302.

BROODTHAERS, MARCEL (1924-1976). Painter. Artist of a complex, anti-conventional and literary-based oeuvre. He is famous for his ironic work with natural materials, such mussels' shells, eggs and coal (q.v.).

BROUWER, ADRIAEN (c.1600-?). Painter. Born around 1600 in Oudenaerde (West-Flanders). He travelled through Flanders (q.v.) to arrive in Amsterdam in Holland, where he became a pupil of the Dutch master Frans Hals. He painted mainly popular and tavern scenes in which he illustrated the unconventional lifestyle of the Flemish people. His painting *De Koning drinkt* (The King Drinks) is typical of his subject treatment and style. His life was described in the last book of the Flemish writer Felix Timmermans (q.v.).

BRUGES. Bruges (Brugge) developed as a port on a large arm of the sea. First known as *pagus Flandrensis,* it became the richest and mightiest town of the County of Flanders (q.v.). In it or in its immediate vicinity, the counts of Flanders usually had their seat. At times, even the Burgundian (q.v.) dukes resided in the town.

Bruges is the town in Belgium that has best preserved its medieval character. It is a living museum town. In the center stands the belfry amid the city hall (13th-15th century), the old-record office (16th century) and the law courts. Its precious reliquary is preserved in the upper chapel (15th century) of the Basilica of the Holy Blood, from which it is removed once a year for a procession through the town. The Saint John's hospital still keeps a Memling (q.v.) collection. The Gruuthuuse house has been transformed into another museum. The paintings of the Flemish Primitives Van Eyck, Van der Weyden, Memling, Van der Goes, and of Bosch (qq.v.) can be admired in the local museums. Bruges also preserved its charming Beguine convent.

BRUSSELS. Brussels in the valley of the Senne River is the capital of Belgium. It owes this position largely to the Burgundian (q.v.) dukes who for long periods held court in the town.

Brussels began its existence as a village that developed around a chapel built on an island in the Senne River during the 10th century. Slower to develop than the Flemish towns, Brussels had become the chief town of Brabant (q.v.) by the 14th century. Under Emperor Charles V it became the capital of the Low Countries. The town participated in the revolt against Philip II in 1576 and was recaptured for the Spanish Habsburgs in 1585. Bombarded by the French during the wars of Louis XIV in 1695, the town suffered significant destruction. The center of the Belgian revolution and capital since 1830, Brussels is officially a bilingual city and became one of the three regions in the new federation of Belgium in 1993.

Its Grand Place is surrounded by old monuments, such as the town hall, the guild houses and the King's House. St. Michael's cathedral on the top of the Treurenberg is a majestic building that dates from the 14th to the 16th century. Vestiges of an 11th-century church were found inside. At the Grand Sablon stands the church dedicated to Our Lady of Victory (15th century). Of the nineteenth-century buildings, the huge courts of justice dominate the surroundings. Outside the city center, among the royal buildings, is the very remarkable chapel of Laeken. There are only a few beautiful remains of the Art Nouveau style, such as the hotels and houses built by Victor Horta.

Brussels also boasts many examples of modern architecture, such as the buildings of the European Union (q.v.). From 1958 to 1969, the executive commission of the Common Market was housed in a building on the Avenue de la Joyeuse Entrée. In 1969, it moved to the huge Berlaimont building, which became also the seat of the European Atomic Energy Commission. In the 1980s, the European Parliament also held some of its meetings in Brussels, as do many other commissions that meet in the city, which serves as the seat of the European Union. In the outskirts of Brussels, at Evere, headquarters were built for the NATO Council after it left France in 1967.

Since 1830, Brussels has been the administrative and political center of Belgium. With regionalization, this status has been somewhat weakened, but not reversed. Along with the federal

Parliament and Brussels's own institutions, the Flemish Parliament (q.v.) also has its seat in Brussels. Brussels also houses both its French-speaking and Dutch-speaking free universities (Université Libre de Bruxelles, ULB and Vrije Universiteit Brussel, VUB), and many other educational and scientific institutions. Precious art collections are preserved in many locations, such as the Museum of Arts and the Museum of History. Moreover, Brussels occupies a central place in Europe and its easy communication networks have convinced many major international businesses to establish their headquarters in the center of the city. *See also* BRUSSELS REGIONAL COUNCIL; MANNEKEN PIS.

BRUSSELS REGIONAL COUNCIL. The Brussels Regional Council (Conseil Régional de Bruxelles, CRB) was established in 1989. It has 75 directly elected members. Article 107 quater of the Constitution (q.v.) endowed the regional councils with important competences in the socio-economic field.

BURGUNDIAN DYNASTY. By diplomatic marriage and by force, the Burgundian dynasty built up a territory, that with the exception of Liège (q.v.), included all of the Low Countries. They were united by the person of the monarch and the culture of the court. Measures toward political and administrative centralization were taken as well, though sometimes resisted by the mighty towns which strove for autonomy and respect for their privileges.

The unification process began with the diplomatic marriage of Philip the Bold (q.v.), Duke of Burgundy, to the daughter of the count of Flanders, Margaret of Male (Marguerite de Male) (q.v.) in 1369. Philip the Bold was the son of the French king Jean II de Valois and by the grace of his father duke of Burgundy. In her dowry, Margaret offered to Philip Flanders, Artois, Franche-Comté, Nevers, Rethel and the towns of Antwerp and Mechelen (qq.v.).

John the Fearless (Jean sans Peur) (1404-1419), Philip the Good (Philippe le Bon) (1419-1467) and Charles the Bold (Charles le Téméraire) (1467-1477) (qq.v.) expanded the Burgundian Duchy.

BURY, POL (1922- ). Surrealist painter. His work embodies an evolution to non-figurative art. Later his interests turned toward sculpture. In 1951, he was nominated for the Award of Belgian Young Painting and, in 1972, he won the Robert Giron Prize.

BUSQUIN, PHILIPPE (1941- ). Socialist Party (Parti Socialiste, PS) (q.v.) politician. In 1978, he was elected a deputy to the Chamber. Since 1980, he has been entrusted with several ministerial portfolios at the federal and regional level. He succeeded Guy Spitaels (q.v.) as president of the PS. At the beginning of March 1997, the Socialist Party congress reelected him to the post for a term of two years.

Busquin was accused of embezzlement in the UNIOP (q.v.) case, but granted immunity from prosecution because the case expired under the statute of limitations. Busquin also came under suspicion that he had knowledge of secret party accounts in the Dassault (q.v.) corruption affair, but he has denied the charge.

BUYSSE, CYRIEL (1859-1932). Flemish naturalist writer. He wrote about the harsh working conditions of the working class. However, he also wrote some humoristic pieces and sometimes treated thematically difficult situations in an ironic way. His best known works are *Het Recht van de Sterkste* (The Right of the Strongest) and *Het gezin Van Paemel* (The Van Paemel Family).

## - C -

CAMPIN, ROBERT (?-1440). Master of Flémalle. He obtained his painter's education in France. Around 1420, he opened an atelier in Tournai (q.v.) that was later taken over as head-master by Rogier van der Weyden (q.v.). Campin introduced bourgeois realism into the art of the late Middle Ages. His most famous work—the Mérode triptych—is on exhibit at the Metropolitan Museum of Art in New York.

CAMPO FORMIO, TREATY OF (1797). Agreement between Austria and France by which France gained the Austrian Low Countries (q.v.) and Austria received Istria, Dalmatia and part of the Italian coast.

CATHOLIC PARTY. The first Belgian unitary Catholic Party was formed in 1888 with the merger of Catholic circles and groups under the leadership of August Beernaert. From then on, the party dominated Belgian politics and it governed alone until 1914. Thereafter, it stayed in power in coalitions, either with Socialists or Liberals (qq.v.). It sat in opposition during the postwar years 1945-1947 and the period from 1954-1958. The Catholic Party had always been the largest party except during the years 1925 and 1936. Since 1987, the Catholics lost their majority position.

The autonomy of the Walloon and Flemish wings grew steadily after 1965. In 1968, a breach took place over the Louvain (q.v.) University affair. The old party split into two new ones, a Flemish Christian People's Party (Christelijke Volkspartij, CVP) and a French-speaking Social Christian Party (Parti Social Chrétien, PSC). The Flemish Christian People's Party remained the largest party in Flanders (q.v.). The French one gained a minority status in Wallonia (q.v.), where the Socialists were dominant.

So far, there have been no asymmetrical federal governments, CVP in and PSC out or the reverse. However, participation in the regional governments has been dictated by regional autonomous policy. In community questions conflicting positions and coalitions have been defended by the Christian sister parties. The latest party congress of the CVP took place on 15 June 1996. Just before, Marc van Peel had succeeded Johan van Hecke as interim party president. On 30 November 1996, Van Peel was confirmed as president with 93 percent of the votes. Charles-Ferdinand Nothomb was the long-term president of the PSC. He was replaced by Philippe Maystadt on 25 May 1998.

CENTRAL ECONOMIC COUNCIL. The Central Economic Council (Centrale Raad voor het Bedrijfsleven, CRB) is one of the consultation and participation institutions of the Belgian economy (q.v.). It was agreed on at meetings in London during World War II (q.v.) and installed in 1948. It brings together the social partners —government, business and labor—on economic matters. Its competence is mainly advisory.

CEPIC. The CEPIC or Political Center of Independents and Christian Cadres (Centre Politique des Indépendents et Cadres Chrétiens) is a right-wing organization in the Christian Democrat political family. A party congress of the Christian Social Party (Parti Social Chrétien, PSC) *(see* Catholic Party) recognized the right of existence of the tendency along with that of the left wing, the Christian Workers' Movement (Mouvement Ouvrier Chrétien, MOC), but urged both to support the party policy. Still, the CEPIC seemed to discredit the party at the end of the 1970s through a close association with the far right and in the early 1980s, the new party president Gérard Deprez obliged both tendencies to suspend their activity. However, the CEPIC was more or less offficially converted into a Center Union (Rassemblement du Centre) and operated from then on in the background.

CHAMBER OF DEPUTIES *See* HOUSE OF REPRESENTATIVES.

CHARLEMAGNE (c.742-814). The son of Pépin the Short, Charlemagne became king of the Franks (768-814) and emperor of the West (800-814). He subjugated the Frisians (Friezen) and incorporated all territories of the Low Countries (q.v.) into his empire. He also supported the Christianization of these lands.

CHARLES, PRINCE REGENT (1903-1983). Count of Flanders (q.v.) and regent of Belgium (1944-1950). He was appointed by the parliament to take over temporarily the functions of his brother, King Leopold III (q.v.), immediately after World War II (q.v.). On the basis of article 82 of the Constitution (q.v.), King Leopold III was declared to have forfeited his right to reign. The king had not returned to Belgium following his imprisonment in Germany because of his dubious role during World War II. Prince Charles on the contrary joined the resistance forces in the Ardennes (q.v.).

Charles assumed office on 20 September 1944 and executed his duty until 20 July 1950. Leopold III returned for less than a year and finally abdicated on 16 July 1951, in favor of his eldest son Baudouin (q.v.). Contradictory evidence has been collected on the intentions and role of Prince Regent Charles. Historians recently revealed that the regent sought the intervention of the Vatican to preserve his prerogatives as regent of Belgium at the expense of Leopold III. On the other hand, other historians have pointed out that Prince Regent Charles backed out of a marriage to the sister-in-law of the Count of Paris, the pretender to the French throne in order to avoid inflaming anti-monarchist passions at the time of the referendum on Leopold's return. After his reign, Prince Charles retired to the royal estate of Raversijde at the sea, which has now been transformed into a provincial historic site that functions as a memorial to the prince. *See also* ROYAL CONTROVERSY.

CHARLES OF LORRAINE, DUKE (1712-1780). He became governor of the Austrian Netherlands in 1744 during the reign of Maria Theresa (q.v.). Under his government, the country enjoyed stability and prosperity. It was one of the happier periods of the Ancien Regime.

CHARLES THE BOLD, DUKE OF BURGUNDY (1433-1477). Son of Isabella of Portugal and Philip the Good (qq.v.). Charles the Bold (Charles le Téméraire) reigned from 1467 to 1477. Even before his Joyful Entrance in 1467 in Flanders, he had himself recognized by military force as hereditary regent of Liège (q.v.). Earlier in 1465, he fought the army of the French king at Montlhéry in Picardy and through vigorous fighting gained his nickname (le Téméraire, the Bold). His Joyous Entry (q.v.) into Ghent and Mechelen (qq.v.) was marred by protests against tax increases.

Charles rigorously continued efforts to centralize the Burgundian (q.v.) territories. He established two central accounting chambers, a State Council for drafting laws and he transformed the Great Council, the high appeal courts for all the provinces, into the so-called Parliament of Mechelen. The name of the court referred to the Parliament of Paris, the high court to which all subjects of the vassal states were liable and toward which Charles wanted to stress his independence. Charles imposed French as the sole administrative language of his territories. Locally, he tried to impose the justice of the ducal courts at the expense of town courts and he placed many of his followers in the local administration and political institutions. By selling many functions, he likewise contributed to corruption and widespread dissatisfaction.

In 1473, Charles succeeded in acquiring Gelre, though at times he had to suppress local revolts. He went to war in 1474 in order to connect the Low Countries with his possessions in Burgundy and he managed to bring under his control the Duchy of Alsace and Lorraine. This project proved fatal. Early in 1477, Charles fell near Nancy in a battle against the Lotharingians and their Swiss allies. Earlier conquered regions resumed their independence and France increasingly threatened the frontiers of the Burgundian state. At this moment, the resistance against his internal centralizing policy came into the open as well. Towns and provinces imposed the so-called Great Privilege (q.v.) on Charles's heir and daughter, Mary of Burgundy (q.v.).

Charles's first marriage was to Catherine of France (1433-1446), sister of the king of France, Louis XI (1423-1483). His second marriage was to Isabella of Bourbon (1435/37-1465). She gave him a daughter and future heir, Mary of Burgundy (q.v.) (1457-1482). In 1468, he was married to Margaret of York (1446-1503) in Bruges.

CHARLES V, THE GREAT (1500-1558). In 1500, Charles V was born at Ghent (q.v.) to Philip the Handsome (q.v.) and Joan of Aragon. On the death of his father in 1506, his aunt Margaret of Austria (q.v.) assumed the regency of the Low Countries (q.v.). Charles came of age in 1515 and in 1517, by the death of the Spanish king, he inherited the Spanish lands. This brought the Netherlands under Spain to center stage in European power politics. In 1542, Charles became Holy Roman emperor as well.

During the reign of Charles V and the regency of Margaret of Austria, the process of the integration of the Low Countries (q.v.) went on. First, Charles completed the territorial unity of the region. In 1521, he took Tournai (q.v.) from the French. He succeeded in imposing his temporal authority in the dioceses of Liège and Utrecht (qq.v.). Finally, he acquired Gelre. Second, Charles constituted the provinces as an autonomous and hereditary unit. By the Treaty of Cambrai of 1529, France gave up all claims to suzerainty over Flanders (q.v.). In 1548, the Imperial Diet adopted the Augsberg Transaction. The Low Countries became independent within the Habsburg Empire. The Pragmatic Sanction of 1549 united the inheritance under one prince of the territory of the Low Countries, from now on named the "Seventeen Provinces." In 1555, Charles V agreed to the Peace of Augsburg, which brought temporary religious peace in Germany, after war with Maurice of Saxony and Henri II of France.

In 1556, Charles V abdicated at Brussels in favor of his son Philip II (q.v.). In 1557, Charles retired to a monastery. During his reign, Spain conquered large parts of the American continent. The conquest was accompanied by missionary activities of Flemish priests, for example, Pedro de Gante (Peter of Ghent), who baptized 300,000 American Indians and Jean de Witte (from Bruges), who became the first bishop of Cuba.

CHARLES VI (1685-1740). Holy Roman emperor and king of Hungary (1711-1740), son of emperor Leopold I (1640-1705). Charles's claim on the Spanish throne caused the War of the Spanish Succession (1701-1713). By the Treaty of Utrecht (1713), Charles VI acquired the former Spanish Netherlands. By the Pragmatic Sanction of 1713, he secured recognition of his daughter Maria Theresa (q.v.) as his successor.

CHRISTIAN PEOPLE'S PARTY. *See* CATHOLIC PARTY.

CHRISTUS, PETRUS (c.1415/1420-1472/1473). He was born in northern Brabant (q.v.) and worked from 1444 as a painter in Bruges (q.v.). He belongs to a late offshoot of the Flemish Primitives. His style is simple and more popular than Jan Van Eyck's (q.v.) aristocratic symbolism. He is known for religious scenes and tender portraits of young women. One part of a triptych depicting Isabella of Portugal (q.v.) and St. Elizabeth can be admired at the Groeninghe Museum in Bruges (q.v.). Christus's delicate portrait of a Carthusian monk can be seen at the Metropolitan Museum of Art in New York.

CLAES, ERNEST (1885-1968). Flemish writer of humoristic naturalistic novels and short stories. The character of his most popular book is *The Witte* (The White One), a young boy who by his nonconformist behavior upsets the serious world of adults and its Catholic religious, mostly hypocritical culture. *See* also FILM.

CLAES, LODE (1913-1997). Flemish nationalist politician. Lode Claes was born at Borgerhout near Antwerp (q.v.) and studied law in Louvain (q.v.), where he participated in the Flemish movement (q.v.). During World War II (q.v.), he became alderman of Brussels (q.v.). After the war, he was condemned for collaboration and went to prison from 1944 to 1949. Afterwards, he worked as a journalist for the newspaper *De Standaard*. In 1958, he became general secretary of the Economic Council of Flanders (q.v.). In 1968, he was elected to the Senate for the People's Union (qq.v.). In 1977, he founded his own party, the Flemish People's Party (Vlaamse Volkspartij). In 1978, he agreed to an election coalition with the Flemish National Party of Karel Dillen. A new party, the Flemish Bloc (q.v.), was born. Only Dillen was elected and Claes returned to journalism and worked for the economic magazine *Trends*.

CLAES, WILLY (1938- ). Socialist Party (SP) (q.v.) politician. Claes was mediator *(informateur)* in 1978, 1980 and 1987. In 1979, he was co-mediator with Charles-Ferdinand Nothomb (PSC). He was appointed minister of economic affairs in several governments. In the Dehaene I (q.v.) government (1992-1995), he was minister of foreign affairs. Claes was elected secretary general of the North Atlantic Treaty Organization (NATO) (q.v.), but before ending his term, he had to resign from his post in October 1995 because he was suspected of fraud in the Agusta case (q.v.). At the end of 1998, he appeared before the Supreme Court (q.v.).

CLAUS, HUGO (1929- ). Flanders' (q.v.) greatest contemporary writer. He is outstanding both in writing poetry *(Oostakkerse Gedichten*, Poems from Oostakker), novels *(Het verdriet van België,* The Sorrow of Belgium) and theater plays *(Vrijdag*, Friday). His plays are often interesting contemporary variations on classical myths; his poems and novels bring symbolical transpositions of his personal experiences in a splendid language. Claus has been proposed several times as a Nobel prize candidate, so far without success.

CLOVIS (466-511). He was born at Tournay (Doornik) in the far southwest of Flanders (qq.v.). Chlodovech—Clovis is his Latin name—took over the throne from his father Childeric in 481. He built up his Merovingian kingdom south of the present Belgian territory and is honored as the father of France. Clovis was baptized around 496. On his death, his land was divided between his four sons.

COAL. Major natural resource of Belgium and mined extensively beginning in the 19th century in the Borinage region southwest of Namur (q.v.) and also in Liège and Limburg (qq.v.) provinces. Squalid living conditions among the coal miners gave rise to demands for social reforms and helped give birth to the Socialist movement. In recent years, the mines have largely been closed.

COBRA (1948-1951). Art movement with roots in Copenhagen, Brussels (q.v.) and Amsterdam. It brought together experimental and cosmopolitan artists who represented the avant-garde of their countries. They launched a new trend in the arts and art criticism.

COCKERILL, WILLIAM (1759-1832). English inventor and manufacturer. He constructed the first wool-carding and spinning machines in continental Europe at Verviers (q.v.) in 1799. In 1807, he built a factory at Liège (q.v.) to manufacture these machines. His youngest son John (1790-1840) developed the business and built a foundry and machine factory at Seraing in 1817. Their efforts contributed to making Belgium the first country in Europe following Britain to experience the Industrial Revolution.

COCOF. Commission of the French Community competent for language questions in the agglomeration of Brussels (q.v.). It is the counterpart of the COCON, the commission of the Flemish Community competent for Brussels.

COEME, GUY (1946- ). Socialist Party (PS) (q.v.) politician. He held the defense portfolio in the Martens (q.v.) VIII government. He was implicated in the UNIOP (q.v.) corruption scandal and had to resign. A parliamentary commission examined the charges and found him liable to appear before the Supreme Court (q.v.).

COLLABORATION. Collaboration in Belgium during World War II (q.v.) was punished as a crime after the war by military courts. The auditor-general of the military court at the time was Walter

Ganshof van der Meersch. Most forms of collaboration were strictly punished, though punishment varied depending on the time period and place of judgment.

Political collaboration with Nazi Germany was treated most severely. The most prominent leaders of the collaboration movement were sentenced to death. Prison sentences were numerous. Most of those convicted lost their political rights.

Economic collaboration could be defined in two ways. In a broad sense, every businessman who continued to operate during the German occupation could be accused of economic collaboration (Article 115 of the Penal Code). However, the first postwar government of the Socialist Prime Minister Achiel Van Acker accepted a narrower definition. Economic collaboration was considered to be any activity that contributed directly to the German war effort. These activities happened to be more widespread in Flanders than in Wallonia (qq.v.). Many Flemish enterprises participated in the construction of the Atlantic wall against an invasion of the Allies on Flanders' soil. Following the narrow definition, 688 files of economic collaboration have been judged since May 1945. Of these, 1,060 individuals were sentenced and one-third of them received a sentence of more than five years of prison.

The extent of military collaboration in Belgium is greatly disputed. Most of the relevant records were burned before the arrival of the Allied armies. In 1945, during the immediate postwar period, judges estimated military collaboration at more or less 100,000 cases. Of the 56,000 convicted collaborators, about 32,000 were charged with bearing arms in uniform against their country. Collaborators lost their political rights and some were imprisoned until the early 1950s. Under an amnesty (q.v.) agreement, several forms of amnesty were granted, depending on the gravity of the facts and the sentences. *See* also FLEMISH NATIONAL UNION; WAFFEN SS.

COLLARD, LEO (1902-1981). From 1932 to 1974, Collard was active in local politics at Bergen and from 1932 to 1971, he held a seat in the Chamber of Deputies as a Socialist representative. He became minister of education. The law of 1955 that carries his name led to a school war. He was president of the Belgian Socialist Party (q.v.) from 1959 to 1971.

COLLEGE FOR APPOINTMENTS AND PROMOTIONS. The College for appointments and promotions (Benoemings- en Bevorderingscollege) in the judicial system has been established in reaction to public criticism of political appointments raised during the protest actions of the White March (q.v.) .

COLLIGNON, ROBERT (1943- ). Minister-president of the Walloon Region since 1994. He is a representative of the Socialist Party (Parti Socialiste, PS) (q.v.) in which he held high offices and for which he was a member of Parliament (q.v.). He was also minister in the Walloon government.

COMIC STRIPS. Though some artists dedicated themselves to comic strips before World War II (q.v.), Belgian comic strips became immensely popular only in the 1950s. Hergé (q.v.) is the pioneer and first well-known master of the school of Belgian comic strip designers. He is the creator of Kuifje/Tintin. His work is known for its clear lines. A contemporaneous figure was Spirou/Robbedoes, brought into life by Jijé (Joseph Gillain) and continued by André Franquin (q.v.). Franquin is also the spiritual father of Gust Flater and the Marsupilami. A third success story was the cowboy Lucky Luke and his faithful horse Jolly Jumper.

A little bit more regionally colored in their early appearances are the stories of Suske and Wiske/Bob and Bobette of Willy Vandersteen and Nero of Marc Sleen.

The younger generation manifested its creativity in the wake of the revolt of 1968 and in the 1970s, when many creations displayed a more explicit aesthetic character. In the 1980s, the absurd comic strips of Kamagurka and Herr Seele in the magazine *Humo* were the absolute trendsetters.

It is a remarkable fact—worthy of deeper anthropological or sociological research—that comic strips have always played and still play a significant role in the life and education of most Belgians. Though of course American influence on Belgian cultural life after the liberation can be identified as a major determinant, it does not tell the whole story.

COMMISSION FOR BANKING AND FINANCE. This state commission (Commissie voor Bank en Financiewezen, CBF) grants and withdraws operating rights of Belgian banking institutions. It regulates the operations of banks to ensure their financial viability and can implement controlling measures. For example, in 1996, it suspended the working license of the Max Fisher Bank in Antwerp (q.v.) on charges of fraud.

COMMITTEE P. The Committee P. (Comité P.) was established to control the police forces and investigation services. For example, the Committee P. made an inquiry into the supposed links of local police forces with the meat mafia and it audited files of the High Inspection Committee (Hoog Comité van Toezicht).

CONFEDERATION OF CHRISTIAN AND FREE UNIONS. The Confederation of Christian and Free Unions of Belgium (Confédération des Syndicats Chrétiens et Libres de Belgique, CSC) was created in 1912. It gathered under one organization earlier Christian syndicalist groups. The first Christian trade unions had been founded in the 1880s as a reaction to Socialist initiatives. The movement was strongly influenced by the papal encyclical Rerum Novarum of 1893. After World War II, the Christian trade union movement expanded widely and became the largest among the unions in Flanders (q.v.). In Wallonia (q.v.), its role is still modest.

As the Christian union ideology more actively encouraged participation and cooperation than did that of the Socialists, it had a significant impact on the economic and social policy of the country.

CONFEDERATION OF THE UNITED BELGIAN STATES (CONFEDERATION DES ETATS BELGES UNIS) *See* BRABANT REVOLUTION

CONGO, BELGIAN. With the help of English explorer Henry M. Stanley, King Leopold II (q.v.) publicized and encouraged exploration of vast regions along the Congo River in central Africa. In 1882, Leopold created the International Association of the Congo, a private commercial venture. In May 1885, a royal decree proclaimed the establishment of the Congo Free State, with Leopold as its ruler. Administered solely for economic gain, the territory was exploited ruthlessly. Slavery and tribal warfare were rife in many areas. Many nations, especially Britain, protested. Belgian public and political opinion, initially reluctant to take responsibility, yielded to growing domestic and international pressure and the government annexed the territory as a colony in 1908.

Administered under tight control from Brussels, which was slow to implement change, the Belgian Congo was swept by sentiment for independence in the 1950s. Although King Baudouin (q.v.) carried out a successful visit in May and June of 1955, the country was racked by riots in 1959 and the government moved quickly to grant independence on 30 June 1960. Rival leaders subbsequently competed for control and a mutiny of the police force in July compelled Belgium to send troops to restore order and protect its citizens. The troops were withdrawn following the arrival of United Nations peacekeeping forces. Diplomatic ties, broken in 1960, were restored in 1964. In 1972, the Congo was renamed Zaire, but returned to the name Congo in 1997. Because of traditional ties, but also in defense of economic interests, the Belgian government tried to maintain a preferential relationship with Congo/Zaire. This came to an end under the Laurent Kabila regime.

CONGRESS OF VIENNA (1814-1815). The Congress of Vienna officially recognized the new state of the Kingdom of the Netherlands, designed by the Protocol of London (q.v.) or the Act of VIII Articles.

CONSCIENCE, HENDRIK (1812-1883). Most popular Flemish-speaking writer of the 19th century. He stimulated Flemish national sentiment by publishing several books on historic and national themes, among others *De Leeuw van Vlaanderen* (The Lion of Flanders, 1838). Hendrik Conscience won the reputation as the Flemish writer who "taught his people to read." He was active in the Flemish movement (q.v.), but his Belgian sympathies were beyond doubt.

CONSTITUTION. The Kingdom of Belgium was established in 1831 as a constitutional parliamentary monarchy. It was constitutionally set up as a unitary state and this remained in effect until 1970. Four constitutional reforms in less than 25 years transformed the country into a federal state. The coordinated text of the latest Constitution was officially published in the State Bulletin of 17

February 1994. It counts 198 articles. Article 1 of the Constitution clearly states that Belgium is a federal state. Seven more special and five ordinary laws define further the main provisions of the Constitution. *See also* CONSTITUTIONAL REFORM; CONSTITUTIONAL REFORM OF 1970; CONSTITUTIONAL REFORM OF 1980; CONSTITUTIONAL REFORM OF 1988; CONSTITUTIONAL REFORM OF 1993.

CONSTITUTIONAL AMENDMENT OF 1993 ON THE SUCCESSION. The constitutional revision of 1993 on the succession allows women to accede to the Belgian throne. Historians hold that this was done at the request of King Baudouin (q.v.) himself. He apparently did not have enough confidence in the capacities of his nephew Laurent, second in line if Laurent's brother remained childless. This move made Laurent's older sister Astrid and her four children second in line. Baudouin's worries seemed misplaced, as unexpectedly his brother Albert (q.v.) and not Philippe was urged by political circles to take the crown.

CONSTITUTIONAL REFORM. For a constitutional transformation of the Belgian unitary state into a federation, identical amendment texts had to be passed in both chambers of Parliament (q.v.) with a two-thirds majority and a simple majority in each language group needed to ensure passage. Moreover, the new parliament had to be declared "constituent" (*grondwetgevend, constituant)* in the last session of the former parliament by passage of a declaration of intention to enact constitutional reform and including a statement listing all the articles to be changed. Sometimes, governments fell unexpectedly or Parliament was not able to do the preparatory work. For example, the 1977 legislature was not "constituent." Sometimes, demands for changes could not be met because the requisite legislative actions had not been taken. For example, in 1996, the Liberal opposition claimed that the reform of the judiciary system implying a change in the powers of the Supreme Court consequent to the Eli Di Rupo case (qq.v.) was not possible along the lines proposed by the government because an article in the Constitution (q.v.) had not been declared subject to change by the previous Parliament.

CONSTITUTIONAL REFORM OF 1970. In 1968, a Christian-Socialist government was formed under Gaston Eyskens (q.v.). In February 1970, the government succeeded in enacting a compromise on a proposal that laid down the basic principles for the nascent federalization of Belgium. The legislation was passed through both chambers of Parliament (q.v.) before the end of the year. Support from the federalist-minded People's Union (q.v.) helped in reaching the two-thirds majority in Parliament needed for the constitutional reform.

The basic new feature of the reform was the legal creation through Article 59 bis of the Cultural Councils (q.v.) of the Dutch-speaking and the French-speaking Communities, and the creation by Article 59 ter of a Council for the German-speaking Community. They were given legislative competences in cultural matters. Moreover, Article 107 quater foresaw regional councils for Wallonia, Flanders and Brussels (qq.v.) with competences in socio-economic matters. However, it was agreed that for the implementation of these articles by ordinary law, again a two-thirds majority would be required. By Article 38 and 38 bis, an alarm-bell procedure (q.v.) was installed, giving two-thirds of a language group the right to block language laws.

Given the need for gradual change necessitated by the political situation in the early 1970s, only the article on the cultural communities was implemented, while the economic regionalization had to wait for action to be taken.

CONSTITUTIONAL REFORM OF 1980. The second constitutional reform, laid down in the Constitutional Amendment of 1980, considerably expanded the powers of the communities. First, welfare policy was included in the package of the earlier Cultural Council (q.v.) for the Dutch Cultural Community, now renamed Flemish Community Council of the Flemish Community. Second, endowed with some new powers on "territory-related" matters, such as the economy, town and country-planning and the environment, the Flanders Region and its council, the Flemish Regional Council, were established. The Flemish Community Council continued to be responsible for the language policy in Brussels (q.v.), but the Regional Council has no legal jurisdiction there, as a local organ was formed. In contrast to the French-speaking Community and the Walloon Region, Flanders (q.v.) preferred to merge its two Councils into the one Flemish Parliament. Under the new regulation, the Parliament also had the right to install its own government.

The Constitutional Amendments of 1988 and 1993 (qq.v.) further increased the powers of the Flemish Parliament.

CONSTITUTIONAL REFORM OF 1988. After the fall of the Martens (q.v.) VII government, the future vice-premier Jean-Luc Dehaene (q.v.) set up a complex negotiating structure with the aim of guaranteeing the necessary majorities—both national and in each language group—to reform the Constitution (q.v.). The coalition agreement signed on 2 May 1988 of the Martens VIII government gave a detailed account of the proposed constitutional reform. It prescribed reforms in three phases.

In the first phase, during July and August 1988, reform of Articles 17, 47, 48, 59 ter, 107 ter, 108 and 115 of the Constitution was undertaken. It included the strengthening of the consultative powers of the regions, the regionalization of education, the establishment of an arbitration court and the regularization of the situation of Brussels (q.v.) and the communes located on the language border. The second phase from January to June 1989 revised Article 59 ter on the German Community and refined some solutions on the arbitration court and on the region of Brussels. Difficult points—such as the international competences of the regions—were delayed to the third phase. A solution had to be found for the question of the exclusive competences of the central government and the direct election of the community and regional councils. The reform of the Senate (q.v.) also had to be regulated. In fact, all proposals designed for implementation during the third phase were temporarily left in abeyance. A large part of these were realized by the Constitutional Reform of 1993 (q.v.).

CONSTITUTIONAL REFORM OF 1993. Until 21 May 1995, the members of the Flemish Parliament were still indirectly elected as they comprised the elected Dutch-speaking members of the National Parliament (q.v.). The double mandate of these members and their conflicting allegiances were considered to be a hindrance to the optimal functioning of an autonomous Flemish Parliament. The Constitutional Amendment of 1993 reversed this situation, so that members of the Flemish Parliament are now directly elected. With the St. Michael's Agreement (q.v.) and the Constitutional Amendment of 1993, politicians expected a communal truce until 1999, when financial regulations of the communities should be reconsidered.

COOLS, ANDRE (1927-1991). Socialist (Parti Socialiste, PS) (q.v.) politician. Mayor of Flémalle in 1964, parliamentary representative from 1958. He became minister for the budget and economy and vice premier. In 1973, he was co-president of the unitary Socialist Party (PSB/BSP). After the split, he became president of the PS. In 1981, he was elected president of the Council of the Walloon Region.

On 18 July 1991, Cools was murdered in Cointe by hired killers, Abdelmajid Ben Ami (31) and Brahim Abdeljelil Ben Regeb (24) from Tunis. The investigation led by the investigating judge Véronique Ancia was lenghty. Finally, the killers were identified by an anonymous witness, who received 10 million BEF for his testimony. So far, the real instigators of the murder have not been identified. It was rumored that they were to be found in the higher circles of the Socialist Party. In fact, ex-PS-minister Alain Van der Biest was arrested and held in preventive detention. He was accused by his former secretary to have actually stated that he wanted Cools done away with. After four months of detention Van der Biest was temporarily released because no further evidence could be found. Van der Biest confessed only that he was regularly drunk and at such times could say anything. Later on, probably in connection with the Dutroux case (q.v.), Véronique Ancia received threats from an anonymous person belonging to a mysterious organization, "La Cagoule" (De bivakmuts).

COUNCIL OF FLANDERS. This council was installed by the German occupier in 1917, in line with the decree on the administrative separation of Flanders and Wallonia (qq.v.).

COUNCIL OF THE BRUSSELS REGION. The Council of the Brussels Region (Conseil de Région Bruxelles Capitale, CBR) was elected for the first time in June 1989 for a five-year term. Its composition has been regulated by a strict proportional representation of language groups: 11 members are Flemish-speaking and 64 are French-speaking. Further guarantees for language groups are foreseen in respect to participation in the executive and in the commissions.

COUNCIL OF THE GERMAN COMMUNITY (RAT DER DEUTSCHEN GEMEINSCHAFT, RDG). The Council of the German Community was created in 1973 and holds its sessions in Eupen, the capital of the German-speaking area. It has 25 directly elected members. The largest fraction is composed of Christian Social Party (Parti Social Chrétien, PSC) *(See* CATHOLIC PARTY) politicians, the second largest consists of five members of the local Party of German-speaking Belgians (Partei der Deutschsprachigen Belgien). It has the same cultural and personal matters' related *(persoonsgebonden)* competences as the Cultural Councils of the French and Dutch language communities, established by the Constitutional Reform of 1970 (q.v.). For economic decision-making, the German area depends on the Walloon Regional Council and its government.

COURT OF APPEAL. There are five Courts of Appeal. They treat the appeals of parties contesting the judgments of ordinary courts. Until 1970, there were three Courts of Appeal. The Constitutional Reform of 1970 (q.v.) created two more. The Courts of Appeal are located in Brussels for the province of Brabant, in Ghent for the provinces of East and West Flanders, in the city of Antwerp for the provinces of Antwerp and Limburg, in Liège for the provinces of Liège, Namur and Luxembourg, and in Mons for the province of Hainaut (qq.v.). The judges of the Courts of Appeal are nominated by the political authorities, the members of the Provincial Council, and judges of the Courts of Appeal themselves. The only appeal possible against the decisions of Courts of Appeal is to the Supreme Court (q.v.), but only on formal procedural grounds.

COURTRAI (KORTRIJK). It is now a little town in the northwest of Belgium. In the early Middle Ages, it was a very important center of the Flemish textile industry. Preserved from this time is a beautiful belfry and a market place. In its vicinity, in 1302, the Battle of the Golden Spurs (q.v.) was fought. It was later superseded as an important trade center by Bruges and Ghent (qq.v.). In the surrounding area, there are still important archaeological sites.

CULTURAL COUNCILS. The Cultural Councils were created by Articles 59 bis and 59 ter of the Constitution (q.v.). The Flemish, Francophone and German Cultural Councils have legislative competences in the cultural field. They were the first officially recognized bodies created in the transformation from centralization to federalization. They were established in the beginning of the 1970s.

CUSTOMS AND MONETARY UNION WITH LUXEMBOURG. Both Belgium and Luxembourg suffered occupation and devastation under the Germans in World War I (q.v.). To promote economic recovery, the two countries signed an agreement on 21 July 1921 to establish a customs and monetary union. Under the agreement, tariff barriers between the two countries were reduced and the Belgian and Luxembourg francs were made equal in value and validity in both countries.

Belgian currency became acceptable everywhere in Luxembourg. Following World War II (q.v.), the two countries renewed the union in 1947. The customs union was extended to the Netherlands in 1948. *See also* BENELUX.

## - D -

DAENS, AUGUST ADOLF (1839-1907). The priest Daens was highly moved by the misery of the industrial proletariat he encountered in Aalst. He founded a political party of Social-Christian tendency, the Parti Populaire Chrétien, and soon came into conflict with the official Catholic Party (q.v.) and hierarchy. At the elections, he won a seat in Parliament and there defended his radical humanistic and Flemish positions.

The figure of Daens was immortalized in a novel of Louis Paul Boon (q.v.) and further popularized in a film (q.v.) of Stijn Coninckx.

DAMME. Bruges's (q.v.) former outer harbor. It has preserved its lovely channels, a monumental church of the thirteenth-fourteenth century and a town hall of the fifteenth century. In 1468, the Burgundian Duke Charles the Bold (q.v.) was married here to Margaret of York.

DASSAULT CASE. Dassault, a French airplane construction firm, secured a contract of 6.5 billion francs from the Belgian state in 1989 following a public tender. It was later claimed that the firm paid black money to the Socialist parties in order to obtain the order for airplane modernization in the Belgian armed forces.

For example, at least 30 million BEF had apparently been secreted to the Socialist Party (PS) (q.v.), then under the presidency of Guy Spitaels (q.v.), to obtain the order. Consequently, in January 1997, the judiciary asked the Walloon Parliament to lift the parliamentary immunity of Spitaels on charges of corruption in the Dassault case. On 26 February, Spitaels resigned as president of the Walloon Assembly. He admitted that he had knowledge of a secret party bank account in Luxembourg. On 7 April 1997, he resigned as mayor of Ath as a consequence of the official charges made against him in the Dassault case. At the end of March his parliamentary immunity was also lifted by the Walloon Region Parliament.

In the case many other public personalities were charged with corruption: Willy Claes, Guy Coëme (qq.v.), Etienne Mangé, Luc Wallyn, Johan Delanghe, Alfons Pulinckx, Merry Hermanus, François Pirot, André Bastien and Jean-Louis Mazy, along with Serge Dassault. All with the exception of Guy Spitaels are also implicated in the Agusta case (q.v.), together with former Agusta boss Rafaelo Teti.

DAVID, GERARD (1450-1523). Late representative of the second generation of Flemish Primitives in Bruges (q.v.). One of his best known triptychs is *The Nativity of Christ.*

DAVID, JAN BAPTIST (1801-1866). Flemish priest, linguist, historian and editor of old Flemish manuscripts. He became a professor at the University of Mechelen (later Louvain). He was one of the leaders of the Flemish movement (q.v.) and as such he participated in many political and juridical actions aimed at securing equal rights for Flemish-language speakers. After his death, his name was bequeathed to the greatest Flemish cultural Christian organization, the *Davidsfonds*.

DE BATSELIER, NORBERT (1947- ). Socialist Party (SP) (q.v.) politician. Former vice president of the Flemish government (1988-1995) and minister responsible for economic matters (1988-1992) and for the environment (1992-1995). He worked out an action plan for the environmental cleanup of the soil that was strongly contested by the farmers. In 1995, he became president of the Flemish Parliament.

DE BROUCKERE, LOUIS (1870-1952). Socialist Party (q.v.) leader and diplomat. He served as Belgian representative to the League of Nations from 1922 to 1930. Brussels's Times Square or Picadilly Circus, the Place de Brouckère, is named for him.

DE CLERCK, STEFAAN (1951- ). Christian People's Party (CVP) (q.v.) politician. Minister of justice since 1995. He played an important role in the reform of the judiciary system after the Dutroux affair and the White March (qq.v.). However, he was forced to resign after the escape of Marc Dutroux on 23 April 1998. His policy was continued by his party colleague and member of the parliamentary Dutroux commission, Tony Van Parys.

DE COMMYNES, PHILIP (c.1447-c.1511). French historian. his *Mémoires* provide a firsthand source for the history of Flanders (q.v.). He described the latter part of Philip the Good's (q.v.) reign from 1440 to 1465 as "good": a period of peace and stability, low taxes and a luxurious court life.

DE CONINCK, PIETER (13th-14th century). Leader of the weavers of Bruges (q.v.). With his companion Jan Breydel (q.v.) and an army of 20,000 men from the Flemish towns, he defeated the French army at the Battle of the Golden Spurs near Courtrai (qq.v.) on 11 July 1302.

DE CROO, HERMAN (1937- ). Liberal (PVV, VLD) (q.v.) politician. Former minister. Herman de Croo succeeded Guy Verhofstadt (q.v.) as president of the Flemish Liberals (Vlaamse Liberalen en Democraten, VLD), and was himself later succeeded by the latter.

DE HERT, ROBBE (1942- ). He was together with Patrik Lebon one of the Flemish innovators of the alternative cinema in the 1960s. With scarce financial resources, he initiated a production house that produced a series of remarkable and socially committed pictures. At the end of the 1970s, he adapted literary classics with much skill, for example *De Witte van Sichem* (The White One from Sichem, 1980) from Ernest Claes (q.v.). In the 1980s, the filmmaker turned to nostalgic films on autobiographical themes *(Blueberry Hill*, 1995). *See also* FILM.

DE LA PASTURE, ROGER. *See* VAN DER WEYDEN, ROGIER.

DE RAET, LODEWIJK (1870-1914). One of the intellectual leaders of the Flemish movement (q.v.). He pleaded for the use of Flemish in Flemish commercial and business life and at the University of Ghent. One of Flanders's (q.v.) educational institutions carries his name (Stichting Lodewijk de Raet).

DEGRELLE, LEON (1906-1994). Born in Bouillon. Editor of a catholic journal in the early 1930s, he founded the Rex movement, which called for reduced powers for Parliament and attacked the excesses of both capitalism and socialism. The Rex won 21 seats in the Chamber in the elections of May 1936. The movement took on a more fascist character and popular support waned, although Dégrelle himself won a seat in the Chamber in the elections of April 1939. He was an enthusiastic collaborator with the Germans following the occupation in 1940. He fought on the German side on the eastern front during World War II (q.v.). After the war, he was sentenced to death. He fled to Spain where he lived until his death. In a well-known interview with a journalist from Belgian television, Maurice De Wilde, he declared that he did not to regret his past policies and behavior. *See also* REX.

DEHAENE, JEAN-LUC (1940- ). CVP politician. Dehaene became vice president of the Young Christian Democrats in 1969 under

President Wilfried Martens (q.v.). From 1965 to 1972, he worked for the Christian Union of Workers. From 1972, he held a seat in the national bureau of the Christian People's Party (CVP) *(See* Catholic Party).

In 1981, Dehaene became minister of social affairs and institutional reforms. In 1982, he was coopted as a member of the Senate (q.v.). In the elections of 1987, he won a seat in the House of Representatives (q.v.). He was then appointed vice premier and minister of communications and institutional reforms in the Martens (q.v.) VIII government (1988-1991).

Since 1992, Dehaene has served as prime minister of the federal government in coalitions with the Socialists (1992-1995, 1995-1999). He secured passage of the Constitutional Reforms of 1993 (q.v.).

DEHOUSSE, JEAN-MAURICE (1936- ). Socialist Party (Parti Socialiste, PS) (q.v.) politician. He was elected to Parliament (q.v.) in 1971. In 1975, he became a member of the Socialist Bureau, the leading body of the PS. In 1997, he was appointed as the minister of French culture and in 1979 minister of the Walloon Region. In 1981, he was minister for the economy of the Walloon Region and in 1982 president of the Walloon government. In this function, he signed the treaty on the Council (later Assembly) of Regions of Europe in March 1985. He also proposed locating the political bodies of the Walloon Region in Namur (q.v.), the economic institutions in Liège (q.v.) and the social institutions in Charleroi. Dehousse scored a victory in the elections of 1991 and became minister of science policy in the federal government of Prime Minister Jean-Luc Dehaene (q.v.). After the communal elections of 1994, he resigned his ministerial duties to become mayor of Liège.

DELAHAUT, JO (1911-1992). Abstract painter and designer. In the 1960s, he evolved toward a more lyric abstract style of painting.

DELVAUX, PAUL (1897-1994). Surrealist painter. He is especially known for his strange compositions of half-naked female figures in train stations.

DEMOCRATIC FRONT OF FRANCOPHONES. The Democratic Front of Francophones (Front Démocratique des Francophones, FDF) was founded on 1 July 1961 from the Front pour la Défense de Bruxelles (Front for the Defense of Brussels). In the parliamentary elections of 23 May 1965, it obtained 10 percent of the votes in Brussels (q.v.), which secured for it three seats in Parliament. The party grew steadily to 18.6 percent in 1968, 34.5 percent in 1971, 39.6 percent in 1974, 34.9 percent in 1977 and 35.1 percent in 1978. Thus, it was the largest party in the Brussels region and held a majority position in one of the three regions of Belgium. The FDF also captured power in the Agglomeration Council of Brussels. It entered the government at the end of the 1970s and stayed in power in the beginning of the 1980s. Then, under pressure from the Christian People's Party (Christelijke Volkspartij, CVP) *(See* CATHOLIC PARTY), it left the government. Afterwards, it sought an alliance with the Walloon Union (Rassemblement Wallon, RW) (q.v.) to strengthen the Francophone front of Brussels and Wallonia (q.v.). However, this caused a split in the RW. The economic crisis turned the electorate away from the community question. The FDF fell back to 20.3 percent in 1981, 10.9 percent in 1984 and 10.8 percent in 1987.

The FDF demanded equal status for the region of Brussels. This was granted in principle by the Egmont Pact (q.v.), but it was afterwards not implemented under pressure from the CVP. Likewise, its demand for an extension of the Brussels region beyond the existing 19 communes has been rejected. In 1989, the FDF participated as one of the parties in the majority coalition on the newly created Council of the Brussels Region (q.v.).

DESTREE, JULES (1863-1936). Walloon Socialist politician. He was born in Marcinelle near Charleroi into a well-to-do family. He studied law in Brussels (q.v.) and, as a young lawyer, he defended Walloon union leaders. He took part in the campaign for universal voting rights and founded the Federalist Association of Charleroi. In 1894, he was elected a Socialist deputy to Parliament (q.v.), where he would hold a seat until the end of his life.

In 1898, Destrée published *Le Socialisme en Belgique* (Socialism in Belgium). He was active as an art critic and sought to define the Walloon characteristics of art. He believed Walloon painters to be more poetic than Flemish or Dutch ones, who he felt excelled in realism. He also accused Flemish art critics of adopting for their own Walloon painters such as Roger de la Pasture (Rogier van der Weyden) who lived in Tournai (Doornik) (qq.v.). In this spirit, he organized an exhibition of Walloon art in 1912.

Jules Destrée will remain famous for his *Lettre au Roi* (Letter to the King) of 15 August 1912, in which he pointedly said: "Majesty, there are no Belgians." He denied any pre-existence of a Belgian nation under the Burgundians (q.v.) and stressed the differences between Flanders and Wallonia (qq.v.). He pleaded for a Belgian federation of two free peoples, the Flemish and the Walloons.

In 1913, he acted as secretary of the Walloon Parliament—a far forerunner of the later federal institution, but of course, then without any official competencies. Due to World War I, all promotion of federalization was abandoned in favor of a Belgian patriotism against the German occupier. During the war, Destrée served in the Belgian diplomatic corps in Russia, Japan and China. After the war, he became minister of science and arts. In 1929, he proposed in vain a compromise with the Flemish, laid down in his publication *Compromis des Belges* (Belgian Compromise). In 1936, Destrée died without having realized his dream of federalization. An important Walloon cultural organization was given his name. *See also* WALLOON MOVEMENT.

DI RUPO, ELIO (1951- ). Socialist (Parti Socialiste, PS) (q.v.) politician. He is one of the vice premiers in the government of Jean-Luc Dehaene (q.v.).

In the middle of 1996, rumors appeared about his supposed homosexual relations with minors. The prosecutor of the Court of Cassation, Van Audenhove—a man of liberal background, the Liberal Party (q.v.) then being in the opposition—felt constitutionally obliged to pass the file to Parliament (q.v.). According to constitutional prescriptions, Parliament had to decide if Di Rupo's parliamentary immunity was to be lifted. Parliament proposed an intermediate solution and, following a limited investigation, the minister was exonerated from the accusations. On this occasion,

Parliament proposed a new law—the Di Rupo Law (q.v.)—that invests the prosecutors of the Court of Cassation with limited investigatory powers without prior consent of Parliament.

DI RUPO LAW. On the occasion of the unproven charge of pedophilia directed at vice premier Elio Di Rupo (q.v.), a new law was proposed. Heretofore, constitutional prescriptions demanded that any charge against a member of government should be considered first by Parliament (q.v.), since only this body could lift the immunity of a politician. This procedure damaged the reputation of politicians, as even minor or false charges led to a public debate. The new law prescribes that the court can start autonomously a discreet investigation of the politician without consent of the Parliament. However, heavy investigatory procedures are not allowed. For these the consent of Parliament is needed as before. Also, if the results of investigation are positive and the charges are upheld, the court must still turn to Parliament in order to lift the immunity of the politician.

DOORNIK. *See* TOURNAI.

DOSFEL, LODEWIJK (1881-1924). Leader of the Flemish movement (q.v.).

DU BOIS, ALBERT (?-1940). Walloon diplomat and writer. He was born into an aristocratic family. He worked as a secretary to the embassy in London, where he was dismissed for his nationalistic writings. He wrote *Belges ou Français?* (Belgians or Frenchmen?) and *Cathéchisme Wallon* (A Walloon Catechism). The first work describes the battle of Waterloo and in the foreword, Du Bois affirms that Belgians are French. Seven characteristics that build a nation are common to French and Walloons: they share the same race, language, habits, history, religion, laws and above all the will to live together. In his eyes, Belgium is an artificial construction that Walloons should leave as soon as possible. More than one million copies of his *Cathéchisme Wallon* were distributed.

Albert Du Bois strongly influenced the thinking of the great leader and father of the Walloon movement, Jules Destrée (qq.v.).

**DUTCH.** Official language of the Low Countries and the Flemish-speaking part of Belgium. The Dutch dialects developed from the Germanic language group as one of the West Germanic languages, along with English, Frisian and German. Around 400 A.D. the Germanic dialects had differentiated themselves into East, North and West Germanic dialects. The Germanic languages belong to the Indo-European family of languages, which also includes the Romance and Celtic language group. As interrelations existed between Germanic, Roman and Celtic tribes in earlier periods, present-day Dutch and Flemish—the southern variant of Dutch—contain some Celtic and Roman elements.

The designation *Nederlands* (Netherlandic, i.e. Dutch) appeared for the first time in 1482. Before that the dialects of the area were known as *Dietsch* or *Duutsch*. *Dietsch* means "of the diet" or people.

It was in Holland, one of the provinces of the Low Countries, that standard Dutch was definitively shaped. The language of the refugees from Flanders and Brabant (qq.v.) who fled the Spanish Inquisition merged with the local dialect of the population of Amsterdam. The standardization of Dutch was further helped by the publication of the States Bible in Leyden in 1637. Also the North-Netherlandic author P.C. Hooft (1581-1647) contributed extensively to the development of a classical language. *See also* FLEMISH LANGUAGE.

**DUTCH COMMUNITY COMMISSION.** *See* FLEMISH COMMUNITY COMMISSION (COCON).

**DUTCH CULTURAL COUNCIL.** *See* FLEMISH CULTURAL COUNCIL.

**DUTROUX CASE (1996).** The Dutroux case was one among a long list of earlier unsolved criminal and political affairs, including the killing of 28 people by the paramilitary forces of the Gang of Nivelles, the corruption in the Agusta case (q.v.) and the abdication of Willy Claes (q.v.), the unsolved murder of the Socialist politician André Cools (q.v.) and others. But because in this case the victims were ordinary young girls, public protest exploded.

The case stems from the discovery of the bodies of four girls—Julie, Mélissa, An and Eefje. Prime suspect Marc Dutroux seems to have also killed his earlier associate Bernard Weinstein. Following the confessions of Dutroux, two girls, Sabine and Laetitia, were found alive, though physically abused and mentally broken. Dutroux was said to be in close contact with a pedophilic network and the role of a key player, Michel Nihoul—who seems to have ties with politicians—is under further investigation.

Public opinion exploded when one inspector on the Neufchâteau team, the investigating magistrate Jean-Marc Connerotte, who substantially contributed to the solution of the case, was removed from the investigation. He had been seen at a solidarity meeting for the victims' families, eating spaghetti. The complaint of the defense attorney for Dutroux was validated by the Court of Cassation (the so-called "spaghetti arrest"). This was seen by the general public as further proof of the lack of will of the judicial system to combat injustice. The public no longer accepted the so-called flight into formalism and seemed to interpret it as a form of self-protection.

There was also widespread criticism of the local inspection team from Liège, headed by Martine Doutrewe, and of the lack of cooperation between the judiciary and police forces in general. A parliamentary investigation of this aspect of the case confirmed that there was indeed reason for criticism.

The inspectors investigated a link with secret witchcraft communities. Rumors circulated that children had been taken for ritual practices. However, no definitive link could be found with the Dutroux case.

Because of presumed irregularities in the investigation of the judiciary and police authorities in the Dutroux case, a parliamentary commission was set up to "investigate the investigation." It held many hearings with all parties concerned. It was confronted with numerous contradictions and members expressed shock at the inefficiency and lack of cooperation among the various investigating services. New juridical action against officials of the judiciary and police was demanded by the president of the commission, Marc Verwilghen (VLD). A preliminary report of the commission at the beginning of March 1997 proved disappointing, a qualification agreed to by its chairman. So-called old political games were played as some members refused to assign concrete responsibilities to officials in the case. The commission then concentrated on the murder of Loubna Benaïssa, a girl kidnapped, raped and murdered by a pedophile, Patrick Derochette. Again, the Brussels judicial police apparatus seemed to have seriously failed.

Dutroux once more surprised all of Belgium by escaping on 23 April 1998 during a judicial procedure in Neufchâteau. The minister of justice, Stefaan Declerck (q.v.), and his colleague at the ministry of the interior, Johan Vande Lanotte, were compelled to resign. If the incident had not occurred just before the final procedures for Belgium's acceptance into the European Monetary Union, even Prime Minister Dehaene (q.v.) and the whole government could have been in danger to resign. *See also* WHITE MARCH.

- E -

ECOLO. Walloon Ecologist Party. It defended the ecological program and organized the ecological movement for political action. the party won a record 370,000 votes in the 1989 elections, but fell back to 190,000 in 1995. *See also* AGALEV.

ECONOMIC UNION. The Benelux (q.v.) countries agreed on an Economic Union by a treaty of 3 February 1958. *See also* EUROPEAN UNION.

ECONOMY. Belgium was one of the first countries to industrialize in Europe and is still one of the most highly industrialized countries in Europe. Belgium's economy depends heavily on its international trade (q.v.) because of its limited size, its geographical location on the sea and its transportation facilities. Belgium is seen by marketeers as an excellent transit and distribution center for reaching the rest of the European market. The country has one of the world's highest gross national products (GNP), delivered by the high productivity of its manufacturing and service industries (q.v.). Its gross national product (in market prices) amounted to 7,936 billion BEF in 1996, national income to 6,422 billion BEF. The Belgian economy in 1995 and 1996 continued its slow recovery from the 1992-1993 recession, the worst since

World War II. Growth slackened in 1996, with real GDP growing by an estimated 1.4 percent in 1996, below the 1.9 percent figure recorded in 1995.

Until 1950, abundant iron and steel provided the raw materials for shipbuilding, railroad, heavy machinery, and structural steelwork industries. These were mostly located in Wallonia (q.v.), in the Sambre and Meuse basin with Liège (q.v.) as its industrial center. In the north, in the province of West Flanders, the textile industry produces fine linens, carpets and synthetic fibers. Belgium's chemical industry led the world in the production of cobalt and radium salts in the 1960s. Diamond-cutting, centered in Antwerp (q.v.), makes Belgium a world production center of industrial diamonds. Belgium's nuclear power plants are the main source of electricity.

Agriculture (q.v.) generates enough revenue to make Belgium self-sufficient and even a net food exporter. Mining and forestry have now become marginal industries. Fishing is still important given Belgium's many ports along the North Sea, with Ostend and Nieuwpoort as its main centers. Antwerp on the river Scheldt (q.v.), and Zeebrugge on the North Sea coast are among the biggest transportation ports in the world. As an integral part of its service (q.v.) industries, Belgium developed an extended financial and banking infrastructure. Most Belgian companies are quoted on the Brussels stock exchange. *See also* INDUSTRY; TRADE.

EDICT OF ABJURATION (1581). The Edict of Abjuration (Plakkaat van Verlatinghe) of 1581 is the formal document on the separation of the northern provinces from rule by Spain.

EDUCATION. The first Constitution (q.v.) of Belgium guaranteed among other civil rights, freedom of education. Belgian citizens are free to choose the education that they prefer for their children. They are free to choose either religious or nondenominational schools with tuition in either French or Flemish. Schooling is compulsory and this requirement has recently been defined as mandatory until age 18. The main school curriculum follows one of several basic patterns: six years at lower school for all, a six-year cycle of secondary school attendance and four to five years of university education or three years of high school attendance; alternatively a six-year cycle of technical education after primary school. Of course, a whole package of diversified educational curricula from child education to university and other post-graduate studies is offered in the educational system of Belgium.

In practice, the individual right of choice of education is exercised through the so called "*Inrichtende machten*" (organizing bodies). Their language and ideological divisions are reflected in Belgium's school system. Following a lengthy political struggle between Catholics and Liberals (q.v.) on the organization of the educational system, a settlement was finally achieved by the School Pact Law of 1959. Both state secular schools and private Roman Catholic schools were given equal standing and still dominate Belgium's educational system. Provincial authorities organized secondary technical education and the communes established primary schools.

This complex network of educational institutions, including leading universities, is thus organized around a specific cluster of determinants: language, ideology and organizing body. For example, within the Flemish Community (q.v.), on the university level, there exists the free Catholic University of Louvain (q.v.), the free University of Brussels (q.v.), the pluralistic State University of Ghent (q.v.) and a mixed pluralistic University of Antwerp (q.v.). A similar mix of institutions exists in the French Community (q.v.).

With the Constitutional Reform of 15 July 1988 (q.v.), organizational responsibilities in relation to the educational system were transferred to the communities. Relatively few powers were reserved to the federal authorities, such as fixing the beginning and end of the compulsory school attendance period, the minimum conditions for granting diplomas and the pension system of educational workers. These exceptions were made to maintain a minimum uniformity and coherence between the educational systems of Belgium. Moreover, pensions are still part of the national social security system. As a consequence, the responsibility for educational matters has been effectively in the hands of the Community Councils and the Community Ministers since 1 January 1989. This does not overrule the previously mentioned language and ideological specifications. The communities have the duty to organize and finance the educational systems, respecting the principles of freedom and organization of the educational system defined above. Nevertheless, the minister of education of the Flemish Community, Luc Van den Bossche, has played a substantial, but also very controversional role in the reform of the high school educational system in recent years.

The influence of students and the degree of student participation in the educational system has been limited so far. The promises and aspirations of the 1969 student reform movement—apart from the language split of the University of Louvain—have not resulted in any major institutional changes. It remains to be seen whether the White March (q.v.), strongly supported by students in secondary education, will produce any lasting effects in the educational participatory structures.

EGMONT PACT (1977). Agreement made among most Belgian political parties that was drafted at a meeting in the castle of Egmont. It is one of the key agreements on Belgian federalization. It produced a government with participation from the Flanders-based People's Union (Volksunie, VU) and the Brussels-based Democratic Front of Francophones (Front Démocratique des Francophones, FDF) (qq.v.) in 1977-1978. The agreement was substantially incorporated into the Constitutional Reform of 1980 (q.v.) following the negotiations at Stuyvenberg (q.v.). *See also* CONSTITUTIONAL REFORM OF 1988, 1993; ST. MICHAEL'S AGREEMENT.

ELSSCHOT, WILLEM (1882-1960). Pen name of Alfons de Ridder. He wrote in a direct and ironic style about the perverse practices of middle-class business in books such as *Kaas* (Cheese). He conveyed fine observations of children *(Tsip)* and he was also a good story teller. Some of his stories were used as film (q.v.) scenarios. He is considered by many to be the best writer of his generation.

ENSOR, JAMES (1860-1949). Modernist painter, born in Ostend (q.v.), a town at the seaside. He began his career with realist-impressionist paintings in which he meticulously represented landscapes, streets and still lives (for example *Rooftops of Ostend,* 1884, *Woman Eating Oysters,* 1882). The study of the outdoors led him to fascinating color experiments. He was deeply impressed by Turner. More and more, Ensor turned to symbolic expressionism. He used skeletons and masks as symbols for death and hypocrisy. They expressed his deeper feelings about the threatening world that did not always recognize his art (for example, *The Intrigue,* 1890; *Skeletons Fighting for the Body of a Hanged Man,* 1891). In some of his pictures, he seems to identify himself with the mocked Christ (for example, *The Entry of Christ into Brussels,* 1888).

ERASMUS, DESIDIRIUS OF ROTTERDAM (c. 1469-1536). Christian humanist. He was chancellor at the Court of Margaret of Austria in Mechelen (qq.v.). In 1515, for the young Charles V (q.v.), he wrote *The Education of a Christian Prince.* Erasmus was known for his wide learning, critical mind, moderation and tolerance.

EUPEN. Town in the province of Liège (q.v.) ceded by Germany together with Malmédy (q.v.) and Moresnet under terms of the Treaty of Versailles in 1919. It is the chief center of the German-speaking population of Belgium.

EUROPEAN UNION (EU). European integration began as a reaction to World War II (q.v.) and the ensuing Cold War. After the war American aid was granted through the Marshall Plan (1948). In the Organization for Economic Cooperation and Development (OECD), recovery and development efforts were administratively coordinated.

The first real European institution to integrate part of the European economy was the European Coal and Steel Community (ECSC). In April 1951, the Benelux (q.v.) countries, France, West Germany and Italy signed the Paris Treaty establishing the ECSC. The aim of the treaty was to abolish all customs barriers on the movement of coal and steel and to equalize conditions of production in the member countries. Institutions of a supranational character were set up. Although during periods of crisis they were not always able to reconcile the national policies of the member countries, a certain success was obtained in the harmonization of trade and production conditions.

On 25 March 1957, the six countries signed the Treaty of Rome, establishing the European Economic Community (EEC) or

Common Market. Paul-Henri Spaak (q.v.), foreign minister of Belgium, was one of the leading initiators of this treaty and Brussels (q.v.) was chosen as the main headquarters. Along with the formation of a customs union, the development of a common agricultural policy was envisaged.

Next, in 1958, the same countries set up the European Atomic Energy Community (EURATOM). It aimed at creating a common nuclear energy industry and research centers.

On 1 July 1967, the executive bodies—the Commission and the Council of Ministers—of the three institutions (ECSC, EEC and EURATOM) were merged as the European Communities (EC).

Europe not only worked toward economic integration but also toward political cooperation. Accordingly, the organization's name was changed to European Union (EU). This was the result of the Maastricht Summit (9-11 December 1991). The European Monetary Union (EMU) will be established in 1999. The groundwork for the new currency was laid by the European Monetary System (EMS), in effect since 1979 and linking the currencies of the member countries. The Maastricht Treaty laid down the conditions for participation in the European Monetary Union (EMU). One of them is the 3 percent limit on the budgetary deficit in 1998. In 1997, Belgium achieved a deficit of 3.4 percent and in 1988, 2.7 percent. Though Belgium did not attain the target ratio for external debt, its efforts in recent years to decrease drastically this ratio convinced the European authorities to admit the country to the European Monetary Union. On 2 May 1998, Belgium along with 10 other European countries was proclaimed a founding member of the EMU.

EYSKENS, GASTON (1905-1988). Christian-Democrat politician of the Catholic Party (q.v.)—since 1968 Christian People's Party (Christelijke Volkspartij, CVP)—and prime minister. Gaston Eyskens studied economics and politics and became a professor at the University of Louvain (q.v.). He began his political career as the head of the cabinet of Minister Van Isacker. In 1939, he was elected to the House of Representatives (q.v.). At the beginning of World War II, he voted in France for the motion that condemned the capitulation by King Leopold III (q.v.). Later, he expressed his solidarity with the government-in-exile in London, but during the war he returned to Louvain where he discreetly supported the resistance (q.v.). After the war, he obtained the portfolio for finance in the first government of Achiel van Acker (1945). The same year, the Christian-Democrats left the government, but Eyskens returned on 20 March 1947 to the same post in the government of Paul-Henri Spaak (q.v.).

After the elections of 26 June 1949, Eyskens formed his first government as prime minister. His government organized the non-binding referendum on the royal controversy (q.v.) on 12 March 1950. Following the divided result, new elections took place on 4 June 1950. Eyskens became minister of economics under Prime Minister Jean Duvieusart. In 1951, he was head of the Belgian delegation to the United Nations General Assembly. After the elections of 1 June 1958, Eyskens formed a new government. This government was charged with making preparations for the independence of the Congo (q.v.). In 1960, Eyskens proposed his so-called Unity Law, a plan for financial recovery. This caused a social upheaval in the form of strikes in December 1960 and January 1961.

The elections of 26 March 1961 led to a new government under Theo Lefevre. Not until 1965 could Eyskens return as minister of finance in the Harmel government. In 1968, he became for the third time prime minister after the Louvain University crisis. The communitarian problems weighed heavily on the government. In 1971, Eyskens resigned, but after the elections, he returned as prime minister. Finally, his proposed laws on community problems were not accepted, and he resigned for the final time. In June 1973, he also left Parliament. He took a job in the financial field and concentrated on his academic activities until the end of his life.

## - F -

FACILITIES. The so-called facilities were introduced by the language laws of 1963 and inscribed in the Constitution (q.v.) of 1988 (Article 129). They gave language facilities to other language-speaking minorities in 21 communes along the language boundary (among them the much disputed Komen and Voeren) and also in six communes around Brussels (q.v.) (namely, Kraainem, Wezenbeek-Oppem, Sint-Genesius-Rode, Linkebeek, Drogenbos, and Wemmel). There were Flemish communes with facilities for the French speakers, French-speaking communes with facilities for the Flemish speakers and French-speaking communes with facilities for the German speakers. These facilities are intended to be a temporary measure, in order to facilitate the adaptation of minority language speakers to the new environment. In October 1997, a Flemish minister Leo Peeters interpreted this as requiring each year a new request by the users of the facilities. This gave rise to vigorous protests by French-speaking politicians of the opposition.

FEDERALISM. In 1830, Belgium was established as a unitary state. It took almost 150 years before Belgium was transformed into a federal state. Four constitutional reforms (q.v.) during the period 1970-1993 transformed it into a federation. By the constitutional reform of 1993 (q.v.) Belgium is no longer a national but a declared federal state *(see* Article 1 of the Constitution). Competences were devolved to cultural communities and regions. These include education (q.v.), culture, so-called personalized matters and some economic and regional competences. These competences could not always be easily delineated. The Arbitration Court (q.v.) was created to decide in case of conflict between the communities in these matters.

So far, residual powers not explicitly devolved to the regions still remain at the national level. In general, the federal level has to safeguard the basic economic and social unity of the country, to preserve its internal and external security and to guide its international policy. Specifically, the remaining competences of the federal government are the following: defense, internal security, justice, external relations, economic and monetary policies, management of public debt, social security, public health and pensions, and residual powers.

FEXHE (PEACE OF). Peace concluded in 1316 by which the prince-bishopric of Liège (q.v.) became semi-autonomous.

FILM. The Belgian film was well represented in the 1930s by the avant-garde documentary school of Charles Dekeukeleire and Henri Storck (q.v.). Storck, in cooperation with the "flying Dutchman" Joris Ivens, made in 1933 the classic documentary film *Misery in the Borinage* about the consequences of a miners' strike.

In Flanders (q.v.), the highly popular feature movie *De Witte* (The White One, 1934) about a farmer boy based on the novel of author Ernest Claes (q.v.) led director Jan Vanderheyden to produce a series of humorous films. They were mostly situated in the harbor town of Antwerp (q.v.). In Brussels (q.v.), Gaston Schoukens directed comedies around the typical local theater characters of Mr. and Mrs. Beulemans. The production of this kind of very cheap and quickly made local film production lasted until the arrival of television in the late 1950s.

In the mid-1960s, the Flanders and Walloon governments created selection committees that subsidized many film projects. In Flanders in 1972, the film *Mira* made by the Dutchman Fons Rademakers was a huge success and stimulated other adaptations from local literature. Both director Roland Verhavert and producer Jan van Raemdonck created a series of so-called "farmer films" that referred to nineteenth-century work and family relations in small rural communities. Others tended toward international co-productions like André Delvaux who made *Un Soir, un Train* (An Evening, A Train) with Yves Montand and *Benvenuta* with Vittorio Gasman and Fanny Ardent. Harry Kumel directed *Malpertuis* with Orson Welles and *The Daughters of Darkness* with Delphine Seyrig. They were followed by younger, successful generations of filmmakers: Benoit Lamy, Robbe de Hert (q.v.) (who did a popular remake of *De Witte*), Jean-Jacques Adrien, Marc Didden, Dominique Deruddere, Jaco van Dormael (who made the much admired film *Toto the Hero),* Chantal Akerman and Marion Hansel.

Recently Belgian films received Oscar nominations: *The Music Teacher* and *Farinelli* by Gerard Corbiau and *Daens by Stijn Coninckx,* an adaptation of an epic novel of writer Louis Paul Boon (q.v.). The Flemish actor Jan Decleir played the main character in the Dutch film *Karakter* (Character) which won the 1998 Oscar for the Best Foreign Film.

Still, the weakness of the Belgian film, especially in Flanders, has meant that only a few films a year are made. Skilled crew and directors cannot profit from production on a regular basis. Nevertheless, many Belgian animated films are of exceptional quality like the ones of Picha, Raoul Servais (q.v.) and Nicole Van Goethem (q.v.). Nor should we forget the great successes enjoyed in Hollywood by actor Jean-Claude Van Damme, the "Muscles from Brussels."

FIRST TREATY OF LONDON (1831). The Belgian revolution (q.v.) represented a violation of the setlement reached at the congress of Vienna (q.v.), under which the united Kingdom of the Netherlands had been created. A conference of the great powers was called in London in November 1830 at which the delegates ordered an armistice in the fighting. In June 1831 the conference approved the choice of Leopold I (q.v.) of Saxe-Coburg as king and drew up the First Treaty of London, or the Eighteen Articles, which regulated Belgian-Dutch separation. King William I (q.v.) of Orange refused to accept the settlement. In October, the conference revised the articles and drafted the Twenty-Four Articles, which embodied conditions more favorable to the Dutch. King William still refused to agree. He finally accepted the terms in April 1839. The independence of Belgium was acknowledged but the teritorial settlement excluded from the new state the eastern part of the province of Limburg (q.v.) and the Grand Duchy of Luxembourg, which remained under the Dutch king. The Scheldt (q.v.) River was open to the commerce of both countries and the great powers guaranteed the neutrality of Belgium.

FLANDERS. The use of the term Flanders has carried more than one meaning in the present day and a different one in history. The most restricted use of the term Flanders designates only the two provinces of East and West Flanders. Today the term is usually used to name the north Flemish-speaking part of Belgium, now recognized as one of the three economic regions of Belgium and one of the three language communities.

Historically, the use of the term Flanders was applied to a county and fief of the king of France. At the time of its greatest expansion in the 10th century, it comprised East and West Flanders, Zealand-Flanders and a section extending into the north of France as far as the Somme River.

FLANDERS (COUNTY OF). Flanders takes its name from the so-called *pagus Flandrensis* (Flemish region), an expression used to designate a district around Bruges (q.v.) in the early Middle Ages. In fact, the early counts enjoyed more power in the more prosperous eastern area around Ghent (q.v.) and later extended their territory towards the west and the south in what is now northeastern France.

The first known Flemish count was Baldwin I (q.v.) "with the Iron Arm," who ruled the region of Ghent from c. 862. He was the son of Audoacer, whose family probably ruled three *pagi* (regions) between the Scheldt (q.v.) and Lys. Baldwin married Judith, the eldest child of Charles II the Bald, Holy Roman emperor and king of West Francia, and received the *pagus Flandrensis* as dowry in 863. This dynastic marriage by which the count of Flanders became influential in circles of both the French and English monarchies laid the basis for the further diplomatic and territorial expansion of the dynasty.

Baldwin II assumed rule over Flanders at the death of his father in 879. He married Elftrude, the daughter of Alfred the Great, himself the stepson of Judith. The beginning of the reign of Baldwin II was characterized by numerous Viking invasions and Baldwin took refuge in the marshes of the *pagus Flandrensis*. When the Norsemen left, Baldwin began a series of successful expeditions to expand his territory to the south and the west. His elder son, Arnulf I the Great (918-965), inherited Flanders and expanded the territory even more to the south. Baldwin V, count of Flanders from 1035 to 1067, added the land between the Scheldt and the Dender to his territory. The lands east of the Scheldt River were part of the Holy German Empire. Robert I, a son of Baldwin V married in 1063 Gertrude, widow of Count Floris I of Frisia, and ruled that northern territory. In 1071, he took over the power from his brother and remained count of Flanders until 1093.

From 1071 to 1206, Flemish power attained its apogee. The region was ruled by Robert II of Jerusalem (1093-1111), Baldwin VII (1111-1119), Charles the Good (1119-1127), Thierry of Alsace (1128-1168), Philip of Alsace (1168-1191), Baldwin VIII (1191-1194) and Baldwin IX of Constantinople (1195-1206). This last count of Flanders is best known for his exploits in the crusades. Baldwin was crowned emperor at Constantinople on 9 May 1204, but he was taken prisoner in 1205 and deported to the land of the Bulgars, where he died. The absence and subsequent death of the count led to a crisis in his homeland Flanders.

Moreover, new regional forces developed in the form of the major towns. Thanks to the expanding cloth industry and trade, Bruges, Ghent and Ypres (q.v.) all developed into strong autonomous centers of power. They were constantly fighting for the preservation of their privileges. More often than not, they opposed the counts of Flanders and their suzerain, the kings of France. The nobility was divided. The "Lily" aristocracy lent support to the French, while the "Claws" took the Flemish side. In 1302, the Flemish leaders Pieter De Coninck and Jan Breydel (q.v.) defeated a French army at Courtrai in the battle of the Golden Spurs (q.v.). It later became a nationalistic symbol for the Flemish movement (q.v.) in its struggles against French language predominance.

However, the battle in 1302 turned out to be a Pyrrhic victory. In the next years, French troops invaded again and Flanders came more firmly under French influence and had to pay a large ransom. Flanders sank into crisis. It was engaged in new military campaigns by Robert of Béthune, count of Flanders from 1305 to 1322. By the marriage of Countess Margaret of Male (q.v.), Flanders came into the possession of the Burgundian dynasty (q.v.). Their centralistic policy led the county of Flanders to slowly develop into an integral part of the Low Countries (q.v.).

FLEMISH BLOC (VLAAMS BLOK). The first postwar Flemish party was the People's Union (Volksunie, VU) (q.v.). Founded in 1954, it united both democratic federalists and former collaborators who pleaded for amnesty (q.v.) following World War II (q.v.). In 1977, the party under the leadership of the moderate

Hugo Schiltz (q.v.) accepted the Egmont Pact (q.v.) and joined the government. This led to a split in the party. The radical right-wingers and anti-Belgians founded a new party called the Flemish Bloc (Vlaams Blok, VL BLOK). The leader became Karel Dillen, a strong sympathizer with the ideas of the conservative nationalist right. He was elected to Parliament (q.v.), but the party failed to gain wider popular support.

A decade later, in 1987, the lawyer Gerolf Annemans and the former journalist Filip Dewinter succeeded Dillen. The party reoriented its program to focus essentially on the immigrant issue. With the economic crisis and growing problems in large urban centers, the party now obtained massive lower-class support. In 1991, the party sent 12 extreme right-wing members to Parliament. In 1994, the Flemish Bloc became the biggest party in the metropolis of Antwerp (q.v.). The other parties were forced into a defensive multiparty bloc. On some issues and on some occasions, the same tactic was used at the national level. However, in the parliamentary election of 21 May 1995, the Flemish Bloc further strengthened its position. The party also abandoned its more or less one issue tactic and gained more credibility by attacking the failings of the governing ruling parties.

FLEMISH COMMUNITY. Language community of the Dutch speaking community in Flanders and Brussels (qq.v.). *See* also CONSTITUTIONAL REFORM OF 1970, 1980, 1988, 1993; FLEMISH COMMUNITY COMMISSION (COCON); FLEMISH CULTURAL COUNCIL; FLEMISH PARLIAMENT.

FLEMISH COMMUNITY COMMISSION (COCON) (Vlaamse Gemeenschapscommissie). Official designation of the community organ of the Flemish-speaking minority of Brussels (q.v.). In contrast to its French counterpart, the COCOF or the community organ of the French speakers in Brussels, it has no autonomous decretal powers and remains strictly under the Flemish Parliament (q.v.). This is a typical feature of the asymmetrical system of federalization in Belgium.

FLEMISH CULTURAL COUNCIL. The change of Article 59 bis of the Constitution (q.v.) due to the Constitutional Reform of 1970 (q.v.) was implemented by the law of 21 July 1971 which created the Dutch Cultural Council (Nederlandse Cultuurraad). It was entrusted with the power to deal with all language-related questions. In the search for a typical Flemish identity, the council was renamed Flemish Cultural Council (Vlaamse Cultuurraad) after the Constitutional Reform of 1980 (q.v.).

FLEMISH ECONOMIC AND SOCIAL CONSULTATION COMMITTEE. The Flemish Economic and Social Consultation Committee (Vlaams Economisch en Sociaal Overleg Comité, VESOC) brings together the Flemish social partners, i.e., the representatives of trade unions and employers and the Flemish government. For example, on 20 November 1996, the VESOC handed down an advisory opinion and reached a consensus on a proposal of the Flemish minister of economics Eric Van Rompuy. The proposal would subsidize Flemish enterprises that preserve or expand employment for jobseekers with limited schooling.

FLEMISH ECONOMIC COUNCIL (Economische Raad voor Vlaanderen). This regional economic council was set up in 1952 as an advisory organ of the national Ministry of Economy and Industry. Following the example of a similar Walloon council, it was an early forerunner of the executive councils of the later economic regions of the linguistic communities. In the asymmetric federalization, the economic powers of the Flemish region are now held by the Flemish Parliament (q.v.).

FLEMISH LANGUAGE. The official language of the Flemish community is Dutch (q.v.). It is a standardized language from Germanic origin that Flanders shares with the Netherlands. However, in the southern regions of this language area, or Flanders, a southern variety is spoken, the so-called Flemish. In fact, it consists of several dialects, more of less mirroring the provinces of the Dutch-speaking area of Belgium. Originally, Brussels was a part of the Flemish-speaking language area, but now Dutch is spoken only by a minority there. This was one reason for the Flemish to fix a language boundary (q.v.) by law in 1962.

FLEMISH LANGUAGE ACTION COMMITTEE. The Flemish Language Action Committee (Taal Aktie Komitee, TAK) joins together Flemish nationalists who support and conduct public campaigns in order to enforce the strict application of laws on the linguistic and community problem. It first came into action on 26 March 1972. It concentrated mainly on the application of linguistic laws in industry and in the communes within greater Brussels and along the linguistic frontier. It is most known for its continuous campaigns conducted against the French-speaking mayor of Schaerbeek, Roger Nols, and against José Happart (q.v.) in Voeren. Recent actions were directed toward the preservation of the Flemish character of Flemish Brabant (q.v.).

FLEMISH LIBERALS AND DEMOCRATS. The party of the Flemish Liberals and Democrats (Vlaamse Liberalen en Democraten, VLD), was the successor party to the Party for Liberty and Progress. The new party name and its orientation were adopted through the efforts of Guy Verhofstadt at the party congress of November 1992. One year earlier, he had published his "citizens manifesto." It rejected the influence of the interest groups in Belgian politics, and he attracted dissenters from most other parties: Catholics, Socialists and even a former president of the People's Union (qq.v.). However, large-scale electoral success eluded him and Verhofstadt had to relinquish the presidency into the hands of the more compromising Herman de Croo. *See also* LIBERAL PARTY.

FLEMISH MOVEMENT. The Flemish movement (Vlaamse Beweging) is a broad political and cultural current that has sought to defend the rights of the Flemish-speaking people in Belgium during the past two centuries. It developed through various stages with different claims and various degrees of success in varying periods.

The original roots of the linguistic problem can be traced back ages ago when the spheres of influence of Roman and Celtic-Frankish civilizations intertwined. In the Middle Ages, the higher circles in Flanders (q.v.) spoke French, especially since Thierry of Alsace ruled as the first of a long line of French counts of Flanders. This culminated in the supremacy of French at the Burgundian (q.v.) court. Even under Austrian rule (q.v.), French as a vehicle of highly civilized culture was maintained in the upper circles. Frenchification of the Flemish middle classes was actively promoted during the French occupation (q.v.) from 1795 to 1815. A short countermovement was introduced by King William I (q.v.) of the Netherlands. However, in addition to the general resistance against his autocratic tendencies, his language policy was rejected by the French-speaking bourgeoisie and the conservative church circles.

One of the early supporters of the official use of the Dutch (q.v.) language was Jan Frans Willems (q.v.). He wrote patriotic poems and plays and published works on the history of the literature in the southern Netherlands. Later generations came to see him as the "Father of the Flemish movement."

Immediately after the Belgian revolution (q.v.) in 1830, the Flemish movement fostered a Flemish national consciousness as part of a broader Belgian patriotism. Flemish intellectuals reacted against the official unilingual administration of the Belgian state. Some of them were linked to the Orangists, supporters of the Dutch regime of King William I, who still governed over the north of the Low Countries (q.v.). The main centers of Orangists in the south were the towns of Ghent and Antwerp (qq.v.). Romantic writers gave ample support to the Flemish movement in this period. The most prominent of them was Hendrik Conscience (q.v.). In 1838, he published a most influential novel, *De Leeuw van Vlaanderen* (The Lion of Flanders). Conscience acquired the reputation of the man who "taught his people to read." A third center of the emerging Flemish movement was the Catholic University of Louvain (q.v.). The church held that the natural and unspoilt soul of the Christian Flemish people had to be preserved. The traditionalist equation of religion, language and fatherland gave the Flemish movement a conservative flavor for a long time. One staunch defender of a well-cultivated Dutch language was the priest and historian Jan Baptist David (q.v.). The Catholic wing of the Flemish movement subsequently honored his name by attaching it to an educational foundation, the so-called *Davidsfonds*.

After 1847, the Flemish movement divided into three ideological wings, which were sometimes in open conflict. Pieter Frans van Kerckhoven (1818-1857) denounced the alignment with the clerical party, as he believed it obstructed the people's enlightenment and progress. In his opinion, the Flemish movement should have been a supporter of the Liberal Party (q.v.). This position was also defended by Julius Vuylsteke (1836-1903) in Ghent, giving the Willems Foundation (q.v.) a liberal underpinning. The Catholic clerical tendency was represented by the priest and great poet Guido Gezelle (q.v.). Based in a seminary in East Flanders, he used the local vernacular in his lyricism. He educated a generation of Catholic Flemish religious idealists. One of his pupils was the poet Albrecht Rodenbach. The student movement under his lead made a decisive contribution to the breakthrough of the Flemish movement. A third tendency tried to transcend the clerical-anti-clerical division and sought to defend Flemish nationalistic values as such. The Flemish movement obtained its first political success with the acceptance of the language laws of 1873.

In the period from 1880 until World War I (q.v.), the Flemish movement allied itself to Christian Democracy. Its gains in this period were meager, with the exception of the Militia Law of 1897 and the Equality Law of 1898. August Vermeylen (1872-1945) wrote in 1896 his well-known critique of the Flemish movement. He introduced a Socialist current into the movement. Professor Julius MacLeod (1857-1919) of the University of Ghent believed in the intellectual emancipation by education and defended the introduction of Dutch as a language of instruction in his university. Lodewijk de Raet pointed to the importance of economic development for cultural life. These intellectuals broadened the scope of the Flemish movement.

World War I (q.v.) seemed to offer new chances to the Flemish movement. In the first place, the Germans developed a Flamenpolitik (Flemish policy). This included a preferential treatment for the Flemings in the occupied part of the country in comparison with the French-speaking population. The Germans even went so far as to create a Council of Flanders (q.v.), thereby inducing the administrative separation of the country. In 1917, the activist parliament of the council even proclaimed the full independence of Flanders. At the same time, at the front on the IJzer the so-called Front Movement (Front Beweging) developed. It agitated against the French-speaking commando structures of the Belgian army and organized numerous Flemish cultural demonstrations. At the end of the war, the leaders of the Front Movement founded the Front Party (Front Partij) to work to achieve self-rule. The defeat of the Germans and the popularity of

King Albert (q.v.) meant a 10-year long drop in support for the Flemish activists. The only achievement in the postwar period was the partial introduction of Dutch at the University of Ghent in 1923.

A new rise of the political movement took place at the end of the 1920s and especially in the 1930s, then again stimulated and supported by German authoritarian forces. In 1928, a former activist condemned to death had obtained the majority of votes in by-elections in Antwerp. In 1929, the Flemish nationalists obtained 12 percent of the votes in Flanders. It was their first massive political success. In the period 1928-1932, language laws were enacted in various spheres of social life. The law of 28 June 1932 recognized the territorial integrity of Flanders as being homogeneously Dutch speaking. The law stipulated that the language boundary could only be adjusted based on the results of a decennial population census. In 1933, Flemish nationalists united into the Flemish National Union (Vlaams Nationaal Verbond, VNV). In the 1936 elections, this party won 14 percent of the votes in Flanders and in 1939 15 percent.

Then the scenario of the period before, during and immediately after World War I was nearly repeated. Again ultra-right circles in Germany devised a Flamenpolitik, which was maintained during the occupation. Shortly before the invasion, Belgian authorities deported unreliable Flemish nationalist leaders to France. This stimulated the activist collaboration (q.v.) policy of Flemish nationalists at the beginning of the war. But annexation plans and the crude oppression by the Germans led to the disintegration of the VNV into different wings. After the defeat of the Germans at the end of World War II (q.v.), repression of collaborators and activists was strong. The Flemish movement was politically beheaded and again the movement fell into inactivity for more than a decade.

It was revived by the founding of the People's Union (Volksunie) (q.v.) and its electoral breakthrough in 1961. In 1962, the language boundary was fixed again, but the continuing disputes over it would characterize the next decade. Belgium was now caught up in communitarian fever and all communitarian parties flourished. One of the crisis points was the turmoil about the splitting of the University of Louvain (q.v.). In 1968, the People's Union won more than 15 percent of the votes in Flanders, one of the highest scores ever obtained by the Flemish nationalists. Traditional national parties took over the federalization ideas and split into language-based wings. Mainstream support for a new governmental configuration led to the federalization of all political structures in Belgium in subsequent steps. From 1970 on, constitutional reforms (q.v.) were accepted on by the political establishment.

In 1977, the active and so-called compromising attitude of the People's Union on occasion of the Egmont Pact (q.v.) led again to a split in the ranks of the Flemish nationalists. Ultra-rightists and extreme Flemish nationalist forces united in the Flemish Bloc (Vlaams Blok) (q.v.). This radical party intends to change the federal structure into a confederal one and ultimately into complete self-rule for Flanders. In the meantime, a Flemish government and a Flemish Parliament (q.v.) were created and are working fully within the contours of the Belgian federal state. For some, the goals of the Flemish movement are nearly achieved, for others there is still a long way to go to achieve full economic and political independence. The Flemish movement continues to show a wide variety of viewpoints on the desired political future of Flanders. This is exemplified by the disputes and incidents that erupt during the IJzerbedevaart, the yearly convocation of the Flemish nationalists.

FLEMISH NATIONAL UNION (1933-1944). The Flemish National Union (Vlaams Nationaal Verbond, VNV) was the prewar Flemish nationalist unity party. It was formed from various formations and founded on 7-8 October 1933 at the initiative of Hendrik Borginon and Staf Declercq. It took an ultra-rightist position in prewar Belgian politics and defended the German corporatist model. At the beginning of World War II (q.v.), some of its prominent members were deported to France. The party opted for collaboration (q.v.) with the Germans. When the leader Staf Declercq died in 1942, his successor Hendrik Elias insisted on distancing the movement from association with the occupying power. The movement slowly disintegrated through internal dissension. Some of its members even joined the Resistance (q.v.). At the end of the war, some of its leaders fled to Germany and some suffered punishment for their collaborationist roles. *See also* AMNESTY; WAFFEN SS.

FLEMISH PARLIAMENT. In 1830, Belgium was established as a unitary French-speaking monarchy. The goal of making a federation of this state, long defended by the Flemish movement (q.v.), was not achieved until a quarter of a century after World War II (q.v.).

In 1970, the First Constitutional Reform (q.v.) on federalization was approved by Parliament (q.v.). It introduced the first officially recognized institutions based on the linguistic identities of the regions, though their powers were still restricted and controlled by national institutions. In essence, the Flemish, French and German Cultural Communities were officially established. The Cultural Council for the Dutch Cultural Community took over legislative powers from the federal Parliament on cultural affairs. In this field, it was given the power to issue decrees. However, actual execution and control were still retained by the ministers of the national government. From 1970 to 1980, the Cultural Council approved 49 decrees, the most important concerning language questions. It worked on a separate Flemish cultural policy and the preservation of monuments and historic buildings. It was also responsible for the Dutch-language institutions in Brussels (q.v.).

The Constitutional Reform of 1980 (q.v.) considerably expanded the powers of the communities. First, welfare policy was included in the package of the earlier Cultural Council for the Dutch Cultural Community, now renamed Flemish Community Council of the Flemish Community (q.v.). Second, also endowed with some new powers on "territory-related" matters, such as the economy, town and country planning and the environment, the Region of Flanders and its Council, the Flemish Regional Council, were established. The Flemish Community Council continued to be responsible for the language policy in Brussels, but the Regional Council has no legal jurisdiction there, as a local organ was formed for the capital region. In contrast to the French-speaking Community and the Walloon Region, Flanders preferred to merge its two Councils into a single Flemish Parliament. Under the new arrangement, this body also held the power to install its own government.

Between 1980 and 1995, the Flemish Parliament installed eight Flemish governments for the region. The Constitutional Reforms of 1988 and 1993 (qq.v.) further increased the powers of the Flemish Parliament. Until 21 May 1995, the members of the Flemish Parliament were still indirectly elected as they constituted elected Dutch-speaking members of the national Parliament. The double mandate of these members and their conflicting allegiances were considered to be a hindrance to the optimal functioning of an autonomous Flemish Parliament. The Constitutional Reform of 1993 reversed this situation, so that members of the Flemish Parliament are now directly elected.

With the St. Michael's Agreement (q.v.) and the Constitutional Reform of 1993, politicians expected a communal truce until 1999, when financial regulations of the communities should be reconsidered. However, in the middle of 1996, demands for fiscal autonomy of the Flemish Community became more and more pressing. Regionalization of children's allowances and funds for health care were considered as the next immediate and urgent step on the way to total fiscal autonomy. These dynamics were overshadowed by the political and judicial scandals and the White Marches (q.v.) that dominated public attention in the second half of 1996.

FLEURUS. Village in the vicinity of Charlerloi (q.v.) in the province of Hainault (q.v.). Here the French under Marshall Jean-Baptiste Jourdan defeated the Austrians in 1794. *See also* FRENCH OCCUPATION.

FOLK DANCE. Contemporary Flemish folk music and dances have most of their roots in the French period (1795-1815). There are a substantial number of local quadrilles, waltzes and polkas. Some Polish influence is also discernible. At present, Flemish folk music and dances are mainly performed by specialized groups on stage with the exception of some dances celebrating the advent of May and the arrival of spring. Some older dances are beautifully depicted in the paintings of Brueghel (q.v.). There is also a revival of amateur societies performing Burgundian (q.v.) court dances.

Walloon folk dances are largely inspired by French examples, imported during the Napoleon period and the French occupation at the end of the 19th century. The most popular Walloon folkdance nowadays is the "Bourrée," originally imported from the region of Auvergne in France, during which partners suddenly change places to the driving rhythm of a beautiful melody; this may be done in long rows of couples.

FOLKLORE. Belgian folklore derives its origins from the rich tradition of religious processions, joyous entries of Burgundian (q.v.) dukes and their court festivities, and various medieval carnivals and fairs. Popular practices were minutely recorded in the paintings of Breughel (q.v.).

All sort of pilgrimages are still popular, religious and pious, such as those to Scherpenheuvel. Processions proceed through Belgium on religious holy days, especially on Palm Sunday. The Procession of the Holy Blood in Bruges (q.v.) is particularly famous. The Car d'Or in Mons, the Procession of the Penitents in Veurne and the Procession of the Plague in Tournai (q.v.) are quite spectacular. There is also the annual Blessing of the Sea in Flanders (q.v.) and the Festivities of the hunters for St. Hubert in the Ardennes (q.v.).

Among the carnival events, the most famous are the Rosenmontag in Eupen, the Dancing of the Gilles in Binche (q.v.), the Chinel Procession at Fosses, the Blanc Moussis at Stavelot and the great festivities at Aalst. Giants are a staple attraction at several fairs and patronal feasts, for example at Ath, and the giant horse Bayard appears in Dendermonde.

Guild celebrations are still lively in small communities and cultural organizations. St. Cecilia, patron saint of the musicians, is the most popular. St. Barbara and St. Eligius are commemorated by mineworkers and metalworkers, respectively.

St. Nicholas's feast day on 6 December is still celebrated in all families, when children receive chocolates and other presents. He is as popular in Flanders as Father Christmas. The year ends with a midnight supper and a dancing party.

Though Flanders and Wallonia (q.v.) still have their own typical folk music and folk dances (q.v.), they are mainly performed by specialized groups on stage.

FOREIGN AFFAIRS. The federalization of Belgium also implied a redistribution of the competences for foreign affairs.

The Constitutional Reform of 1970 (q.v.) created the Cultural Councils and the Special Bill of 1978 prescribed that international treaties on cultural and educational matters had to be approved by them, though the national government retained the power to conclude them. By the Constitutional Reform of 1980 (q.v.), this state of affairs was extended to other so-called personalized matters—guaranteed rights that concern typical personal rights defined by the law. The national state retained authority for the international regulation of the economic powers that were internally delegated to the regions. This was reversed by the Constitutional Reform of 1993 (q.v.). The reform transferred the responsibility to conclude treaties and handle international affairs to the Cultural and Regional Councils on matters on which they were competent internally.

Article 81 of a special law on international affairs also decrees coordination of policy and cooperation between all levels of government competent in the field of international affairs. Moreover, the Constitution (q.v.) of 1993 provided that the competence in matters concerning overall foreign policy should remain with the king, which means at the level of the federal government. However, there is still some lack of clarity on the precise powers of the federal and regional organs. Discussions on this matter are ongoing.

FOURONS, LES. *See* VOEREN.

FRANCHIMONTESES, SIX HUNDRED. On 29 September 1467, 600 Franchimonteses attacked during the night the camp of the Burgundian duke Charles the Bold (q.v.) and the king of France. The attack failed and all the warriors were executed. Nevertheless their brave and patriotic act was praised for centuries and finally canonized in national history by Henri Pirenne (q.v.). The event was at times honored as the expression of the Walloon drive for autonomy and independence. However, as it remained a memory of a defeat, it could not serve as the symbol for the Walloon national holiday. In any case, this was so decided by the newly installed Walloon Regional Council (q.v.). *See also* LIEGE.

FRANCK, CESAR (1822-1890). Composer and organist. He wrote remarkable symphonic pieces for violin and piano.

FRANQUIN, ANDRE (1924-1977). Comic strip designer, born in Brussels (q.v.), where he visited the drawing academy. He worked for the magazine Spirou/Robbedoes of the French comic strip artist Rob-Vel and the Walloon Jije (Joseph Gillain). His most successful creations are the chaos-maker Gaston Lagaffe/Guust Flater and the Marsupilami, a character combining a monkey and a leopard. Specialists appreciate his style of dynamic drawing even more than that of the more popular "Kuifje/Tintin" of Hergé (q.v.).

FRENCH COMMUNITY. Language community of the French speakers in Wallonia and Brussels (qq.v.). *See also* CONSTITUTIONAL REFORM OF 1970; FRENCH COMMUNITY COMMISSION; FRENCH COMMUNITY COUNCIL; FRENCH LANGUAGE.

FRENCH COMMUNITY COMMISSION. The French Community Commission (Commission de la Communauté Française, COCOF) is the organ of the French-speaking Community in Brussels (q.v.). It has only decretal competences as an organ ranking lower than Parliament.

FRENCH COMMUNITY COUNCIL. Article 59 bis of the Constitution (q.v.) entered into effect under the law of 21 July 1971 and stipulated the creation of the French Cultural Council (Conseil de la Communauté Française, CCF) as the executive organ of the French Community (q.v.). *See also* FRENCH COMMUNITY COMMISSION.

FRENCH LANGUAGE. French is the official language of the French Community (q.v.). The French-speaking Community of Belgium is a member of the Francophone World Congress. French is spoken in the regions of Wallonia and along with Dutch in the capital region of Brussels (q.v.). In addition, in Wallonia (q.v.), several Walloon dialects of Roman origin are still spoken around the major industrial towns and in the countryside.

FRENCH OCCUPATION (1795-1815). At the battle of Fleurus (q.v.) on 26 June 1794, the French Marshall Jourdan defeated the Austrians. The next year the National Convention in Paris decreed the annexation of Liège (q.v.) and the Austrian Low Countries (q.v.). For the future Belgium, it meant among other things that almost all of its regions were united under France. France organized the territories into an administrative structure that was to be adopted almost intact by the future Belgian state. The territory was divided into four Flemish and four Walloon provinces and the linguistically mixed province of Brabant (q.v.). This arrangement continues today with the only exception that the province of Brabant was split in 1995 into Flemish and French entities. Much progressive legislation was introduced by the French, for example the Napoleonic Code, and survived the French regime. The church and the conservative peasantry resisted the changes during the Peasants' Revolt (q.v.) of 1798, but they were defeated. The French period ended with the defeat of Napoleon at the battle of Waterloo (qq.v.) of 1815.

FRERE-ORBAN, HUBERT (1812-1896). Leading 19th-century Liberal Party (q.v.) member of the House of Representatives (q.v.). A lawyer from Liège (q.v.), he founded the National Bank and implemented free trade policies as minister of finance (1848-1852, 1857-1870). As prime minister, he established a secular primary school system in 1879 that aroused a storm of protest from devout Catholics and local authorities resentful of central government mandates. He sponsored an extension of the franchise in 1883, but a year later suffered a crushing electoral defeat at the hands of Catholic opponents.

FRONT NATIONAL (FN). Party of the extreme right in the French-speaking part of Belgium, ostensibly influenced by the example of the Front National of Le Pen in France.

## - G -

GALLIA BELGICA (BELGIAN GAUL). Roman province covering more or less the present territory of Belgium and the Netherlands and established some time after the conquest by Caesar (58-51 B.C.). Gallia Belgica (Belgian Gaul) was divided into *civitates*, administrative units that corresponded to the earlier territories of the different tribes. Roman immigrants influenced the habits of local Gallic tribes and this process produced a Gallo-Roman culture. On the crossings of major roads, fortifications and Roman towns appeared, such as Tournai, Arlon and Tongres (qq.v.).

GARD SIVIK. Literary journal founded by Paul Snoek and Gust Gils. It has been regarded as the heir of *Tijd en Mens* (q.v.), the avant-garde periodical that ceased production in 1955.

GENERAL FEDERATION OF BELGIAN TRADE UNIONS. The General Federation of Belgian Trade Unions (Algemeen Belgisch Vakverbond, ABVV/Fédération Générale du Travail de Belgique, FGTB), the leftist trade union, is the national, but also the federalized, organization of the Socialist workers. It grew out of the merger of several workers' organizations and was officially founded under its present name at a unification congress in Brussels (q.v.) on 28-29 April 1945. The Socialist trade union is still the largest in Wallonia, while in Flanders (qq.v.) it is now second in size after the Christian Trade Union. *See also* TRADE UNIONS.

GERMAN COMMUNITY COUNCIL. Under Article 59 tris of the Constitution (q.v.), the council was established by the law of 10 July 1973. Its members are directly elected and serve the interests of the German-speaking residents in extreme eastern Belgium. *See also* CONSTITUTIONAL REFORM OF 1970.

GERMAN-FLEMISH UNION FOR COOPERATION "DE VLAG." This Flemish organization promoted cultural ties with Germany before World War II (q.v.) and during the war it adopted the National Socialist ideology. It unconditionally supported the German occupier under the leadership of Jef Vandewiele and declared itself in favor of incorporation into the Greater German Empire. After the liberation in September 1944, tens of thousands of its supporters received prison sentences and were deprived of their civic rights.

GEZELLE, GUIDO (1830-1899). Priest and poet, born and worked in West Flanders. He used the vernacular of this region in his lyricism. He educated a generation of Catholic Flemish religious idealists and as such played an important role in the Flemish movement (q.v.). One of his pupils was the poet Albrecht Rodenbach. Some critics praise him as the greatest Flemish poet of the nineteenth century.

GHENT (GENT). Ghent was founded at the confluence of two major rivers, the Lys (Leie) and the Scheldt (Schelde) (q.v.). Its origins go back to the St. Bavon Abbey. It was founded by St. Amand from Aquitaine in the first half of the seventh century as the Ganda monastery. Later remains can still be visited on the same site. Somewhat to the north, a second abbey, the Blandinium (now St. Peter's Abbey) was erected by Amand's follower John. Thanks to the support of the Frankish king Dagobert, the abbeys acquired important estates in the region. Charlemagne (q.v.) had a fleet built nearby at St. Bavon's Abbey. However, the abbeys were destroyed by the Vikings in the years 879-883. The population regrouped around a fortification on the left bank of the river Lys built against the Vikings in 876 by Baldwin I (q.v.), the count of Flanders. In 942, the bishop of Tournai (q.v.) inaugurated the Church of St. John (now St. Bavon).

Ghent developed at the same time as and after the decline of Bruges (q.v.), its sometimes rival but more usually together in fighting against the authority of the counts of Flanders (q.v.). The counts resided in the Count's Castle that was erected in 1180 by Count Philip of Alsace. St. Nicholas Church was built in the 13h century, as was the belfry. At the same time, the building of St. Bavon Cathedral began and was finished in the 15th century. It houses the triptych of the Mystical Lamb by the Van Eyck brothers (q.v.). In 1302, Ghent took a leading role in the Battle of the Golden Spurs (q.v.).

Around 1340, Ghent became the largest city in Western Europe after Paris. It took over the leading role in Flanders from Bruges, a role that later passed to Antwerp in Burgundian Brabant (qq.v.).

Economically, Flanders was dependent on the wool of England, so Jacob van Artevelde (q.v.), "the wise man of Ghent," invited the English king Edward III to Ghent to be crowned king of France. After a few years, he was murdered by his own citizens and the dependence on France was restored.

In 1500, Charles V (q.v.) was born in Ghent's Prince's Court (Prinsenhof). In 1540, he entered into conflict with his native town and replaced St. Bavon's Abbey with a Spanish fortification. The inhabitants had to appear publicly before him confessing their guilt with a noose around their necks. The event is commemorated in the nickname of the inhabitants of Ghent, the "Noose-bearers" (Stropkens), and in an annual public manifestation during the Ghent festivities. The Prince's Court and the Spanish fortification were later completely destroyed by the inhabitants of Ghent.

Calvinism and the iconoclastic movement made their way through the rebellious city in 1566. By the Pacification of Ghent (q.v.) in 1576, local rulers tried to stabilize the situation. However, in 1579, the Calvinist Republic was proclaimed in Ghent. The Spanish regent, the Duke of Parma, Alexander Farnese, reconquered the town in 1584 and restored the Catholic regime. Repression and decay followed over many decades. The town revived during a short period under the Austrian rule of Maria Theresa (1748-80) (q.v.). Some houses of the burgers of this period are preserved in the town center. In the nineteenth century, Ghent was again in the European forefront as a leading center of industrialization. It was also here that, at the end of the nineteenth century, the Belgian workers' movement took root.

Ghent was the scene of the signing, on 24 December 1814 of the treaty that marked the end of the War of 1812 between Britain and the United States.

Nowadays Ghent remains a seaport and it is the administrative center of East Flanders Province. It houses the only Flemish state university.

GEWESTELIJKE INVESTERINGSMAATSCHAPPIJ VOOR VLAANDEREN (GIMV). *See* REGIONAL INVESTMENT COMPANY OF FLANDERS.

GOL, JEAN (1942- ). The liberal PRL-politician entered the House of Representatives in 1972. From 1972 to 1974, he was state-secretary for the economy of the Walloon region. From 1979 for three years, he was the president of the Liberal Reformist Party (Parti Réformateur Libéral, PRL) and since 1981 vice premier and minister of justice and of institutional reforms in the Martens's (q.v.) governments. In 1992, he resumed the presidency of the party.

GREAT PRIVILEGE (1477). In 1477, the Burgundian Duke Charles the Bold (q.v.) fell near Nancy in a battle against the Lotharingians. His daughter and heiress to the Low Countries, Mary of Burgundy (qq.v.), was forced to grant the Great Privilege in order to obtain the continued support of her subjects. This temporarily reversed the secular trend toward unification and centralization under the Burgundian dynasty (q.v.).

The Great Privilege contains 20 articles. Seven of them deal with the organization of the central financial and judicial institutions. Governing powers are brought back under control of the regional and local authorities. Four articles concern the observance of local and regional privileges. Four others point to the use of the language of the defendants and other concerned parties in law suits. Further articles treat the issues of selling of functions, tolls, obstruction of free trade and abuse of feudal services. At the same time, the Estates acquired for themselves the right to free assembly and to participate in decisions on the declaration of war. All this signified a tightened control of and restriction on the ducal power. The Great Privilege was followed by regional special editions for the Estates in the various provinces (Flanders; Brabant; Holland, Zeeland and West Friesland; Namur) and several towns.

In the long run, the division between the councils of the ducal court and the juridical court and the regionalization of the Accounting Chambers tended to become a permanent feature of the institutional structures. However, Mary's new husband and regent of the Low Countries, Maximilian of Austria (q.v.), tried to reverse this decentralizing tendency. Though confirmed by the peace of Arras (1482), he attacked the legitimation of the Great Privilege (and the ensuing regional privileges) in 1485 by arguing that they were won from Mary by force and violence. In 1494, he had them removed from the official acts of accession of his son Philip the Handsome.

## - H -

HABSBURG DYNASTY. In 1477, the Burgundian Duke Charles the Bold (q.v.) was killed at Nancy. He was succeeded by his daughter Mary of Burgundy. She encountered resistance from the union of the Flemish towns, the so-called Members of Flanders, which included Ghent, Bruges and Ypres (qq.v.). They compelled her to grant the Great Privilege (q.v.). Under this, she was supervised by a newly established Great Council. This strenghtened the trend toward unification of the territory because it created a constitution and political institutions for the whole of the Netherlands. Mary then entered into a dynastic marriage with Maximilian of Habsburg, which brought the Austrian dynasty to Flanders.

On Mary's death in 1482, Maximilian of Austria assumed the regency over the Low Countries. He tried to subject the towns to royal control, and he fought a continuing effort by the town to reassert their independence and once was even held prisoner in Bruges. However, in 1494, the towns finally submitted and they lost their privileges in the Peace of Cadzand. In 1493, Maximilian became Holy Roman Emperor and the next year, he delegated the rule of the Netherlands to his son Philip of Clève. Philip married Joan of Aragon, the daughter of the Spanish king, and their son Charles of Luxembourg became heir to the Spanish Crown, as well as to the Austrian Habsburg lands. At the death of Philip in 1506, Charles was only six. Margaret of Austria (q.v.) assumed the regency until Charles came of age. In 1517, Charles V (q.v.) inherited the Spanish Habsburg lands. In 1542, he obtained the crown of the Holy Roman Empire. In 1555, he abdicated in favor of his son, Philip II of Spain. Spanish rule continued in the south of the Low Countries (q.v.) until 1713, when the Austrians took over. *See also* AUSTRIAN RULE; CHARLES VI; JOSEPH II; MARIA THERESA.

HAINAULT. Province in the southwest. A medieval county dating from the late ninth century, Hainault was united with the county of Flanders (q.v.) several times from the 11th to the 13th centuries. Acquired by Philip the Good (q.v.) in 1433, it became part of the Spanish and Austrian Netherlands. Southern sections, including the towns of Lille and Cambrai, were acquired by France in the 17th and 18th centuries.

HANSENNE, MICHEL (1940- ). Social Christian Party (PSC) politician. Former Minister of labor in the eighties and from 1989 on director of the International Labour Organisation.

HAPPART, JOSE (1947- ) In the local elections of 1982, the French-speaking Action Fouronnaise under José Happart won 10 of the 15 seats in the Council of Voeren (Les Fourons) (q.v.). He was elected mayor and refused to speak Dutch. This provoked a violent reaction not only from Flemish extremists but also from Flemish politicians in general. However, he was supported by the president of the Socialist Party (PS), Guy Spitaels (qq.v.). In 1984, Happart headed the Socialist Party election list to the European Parliament and obtained an overwhelming number of preference votes.

HENNEPIN, LOUIS (1626-1701). Franciscan missionary born in Ath. He journeyed to Canada in 1675 and three years later joined the expedition of the explorer Robert Cavalier, sieur de La Salle, who with a small group of companions explored the Great Lakes and upper Mississippi River areas. Hennepin wrote several books on his travels, including *Nouvelle Découverte* (1697), which contains the earliest written description of Niagara Falls.

HERGE (1907-1983). Hergé was the pseudonym of Georges Remi, a famous comic strip designer. He is the creator of Kuifje/Tintin. He is known for his clear line. He is regarded as the pioneer and first great master of the school of Belgian comic strip designers. *See also* COMIC STRIPS.

HIGH COUNCIL OF FINANCE. This council is an advisory body on financial matters. On request, it gives advice to the government and proposes needed policy. For example, the Minister of Finance Philip Maystadt asked for advice on the reform of taxes on incomes from renting. The council produced a study of the consequences of alternative measures, taking into account the results of similar measures in neighboring countries.

HIGH COUNCIL OF JUSTICE. In the aftermath of the political and judicial scandals of 1996, the government decided to reform the judiciary system (q.v.). The installation of a High Council of Justice (Haut Conseil de la Justice/Hoge Raad voor de Justitie) was one of the first proposals discussed at the end of 1996 and delivered to Parliament (q.v.) at the beginning of 1997. Until then, political practice rigorously respected the constitutional principle of the strict division of powers. To correct some dysfunctional operations of the judiciary system, a higher degree of external political control over the organization and functioning of justice were to be introduced.

The High Council of Justice will be composed half by judicial magistrates and half by persons external to the judiciary. The council will function as an ombudsman that gathers grievances from the public. The council can decide to investigate the cases itself or delegate them to other judicial organs. However, its main task is reporting and advising on the general functioning of the judiciary system. On request, judicial organs will have to report to the council. The reports of the council will be sent to the government and Parliament and they can be adopted as legislative initiatives, if necessary. The council also has some limited controlling power over the judiciary. The High Court of Justice will not interfere in questions of appointments and promotions. This will be entrusted to another new body, the College for Appointments and Promotions (q.v.). *See also* REFORM OF THE JUDICIARY SYSTEM.

HOUSE OF REPRESENTATIVES. Since 1830, the House of Representatives (or Chamber) has served as one of the two bodies of the Belgian parliamentary system. All proposed laws had to be approved by the Chamber and the other legislative body, the Senate (q.v.), in identical version. The Constitutional Reform of 1993 (q.v.) differentiated the roles of the Senate and Chamber and made the House of Representatives solely responsible for most ordinary legislation. It is no longer required that identical draft laws be voted by both the Senate and Chamber. It is now also the exclusive prerogative of the House of Representatives to control the government and to give or withhold its confidence. The Chamber is also exclusively competent to propose budgets and approve accounts. It also decides on the numerical strength of the army.

However, for a series of important institutional matters, the bicameral system has been maintained. Both Senate and Chamber have equal rights in initiating and finalizing the reform of the Constitution (q.v.), in preparing the legislation that according to the Constitution belong to the competence of both Senate and Chamber such as proposals about dynastic matters, laws that regulate the relations between communities and regions (qq.v.) and their supranational representation, and laws concerning the Supreme Court (q.v.) and the organization of the judiciary system (q.v.). Moreover, the list of legislation subject to the bicameral system can again be extended by a special law that must be approved by a two-thirds majority vote in both legislative houses.

Since the 1995 elections, the House counts 150 members elected by proportional representation. *See also* PARLIAMENT (ROLE OF).

HUGO VAN DER GOES (c.1430-1482/83). Painter living in Ghent (q.v.), dominating the generation after Rogier van der Weyden (q.v.). One of his preserved works is *Death of the Lady,* now at the Groeninghe Museum in Bruges (q.v.).

HUYSMANS, CAMILLE (1871-1968). Socialist leader. He was a member of the Socialist International. He became a member of Parliament (q.v.) and minister of arts and science before World War II (q.v.). From 1932 until 1942, he was also mayor of Antwerp (q.v.). He was prime minister from 3 August 1946 until 12 March 1947. He then took the portfolio of minister of education. In 1965, he clashed with the Belgian Socialist Party (q.v.) and no longer played an active role on the political scene.

HYMANS, PAUL (1865-1941). Politician and diplomat, member of the House of Representatives (q.v.) and a leader of the Liberal Party (q.v.). He entered the House in 1900 and held ministerial posts in several coalition governments. Hymans was ambassador to Britain during World War I (q.v.) and served as president of the first General Assembly of the League of Nations in January 1920.

## - I -

IGUANODON. *See* BENISSART.

INDUSTRY. Being a small country with a relatively limited domestic market, Belgium's industry has been heavily dependent in the choice of its product mix on international markets.

Chemicals, light engineering and food and drink processing were the leading industrial sectors of the last decade. Thanks to earlier American investments, the petrochemical industry flourishes in the ports of Antwerp and Ghent (qq.v.). The industry imports almost all of its raw materials and exports around 80 percent of its output. Belgium is still an important producer of zinc, silver, lead and other nonferrous metals. But mining has practically died out, the last coal mine pit being closed in 1991. The steel industry has also suffered from overproduction and is now in decline, consuming large subsidies. The closing of the blast furnace plant Forges de Clabbecq near Liège (q.v.) is a case in point. The processing industry, such as car assembly lines, have also seen a drop in production, as exemplified by the closing of the Renault factory in Vilvoorde.

The food, drink and tobacco sector has been successfully managed in medium-sized enterprises, not in the least because of good infrastructure and transportation facilities. Traditionally, Antwerp with its Jewish community has been a stronghold of the diamond industry. The paper and printing industries perform quite well. In graphics, a modest breakthrough onto the international market has been achieved.

Belgium has taken action to stimulate small and modern service industries, such as computer and information technology. The authorities have established small industry centers offering substantial infrastructe and transportation facilities and granting tax rebates. The share held by heavy industry in both GDP and employment will likely continue to decline. *See also* AGRICULTURE; BANKING; COAL; ECONOMY.

ISABELLA OF PORTUGAL (1397-1473). She was the daughter of the king of Portugal Joao I of Aviz. She was the third wife of Philip the Good (q.v.) and the mother of Charles the Bold (q.v.).

## - J -

JACOB VAN MAERLANT (c.1230-c.1293). He was born at Damme near Bruges, where he was a pupil of the chapter school.

He was author of didactic works, such as his *Spiegel Historiael,* an encyclopedic history in 91,000 verses written between 1284 and 1290. The only preserved version of the beautiful illuminated manuscript dates from 1300. Van Maerlant popularized the early Renaissance insights of the 12th century. Jan van Boendale, another Flemish writer of the Middle Ages, called him *de Vader der Dietser Dichtern Algader* (The Father of All Flemish Poets). His expression *om datic Vlaminc ben* (because I'm a Fleming), an apology by the writer for the use of Flemish rhyme-words that were not understood in Holland, was adopted as a motto by the modern-day Flemish movement (q.v.).

JAN VAN BOENDALE (1280-1365). Born at Boendale in the Netherlands, he lived in Antwerp (q.v.) as the town's secretary. He was a pupil of Jacob Van Maerlant (q.v.). Van Boendale wrote a history of Brabant (q.v.) *(Brabantse Yeesten)*, and encyclopedic and highly speculative works *(Der Leeken Spieghel, Jans Teestye)*.

JAN VAN EYCK (c.1390-1441). Jan and his brother Hubert van Eyck (c.1370-1426), master painters of the school of Flemish Primitives, were born in Maaseik. They introduced "modern" modelling, perspective and lighting. They worked in the service of the Burgundian (q.v.) court and made many portraits of dukes, duchesses and important nobility. In 1428, Jan Van Eyck travelled in a royal delegation to Portugal to portray the future wife of Duke Philip the Good, Isabella of Portugal (qq.v.).

The brother's paintings show a deep religious inspiration. Their masterpiece, *The Adoration of the Lamb* (1432), can be admired in the church of St. Bavon at Ghent (q.v.). One panel called *The Righteous Judges* disappeared before World War II (q.v.) and was the subject of much speculation on who had taken it and where it could have been hidden.

Jan van Eyck's portraits are noted for precision of execution and clear consistency. They include *Giovanni Arnolfini and his Bride* (1434) and *Man in a Red Turban* (1433), possibly a self-portrait. In 1436, van Eyck painted *The Madonna with Canon Joris Van der Paele.* At the end of his life in 1439, he made a famous portrait of his 33-year old wife Margaret van Eyck. Both pictures can be seen at the Groeninghe Museum in Bruges (q.v.).

JAN VAN RUYSBROECK (c. 1293-1381). Greatest Flemish medieval mystical writer. He was a priest in St. Goedele cathedral in Brussels (q.v.) and then retired to an abbey in the Forest of Soignes. He wrote *Die Chierheit der geistlicher Brulocht* (Elegance of a Spiritual Marriage).

JEAN I of BRABANT, DUKE (?-1294). The duke of Brabant (q.v.) arranged two diplomatic marriages for himself. First he was married to Margaret, daughter of King Ludwig the Holy, and later to the daughter of the Flemish Count Gwyde of Dampierre. He bought the Duchy of Limburg (q.v.) from its heir Hendrik. Jean defeated the archbishop of Cologne, Duke Hendrik of Luxembourg (q.v.) and Duke Reinout of Gelre at the battle of Woeringen in 1288. Duke Jean I of Brabant and Lower Lotharinga (q.v.) was mortally wounded during a tournament and buried in the cloister church of the Minor Brothers in Brussels (q.v.).

JOHN OF AUSTRIA (1547-1578). Spanish general and regent of the Netherlands. He was the son of Emperor Charles V (q.v.). Commonly known as Don John, he was appointed regent of the Netherlands in 1576. Faced with united opposition to Spanish rule, he was forced to make concessions acknowledged in the Pacification of Ghent (q.v.). However, he quickly resumed hostilites and, in command of Spanish armies, he entered Brussels in 1577. He defeated Dutch rebels at the battle of Gembloux in 1578 but failed to follow up the victory because of lack of support from king Philip II. He died suddenly in camp at Namur (q.v.). Alexander Farnese succeeded him as regent.

JOHN THE FEARLESS (1371-1419). John the Fearless (Jean sans Peur, Jan zonder Vrees), duke of Nevers, (1404-1419) was the son and heir of Philip the Bold (q.v.). In his youth, he was most interested in military strategy. He fell a prisoner to the Turks during a crusade at Nicopolis in 1396 and was ransomed at a high price by his vassals of Flanders (q.v.) and Burgundy. He married Margaret of Beieren-Holland (1385-1426).

On the death of his father Philip in 1404 and his mother Margaret of Male (q.v.) in 1405, John acceded to power in Flanders and Artois. He directed most of his attention to the efforts to secure the French throne and its financial resources. He entered into numerous intrigues, physically eliminated his main rival, the Duc Louis d'Orléans in 1407, but he was murdered himself in 1409. His son Philip the Good (q.v.) concentrated on building up an autonomous Burgundian state.

JORDAENS, JACOB (1593-1678). He was a pupil of Peter Paul Rubens (q.v.) and a representative of baroque naturalism. He painted both altar pieces and scenes of everyday life. His renowned *The King Drinks* hangs in the Museum of Fine Arts in Brussels (q.v.).

JOSEPH II (1741-1790). Son of Maria Theresa (q.v.), Holy Roman emperor and archduke of Austria (1765-1790). He was called an enlightened despot. After the death of his mother in 1780, he initiated a series of sweeping reforms in the fields of law, trade, taxes, education and religion. The resistance against his rule in the Austrian Netherlands was canalized into the Brabant Revolution (1789-90) (q.v.). In 1790, the revolutionaries proclaimed the independence of the Confederation of the United Belgian States (Confédération des Etats Belges Unis). The rivalry between conservative and progressive factions in the rebellious forces enabled the Austrians to restore their rule. *See also* AUSTRIAN RULE.

JOSQUIN DES PRES (c.1450-1521). Flemish polyfonist at the court of Margaret of Austria (q.v.). He wrote mainly motets, masses and other church music.

JOYOUS ENTRY OF BRABANT (1356). A charter dating from 1356 in which the Burgundian dukes guaranteed all citizens of the province equality before the law, impartial justice, linguistic freedom, and no taxation without popular consent. Similar charters were accorded to towns in Flanders (q.v.), including Ghent (q.v.).

JUDICIARY SYSTEM. The judiciary is one of the three state powers and, rather than aiming to secure a balance, the Constitution (q.v.) and Belgian practice until recently rigorously upheld the principle of division of powers. In general, political involvement in justice was limited to the appointment of judges to some of the higher courts. On the other hand, with the exception of the State

Council and later the Arbitration Court (qq.v.), courts have no general right of judicial review of laws. The Supreme Court (q.v.), the highest in the hierarchy of ordinary courts, which in theory must judge appeals on strictly formal legal grounds, must proceed case by case and has no general right of interpretation. This is reserved for Parliament (q.v.) as law maker.

The system of ordinary legislation has a strict hierarchical structure. At the basis in each canton or judicial area, magistrates (Vrederechters, juges de paix) try to reconcile disputes between citizens or apply sanctions for minor violations of the law. At the district level, there are the so-called courts of first instance with sections for civil, criminal and juvenile cases. Special labor and commercial courts also work on this level. Apart from these there are police and military courts. Serious criminal cases such as murder pass before a special court where professional judges are assisted by a jury of 12 citizens (Hof van Assisen, Cour d'Assises). There are five Courts of Appeal (q.v.), located in Brussels (2), Ghent, Antwerp, and Mons (qq.v.). They treat the appeals of parties contesting the judgments of the ordinary lower courts.

The Supreme Court (Hof van Cassatie, Cour de Cassation) is the highest court. It treats the appeals from parties judged by all lower courts, included the five Courts of Appeal. Appeal to the Supreme Court can only be made on formal procedural grounds. The Supreme Court will not reconsider the factual evidence of the cases. The Supreme Court also takes decisions on the removal of poorly functioning judges. Finally, it decides on the impeachment of ministers of the federal and community governments. Prior to 1996, it had first to inform Parliament (q.v.) before it could take any investigative step. As a consequence of the Di Rupo (q.v.) case, it now may take some limited steps of investigation before it informs Parliament. Any official charge still has to pass Parliament.

There is also a sharp division of competences between the Supreme Court, which functions at the top of the judicial hierarchy, and two other high-level organs with judicial competence: the State Council and the Arbitration Court (qq.v.). The State Council is the sole body that determines the legality of laws and decrees and hands down interpretations of the latter. The Arbitration Court serves as the last resort for disputes between the linguistic communities.

Following the Dutroux case (q.v.) and massive popular protests politicians announced that the judiciary system would be reformed and took steps to implement reforms at the end of 1996. *See also* ST. NICHOLAS PLAN.

## - K -

KAREL, PRINS REGENT. See CHARLES, PRINCE REGENT.

KHNOPFF, FERNAND (1858-1921). Symbolist avant-garde painter. He was one of the founders of the progressive movement "Les XX" (1883).

KING (ROLE OF). According to the oath constitutionally required of the Belgian king, the sovereign must govern the country with respect for its laws and with intent to preserve the sovereignty and the integrity of its territory against external threats.

Historically, the importance of the role of the king in the political system has declined steadily since 1831. The first kings made full use of their prerogatives and even exceeded them whereas after World War I and especially after World War II (qq.v.), the king played a more symbolic role. The growing importance of the parties and of the governments and their cabinets reduced the actual power of the monarch.

According to the Constitution, the king appoints and dismisses his ministers. The first king Leopold I (q.v.) did so actively, while the competence of King Baudouin (q.v.) was reduced to giving advisory consent only. Some of his preferences for appointments and dismissals met with a flat refusal from the prime minister. Article 64 of the Constitution says that no act of the king can have effect if not countersigned by a minister, who takes the responsibility for it. This severe limitation of the political power of the monarch has generally been observed. Two important exceptions can be pointed to in the history of Belgium: the creation of the Congo empire by Leopold II (q.v.) and the military actions undertaken without co-signing of ministers.

In wartime, the king constitutionally takes command of the army. Albert I (q.v.) did so and accompanied his troops in the fields of the IJzer during World War I. During World War II, Leopold III (q.v.) did so also, but ordered the surrender without consulting his government. He did not follow his government into exile. He defended his decision in saying that he could better defend the interests of his people while physically present in Belgium. He negotiated with the occupying forces and Hitler personally. Later, he was detained as a prisoner of war in Germany and Austria. After the war, these developments led to the so-called royal controversy (q.v.) and ultimately to his abdication in favor of Prince Baudouin.

This certainly weakened the dynasty's popularity. During the strikes of 1960-1961, republican forces were strong, especially in Wallonia (q.v.). However, by his long and cautious policy, Baudouin restored sympathy and loyalty to the monarchy. His break with his stepmother Princess Liliane and his marrige to Fabiola di Aragon contributed to restoring the prestige of the monarchy. One recent incident disturbed the new harmony. In 1990, a coalition of Liberals, Socialists and Greens passed an abortion act (q.v.) in Parliament (q.v.). King Baudouin wrote the prime minister that he should not sign the law. A devout Catholic, he had personal religious objections to the law. Consequently, the king stepped down from office for 36 hours. The cabinet assumed his functions and signed the bill. Discussions followed whether or not to change the Constitution and ascribe to the monarchy a purely ceremonial function, as in the Nordic countries.

However, no quick change was enacted and after the unexpected death of King Baudouin, his brother Albert II (q.v.) was asked by the top party leaders to take over. Following the White March (q.v.), Albert seems willing to undertake a more active role in public life.

KING ALBERT. *See* ALBERT, KING.

KING BAUDOUIN. *See* BAUDOUIN, KING.

KING LEOPOLD. *See* LEOPOLD, KING.

KORTRIJK. *See* COURTRAI.

## - L -

LABOR PARTY. The Labor Party (Partij van de Arbeid/Parti du Travail Belge), previously AMADA (Alle Macht aan de Arbeiders), is a Communist-inspired Party of Maoist allegiance. It mildly flourished in the heady days of the 1968 movement. It launched major ideological campaigns and enjoyed some local support, but its overall electoral success remained insignificant.

LANGE WAPPER. Lange Wapper (Lanky Flop) is a folkloristic personage, popular in the old town of Antwerp (q.v.). He would suddenly appear as a giant to scare the children and good people of the town. In recent times, he reappeared as a popular figure in tales and especially in the local puppet theater.

LANGUAGE. There exists no common Belgian language. The official languages of Belgium are Dutch (q.v.), French and German. Along with these standardized languages, the inhabitants of Belgium speak local dialects, for example Flemish in the north and Walloon in the south. *See also* FLEMISH LANGUAGE; FRENCH LANGUAGE; LANGUAGE BOUNDARY.

LANGUAGE BOUNDARY. After the conquest by Caesar (58-51 B.C.), Gallia Belgica (Belgian Gaul) was established. It was divided into *civitates*, administrative units that corresponded to the earlier territories of the different tribes. Along the great roads and at the site of Roman fortifications, Roman towns appeared, such as Tournai (q.v.), Arlon, Tongeren, Maastricht, Nijmegen. For some time, the Romans tried to defend their eastern frontier along the Rhine. From the third century on, Germanic tribes invaded the Roman Empire and assimilated the Celtic tribes, as well as the fewer Romanized elements. Out of this melting pot developed the Flemish (Dutch) language.

Most Romans withdrew southwards of the main Bavai-Cologne road. The southern regions of the present territory of Belgium were therefore much more Romanized. The road grew into an early forerunner of the present language frontier, as

French (and Walloon) developed from the language of the Romanized population.

Consequently, in the territory that would later become Belgium, there were always at least two language groups and a common Belgian language never existed. *See also* FLEMISH LANGUAGE; FRENCH LANGUAGE; LANGUAGE LAWS.

LANGUAGE LAWS. Belgium began independence in 1830 with French decreed as the official language both in Flanders and Wallonia (qq.v.).

On 17 August 1873, the Belgian Parliament (q.v.) voted the first law on the official use of the Flemish language (q.v.). The law permitted the use of Dutch (q.v.) in the courts of Flanders (q.v.).

In 1893, the Equality Law recognized the Dutch language as one of the two official languages of Belgium. In 1930, the State University of Ghent adopted Dutch as its language of instruction. In 1932, Dutch became the exclusive language of instruction in primary and secondary education in Flanders.

In 1962-1963 the language boundary (q.v.) was fixed with the Law of 8 November 1962 defining the boundary in the communes of Voeren and Comines and in 1963 with the Law on Brussels and its neighboring communes establishing facilities for French speakers only in the following communes: Kraainem, Wemmel, Linkebeek, Drogenbos, Sint Genesius-Rode and Wezenbeek-Oppem. (Since 1954, facilities existed in additional communes, as a consequence of the language poll of 1947, and in 1963 conditions allowing access for French speakers were strengthened).

In 1973, the Cultural Council of the Dutch-language Community issued a decree stipulating Dutch as the only language to be used in employer-employee relations in Flanders.

In addition, the Decree of 10 December 1973 defined the official designation of the language spoken in Flanders as "Dutch, or the Dutch language."

However, linguistic problems and language-community conflicts still arise around the language boundary of Brussels and its environs and around Comines (Komen) and especially Voeren (Les Fourons) (q.v.). The strong opposition to the existing laws on Voeren, led by its mayor Joseph Happart (q.v.), succeeded in securing changes with the support of the French-speaking Socialists (Parti Socialiste, PS) *(see* Socialist Party) and resulted in the fall of the government of the Flemish Christen Democrat Wilfried Martens (q.v.) on 15 October 1987. Although a complicated compromise was found, the situation has not been totally stabilized and can erupt again at any moment. The problem, however, is now again integrated in the difficult modus vivendi of the French and Dutch language-community politics.

In summary, the history of language laws in Belgium is largely one of gradual success by Dutch speakers in securing equal and then preferential rights for the language in Flanders and the capital district. Walloon as a spoken dialect has not received an official status, as it was always subsumed by the official French language (q.v.). *See also* CONSTITUTIONAL REFORM OF 1970; LANGUAGE BOUNDARY.

LANOYE, TOM. Publicist and writer. He made his debut with the collection of poems *In de piste* (At the Ring, 1984). His real artistic breakthrough was his nostalgic novel *Kartonnen Dozen* (Cardboard Boxes, 1991).

LASSUS, ORLANDUS (c.1530-1594). Flemish polyphonist. He wrote madrigals, motets and masses.

LATEM. *See* ST. MARTENS LATEM.

LEAGUE OF SUPPORTERS OF DUTCH NATIONAL SOLIDARITY (VERDINASO). The League of Supporters of Dutch National Solidarity (Verbond van Dietsche Nationaalsolidaristen) was a Flemish nationalistic movement founded by Joris van Severen in 1931 together with supporters of the so-called Dutch National Solidarity. It was a paramilitary organization. The movement's ideological commitment moved slowly from an anti-Belgian and anti-parliamentary attitude toward a national patriotic position and it worked with the Resistance (q.v.) against the Germans during World War II (q.v.).

LEOPOLD I, KING (1790-1865). First king of Belgium. Leopold of Saxe-Coburg was not the first candidate to the Belgian throne. Rather, the vice president of the National Congress proposed to offer the Belgian throne to the French royal family. Members of Parliament sought a union with France. Under English pressure the French King Louis-Philippe declared he could not accept the throne. On 3 February 1831, the Congress voted in favor of the fourth son of the French king, the Duke of Nemours. Again, the allies pressed the French royal house not to accept the throne. Finally, the English candidate, Leopold of Saxe-Coburg, was put on the throne. Walloon discontent was tempered by the fact that the new king of Belgium married Louise-Marie, daughter of the French king.

In the first years of his reign, Leopold tried with success to consolidate the sovereignty of the new kingdom. Immediately after independence, he allowed several governments of national union to be formed. In the 1850s and 1860s, the Liberal and Catholic parties (q.v.) were founded and the parliamentary politics became more complicated. The country passed through a severe economic crisis. Leopold tried to alleviate this situation by massive infrastructure works. The first railway on the continent between Brussels and Mechelen (qq.v.) was opened under his reign. Leopold I was succeeded by his son Leopold II (q.v.).

LEOPOLD II, KING (1835-1909). Leopold II succeeded his father Leopold I (q.v.) on 17 December 1865. His reign was characterized by the further industrialization of Belgium, especially of the Walloon region. The poverty-stricken proletarians organized their first trade unions and a Socialist Party (q.v.) was founded. In the political field, the division between Catholics and Liberals materialized in the so-called "school war." However, the reign of Leopold II is largely remembered for his great adventure on another continent: he became the ruler of the Congo (q.v.).

LEOPOLD III, KING (1901-1983). The eldest son of King Albert I (q.v.) succeeded to the throne on 23 December 1934. After one year of reign, he lost his popular wife, Queen Astrid, in a car accident. At the outbreak of World War II (q.v.), he commanded the Belgian army during the 18-day campaign in May 1940. He played a controversial role during the war stemming from his decision to stay in the country.

An advisory plebiscite was organized in which the majority of the Flemish Catholic people approved and the Walloon Socialist population strongly rejected the return of King Leopold III. The conflict ended with the abdication of Leopold III in favor of his son Baudouin (q.v.). *See also* ROYAL CONTROVERSY.

LEUVEN. *See* LOUVAIN.

LIBERAL PARTY. The Liberal Party (Parti Libéral) was the first party to be organized in Belgium. In the early years following independence, the country was governed by united factions, composed of both Catholic and liberal tendencies. The Liberal Party was formed as an outcome of the First Liberal Congress of 1846, itself organized by the Alliance Libérale of Brussels (q.v.). From then on the Liberals led the government with rare exceptions until 1884, when a period of unilateral Catholic dominance set in until World War I (q.v.). The introduction of proportional representation in 1889 undercut the Liberal majority and the rise of Socialist representation in parliament reduced the Liberals to third place. After the war, the Liberals could return to power only in coalition governments.

Like all other national parties, the Liberal Party was shaken by the community problem and the federalization of Belgium. In December 1969 the Flemish "Blue Lions" (Blauwe Leeuwen) in Brussels withdrew from the unitary Party for Freedom and Progress (Partij voor Vrijheid en Vooruitgang, PVV/Parti de la Liberté et du Progrès, PLP). Thereupon, the PVV and PLP became autonomous and held separate congresses. In 1972, the separation into two parties was complete. In Brussels, several splits and new alliances of French-speaking Liberals led to new formations. However, the Liberal electoral success in Brussels declined and in 1979, they decided to join their Walloon compatriots, creating the Liberal Reformist Party (PRL, q.v.). Jean Gol was elected president. The Liberals also tried to reestablish cooperation on the national level by electing the national chairman Pierre Deschamps (PRL).

LIBERAL REFORMIST PARTY. The Liberal Reformist Party (Parti Réformateur Libéral, PRL) came to life in 1979 as a fusion of earlier liberal parties in Brussels and Wallonia (qq.v.). Its president was Jean Gol. It functions as the French-speaking counterpart to the Flemish Liberals and Democrats (q.v.) (Vlaamse Liberalen en Democraten, VLD). Both are heirs of their nineteenth-century mother party, the Liberal Party (q.v.) (Parti Libéral).

In the two decades following World War II (q.v.), the Liberals had traditionally been the third party in Wallonia after the Socialists and Christian Democrats. In 1981, the new formula proved successful and the Liberals took second place. The 1985 election saw its share of votes increase to 24.2 percent. In 1987, it fell back to 22.2 percent and lost its second place to the Christian Social Party (PSC) (*see* Catholic Party). The decrease continued in 1991 when it obtained 19.8 percent of the Walloon votes. A similar evolution took place in Brussels, though the losses stabilized on a high level there. After the crisis at the end of the 1970s, the election results in Brussels recovered amazingly due to the fading away of rival formations. In 1985, the PRL obtained 26 percent. In 1987 and 1991, it fell to 25.3 percent and 21.7 percent

LIBERAL UNIONS. The General Confederation of Belgian Liberal Unions (Confédération Générale des Syndicats Libéraux de Belgique) was established in 1930. The Liberal unions are in members, strength and influence significantly less strong than the Socialists and Christian Democrats. However, the liberal confederation plays a full part in the Belgian participation and consultation system. At the grassroots level, it has a more corporatist character. Ideologically, it fully accepts the competition of the capitalist system, but supports social measures to alleviate inequities.

The Liberal trade unions followed the federalizing movement in Belgium and now have a French and a Flemish wing.

LIEGE. Town on the Meuse and capital of the province of the same name. In the early Middle Ages Liège was the seat of an autonomous prince-bishopric.

The origin and significance of Liège is connected with the murder around 700 of the Bishop of Tongres (q.v.), Lambertus. His follower, Hubertus, transferred his relics to Liège and it became a frequently visited place of pilgrimage.

In 980, Notger, the first prince-bishop of Liège, received from the German emperor the right to wield religious and temporal control over the bishopric. Notger and his followers continually extended their possessions, so that at one time Liège controlled the whole of Wallonia with the exception of the region of Tournai (qq.v.). Liège became a famous center of learning and devotion, with a cathedral school at its core.

In 1212 and again in 1213, the duke of Brabant (q.v.), Hendrik I, tried to conquer the town. A coalition of the prince-bishop of Liège and the citizens of Liège, Huy, Dinant, Ciney and Fosses defeated the duke in the municipality of Steppes. It was the same type of conflict that the town of Flanders fought against the French crown at the Battle of the Golden Spurs (qq.v.).

In the 14th and 15th centuries internal struggle characterized the changing pattern of power in the city. The "Littles" fought under the leadership of their mayor, Henri de Dinant, father of the people, against the "Greats" and their prince-bishop. Henri de Dinant introduced incipient forms of democracy and strived toward securing the equality of all citizens. In the end, he was defeated and banned. His historical role can be compared to that of Jacob van Artevelde in Ghent (qq.v.).

But the struggle between "Greats" and "Littles" was not over. During the night of 3-4 August 1312, the "Littles" set fire to the church of Sint-Maarten. The "Greats," who had fled to the church, were burnt alive. The memory of these events is still vivid and, even today, the streets are filled with noisy commemorative crowds on the night of 3-4 August.

In 1316, the Peace of Fexhe (q.v.) affirmed the rights of the citizens. Prince-bishop Adolphe de la Marck recognized the right of the citizens to revolt if he failed to respect their rights. The only exception allowed the prince-bishop to supersede citizens' rights when necessitated by "the interest of the country." In some sense, the prince-bishop was factually "judicially irresponsible" in power relations with the citizens. This embodies a judicial forerunner of Article 82 of the Belgian Constitution (q.v.) which constitutionally defines the position of the king (q.v.) in exceptional circumstances, such as the occupation of the country by foreign powers.

During the next centuries, the struggle continued between the "Greats" with the prince-bishop at their head and the "Littles." In 1390 the pope of Rome, Boniface IX, installed Jan van Beieren on the throne. He formed an alliance with his brother- in-law, the Burgundian Duke John. They defeated rebellious popular forces at the Battle of Othée in 1408, where John acquired his nickname "Jean sans Peur" (John The Fearless) (q.v.).

In conjunction with his plans to bind Liège to the counties of Flanders and Hainaut (qq.v.) and the duchies of Brabant (q.v.), Limburg and Luxembourg (q.v.), already under Burgundian influence, Philip the Good (q.v.) invited the pope to put a French prince on the throne of Liège, Louis the Bourbon. This Bourbon called upon the Burgundian Duke Charles the Bold (q.v.) to discipline the citizens of Liège. After several campaigns and fierce battles, Charles the Bold finally conquered the town. He repressed its citizens and destroyed their national symbols. The "Perron," an age-old monument of freedom, was sent to Bruges (q.v.). Two years later, the struggle revived. Charles the Bold resumed the fight against the citizens of Liège. He brought with him the king of France, more or less as a hostage. Charles's army threatened to defeat the citizens of Liège again. In the night of 29-30 October 1467, the army of the duke and the king's escort camped on the heights of Walburgis. Six hundred citizens of the village of Franchimont decided to make a desperate attack and to take the king and the duke hostage. They failed to do so, and were all murdered. However, the courage of the "six hundred Franchimonteses" (q.v.) grew into a national myth. Duke Charles the Bold destroyed Liège. It was consumed by fire for nine weeks. From this event, the town got its nickname "fiery" or "ardent" town, interpreted later in a more psychological and figurative sense.

In 1493, Liège under Mayor Erard de la Marck secured recognition of its neutrality towards France and the Low Countries (q.v.) by the Treaty of Senlis.

In 1795, Liège lost its autonomy and was annexed to France with other parts of the southern Low Countries. From then on it remained an integral part of the future Belgian territorial configuration.

During the industrialization process, Liège grew into an important industrial center and a river port connected with Antwerp (q.v.) by the Albert Canal.

The city is full of testimonials to the city's past, such as the St. Barthélémy Church with its baptismal font made by Renier de Huy, the St. John Church with the shrine of Charles the Bold and the St. Croix Church of the 13th century. Liège also possesses one of Belgium's finest Renaissance monuments: the Palace of the Prince-Bishops that dates from the 16th century. The existing "Perron" that dates from the 18th century is the symbol of the freedom of Liège.

Liège is the cultural center of French-speaking Belgium.

LIMBURG. Province lying along the west bank of the Maas (Meuse) River. Together with adjoining lands on the east bank of the river, now in the Netherlands, the territory formed part of Lower Lotharinga (q.v.), and passed to the duchy of Brabant (q.v.) in the late 13th century. Incorporated into the duchy of Burgundy and the Spanish-ruled Netherlands, eastern portions passed to the Dutch Republic by the Peace of Munster (q.v.) in 1648. The province was reunited in the Kingdom of the Netherlands in 1815 but again divided with acknowledgement of Belgian independence in 1839.

A coal-mining and dairying region, Limburger cheese was first produced in the province near the border with the province of Liège (q.v.).

LIPSIUS, JUSTUS (1547-1606). He is one of a series of great humanists and scientists who lived in the Netherlands in the second part of the sixteenth century. Born in Overijssel, he spent most of his life in Louvain (q.v.) and was a good friend of Christoffel Plantijn (q.v.), who printed his books in Antwerp (q.v.). Lipsius is especially known for his interpretation of Latin writers such as Tacitus.

LOBBES SUR SAMBRE. Walloon locality where the pre-Romanesque church of St. Ursmar has been preserved.

LODEWIJK VAN MALE. *See* LOUIS OF MALE.

LOTHARINGA. After the death of Louis the Pious (840), his sons divided the Holy Roman Empire into three parts by the Treaty of Verdun (q.v.). To the west and including Flanders (q.v.), a Frankish kingdom developed that would eventually grow into modern France. To the east, Francia Orientalis would become the German imperial lands. The middle territories—Francia Media—would become a much divided and contested area. In 855, this region was split into an Italian kingdom, into Provence and Burgundy and into Lotharinga, the area between the Rhine and the Meuse. In 959, it was divided again into Lower Lotharinga that covers present-day Wallonia (q.v.) and Upper Lotharinga. In 1012, Emperor Henry II gave Lotharinga to Godefroi I. After 1100, local dukedoms flourished here, such as Brabant (q.v.), the counties of Hainaut, Luxembourg and Limburg (qq.v.) and the independent bishopric of Liège (q.v.).

LOUIS OF MALE (LODEWIJK VAN MALE) (1346-1384). Count of Flanders (q.v.), Rethel and the towns of Antwerp and Mechelen (qq.v.). His mother possessed Artois and Franche-Comté and together they reigned over Nevers. He married his daughter Margaret to the Burgundian Duke Philip the Bold (q.v.). In 1357, he conquered Antwerp and Mechelen and incorporated them into Flanders. He won a battle against the Ghent (q.v.) townsmen at Nevele, but he could not conquer Ghent, defended by Pieter van den Bosch. Moreover, he was defeated at Bruges (q.v.) by Philip van Artevelde of Ghent. However, he subsequently secured the support of the French king Charles VI and defeated Artevelde at West-Rozebeke in 1382.

LOUVAIN (LEUVEN). Town in Brabant (q.v.). It was already a textile center in the 13th century. It was incorporated into the Burgundian and Habsburg (qq.v.) lands. Its flamboyant Gothic town hall dates from 1445-1463. Louvain became the seat of the first university on what would later become Belgian territory with the founding of the Roman Catholic theological center in 1426.

In 1968, a student revolt broke out aimed at splitting the Catholic University into a Flemish and French section. The managing authorities of the university, among them the bishops, rejected this idea. However, student protests continued and the issue raised sufficient controversy to cause the government to fall. The French section of the university moved to Louvain-La-Neuve (q.v.) in French-speaking Brabant.

When the province of Brabant split into a Flemish- and French-speaking part, Leuven became the capital of Flemish Brabant.

LOUVAIN-LA-NEUVE. University site near Ottignies in French Brabant (q.v.) where the French branch was located after the Catholic University of Louvain (Leuven) (q.v.) split in 1968. It is now an autonomous, modern and well-equipped university with world-famous scholars in economics and science.

LOW COUNTRIES. This is the collective name for Belgium (België, Belgique), Luxembourg (q.v.) and the Netherlands (Nederland). The Low Countries (De Nederlanden) were first united under Charles V (q.v.) in the 16th century. The 17 "United Provinces" were constituted in 1548 as an administrative unit and were placed under the administration of Spain in 1555 at Charles's abdication in favor of his son Philip II. The new Spanish king and his regent, the Duke of Alva (q.v.), bloodily suppressed the rising Protestant movement in the Low Countries and provoked a war of secession of the northern provinces. In 1579, the seven northern provinces concluded the Union of Utrecht. The southern provinces joined, but were reconquered by the Spanish Duke Alexander Farnese and were forcibly separated from the north. By the Twelve Year's Truce of 1609, Spain implicitly recognized the independence of the northern provinces, made official by the Treaty of Munster in 1648. At the end of the War of the Spanish Succession in 1713, the Low Countries were united again briefly prior to placement of the southern provinces under Austrian rule (q.v.). They also shared a common fate under the French occupation (q.v.) (1795-1815). After the defeat of Napoleon (q.v.) in 1815, the Low Countries were united under the rule of the Dutch King William I of Orange (q.v.). Finally, the Belgian revolution (q.v.) of 1830 separated Belgium and the Netherlands again. Luxembourg was split into a Belgian province and a dukedom, then still under the Dutch king.

After World War II (q.v.), the Benelux (q.v.) Treaty did much to unify the economies of the Low Countries, which also resulted in some cooperation on foreign policy matters.

LUXEMBOURG. Capital town of the southernmost province of Belgium of the same name. The region has belonged to the Kingdom of Belgium since 1839 when it was handed over by William I of Orange (q.v.), king of the Netherlands. William retained half of the region, which was to become the independent Grand Duchy of Luxembourg and of which he was the first duke.

## - M -

MAETERLINCK, MAURICE (1864-1949). Flemish symbolist and French-language author. Poet, dramatist and essayist. He produced some 60 volumes of work. His best known works are *Pelléas et Mélisande* (1892) and *L'Oiseau bleu* (The Blue Bird, 1908). He was the only Belgian writer to receive a Nobel prize for literature, awarded in 1911.

MAGRITTE, RENE (1898-1967). Surrealist painter. He was influenced by the metaphysical painting of Giorgio de Chirico. From Brussels, he moved to Paris where, in 1934, he illustrated the edition of a lecture of André Breton. Some critics hold that he evolved to a form of anti-painting in which pure aesthetics played a secondary role to the emotions stirred up by the work.

MALMEDY. Town in the province of Liège (q.v.). It was ceded by Germany to Belgium under the terms of the Treaty of Versailles in 1919. Scene of the "Malmédy Massacre" of approximately 100 U.S. soldiers in World War II (q.v.). *See also* BATTLE OF THE BULGE.

MANNEKEN PIS. International symbol of Brussels (q.v.). The statue stands not far from the Grand Place. Its mythical origin goes back to the Spanish occupation in the sixteenth century. The city's little hero is said to have extinguished a fire caused by drunken Spanish soldiers in his own natural way.

MARCHE-LES-DAMES. Locality on the Meuse between Namur (q.v.) and Dinant. Prehistoric caves were found here. Tradition says the ladies of the crusaders waited here for the return of their knights. On 17 February 1934, King Albert (q.v.) fell to his death from a rock at Marche-les-Dames.

MARCINELLE. Coal mine location in Wallonia (q.v.). In an accident in 1956, 262 workers, including many Italian immigrants, died here in the underground shafts.

MARGARET OF AUSTRIA (1480-1530). Regent of the Low Countries (q.v.) (1506-1515, 1518-1530). Second child of Mary of Burgundy and Maximilian of Austria (qq.v.). Margaret of Austria acted as regent in the Low Countries after the death of her brother Philip the Handsome, when his son, the future Charles V (q.v.), was still a minor (1506-1515), and when he was absent from the Netherlands as king of Spain (1518-1530).

In 1508, she concluded the peace of Cambrai (Kamerijk) with the French king Louis XII. In 1529, the French king François I relinquished his claims over Artois and Flanders (q.v.) by the Treaty of Cambrai. Margaret's regency is remembered as a period of peace and stability and is compared to the last period of the reign of Philip the Good (q.v.).

MARGARET OF MALE (MARGARETA VAN MALE) (1384-1405). Margaret was the daughter of the count of Flanders, Louis of Male (q.v.). On 20 July 1369, she married Philip the Bold (q.v.), the fourth son of the French king and duke of Burgundy.

When her husband Philip the Bold died in 1404, Margaret continued to reign over her hereditary lands Flanders (q.v.) and Artois.Her son and heir John the Fearless (q.v.) ruled these lands at her death in 1405.

MARY OF BURGUNDY (1457-1482). Daughter of Charles the Bold (q.v.) and his second wife Isabella of Bourbon.

In 1477, her father, the Burgundian Duke Charles the Bold was killed at Nancy. Mary as the only heir succeeded as ruler. She met resistance from the union of the Flemish towns (The Members of Flanders: Ghent, Bruges and Ypres) (qq.v.) and was compelled to grant "The Great Privilege" (q.v.). She submitted to supervision by a newly established Great Council. Though the power of the duchess was curtailed, a territorial unifying entity was created through a constitution and other political institutions for the whole of the Low Countries (q.v.). Under permanent threat from France, Mary contracted a dynastic marriage with Maximilian of Habsburg, son and heir of the Holy Roman emperor. This marriage was in fact arranged earlier during a meeting in 1473 at Trieste by her father Charles the Bold and Holy Roman Emperor Frederick III. It brought Flanders (q.v.) under the Austrian dynasty at Mary's death in 1482, when Maximilian of Austria assumed the regency over the Low Countries and when their son and heir Philip the Handsome was still a minor. *See also* AUSTRIAN RULE.

MARIA THERESA (1717-1780). Archduchess of Austria, daughter of Holy Roman Emperor Charles VI (1685-1740). Maria Theresa ruled over the Austrian lands from 1740 to 1780. In 1744, Duke Charles of Lorraine became governor in the Austrian Netherlands during her reign. Under their rule, the country experienced stability and prosperity, constituting for the southern Low Countries (q.v.) one of the happier periods of the Ancien Regime. *See also* AUSTRIAN RULE.

MARIBEL. Economic policy program that incorporates measures to stimulate employment, especially of export firms. The Commission of the European Union (q.v.) protested at the end of 1996 against these measures which it claimed were discriminatory. In 1997, a new program was devised that gave advantages to all firms employing manual labor.

MARTENS, WILFRIED (1936- ). Politician of the Christian People's Party (Christelijke volksparty, CVP) (q.v.) and former prime minister. Martens studied law in Louvain. He became president of at least two important Flemish student unions.

In 1965, Martens began his political career with a post in the cabinet of Prime Minister Pierre Harmel. In 1967, he became president of the Young Christian Democrats and defended the regionalization of Belgium, along with other radical proposals. In 1969, Martens entered the high committee of the CVP. In 1972, he was chosen president of the CVP, a function he occupied with caution and authority until 1979. After the elections of 1979, Martens became the head of a coalition of the CVP with the Socialists and the Democratic Front of Francophones (Front des Francophones, FDF) (qq.v.).

From 1979 until 1992, he led several coalition governments, alternatively with Socialists and Liberals. Together with Jean-Luc

Dehaene (q.v.), he was the architect of the constitutional reforms (q.v.) that made Belgium a federal state.

In the later period, Martens concentrated on European politics. Beginning in June 1994, he was a member and played a dominant role in the bloc of Christian-Democrats in the European Parliament. He was also president of the European People's Party.

MAX, ADOLPHE (1869-1939). Mayor of Brussels (q.v.) at the start of World War I (q.v.). In August 1914, he became a national hero when he refused to cooperate with the invading German forces, who demanded requisitions. He was imprisoned in Germany throughout the war.

MAXIMILIAN I OF AUSTRIA (1459-1519). Regent of the Low Countries (1482-1493), king of Germany (1486-1519) and Holy Roman Emperor (1493-1519). His father Frederick III, emperor of the Holy Roman Empire, arranged a dynastic marriage to Mary of Burgundy (q.v.). Until her death in 1482, he assisted her in protecting the country against French attacks and restoring internal order in the rebellious provinces and towns of the Low Countries. Maximilian regularly intervened in the province of Holland, he brought the diocese of Utrecht under his control and he reconquered the duchy of Gelre. After Mary's death, he assumed the regency for his minor son, the future Philip the Handsome (q.v.). Maximilian was constantly occupied in battling to break the resistance of the Flemish towns. Not until 1485 was he able to achieve his Joyous Entry into Ghent (q.v.). A month after his arrival, there was a new revolt. In 1487, he was taken prisoner in Bruges (q.v.) and it took the imperial army to free him. Maximilian then devastated the region and ordered foreign traders to move from Bruges to Antwerp (q.v.). This was a significant factor in causing the center of economic gravity to shift from the county of Flanders to the duchy of Brabant (qq.v.).

Maximilian continually strived to regain the monarchical power lost by granting the Great Privilege (q.v.) and by the concessions he himself had made to be accepted as regent of the Netherlands. He tried to restore the power and position of centralizing institutions, such as the Parliament of Mechelen (q.v.). In 1493, when his son Philip the Handsome acceded to power, Maximilian had finally achieved his centralizing aims by bringing the towns back under control. Maximilian's daughter, Margaret of Austria (q.v.), was installed as regent of the Netherlands (1506-1515) at the death of Philip the Handsome. Philip's son, the future Charles V (q.v.), was still a minor.

MECHELEN (MECHLIN). Mechelen was a small independent region in the dowry of Margaret of Male (q.v.) and as such was incorporated into the Burgundian Low Countries (q.v.). Charles the Bold (q.v.) located his High Court, the Parliament of Mechelen, two central Accounting Chambers and other centralizing institutions here. Mechelen was to remain the main town of the Low Countries until 1530, as the regent Margaret of Austria (q.v.) chose it as her central seat. It suited the purposes of the last Burgundians and the first Habsburgs to make Brabant (qq.v.) the center of their state in order to weaken the rebellious Flemish towns. In the same years, the town and port of Antwerp (q.v.) grew to great wealth and prominence.

The court life in Mechelen during this period was luxurious and many treasures of architecture, painting, tapestry, manuscript-writing and music are preserved. Examples of early Gothic and Renaissance architecture are the Palace of Margaret of Austria, the House of the Busleyden family and St. Rombaut's Cathedral. At the court of Margaret, Josquin des Prés (q.v.) composed his polyphonic church music.

Since 1559, Mechelen has been the see of Belgium's only archbishopric. It remains today the seat of Belgian religious authority.

MEMLING, HANS (c.1435/40-1494). Painter belonging to the school of the Flemish Primitives. Born in Germany, he worked from 1465 in Bruges (q.v.) and developed his own mystic religious style. He was influenced by Rogier van der Weyden (q.v.). One of Memling's preserved works is the *Moreels Triptych,* now at the Groeninghe Museum at Bruges. His sacred works *Adoration of the Magi* and *The Mystic Marriage of St. Catherine* are also famous.

MERCATOR, GERARDUS (1512-1594). Latin name for Gerhard Kremer. A Flemish cartographer who studied at Louvain. He produced a map of the world in 1538 and of Flanders (q.v.) in 1540. He later worked at the court of the Duke of Cleve in Germany and produced maps of many European countries. He is known especially for his map of the world drawn in 1569 using his Mercator projection.

MEUNIER, CONSTANTIN (1831-1905). Painter and sculptor. He is known for his realist and naturalist sculptures of working people such as miners and carriers. *See also* NATURALISM.

MINA. Environment policy plan of the Flemish region. (MINA I: 1990-1995. MINA II: 1997-2002).

MOCKEL, ALBERT (1866-1945). Poet and journalist, early advocate of the Walloon movement (q.v.). He began promoting Walloon rights with the publication of the magazine *La Wallonie.* In 1897, he pleaded for the introduction of a federal system. Later, he became a collaborator of Jules Destrée (q.v.).

MODERN ART MOVEMENTS. Three main currents characterized the art of the new Belgian state in the 19th century. First, neoclassicism, taking as a model the French classicist painter David, who also worked in Belgium. Second, romantic nationalism as represented by the painters Wapper and Leys. And thirdly, realism with Jacob Smits, Eugene Laermans, Richard Minne and Constantin Meunier (q.v.). At the end of the century, Belgian art circles opened up to impressionism and symbolism with Fernand Khnopff and James Ensor (qq.v.). The Art Nouveau of Victor Horta and others was the last stylistic movement that can be considered as bearing a national Belgian character. In the twentieth century, art movement would display a more regional and individualistic character. For example, expressionism had a typical Flemish expression in the Latem school *(see* St. Martens Latem), and contemporary Belgian art is highly individualistic.

MONS (BERGEN). Capital of the Province of Hainaut (q.v.). After the reign of Charlemagne (q.v.), it became the seat of the counts of Hainaut. The origin of the town goes back to a monastery dedicated to Saint Walburgis (Saint Waudru).

In the 13th century, the cloth industry brought the town prosperity. It was also a canal port in the coal belt. In 1348, it was ravaged by the plague. The plague's end is commemorated in a yearly procession at which a golden chariot *(Char d'Or)* rides around the town and a fight between Saint Joris and the Dragon "Lumeçon" takes place. During World War I (q.v.), on 23 August 1914, the retreat of the British began here following a stubborn resistance in a battle against the Germans.

Of the preserved monuments, the St. Calixte Chapel dates to the 11th century. Some 13th century vestiges of the count's residence are still there. The St. Marguerite Chapel dates from the same period. St. Walburgis' collegiate church and the town hall were built in the 15th century.

MOUREAUX, PHILIPPE (1939- ). Socialist Party (PS) (q.v.) politician. He defended radical positions on the issue of federalization of the state, such as the equality of the three regions. He became vice premier holding the institutional reform portfolio within the Martens (q.v.) VIII government (1988-1991). In 1982, Moureaux was president of the executive of the French community (q.v.). He vigorously defended the international competences of the communities.

MUNSTER, PEACE OF (1648). In 1648, by the Peace of Munster, Spain officially recognized the independence of the northern United Provinces and acknowledged the loss of territories near Breda and Maastricht and a part of northern Flanders (q.v.) (Axel and Hulst). Under the peace terms, the mouth of the Scheldt River was closed in favor of the Dutch, which contributed significantly to the ruin of the port of Antwerp (q.v.). Artois (q.v.) and the fortresses in the Sambre-Meuse valley were ceded by Spain to France.

## - N -

NAMUR (NAMEN). This town lies at a strategic point at the confluence of the Sambre and Meuse. It is now the capital of the province of the same name and of the Walloon Region. It has frequently been subordinated to Liège (q.v.). The Romans build a *castrum* (castle) at the place. Caesar wrote in his diary that he defeated here the tribes of the Condruzi and Aduatuci. The county was sold to Liège by Count Gwijde of Dampierre and acquired by Philip the Good (q.v.). It thus came into the possession of the Burgundians (q.v.), and afterwards it passed into Austrian, Spanish, French and Dutch hands.

NAPOLEON I BONAPARTE (1769-1821). In 1796-1797, Napoleon commanded the Italian campaign against the Austrians. In the Austrian Netherlands, the Austrians were defeated at Fleurus (q.v.) and by the terms of the Treaty of Campo Formio (q.v.) France acquired the territory gained.

By the coup d'état of 9 November 1799, Bonaparte became First Consul. He was winning some sympathy in Flanders (q.v.), where pious Catholics supported the 1801 Concordat with the papacy. The port of Antwerp was expanded. The southern Low Countries also served his military strategy, whose location served "as a pistol directed towards England." In 1804, Bonaparte proclaimed himself emperor. After a period of stability, he launched his series of European wars and the war against Russia. In 1813, Napoleon was defeated by the Allies and abdicated. He was exiled to Elba, but in 1815 he returned. At the end of his last Hundred Days, he was finally defeated at Waterloo (q.v.).

The Napoleonic Code was introduced also into Belgium and its civil law prescriptions remain in force with minor adaptations today. *See also* FRENCH OCCUPATION.

NATIONAL LABOR COUNCIL. The National Labor Council (Nationale Arbeidsraad, NA) is a national organ of the Belgian consultation and participation structure. It brings together social partners on social matters, especially working conditions. It has mainly advisory competence. The Law of 5 December 1968 gave the National Labor Council the competence to conclude collective labor agreements, which it has done frequently.

NATURALISM. This art movement was very popular in Belgium at the end of the 19th century. Naturalist artists mostly chose as their subjects ordinary working people in their working environment. Among Belgium's most important naturalists were Léon

Frederic, Constantin Meunier (q.v.), Frans van Leemputten and Eugène Laermans.

NEYTS-UYTTEBROECK, ANNEMIE (1944- ). Liberal politician (PVV, VLD) of Brussels. She represented the more social-minded currents in the Party for Freedom and Progress (Partij voor Vrijheid en Vooruitgang, PVV) (see Liberal Party). At a tragic moment of her political career, she lost the party presidency battle to the doctrinaire Guy Verhofstadt (q.v.).

NOBEL PRIZE WINNERS (BELGIAN). Belgian scientists and writers were awarded the Nobel prize 10 times. Belgian laureats include: Chemistry: I. Prigogine (1977). Literature: Maurice Maeterlinck (1911). Peace: Institute for International Law - Ghent (1904); A. Beernaert (1909), H. La Fontaine (1913), G. Pire (1958). Physiology and medicine: J. Bordet (1919), C. Heymans (1938), A. Claude (1974), Chr. De Duve (1974).

NORSEMEN. After the death of Charlemagne (q.v.) in 814, the Norseman sailed up the major rivers and ravaged the towns, including Ghent at the Scheldt (qq.v.). They were expelled from the territories of the Low Countries (q.v.) after their defeat at Louvain (q.v.) in 912.

NORTH ATLANTIC TREATY ORGANIZATION (NATO). Belgium and its minister of foreign affairs Paul-Henri Spaak (q.v.) assisted in the creation of NATO in hosting the meeting at which was signed the Brussels Treaty in March 1948, uniting the Benelux (q.v.) countries, France and Britain in a defense association. A year later, the United States and Canada joined and NATO was born. In 1967, the Supreme Headquarters of the Allied Powers in Europe (SHAPE) established headquarters in the area of Chièvres-Casteau, near Mons (Bergen) (q.v.), after its eviction from France by General de Gaulle.

## - O -

ORDER OF THE GOLDEN FLEECE. Order of chivalry founded by Philip the Good (q.v.), duke of Burgundy, in Bruges (q.v.) on 10 January 1430 on the occasion of his marriage to Isabella of Portugal (q.v.). It was inspired by the tradition of the King Arthur legend and symbolized aspirations of the Burgundian dynasty (q.v.) to be recognized as kings. It sought to create a strong bond among the noblemen elite around the monarch. Fifteen official meetings of the order were held in all the important towns of Flanders, Brabant (qq.v.) and Burgundy.

OSTEND. Major commercial and fishing port on the North Sea in Flanders (q.v.). A port by the time of the First Crusade in the 11th century, the town played a leading role in the Dutch struggle for independence. A rebel stronghold, the city was taken by the Spanish in 1604 after a three-year struggle in which it was almost totally destroyed. It was seized and plundered by the French in 1745 and heavily damaged by Allied bombardment in World War II (q.v.). From the mid-19th century until World War I (q.v.) it was one of Europe's most fashionable resort centers. Its casino continues to draw many visitors today.

OSTEND EAST INDIA COMPANY. Trading company formed in the 17th century to compete in overseas commercial ventures with the Dutch East India Company. Its efforts proved largely unsuccessful and it was abolished in 1731 in return for Dutch acceptance of the Pragmatic Sanction (q.v.) of Austrian Emperor Charles VI (q.v.).

## - P -

PACIFICATION OF GHENT (1576). The Pacification of Ghent was an agreement that created a federation of the Seventeen Provinces. It decreed a general amnesty and adopted a compromise in religious matters, including considerable tolerance toward the Protestants. Two provinces, Holland and Zeeland, were openly recognized as Protestant.

PARLIAMENT (ROLE OF). According to the Constitution (q.v.) of 1830 Belgium is a parliamentary monarchy. In the liberal tradition, all power emanates from the nation, but a choice was made to create representative democracy rather than a direct democracy. Parliament consists of two bodies, the Senate and the House of Representatives (Chamber of Deputies) (qq.v.).

In principle, the government is responsible before the Parliament. The Parliament is elected for four years, but it can be dissolved—formally by the king (q.v.). In practice, Parliament is dissolved when a government meets a vote of no-confidence, mostly because the coalition parties can no longer agree on a governing agenda. The electors can then decide on the new coalition to be formed.

Two tendencies have fundamentally reduced the role of the Parliament in the political system of Belgium. First, the growing power of the parties shifted the true power of decision-making to a great extent to party secretariats. Second, and associated with this first trend, the preponderance of the government over Parliament has grown. Extraordinary powers *(volmachten)* are routinely asked for and granted by the party-ruled Parliament. Also, in ordinary government conditions, ministerial cabinets and consensus seeking meetings of government members work out political solutions, which Parliament can only confirm or reject. The nexus of political decision-making has shifted heavily toward the deliberations on the formation of a new governments. Third, the trend to regionalization has complicated and perhaps obscured the process of political decision-making. The Constitutional Reforms of 1970, 1980, 1988 and 1993 (qq.v.) transformed Belgium into a federal state of three regions, each invested with legislative power and a parliament. The shift to regional governing bodies of powers that are not always clearly defined has made political decision-making, at least for the public, a difficult and confusing process. This contributed to the sudden outburst of political distrust during the White Marches (q.v.).

PEACE OF FEXHE. *See* FEXHE.

PEACE OF MUNSTER. *See* MUNSTER.

PEACE OF UTRECHT. *See* UTRECHT.

PEASANTS' REVOLT (BOERENKRIJG) (1798). The Peasants' Revolt (Guerre des paysans, Boerenkrijg) was a revolt against the French occupation (q.v.) and its revolutionary measures. Obligatory conscription proved especially onerous. The anticlerical character of the French regime aroused the ire of the Roman Catholic clergy, who wielded considerable influence among the peasants, especially in Flanders. This is exemplified in the rising's motto "Voor Outer en Heerd" (For Altar and Hearth). The revolt was severely repressed by the French.

PEOPLE'S UNION. The People's Union (Volksunie, VU) was founded in 1954. The party advocated the autonomy of Flanders (q.v.) in a federal Belgium. It grew quickly into a medium-sized party under the leadership of the Brussels (q.v.) lawyer Frans van der Elst. Along with a democratic left wing, the party represented the former collaborators who pleaded for amnesty (q.v.) following World War II (q.v.). In 1970, the federal-minded People's Union eagerly sought to contribute to the two-thirds parliamentary majority needed by the Christian-Socialist coalition to push through the constitutional reform (q.v.) of that year. In 1977, the party, now under the leadership of the moderate Hugo Schiltz (q.v.), even joined the government. This led to a split. The radical right wingers and anti-Belgians founded a new party, the Flemish Bloc (q.v.) (Vlaams Blok).

From then on, the People's Union weakened and some of its most respected democratic members left for other parties. The former president of the party, Jaak Gabriëls joined the liberal Party for Freedom and Progress (Partij voor Vrijheid en Vooruitgang, PVV) *(see* Liberal Party). Others joined the Christian People's Party (Christelijke Volkspartij, CVP) *(see* Catholic Party). A very young leader, Bert Anciaux, worked to eliminate any remaining vestiges of the older authoritarian and rightist images of the People's Union and by stressing the democratic and pluralistic outlook of the party. Anciaux openly challenged the anti-Belgian and anti-politics as usual views of the Flemish Bloc, though without too much electoral success.

PERMANENT COMMISSION FOR LANGUAGE SUPERVISION. The Permanent Commission for Language Supervision (Vaste Commissie voor Taaltoezicht, Commission Permanente de Contrôle Linguistique)—it has both a Dutch-speaking and French-speaking section—supervises the correct enforcement of the language laws (q.v.). For example, at the beginning of 1997, Vic Anciaux, secretary of state of Brussels (q.v.), delivered a complaint before the Commission on the charge that seven communes of Brussels did not properly apply the law that obliges them to distribute information for the general public in both languages. The local authorities of the communes of Anderlecht, Elsene, Vorst, Sint-Pieters-Woluwe, Sint-Lambrechts-Woluwe, Watermaal-Bosvoorde and Ukkel edited information sheets that were not wholly bilingual.

PERMEKE, CONSTANT (1886-1952). Flemish expressionistic painter. Member of the school of St. Martens Latem (q.v.) school. He is especially known for his voluminous peasant figures.

PERSONALIZED MATTERS. The powers of the cultural communities include, along with education (q.v.) and cultural matters, the so-called "personalized" matters. These are health and social assistance, including hospitals and family policy. However, some reserve competences were maintained at the federal level, such as basic legislation on health care, the handicapped, the rehabilitation of prisoners and youth policy.

PETRUS CHRISTUS. *See* CHRISTUS, PETRUS.

PHILIP DE COMMYNES (c.1447-c.1511). Writer of chronicles and diplomat. In 1472, during the rule of Charles the Bold (q.v.), he transferred his allegiance from the Burgundian dukes to the king of France. His *Mémoires* are a firsthand source of the history of Flanders (q.v.). He described the latter part of Philip the Good's (q.v.) reign from 1440 to 1465 as truly "Good": it was a period of peace and stability, low taxes and a luxurious court life. He implicitly criticized the regime of Charles the Bold (q.v.) for its many wars and heavy taxes.

PHILIP OF ALSACE, COUNT OF FLANDERS (1143-1191). Son of Thierry of Alsace (q.v.). Before his third journey on crusade to Palestine, in 1157, Thierry installed his 14-year old son Philip of Alsace (q.v.) as count. He married Elizabeth, sister of Count Ralph V of Vermandois, and inherited that county after 1164. His territories encompassed the largest ever assembled by a Flemish count. This initiated a long period of hostility between Flanders (q.v.) and France. In 1189, Philip of Alsace accompanied the kings of France and England on crusade and died at Acre in 1191. Philip of Alsace was one of the most important law-giving counts of Flanders. He tried to unify the penal law and procedures over his whole territory.

PHILIP THE BOLD, DUKE OF BURGUNDY (1341-1404). Son of the French king Jean II of Valois (1319-1364). By his conduct against the English on the battlefield of Poitiers in 1356, Philip was called the Bold (le Hardi). By the grace of his father, he became duke of Burgundy in 1363. His father also arranged a diplomatic marriage to the daughter of the count of Flanders, Margaret of Male (q.v.). It took place on 20 June 1369 and the dowry included Artois (q.v.), Franche-Comté, Nevers, Flanders, Rethel and the towns of Antwerp and Mechelen (qq.v.). The duke reigned from 1384 to 1404 and initiated the integration of the regions under his personal rule. In 1386, he created in Flanders a Chamber of Accounts (Rekenkamer) for financial matters and a central court as general Court of Appeal. By the installation of a prosecutor-general cases from the courts of the towns were redirected to that of the count. Philip the Bold was succeeded by his son John the Fearless (q.v.).

PHILIP THE GOOD, DUKE OF BURGUNDY (1396-1467). Philip the Good (Philippe le Bon) was the son of John the Fearless (q.-v.). In 1419, his father was murdered as a consequence of his numerous intrigues to secure the throne of France. Philip the Good concentrated on building up a strong Burgundian (q.v.) state as duke from 1419-1467. He considerably extended the possessions of the Burgundians in the Low Countries (q.v.). He incorporated Namur (1429) and Brabant (1430) (qq.v.). In a stop-go process, he integrated Zeeland, Holland and Hainaut in 1433. In 1441, he was able to buy the duchy of Luxembourg/Limburg and in 1451, at the death of his aunt Elizabeth of Görlitz, he actually brought it under his control. Nearly all the territories of the Low Countries (q.v.) were now under one ruler. Only the dioceses of Utrecht and Liège (q.v.) remained outside Burgundian control. They were under church protection. However, Philip managed to put his bastard son as bishop on the throne in Utrecht. Liège remained under French influence.

In 1430, Philip founded the Order of the Golden Fleece (q.v.) in order to bind his fellow noblemen to himself. In 1433-1434, he introduced a common monetary unit for Flanders (q.v.), Brabant, Holland, Zeeland and Hainaut. By the Treaty of Arras (q.v.) of 1435, Philip was recognized as an independent European sovereign. He was freed from his obligations as vassal to the French king. His subjects were no longer liable to the highest court of Paris, but to the Burgundian Great Council. While the Arras Treaty brought reconciliation with France, it resulted in tensions with England and with the Flemish townsmen who were dependent on the import of English wool. Resistance in Flanders hardened and Philip expended considerable time and resouces in pacifying the territory.

The latter part of Philip's reign from 1440 to 1467 has been labelled a "golden age" chracterized by low taxes and a luxurious court life. The lifestyle at the court of the Burgundian dukes, copied from the French example, was one of active encouragement of the arts. Sculpture, tapestry, music, literature and especially painting attained unprecedented levels of excellence under court patronage. For example, Rogier van der Weyden and Jan van Eyck (qq.v.) were both employed in Philip's service.

Philip's first marriage was to Michelle of France (1395-1422), sister of the French King Charles VII (1402-1462). His second marriage was to Bonne of Artois (1397-1425). The third marriage was to Isabella of Portugal (q.v.) (1397-1473), the mother of his heir Charles the Bold (1433-1477) (q.v.).

PHILIP THE HANDSOME (1478-1506). Son and heir of Maximilian of Austria and Mary of Burgundy (qq.v.). He reigned in the Netherlands from 1493 to 1506. He was married to Joan of Aragon and became king of Spain in 1506 as Philip I. His son Charles V (q.v.) succeeded him. These dynastic events brought the Low Countries (q.v.) under Spanish rule and subject to Spanish diplomacy.

PIRENNE, HENRI (1862-1935). Widely acknowledged historian of the Belgian nation. A professor at the University of Ghent (q.v.), he was a leader of passive resistance in World War I (q.v.). In his monumental work *Histoire de la Belgique* (History of Belgium), he showed how historical and economic interests had drawn Flemings and Wallons together. He thus sought to promote Belgian nationalism. However, Pirenne did not accept the notion of the existence of a "Belgian soul," an idea sometimes wrongly ascribed to him.

PLAKKAAT VAN VERLATINGHE. *See* EDICT OF ABJURATION.

PLANCENOIT. Small locality near Waterloo (q.v.). Every year there is a memorial gathering at this site commemorating the battle of Waterloo (q.v.) by French national and linguistic sympathizers, similar to that of the Dutch speakers at the IJzertoren (q.v.) in Diksmuide.

PLANTIJN, CRISTOFFEL (1520-1589). Famous printer in Antwerp (q.v.) in the 16th century. In 1555, he began a printing house in Antwerp. In 1572, he published a multilingual bible, the Biblia Polyglotta. He obtained the monopoly right from king Philip II to print religious works in the Spanish-ruled lands. After his death, his work was continued by Jan Moretus. His printing workshop at the center of Antwerp has been turned into a much visited museum.

POUSSEUR, HENRY (1929- ). Avant-garde composer. Influenced by Stockhousen. He worked at the Studio of Electronic Music of Brussels (q.v.) and at the Center for Music Research of Wallonia in Liège (q.v.). *See also* BOESMANS, PHILIPPE.

PRAGMATIC SANCTION (1549). The Pragmatic Sanction of 1549 unified the inheritance of the Seventeen Provinces under one prince. It was approved by the Imperial Diet one year after the same organ adopted the Augsburg Transaction whereby the Low Countries (q.v.) became independent within the Habsburg empire.

PROTOCOL OF LONDON (1814). By the Protocol of London or "The Act of the VIII Articles," the Allies set up the Kingdom of the Netherlands, uniting all former provinces of the Low Countries and the principality of Liège (qq.v.). William I of Orange (q.v.) was ackowledged king of the new united country.

PROVINCES. Belgium's traditional nine - now 10 - provinces trace their origins to the administrative division of the Belgian territory under the French occupation (q.v.), though the existence of some of them have roots that date to the medieval area. There are four Flemish-speaking provinces: East Flanders, West Flanders, Antwerp, and Limburg. Historically, they correspond to lands that formed part of the county of Flanders, and the duchies of Brabant and Limburg (qq.v.) . There are also four French-speaking provinces: Hainaut, Liège, Namur and Luxembourg (qq.v.). The province of Brabant, now much smaller than its historical counterpart, is bilingual. It still has one governor, but it has been split into a Dutch-speaking northern part and a French-speaking southern part. In the center are the bilingual 19 communes of Brussels (q.v.). Provincial competences here were transferred to the Brussels Regional Council (q.v.). Each province has a provincial council and executive. They have no legislative competences.

PROVISIONAL GOVERNMENT (1830). A day after the revolt against William I in Brussels (qq.v.) on 23 September 1830, a Provisional Government was formed of nine members. On 4 October, independence was proclaimed and two days later, the Provisional Government began the drafting of a new constitution (q.v.). It also decided that the official language of the new state would be French. *See also* BELGIAN REVOLUTION.

PUBLIC FINANCE. Public finance is partly regulated by the Constitution (q.v.). No taxation may be levied except by an act of Parliament (q.v.). In practice, a royal decree, designed by a competent minister and signed by the king, may do. The state budget must be voted annually.

## - Q -

QUETELET, LAMBERT ADOLF (1796-1874). Mathematician, astrologer and statistician. He introduced numerous methodological refinements into statistics. In his practical research, he documented that during the nineteenth century, the Walloon part of Belgium was much wealthier than the Flemish.

The library of the Belgian Ministry of Industry has been named in his memory.

## - R -

REFORM OF THE JUDICIARY SYSTEM. In the aftermath of the political and judicial scandals in 1996, the government decided to reform the judiciary system (q.v.). The installation of a High Council of Justice (q.v.) was one of its first proposals at the beginning of 1997. Before, political practice rigorously respected the constitutional principle of the division of powers. To correct some dysfunctions of the judiciary system external political control of the organization and functioning of the judiciary will be introduced. Other aspects of reform in the aftermath of the Dutroux case (q.v.) concern aid to victims, depolitization of the appointment of judges and modernizing and control of the execution of penal policy. *See also* COLLEGE FOR APPOINTMENTS AND PROMOTIONS.

REFORM OF THE POLITICAL SYSTEM. In the aftermath of the political and judicial scandals in 1996, the government decided to reform political practices. Corruption, party appointments in administration and the juridical system and inefficiency stemming from politicians' remoteness from citizens concerns were identified as the main shortcomings and detonators of massive popular protests. Talk in favor of a new political culture came into fashion. Following repetitious promises, some new actions were taken to forge the necessary changes.

The president of the federal Parliament, Raymond Langendries, took one of the first initiatives for bringing about the reform of the political system. He called together a States General (q.v.) (Staten Generaal). He invited all the presidents of all the parties except the Flemish Bloc (q.v.) (Vlaams Blok), widely considered as an anti-democratic party that seeks to destroy the current political system. The objective was to give a new democratic impulse to political life in Belgium and to refresh political and democratic practices. The Greens did not take part in the first conversation, as they considered that the crisis stemmed the practices of the traditional parties, of which they did not consider themselves to be part. After the first discussion, optimism reigned, even in the ranks of the opposition whose support is necessary for any structural reforms.

However, the attitude toward the Di Rupo (q.v.) case produced division between governmental parties and opposition. The Liberal parties withdrew their cooperation at least temporarily. The People's Union (Volksunie, VU) defined in stricter terms the conditions under which it wanted to participate in the talks. Langendries decided to delay temporarily the second meeting of the States General. Later the meeting was held, but in the meantime, it had become clear that this was not the way a breakthrough should be achieved. Most of the discussions on political reform returned to the Parliament (q.v.) and its various commissions. The White Movement expressed its disillusion, but itself seemed incapable of channeling the energy it aroused in the White March (q.v.) into far-reaching political reforms. Paul Marchal, the father of murder victims An and Efje, founded his own party, while some parents of victims openly supported traditional parties.

REGIONAL COUNCILS. Article 107 quater of the Constitution (q.v.) created Regional Councils for Flanders, Wallonia and Brussels (qq.v.) with legislative competences in socio-economic matters.

REGIONAL INVESTMENT COMPANY OF BRUSSELS. The Gewestelijke Investeringsmaatschappij voor Brussel (GIMB) is the regional investment company for the 19 communes of Brussels. The Region of Brussels owns 75 percent of the company's capital. The other quarter is in the hands of private banks. The Investment Company finances projects ordered by decree or entrusted by the regional government.

REGIONAL INVESTMENT COMPANY OF FLANDERS. The Gewestelijke Investeringsmaatschappij voor Vlaanderen (GIMV) is the investment company of the Flemish region. It specializes in new technologies and stimulates and supports startups and promising enterprises. Cases in point were plant genetics systems and applied speech programs. The government of the Flemish region owns 85 percent of the funds, while two banks, ASLK and Communal Credit (Gemeentekrediet) hold 10 percent of the capital and 5 percent is placed with institutional investors. In mid-1997, the company asked for the listing of half of its portfolio on the stock market. For the execution of specific projects of the regional government ordered by decree, another body, the Flemish Participation Society (Participatiemaatschappij Vlaanderen, PMV) was created, owned by the regional government. The institution is the counterpart of the Regional Investment Companies of Wallonia and Brussels (qq.v.).

REGIONAL INVESTMENT COMPANY OF WALLONIA. The Société Régionale d'Investissement de Wallonie (SRIW) is the limited liability company of public utility that supports the execution of economic policy in Wallonia (q.v.). It stimulates regional development and acts as a development bank, both financing private and government initiatives. It does not interfere in the management of private companies. The investment company has its seat in Liège (q.v.), the economic capital of the Walloon region. It is the counterpart of the Regional Investment Companies of Flanders and Brussels (qq.v.).

RELIGION. The population on the territory of what is present-day Belgium—then a part of the Frankish empire—was first Christianized in the seventh and eighth century. Missionaries such as St. Amand and St. Bavo founded abbeys in larger centers of the territory. This movement was actively supported by the Merovingian kings and later by Charlemagne (q.v.). The abbeys suffered a serious setback with the incursions of the Norsemen (q.v.), but religious life returned from the 10th century on. The Burgundian dynasty (q.v.) endorsed publicly the Catholic religion and sponsored many religious-inspired works of art. Its territory was also united by family bonds to the bishopric of Liège (q.v.), which at that time comprised almost the whole of the territory of Wallonia and Limburg (qq.v.).

In the 16th century, Lutheran and Calvinist beliefs spread rapidly in Flanders (q.v.), especially in the larger towns of Ghent and Antwerp (qq.v.). In 1566, the iconoclastic movement destroyed Catholic images in churches in Flanders. In Antwerp, Protestant tracts were printed and distributed. In Ghent, a Calvinist republic was proclaimed in 1577. The movement was connected to the independence struggle against the Spanish oppressors, who defended Catholic orthodoxy. When the Spaniards succeeded in crushing the resistance in the south of the Netherlands, the larger part of Protestant intellectual circles fled to the north, which liberated itself from Spanish rule and remained Calvinist. In the southern part of the Netherlands, the Counter-Reformation set in and the bulk of its population would remain Roman Catholic until today.

The Catholic faith was sustained by the Austrian dynasty (q.v.), though the clergy fought the modernizations of Joseph II (q.v.). The French regime at the end of the eighteenth century tried in an anticlerical republican spirit to undermine the position of the church. In fact, the resistance aroused against a foreign power strenghtened rather than weakened the traditional Catholic beliefs among the broad masses of peasants. A Peasants' Revolt (q.v.) ensued with a victory for Church-supported traditional authorities.

In the Constitution (q.v.) of 1831 of the new kingdom of Belgium, freedom of religion was inscribed among other liberal principles. In political practice, the Catholic Party (q.v.) was backed by the church and vice-versa. As a result, education (q.v.) remained in the hands of the Catholic clergy.

Nowadays, the great majority of the Belgian people—according to some sources the figure stands at 84 percent—are Roman Catholic. This fact is more pronounced in Flanders than in Wallonia (q.v.), where the influence of socialism led to higher instances of atheism. Moreover, as in most modern societies, regular attendance at church has drastically decreased, even in Flanders. This is most clearly demonstrated in the difficulties of the church to attract new priests. On the other hand, a renewal of religious life in recent years seems to have counteracted somewhat the long-term trend toward secularization.

Other religions are only marginally represented in Belgium. There are a few isolated small communes in Flanders with an outspoken Protestant image. Jews traditionally had their quarters in the commercial centers of Antwerp and Brussels (qq.v.). Though decimated during World War II (q.v.), especially in Antwerp, the Jews managed to preserve their traditional city district. A religion new to Belgium is Islam, due to immigration from the Middle East and orth Africa into the Brussels (q.v.) area in recent years.

RENARD, ANDRE (1911-1963). Trade union and Walloon leader. He organized the strikes in the Walloon region during the royal controversy (q.v.). He pushed the movement for autonomy of Wallonia (q.v.) and was engaged in setting up a provisional independent government in Wallonia in the summer of 1950.

In the 1960-1961 period, Renard organized the biggest strike in postwar Belgian history. The strike was occasioned by the economic decline of the Walloon coal mines and coal-processing industry. The strike was directed against the government of the Flemish prime minister Gaston Eyskens (q.v.), who strived for stronger executive powers through his so-called Unity Law. On 21 November 1960, 50,000 union members demonstrated and the strike spread rapidly. The protest movement called for structural reforms in industry and for Walloon independence. However, the strike failed and the Unity Law was voted in Parliament.

At the end of his life, Renard was the driving force behind the pressure group Walloon Popular Movement (Mouvement Populaire Wallon, MPW) (q.v.).

RESISTANCE (1940-1944). The Resistance in Belgium during War II (q.v.) proved to be a complex phenomenon with both spontaneous and isolated actions by individuals, concerted actions by small resistance groups, and attempts to organize a united independence movement and a general uprising. Of course, the Resistance worked secretly and the activities of many organizations were revealed only after the war, sometimes misrepresented or idealized in the light of postwar power struggle.

Following the sudden defeat of the Belgian forces against the German invader in the spring of 1940, acts of resistance were sparse during the first year of the occupation. The first isolated sabotage acts were undertaken mostly by Belgian nationalists who remembered and resented the first German occupation of World War I (q.v.). By the end of the year, members of the Belgian government who had first fled to France formed a government-in-exile in London. The British allies organized within their intelligence service a special operations executive charged with armed actions and sabotage acts against the German occupier. A military intelligence service (number 9) set up escape lines to England for escaping prisoners. A psychological war executive tried to influence the population of the occupied country by propaganda, support of the resistance press, demoralization of the enemy, etc. Men were dropped by parachute behind the enemy lines in order to contact emerging local resistance groups.

Immediately after the German invasion of the Soviet Union on 22 June 1941, the Belgian Communists took the leading role in the resistance. They tried to set up a unity front. The Communists likewise dominated partisan activities. In 1943, the Independence Front assumed a more pluralistic character, as the Resistance movement had grown and as many Communists had died or been arrested during Resistance activities.

Apart from the Communist partisans, active Resistance organizations included the White Brigade (Fidelio), the Belgian National Movement, the National Royal Movement and the Liberation Army. The White Brigade (Witte Brigade) was the best known Flemish movement. It originated in liberal academic circles in Antwerp (q.v.) but soon gained both a broader membership and a regional expansion toward Lier, Ghent (q.v.), Aalst, Brussels and even into Wallonia (qq.v.). Its founder, Marcel Louette, emerged as a symbolic leader of the resistance in this part of the country. Many members of the organization were arrested and deported. The Belgian National Movement was founded on 17 December 1940 by Aimé Dandoy. After his arrest, the leadership was assumed by a high official of the previous state administration, Camille Joset. The main activities of the organization consisted in supporting the clandestine press and aiding the Allied forces behind the enemy lines. It also had its own publication, *La Voix des Belges* (The Voice of the Belgians). In

1944, about 100 members were arrested. The National Royal Movement developed from a Rexist group located in the Flemish town of Aarschot. Its leaders broke with the collaborationist sentiments of the Rex (q.v.) leadership. Its activities were carried out mostly in the region of Louvain (q.v.), where it recruited students from the university. It remained an authoritarian and royalist organization and counted in its ranks many military pensioners. About 166 members lost their lives in executing their duties; 300 returned alive from the German concentration camps.

The Liberation Army had its roots in the Christen Democratic environment of Liège (q.v.). It was founded by Minister Delfosse, Léon Servais, Joseph Fafcamps and Pierre Clerdent, among others. Colonel of the National Guard Bartholomé joined its ranks. The organization collaborated with André Renard—who created an autonomous Socialist organization—and the Secret Army (Het Geheime Leger), another important resistance movement of former military members. The Liberation Army operated not only in Liège but also in Flanders (q.v.). In September 1944, it played an important role in the liberation of Wallonia. This was not so for most resistance movements, as elsewhere in Belgium, the liberation proceeded rapidly under the command of the Allies. The resistance movements had hoped to play an active role in shaping new postwar policies in the country, but they found their plans frustrated. The government-in-exile returned quickly from London and the political parties and their parliamentary procedures were restored. Only in the work of identifying and punishing collaborators immediately after the war did the Resistance have a free hand. A collective uprising of the population and the establishment of a new regime—a dream of the Communist resistance—turned out to be an illusion. These sentiments did play a part in the formations of public attitudes toward the royal controversy (q.v.).

REVOLUTION. *See* BELGIAN REVOLUTION.

REVOLUTIONARY LABOR LEAGUE. The Revolutionary Labor League (Revolutionary Arbeiders Liga (RAL)/ Ligue Révolutionnaire Communiste (CRL)) is a Trotskyite organization. It has a tradition of intellectualism, but never took root in the labor movement. After World War II, it was active in university circles and trade unions of major urban centers. The organization participated in the student uprisings of 1969, but its influence gradually declined in the seventies and eighties.

REX. Ultra right-wing party active before and during World War II (q.v.). It began as a Catholic rightist-populist movement, but inclined in the 1930s toward fascism. It won 11.5 percent of the votes in 1936. It collaborated with the occupying Germans and its members were punished severely after the war. Its main leader was Léon Dégrelle (q.v.), who became during the war a volunteer in the Waffen SS (q.v.).

RODENBACH, ALBRECHT (1856-1880). Flemish poet and playwright. He was the author of the *Kerelslied* (Fellow Song) and other works of Flemish nationalist inspiration. He had a lasting influence on the Catholic youth movement.

ROGIER, CHARLES LATOUR (1800-1885). Politician and revolutionary leader. He founded a journal in 1824 that promoted Belgian national sentiment. Arriving in Brussels (q.v.) with 300 armed volunteers from Liège (q.v.) in September 1830, he quickly became leader of the Belgian revolutionaries. Under his direction, state funds and ministeries were seized, Dutch civil servants dismissed, and an appeal made to the provinces for support, which transformed the resistance in Brussels into a national effort. A Liberal Party (q.v.) leader after independence, Rogier served as prime minister from 1847 to 1852 and again from 1857 to 1867.

ROPS, FELICIEN (1833-1898). Born at Namur (q.v.). Rops worked in Paris and illustrated the work of Baudelaire. He became known especially for his erotic paintings. There is a museum in Namur devoted to him.

ROYAL CONTROVERSY (1950). After World War II (q.v.), criticism of King Leopold III (q.v.) arose because he had not followed his government into exile abroad and because many believed he had cooperated too closely with the German occupiers. Following the defeat of Belgian forces on 28 May 1940 he remained in the country under house arrest. As commander in chief of the armed forces he felt it his duty not to leave the country as did monarchs in other German-occupied countries. He left the country on 7 June 1944 as a prisoner of the Germans. The Parliament that convened on 20 September following liberation decided that the royal powers should be assumed by a regent, Prince Charles (q.v.), brother of the king. The country remained divided as to whether or not the king should return. In 1950, an advisory plebiscite was organized. A majority of more than 70 percent of the Flemish welcomed the return of the king, but 57 percent of the Walloon and 51 percent of the population of Brussels (q.v.) voted against this. Unrest spread through the country. Between 26 July and 1 August, 55 acts of sabotage on the railway between Brussels and Wallonia (q.v.) were noted. On 30 July, four workers were shot down near Liège (q.v.). Leading Walloon politicians and administrators came together from 28 to 31 July and decided to form an autonomous Walloon government. The king resigned during the night of 31 July - 1 August. He abdicated in favor of his son Baudouin (q.v.).

RUANDA-URUNDI. Colonial territories in central Africa transferred from German to Belgian authority under a League of Nations mandate in 1919. The colonies were granted independence on 1 July 1962, becoming Rwanda and Burundi, respectively.

RUBENS, PETER PAUL (1577-1640). Master painter of the baroque art of the Counter-Reformation. In his youth, he travelled to Italy to study Renaissance Italian painting (1600-1608). He settled in Antwerp (q.v.) where he worked as a portraitist and painter of allegorical and mythical compositions. Among his monumental pieces *The Raising of the Cross* (1610) and *The Descent from the Cross* (1612), both in the Cathedral of Our Lady in Antwerp, excel. One of his later beautiful portraits depicts his second young wife, Hélène Fourment. After a busy diplomatic and painting career, he lived a quiet life with her at the castle of Elewijt, which still exists.

One of Rubens's most talented pupils was Antoon Van Dijck (q.v.).

RUYSBROECK. *See* JAN VAN RUYSBROECK.

## - S -

SAX, ADOLPHE (1814-1894). Born in Dinant. Inventor of the saxophone.

SCHELDT, THE (DE SCHELDE, L'ESCAUT). River flowing from its sources near St. Quentin in France to its mouth in the Netherlands. Its length is 370 kilometers. On the confluence with a major branch, the Lys (Leie), Ghent (q.v.) was founded. Ghent and Antwerp (q.v.) are still its major ports in Belgium.

By the Treaty of Verdun (q.v.), it became one of the main boundaries between Flanders (q.v.) under French influence and Brabant (q.v.) under German influence. In 1648, the Peace of Munster recognized the northern provinces as an independent state and authorized the cession of Axel and Hulst, lying north of the Scheldt, to the Dutch. At the same time, the blockade of the mouth of the Scheldt was initiated. It brought the port of Antwerp to near ruin. Under the French and William I (q.v.), Antwerp revived and new docks were constructed. The blockade problem reappeared after the secession of the Kingdom of Belgium from the Kingdom of the Netherlands. Only in 1863 did King Leopold I (q.v.) succeed in buying back from Holland the toll rights on the Scheldt. From then on, free navigation was resumed and the port of Antwerp expanded anew.

SCHILTZ, HUGO (1927- ). Politician of the People's Union (Volksunie, VU) (q.v.). He held the budget portfolio in the Martens (q.v.) VIII cabinet as vice prime minister.

SCHMITZ, FRANZ-JOSEPH (1934- ). Former high magistrate and advisor for the German-speaking area of several Christian Democrat prime ministers. He was charged with corruption, as he pocketed large sums of money that he collected for charitable purposes. He allegedly protected a direct subordinate, Marc de la Brassine, who was under investigation for sexual offenses, corruption and illegal possession of weapons.

SENATE. The Constitution (q.v.) of 1830 established a two-chamber parliamentary system. Until recently, both bodies were invested with the same legislative competences and the same version of law bills had to be accepted by both organs. The federalization of Belgium introduced a new format for the law-giving institutions. The St. Michael's Agreement (q.v.) provided for a reform of the composition and functioning of the Senate.

Since 1994, the Senate has consisted of various member categories: 40 are directly elected senators of which 25 are Flemish speaking and 15 French speaking; 21 senators are elected by the community councils from their own ranks, including 10 each by the French and Flemish Community Councils and one by the German Community Council; 10 are co-opted, including six from the Flemish region and four from the Francophone; along with these 71 members, there are ex officio senators from the Royal House. The community senators are supposed to represent community interests, the directly elected to represent the broad public and the co-opted are chosen on the basis of their expertise in specific fields.

The new Senate is designed to play a more detached role. It is no longer the primary function of the Senate to control the government. Before, identical texts had to be passed by both houses. In 1830, the Senate was conceived as a conservative check on the House of Representatives (Chamber) (q.v.). Now, both houses have their own role. The Senate's role at present is one of reflection and coordination. The body is charged with study and coordination of new laws and deals with constitutional revision, if necessary. It is conceived as a place for encounter and dialogue. It functions also as a mediator and arbitrator in community debates.

The first president of the Senate in its new role was Frank Swaelen (Christian People's Party, CVP) *(see* Catholic Party). Two important investigation commissions set up by the new Senate were a commission on the Belgian UN mission and genocide in Rwanda in 1994 and a commission on organized crime. *See also* PARLIAMENT (ROLE OF).

SERVAIS, RAOUL (1928- ). Father of the Flemish animation film. He won several international prizes for his creations. They include the short films *Harbour Lights, The False Note, Chromopho-*

*bia, To speak or not to speak, Operation X-70, Pegasus, The Song of Halewijn, Harpya* and the long animation picture *Taxandria*. In Ghent (q.v.), Servais set up an animation film school. Its students included Paul Demeyer (*The Wonder Shop)* and Frits Standaert.

SHAPE. *See* NORTH ATLANTIC TREATY ORGANIZATION (NATO).

SIMENON, GEORGES (1903-1989). Journalist and writer. He is the creator of Jules Maigret, the detective and commissioner of the judicial police in Paris, who was immortalized in a seemingly endless series of novels starting with *Piotr le Letton* in 1930.

SOCIALIST PARTY (SP/PS). The Belgian Workers' Party (q.v.), founded in 1885 and led for a long time by Emile Vandervelde was dissolved by its succeeding chairman Hendrik De Man on the eve of World War II (q.v.).

The future postwar Belgian Socialist Party (Parti Socialiste Belge, PSB/Belgische Socialistische Partij, BSP) was organized during the war under the guidance from London of Paul-Henri Spaak (q.v.) and with organizational input from the resistance (q.v.). In 1967, the Flemish- and French-speaking wings held separate congresses. In 1978, the Belgian Socialist Party split formally into a Flemish and a Walloon wing. The Dutch-speaking party is called Socialistische Partij (SP), the French-speaking Parti Socialiste (PS). Both are totally independent of each other. Especially in the initial period after the split, communal differences appeared to outweigh devotion to the same ideological principles. The situation has been scrupulously avoided in which one party is in the government and the other in the opposition, although rumors persist that it will happen.

In 1981, the PS obtained 12.7 percent of the overall Belgian vote, including 37.1 percent in Wallonia and 12.8 percent in Brussels (q.v.). However, at the national level a Catholic-Liberal government was formed under prime minister Martens of the Flemish Christian People's Party (Christelijke Volkspartij, CVP) (qq.v.). In February 1982, in the elections for the party presidency of the French-speaking Socialist Party (PS) to succeed André

Cools, Guy Spitaels (q.v.) obtained a victory with 53 percent against 47 percent for the leftist Ernest Glinne.

Spitaels set the direction of the PS for the next 20 years. He put the party on the track to federalism. By supporting José Happart (q.v.), he endorsed the Francophone cause. He discarded all the remnants of leftist ideology for a very moderate and pragmatic socialism. He further weakened the alliance with the leftist socialist trade union General Federation of Belgian Trade Unions (FGTB) (q.v.). The strategy for a PS return to power under Spitaels missed its goal in 1985, but it was successful in 1987. Coalition negotiations were tight and there was strong opposition from the federations of Liège (q.v.) and Charleroi in the PS party congress that finally approved participation in the government. Philippe Moureaux became vice president, but Spitaels remained influential as party president.

Whereas the Socialists in Wallonia (q.v.) remained the largest party, they were always a minority in Catholic Flanders (q.v.). After the split and without both the protection and the tutelage of their Walloon brothers, the SP embarked on a more reformist and Flemish course. Under the chairmanship of Karel Van Miert, the party opened itself to increased cooperation with Catholics, environmentalists and grassroots groups. This trend was confirmed by his successor Frank Vandenbroucke (q.v.), when Van Miert left for the European Commission in 1989. In 1981, the SP obtained 12.4 percent of the national vote or 21.1 percent of the Flemish voters. In 1987, it won 24.2 percent of the Flemish vote and, in 1991, it fell back to 19.6 percent. In Brussels (q.v.), it won only 3 percent of the votes that year. In the mid-1990s, the party was plagued by the Agusta (q.v.) scandal. An electoral debacle was feared, but the SP stabilized its position under the strong leadership of Louis Tobback (q.v.).

SPA. Town in the province of Liège (q.v.). Located in the Ardennes (q.v.), its therapeutic mineral springs and baths have made it a fashionable resort since the 16th century. Its fame became so well known that its name is used to designate any health resort.

At the Spa Conference in 1920 the Allies accepted a German plan for the payment of World War I (q.v.) reparations.

SPAAK, PAUL-HENRI (1871-1936). Socialist politician and statesman. He was a member of the Parliament (q.v.) from 1932 to 1957 and from 1961 to 1966.

Before World War II (q.v.), Spaak became minister of post and traffic in 1935, minister of foreign trade in 1936 and minister of foreign affairs in 1939. In 1938, he formed his first government as prime minister (1938-1939). An incident with the king over the leaked nomination of a World War I (q.v.) collaborator as member of the Flemish Academy caused the fall of his government. Nevertheless, in 1939, Spaak was appointed minister of foreign affairs in the third government of prime minister Hubert Pierlot.

During World War II, following the break in 1940 with King Leopold III (q.v.), Spaak joined the government-in-exile in London. After the war, he served in the postwar government as minister of foreign affairs. Beginning in 1946, Spaak became prime minister of several governments (1946-1949). In 1954, Spaak returned as minister of foreign affairs in the government of Achiel Van Acker.

In 1961, the Socialists begged Spaak to head again a difficult electoral campaign. He did so successfully and entered the new government of Théo Lefèvre as vice prime minister and again minister of foreign affairs. In that role, he articulated Belgium's position in the aftermath of the Congo (q.v.) crisis, such as the military intervention on Stanleyville in 1964.

In 1966, Spaak left the Socialist Party and Parliament and took up a career in international business.

On the international scene, Spaak played an eminent role as longtime Belgian minister of foreign affairs. He took the initiative in the creation of Benelux (q.v.) and was one of the moving forces behind the foundation of the Council of Europe in 1949. He was the first to occupy the seat of chairman of the Consultative Assembly of the Council of Europe (1949-51). Belgium was also one of the first signatories of the United Nations (UN) charter and Spaak was chosen first president of the UN General Assembly (1946). He also participated in the negotiations leading to the creation of the European Common Market and was a co-signer of the Treaty of Rome on 25 March 1957. In his last international post, he was appointed secretary-general of the North Atlantic

Treaty Organization (NATO) (q.v.) (1957-1961). *See also* EUROPEAN UNION.

SPECIAL TAX INSPECTORATE. This control and investigating state organ (Bijzondere Belastingsinspectie, BBI) works to recover taxes in cases of irregularities. For example, in 1996, it was announced that the BBI should collect more than 1,500 million BEF at the expense of the Kredietbank, a private institution that facilitated the transfer by its clients of large sums of money to foreign banks in order to avoid payment of taxes.

SPITAELS, GUY (1931- ). Politician of the Socialist Party (q.v.) (Parti Socialiste, PS). Spitaels was a professor at the Free University of Brussels (ULB) and became a senator in 1974. In 1977, he was elected mayor of Ath. Since 1979, he was twice appointed vice prime minister and minister of the budget and traffic. In 1981, the Socialist Party left the government and, in the 1982 elections for the party presidency, Spitaels succeeded André Cools (q.v.) in a victory over the leftist candidate Ernest Glinne. Spitaels defended a more pragmatic socialism in a thoroughly federalized Belgium. He also expressed his solidarity with José Happart (q.v.) in support of the Francophone cause.

Following the 1991 elections, Spitaels became the president of the Walloon executive. He resigned from this function on 21 January 1994 as a consequence of the affair of the three Guy's (Spitaels, Coëme and Mathot), all suspected of corruption in the Agusta case (q.v.). After the 1995 elections, Spitaels became president of the Walloon Parliament. In January 1997, the judiciary asked the Walloon Parliament to lift his parliamentary immunity on charges of corruption in the Dassault case (q.v.). On 26 February, Spitaels resigned as president of the Walloon Assembly. He admitted that he had been aware of a secret party bank account in Luxembourg (q.v.). On 7 April 1997, he also gave up his function as mayor of Ath as a consequence of the official charges made against him in the Dassault case.

SPY (MAN). Prehistoric skeletons of a man and a woman were found in a cave at Spy, a small locality on the Sambre between Namur and Charleroi. The anthropologists Max Lohest and Marcel De Puydt concluded the skeletons were of the Neanderthal type from the Aurignocean period and labelled them Homo sapiens.

STATE. According to the Constitution (q.v.) of 1830 and following Western traditional concepts of democracy, state power resides in three bodies. Constitutionally, there exist separate legislative (parliament), executive (king and government) and judicial (courts) organs.

The supreme head of the Kingdom of Belgium is the king (q.v.), who rules in principle for a life-term. At present, the king has rather limited and only slightly more than representative power, but at independence in 1831, the monarch held more substantive powers. The king's power eroded especially in the past half century, not in the least due to the convulsions engendered by war and occupation and their consequences.

According to the Constitution, the king appoints the prime minister and, on proposal of the prime minister, other ministers of government. These appointments are subject to confirmation by the House of Representatives (q.v.).

STATE COUNCIL. The State Council (Raad van State/ Conseil d'Etat) has the important competence of judging the legality and validity of all laws and decrees. It is usually consulted by legislators when questionable new laws are devised and its advice is regularly requested in legal disputes by ordinary citizens. Its advice is binding and general. Laws rejected by the State Council are declared to be invalid. For example, a decree proposed by the minister of education of the Flemish community Luc Van den Bossche on the goals of lower education was invalidated even before its application.

STATES GENERAL (STATEN GENERAAL). Raymond Langendries, the president of the House of Representatives (q.v.), convened the States General on the new political culture for the first time on 7 December 1996. This was largely interpreted as a political response at the federal level to the White March (q.v.). The party presidents accompanied by a second member were invited, but not the representatives of the Flemish Bloc (q.v.) (Vlaams Blok), which was excluded because of its perceived opposition to the existing political system. The Greens did not attend the meeting either. They held that problems of reform of the political system (q.v.) should be tackled by Parliament (q.v.). The Liberals (q.v.), the most important opposition party, attended the first meeting, but did not appear later. They were said to be offended by parliamentary developments surrounding the Di Rupo (q.v.) case. During the second meeting, four committees were formed to work on problematic aspects of the new political culture: on the cumulation of political and other offices (president: Philippe Busquin, PS); on the public referenda (Louis Michel, PRL); on party financing (Bert Anciaux, VU); and on the functioning of the administration and the provision of political services (Marc Van Peel, CVP). Expectations that the committees would produce recommendations for real change were dashed when traditional political divisions prevailed and no substantive reforms were forthcoming. *See also* REFORM OF THE POLITICAL SYSTEM.

STEENOKKERZEEL. The castle where consultations on community relations took place in 1974. No definitive solution could be found, but the deliberations paved the way for similar meetings, such as the Stuyvenberg-Egmont discussions and the later talks that led to implementation of federalization. *See also* CONSTITUTIONAL REFORM OF 1980, 1988, 1993; EGMONT PACT; ST. MICHAEL'S AGREEMENT.

ST. MARTENS LATEM. Rural artistic village on the Lys (Leie) in the vicinity of Ghent (q.v.). Several generations of Flemish artists lived here in the first part of the twentieth century and gave vent to their personal visions through a variety of impressionistic, expressionistic and symbolic styles. To the first generation belong the sculptor/drawer George Minne and the painters Gustave van de Woestijne, Albert Servaes and Valerius De Saedeleer. The second movement consisted of Constant Permeke (q.v.), Gustave de Smet and Fritz van den Berghe.

ST. MICHAEL'S AGREEMENT (1992). The St. Michael's Agreement, given this name because it was concluded on 28 September, contained the agreed proposals to transform Belgium into a full-fledged federal state. The agreement's main provisions strengthened the role of regional parliaments (henceforth directly elected) and expanded the powers of the regional governments. At the federal level, it also reformed the Senate (q.v.). Most of the proposals of the St. Michael's Agreement were put into law by the Constitutional Reform of 1993 (q.v.).

ST. NICHOLAS PLAN. The government plan presented by federal Prime Minister Jean-Luc Dehaene (q.v.) on 6 December 1996. It aimed at reforming the relations between politics and the judiciary system, which was regarded as a political necessity after the White March (q.v.). *See* REFORM OF THE JUDICIARY SYSTEM.

STORCK, HENRI (1907- ). Film director. Though a Fleming, he can be called the father of the Walloon cinema. His classic film *Misère au Borinage* (Misery in the Borinage, 1933-34) is a socio-political documentary on the crisis in the 1930s. *Le Banquet des Fraudeurs* (The Banquet of Fraud) treats of the same socio-political problems in a fictional way. *See also* FILM.

STRUCTURAL PLAN FLANDERS. The structural plan lays out the conceptual basis for future socio-economic development of Flanders, an explicit competence of the Flemish Community (q.v.). The plan defines residential and commercial areas and designates land for recreational, forest and agricultural use. The plan begins with an overview of past trends and current conditions. As such, it serves as a guide for future policy. The plan includes proposals for future land use that must be approved by the Flemish Parliament before action can be taken. Critics contend that plans are often too vague and abstract.

STUYVENBERG AGREEMENT (1977-1978). The deliberations at Stuyvenberg castle between 24 September 1977 and 17 January 1978 were needed to implement the Egmont Pact (q.v.). They led to an action plan for the further federalization of Belgium. The Stuyvenberg agreement was annexed to the government declaration of February 1978. Its main objective was a concretization of Articles 59 bis on the extension of the competences of the Cultural Councils and Article 107 quater on the establishment of the Regional Councils.

SUENENS, JOSEPH (1905-1996). Primate of Belgium from 1962 to 1980. He played an important role in the Second Vatican Council (1962-1965).

SUPREME COURT. The Supreme Court (Hof van Cassatie/Cour de Cassation) receives appeals from parties judged by lower courts, the five Courts of Appeal (q.v.) included. The Supreme Court only considers formal legal questions and does not reopen the files of lower jurisdictions. It also decides on the removal of incompetent judges. Finally, it decides on the impeachment of ministers of the federal and community governments. Heretofore, the Supreme Court had to inform Parliament (q.v.) before it could take any investigatory step. As a consequence of the Di Rupo (q.v.) case, it can now make a preliminary investigation without informing Parliament. The request for a detailed investigation and for any official accusation of the members of federal or regional governments or parliaments still has to be presented to the parliaments concerned. The judges of the Supreme Court are appointed by the Senate (q.v.) and the Court itself.

There is a sharp division of jurisdiction between the Supreme Court and two other higher bodies with juridical competence: the State Council (q.v.) is the sole body that decides on the legality of laws and decrees and the Arbitration Court (q.v.) considers the disputes between the separate political communities.

## - T -

TAXANDRIA. Region during the Roman period comprising roughly the present territory of Brabant (q.v.). The Romans allowed the Franks to settle here within their empire.

THIERRY OF ALSACE, COUNT OF FLANDERS (?-1168). Grandson of Robert I the Frisian and son of Thierry, Duke of Lorraine. Thierry of Alsace was accepted in 1128 as count of Flanders (q.v.) over his rival William Clito by promising the towns that he would respect their privileges. With their status recognized, the towns would play a dominant role in the history of Flanders. Thierry was the first French count of Flanders in a line that would last until 1482. His reign was prosperous with the exception of the year 1148, when Baldwin IV of Hainaut invaded Flanders. In international politics, Thierry preserved the county's neutrality between France and England. In 1134, Thierry married Sybilla, daughter of Fulk V of Anjou, King of Jerusalem. In this way, Thierry became involved in the Crusades and went to Palestine four times. Before his third journey, in 1157, he installed his 14-year-old son Philip of Alsace (q.v.) as count.

THYS, JEAN-LOUIS. Former Brussels (q.v.) Region minister and mayor of the Brussels commune of Jette. The Supreme Court (q.v.) asked the Parliamentary Assembly of the Brussels Region to lift his parliamentary immunity. There were charges that he demanded commissions from public works contractors and that he used the funds to finance election campaigns of his Social Christian Party (Parti Social Chrétien, PSC). *See* Catholic Party.

TIJD EN MENS (1949-1955). Journal founded in 1949. It defended avant-garde positions in Belgian art. It was influenced by existentialism and surrealism. The main collaborators were Jan Walravens, Hugo Claus (q.v.), R. Van de Kerckhove, Louis Paul Boon (q.v.) and A. Bontridder. One of its main theoretical contributions was the essay "Phenomenologie van de Moderne Poëzie" (1951) of Jan Walravens.

TIMMERMANS, FELIX (1886-1947). Flemish writer of popular literature. His main character Pallieter has become the model of the Flemish man who enjoys life and nature in a country environments of farmers strongly influenced by the church and the local pastor, but who retains his independence. In *Boerenpsalm* (Song of the Landman), the author relates the tragic reality of the peasant's existence. Timmermans also carefully observed and romanticized the life of animals, as in *Floere, het Fluwijn* (Floere, the Marten). In his last book, he depicted the adventures of the popular painter Adriaen Brouwer (q.v.).

TINDEMANS, LEO (1922-  ). Politician of the Christian People's Party (Christelijke Volkspartij) (q.v.) and prime minister of three governments during the period 1974-1978 in coalitions with several parties.

Tindemans began his political career as national secretary at the study center of the Christian Democrats. He became a representative in the Chamber in 1961, where he succeeded Frans Van Cauwelaert. From 1965 to 1973, Tindemans was secretary-general of the European Union of Christian Democrats. In 1968, he was asked by Prime Minister Gaston Eyskens (q.v.) to be minister of communitarian relations and in 1972 minister of agriculture. In 1973, during the government of Edmond Leburton, Tindemans was vice premier and minister of the budget. In 1974, Tindemans won the elections and became prime minister. In 1975, he also produced a report on European integration. The government fell because of continuing communitarian problems. Tindemans again won the elections of April 1977 and formed a new government. In 1978, communitarian problems again led Tindemans to resign. He returned in 1981 as minister of foreign affairs in the Martens (q.v.) V and VI governments.

In 1989, Tindemans was elected a member of the European Parliament. With others, he led an investigatory commission to the Balkans.

TOBBACK, LOUIS (1938- ). Socialist Party (Socialistische Partij, SP) (q.v.) politician. In 1974, he was elected a deputy in the Chamber. In the period 1978-1988, he assumed the leadership of the parliamentary section of the Socialist party. In 1988, he obtained the portfolio of minister of the interior under Prime Minister Wilfried Martens (q.v.). He won a seat in the Senate (q.v.) in the elections of 24 November 1991, while he remained minister of the interior in the government of Jean-Luc Dehaene (q.v.). Following the communal elections of 1994, he was appointed mayor of Louvain (q.v.). He also assumed the presidency of the Socialist Party (Socialistische Partij, SP) from Frank Vandenbroucke (q.v.), who was implicated in the Agusta case (q.v.). In this role, he succeeded in limiting the damage inflicted on the Socialist Party during the parliamentary elections of 1995. Since then, Tobback has become the undisputed Socialist leader within and without the party. With an overwhelming majority, he was confirmed as president of the Socialist Party. On 24 April, Tobback replaced the resigning socialist minister of the interior J. Vande Lanotte after the tragic escape of Dutroux (q.v.).

TONGRES (TONGEREN). Small town in Limburg on the river Jeker. It has the best preserved Roman site in Belgium and the most important archeological museum on Roman times in the country. A town grew around a fortification built in the time of Emperor Augustus. It served as a supply center for Roman troops on the Rhine. The foundations of a five kilometer long aqueduct are still present. Likewise, the foundations of a temple have been uncovered. A five kilometer wall with watchtowers built around the town in the second century has been partly preserved. The new basilica of Our Lady is constructed on the foundation of the old one and fragments of older Roman sculptures. A route was built from Tongres to Bavai, which can still be followed. Several tumuli can be seen at the roudside along the old route.

TOURNAI. Tournai (Doornik) is a town on the river Scheldt (q.v.) in the province of Hainaut (q.v.). It was the capital of the early Frankish kingdom. In 466, Clovis (q.v.) was born here. It was also the home town of Rogier van der Weyden (q.v.). It was frequently occupied by the French. In 1526, Charles V (q.v.) reconquered the town from the French and integrated it into the Low Countries (q.v.).

Tournai has the oldest belfry in Belgium, dating back to the 13th century. A Romanesque-Gothic cathedral from the 12th to the 13th centuries has also been preserved.

TOWER ON THE IJZER (IJZERTOREN). Flemish national symbol. Each year a large gathering of Flemish nationalists takes place at this monument. On this occasion Flemish nationalist political statements are made. Immediately after World War II (q.v.), the monument was destroyed by unknown persons, hostile to the Flemish movement (q.v.).

It was rebuilt with support from Christian Democrat politicians and carries the inscription AVK—VVK (Alles voor Vlaanderen: Vlaanderen voor Kristus / All for Flanders: Flanders For Christ).

TRADE. Foreign trade plays a vital role in a small, open economy (q.v.). In 1997, imports accounted for 5,575 billion BEF, exports for 6,018. Belgium's main trading partners are its immediate neighbors: Germany, the Netherlands, France and Britain. Together, they constitute more than a 60 percent share of Belgium's foreign trade. Belgian exports consist mainly of manufactured goods, machinery, chemicals and food and drink. Imports are fuel and raw materials. Invisibles (services) also contribute to a positive current account balance. These services are transport, insurance and other financial services, government services and legal and consulting services. *See also* APPENDIX 6.

TRADE UNIONS. Unionism in Belgium developed historically along pluralistic lines. The organizations followed the same political-philosophical lines as the political parties and the mutualities for medical care. Trade unions developed before working-class-based political parties. In 1857, the weavers in Ghent (q.v.) founded a mutual aid organization. Other professional groups formed their own around the same time and in 1860, the Workers' Association (Werkersbond), the first interprofessionnal Socialist union was founded. In response, Christian workers of the cotton industry in Ghent formed their Catholic union in 1886. The Christian union movement was given new impetus by the 1893 papal encyclical *Rerum Novarum*. It lasted until 1912 when the national Confederation of Christian and Free Trade Unions of Belgium (Confédération des Syndicats Chrétiens et Libres de Belgique, CSC) was formed. Liberal trade unions developed much later: in 1930, the General Confederation of Liberal Trade Unions was founded. It is still the smallest in membership.

During World War II (q.v.), the occupation put the trade-union organizations under strong pressure to merge into one organization with a collaborationist flavor. This was proposed by the Socialist leader Hendrik de Man, but ultimately refused by trade union leaders. In fact, the unions ceased to exist and many union members rejected collaboration and joined the Resistance (q.v.). One of its early achievements was a massive strike in 1941 in the steel industry of Liège (q.v.). During the occupation left-wing committees took over the role of the trade unions, notably in Wallonia (q.v.).

After the war, a new Socialist trade union was officially established, the General Federation of Belgian Trade Unions (Algemeen Belgisch Vakverbond, ABVV/Fédération Générale du Travail de Belgique) (q.v.) at a unification congress in Brussels (q.v.) on 28 and 29 April 1945. During the war, representatives of trade unions and employers had met in exile in London and agreed on a new social pact after the liberation. A whole system of social concertation and participation was projected and effectively brought into practice in the 1950s. The three national trade union organizations were officially recognized as the representatives of the workers and had seats in the Economic and Social Council and other participation organs. Officially, this is the immediate and tolerated power base of the trade unions, along with the legally recognized rights vested in the trade union organizations. In fact, much of their influence was gained through the affiliation with political parties of their own ideological family.

## - U -

UNION WALLONNE DES ENTREPRISES (UWE). Walloon organization of employers. It functions as an official social partner. It was founded in 1967 as the heir to a previous organization with a similar name.

UNIOP. University Institute of Opinion Polls (Universitair Instituut voor Opiniepeilingen) of the Free University of Brussels (q.v.) (Vrije Universiteit Brussel, VUB/ Université Libre de Bruxelles, ULB). The institute obtained counterfeit commissions for 250 million BEF from the Belgian Socialist Party (q.v.). Because of these practices, the former Socialist Party (Parti Socialiste, PS) minister Guy Coëme was condemned conditionally to two years in prison.

UNITED KINGDOM OF THE NETHERLANDS (1815-1830). After the defeat of Napoleon, the allied powers occupied Belgium. The Netherlands regained independence as a kingdom under the government of William of Orange. The powers decided on March 1814 to unite the Low Countries (q.v.) into a United Kingdom of the Netherlands under King William I (q.v.).

UTRECHT, PEACE OF (1713). The Peace of Utrecht ended the War of the Spanish Succession. One of its treaty clauses transferred the Spanish Netherlands to the rule of the Habsburgs of Austria. France secured maritime Flanders (Duinkerke/Dunkerque), Gallician Flanders (Valenciennes), and the towns of Philippeville and Thionville. *See also* AUSTRIAN RULE; CHARLES VI; LOW COUNTRIES.

## - V -

VAN ARTEVELDE, JACOB (c. 1295-1345). Leader of the municipal government of Ghent (q.v.) and an active proponent of local liberties and privileges. At the outbreak of the Hundred Years' War he sided with King Edward III of England, with whom Flanders (q.v.) maintained close economic ties as a central source of wool for its cloth industries. Van Artevelde was murdered by the citizens during a riot in 1345. His son Philip (1340-1382) led the revolt of Ghent against Louis of Male (q.v.), the count of Flanders and his French allies. The rebels were defeated at the battle of West-Rozebeke and Philip was killed.

VAN DEN BRANDE, LUC (1945- ). Christian People's Party (CVP) (q.v.) politician. Minister-president and minister of foreign policy, European affairs and technology of the government of Flanders (q.v.).

VAN DEN VOS, REYNAERDE (REYNARD THE FOX). Animal epic from the 13th century, written in Dutch (Dietsch) by the anonimous Willem—who made the *Madoc*—after the French example. It is one of the best preserved and literarily most appreciated works of Flemish medieval literature.

VAN DER BIEST, ALAIN. Socialist Party (PS) (q.v.) politician and former PS-minister. He was accused by associates of having given the order to murder the former Socialist vice prime minister and party president André Cools (q.v.) in 1991.

VAN DER GOES, HUGO (c. 1440-1482). One of the followers of the so-called Flemish Primitives. One of his most renowned paintings is the *Triptych of the Adoration,* now hanging in the Uffizi Gallery at Florence.

VAN DER WEYDEN, ROGIER (ROGER DE LA PASTURE, 1399/1400-1464). He was born in Tournai (q.v.). In 1424, he entered the workshop of Robert Campin (q.v.), the so-called master of Flémalles. Around 1433, he became the official painter of the city of Brussels and the Burgundian (qq.v.) court. His art can be characterized as aristocratic-symbolic. One of his authenticated paintings is *The Descent from the Cross,* now hanging in the Prado Museum of Madrid.

VAN DIJCK, ANTOON (1599-1641). Painter of the baroque period. He went to Italy to study Renaissance painting. Later, he worked in the workshop of Peter Paul Rubens (q.v.) and became court painter at Antwerp (q.v.). In 1632, Van Dijck was asked by Charles I to come to London, where he spent most of the remaining nine years of his life making portraits of members of the English royal court. He was overwhelmed with commissions and was knighted.

VAN EYCK, JAN AND HUBERT. *See* JAN VAN EYCK.

VAN GOETHEM, NICOLE. Creator of animated films. She cooperated in the film projects *Tarzoon* and *The Missing Link.* Her six-minute long animation film *A Greek Tragedy* (1985) won an Oscar. Her second film *Full of Grace* was controversial and aroused protests in conservative circles. It deals with candles, nuns and a sex-shop.

VAN HECKE, JOHAN. He was elected president of the Christian People's Party (Christelijke Volkspartij, CVP). He set in motion the renewal of his party. On 6 June 1996, he resigned from a second term for personal reasons. *See also* CATHOLIC PARTY.

VAN ISTENDAEL, GEERT. Flemish-speaking contemporary journalist and writer in Brussels (q.v.). He collected old Flemish stories and wrote critical essays about the art and literature of Brussels.

VAN MAERLANT. *See* JACOB VAN MAERLANT.

VAN MIERT, KAREL (1942- ). Former president of the Socialist Party (q.v.) (Socialistische Partij, SP) and now a member of the European Commission.

Van Miert took a degree in diplomatic sciences at the University of Ghent. He entered the National Scientific Research Fund (Nationaal Fonds voor Wetenschappelijk Onderzoek) and worked with Sicco Mansholt. From 1971 to 1973, he was assistant in international law at the Free University of Brussels (Vrije Universiteit Brussel, VUB) (q.v.). In 1973, he became a member of the office of Henri Simonet, then vice president of the European Commission. In 1976, he was chosen international secretary of the Belgian Socialist Party (BSP/PSB). In 1977, he was appointed head of the private office of Willy Claes (q.v.), then minister of economic affairs. In 1978, Van Miert was elected chairman of the Socialist Party. From 1979 to 1985, he was a member of the European Parliament. In 1989, he was appointed member of the European Commission, responsible for transport, credit and investment and consumer policy. From July 1992 on, he was also responsible for the environment. Since 1993, Van Miert has held responsible for competition policy, personnel and administrative policy, translation and in-house computer services.

VAN NOPPEN, KAREL (? -1995). Inspector of the Institute for Veterinary Control (IVK). He was murdered on 20 February 1995, probably by the mafia of hormone sellers. This is one of the unsolved judiciary problems of Belgium.

VAN ZEELAND, PAUL (1893-1973). Economist and statesman. He became prime minister in 1935 under a government of national unity and instituted social and reform legislation. In 1936, he suppressed members of the Rex (q.v.) movement, after proclaiming martial law. During his administration, Belgium renounced its military alliance with France, established after World War I (q.v.), and returned to a policy of neutrality. During World War II (q.v.), he served in London as a high commissioner for the repatriation of Belgians uprooted by the war. A leader of the Catholic Party (q.v.), he served as foreign minister in several cabinets after the war and as a financial advisor to the Belgian government and the North Atlantic Treaty Organization (q.v.).

VANDEN BOEYNANTS, PAUL (1919- ). Christian-Democrat politician and prime minister. Vanden Boeynants was taken prisoner during World War II (q.v.) and deported to Germany. After the war, he launched a professional career and entered politics. In the elections of 26 June 1949, he obtained a seat in the Chamber. In 1953, he became an alderman of the town of Brussels (q.v.). After the elections of 1 June 1958, Vanden Boeynants got the portfolio of minister of middle classes—a section of the ministry of economic affairs—under Prime Minister Gaston Eyskens (q.v.). On 27 May 1961, he was elected president of the Christian People's Party (Christelijke Volkspartij, CVP).

In 1966, Vanden Boeynants formed his first government as prime minister. He struggled with the communitarian problems and his government fell over the split of the University of Louvain (q.v.) in 1968. From 1972 on, Vanden Boeynants was entrusted with the portfolio of defense, successively in the governments of Gaston Eyskens, Edmond Leburton and Leo Tindemans (q.v.). On 20 October 1978, he became prime minister again. His government prepared a revision of the Constitution (q.v.). In the next government, Vanden Boeynants reappeared as vice-prime minister and minister of defense. However, on 8 October 1979, the Social Christian Democrats (PSC) chose him as party president and a week later he left government.

In 1982, Vanden Boeynants was charged with an affair of corruption, which did not leave him unaffected. In vain, he tried to become mayor of Brussels. Finally, he got involved as victim in a case of kidnapping, apparently with political intentions. *See* CATHOLIC PARTY.

VANDENBROUCKE, FRANK (1955- ). In his youth he militated in the Trotskyist movement. He later joined the Socialist Party (Socialistische Party, SP) (q.v.) and was pushed by Louis Toback (q.v.) to the party top. In 1989, he succeeded Karel Van Miert (q.v.) as president of the party. He became minister of foreign affairs and vice premier when Willy Claes left to head NATO (qq.v.). He will remain famous for his order to burn black money found in the Socialist Party safe. In 1995, he temporarily left active politics subsequent to his unhappy intervention in the Agusta case (q.v.) and to write a doctoral dissertation on social security at the University of Oxford. It is rumored that he will return in the elections of 1999.

VANDERVELDE, EMILE (1866-1938). Theoretician of the Socialist movement and longtime president of the Belgian Socialist Party (q.v.). He served as president of the Socialist Second International in 1900. He held posts in the cabinet during World War I (q.v.) and served as minister of justice from 1919 to 1921 and as foreign minister from 1925 to 1927.

VERDINASO. See LEAGUE OF SUPPORTERS OF DUTCH NATIONAL SOLIDARITY.

VERDRONKEN WEIDEN. Important archaeological site near Ypres (q.v.) originating from the period just before 1383 when the siege of Ypres destroyed the area. Materials—especially textiles—have been very well preserved because the area was regularly covered by water.

VERDUN, TREATY OF (843). The sons of Louis the Pious divided his empire into three parts by the Treaty of Verdun. In the west a kingdom was established under Charles II "The Bald" that was later to become modern France, in the east Francia Orientalis under Louis II "The German" or the future Holy German Empire and in the middle Francia Media or Lotharinga (q.v.) under Lothair I. The Scheldt (q.v.) was to become an important boundary line. Beginning in 879, the river formed the dividing line between Flanders (q.v.) under French influence and Brabant (q.v.) and other eastern provinces of the Low Countries (q.v.) under German influence.

VERHAEREN, EMILE (1855-1916). Flemish French-writing author, born in St. Amands on the Scheldt (q.v.). He belonged to the symbolist school. In his verses, he sings about the beloved Flemish soil.

VERHOFSTADT, GUY (1953- ). Mediator *(informateur)* in 1991, but he failed to construct a coalition with either Christian Democrats or Socialists or both. He became president of the Party for Freedom and Progress (Partij voor Vrijheid en Vooruitgang, PVV) by defeating another candidate Annemie Neyts (q.v.), a politician from Brussels (q.v.) with a more social-liberal profile. Then he was temporarily replaced by the more traditional and the equally more social-liberal Herman Decroo (q.v.), but succeeded in becoming president again. In fact, he is a proponent of a strict Liberal Party ideology and he provoked the resistance of union interest groups, even those that support the party.

In 1991, he published a "citizens' manifesto." In 1992, he opened the party to other so-called "democrats" and at a congress in November replaced the PVV with a new party—the Flemish Liberals and Democrats (Vlaamse Liberalen en Democraten, VLD). Some dissenters from among Socialists, Catholics and People's Union (q.v.) (Volksunie, VU) adhered, but at the next elections, the success was limited. Verhofstadt chose to step down temporarily and left the party presidency to Herman Decroo. In 1997, he made his comeback as party president. *See* LIBERAL PARTY.

VERLOOY, JAN BAPTIST (1746-1797). Brussels (q.v.) lawyer and early forerunner of the Flemish movement (q.v.). He ascribed the cultural decline of Flanders (q.v.) to the neglect of the Dutch in favor of the French language (q.v.). He defended this idea in a controversial essay, published in 1788 under the title: *Verhandeling op D'onacht der Moederlyke tael in de Nederlanden* (Treatise on the Neglect of the Mother Tongue in the Low Countries). For a long time, it remained the reference point for the Flemish cultural emancipation movement.

VERMEYLEN, AUGUST (1872-1945). Writer, art critic, professor and politician. He is best known for his book *Kritiek op de Vlaamse Beweging* (Criticism of the Flemish Movement, 1896). After his death, his name was given to a Socialist Flemish cultural organization, one of the three traditional Flemish cultural organizations. *See also* FLEMISH MOVEMENT.

VERSCHAEVE, CYRIEL (1874-1949). Curate of Alveringem. He wrote literature and critiques. During World War I (q.v.), he was dean of the Flemish-Catholic youth movement on the IJzer front.

He became the spiritual leader of the movement. On his experiences at the front, he wrote *Oorlogsindrukken* (War Impressions, 1914-1917). He was accused of collaboration (q.v.) with the Germans.

VERVIERS. Industrial town on the Vesdre River in Wallonia (q.v.). It became one of the first industrial centers in continental Europe after William Cockerill (q.v.) introduced a mechanical weaving loom here in 1799.

VLAAMSE BEWEGING. *See* FLEMISH MOVEMENT.

VLAAMS BLOK. *See* FLEMISH BLOC.

VOEREN (LES FOURONS). The region of Voeren contains several French-speaking villages in the Flemish region along the language boundary (q.v.). After long debates and drawn out consensus-making, the region of Voeren was administratively transferred in 1963 from the Walloon province of Liège (q.v.) to the Flemish province of Limburg. However, the decision engendered continuing friction between the linguistic communities and provoked the fall of a government.

The French-speaking Action Fouronnaise under José Happart (q.v.) won 10 of the 15 seats in the communal council. He was elected mayor and refused to speak Dutch. This provoked a violent reaction not only by Flemish extremists, but also by mainstream Flemish politicians. In 1986, José Happart was disqualified as mayor. However, his removal again led to high tensions between French and Flemish government members. Administrative solutions to the problem failed. The PSC-interior minister Charles Nothomb resigned. On 15 October 1987, the government of Wilfried Martens (q.v.) VI resigned.

Only the following government, mediated by Jean-Luc Dehaene (q.v.) and again led by Wilfried Martens, was finally able to settle the Voeren problem by a complicated but ingenious compromise, which encompassed a guarantee that both language groups be involved in decision-making. Members of the local executive of Voeren were to be elected by a direct vote on a proportional basis.

VOLKSUNIE. *See* PEOPLE'S UNION.

## - W -

WAFFEN SS. Most Belgian SS regiments during World War II (q.v.) fought on the Eastern Front against the Red Army. Only a few Flemish volunteers fought against the Allies in the Walcheren battles during the last months of the war. The Walloon leader of the Rex (q.v.) movement, Léon Degrelle (q.v.), was a volunteer in the SS. After the war, SS members in Belgium were severely treated. Some 324 Belgian citizens who fought for the Waffen SS were still receiving German pensions in 1996.

WALLONIA. The name *Wallonie* appeared in the pamphlet *Wallonades* (1845), written by the poet Joseph Grandgagnage. The identity of Wallonia within the independent kingdom of Belgium was upheld by the Walloon movement (q.v.), which itself developed under the pressure of the Flemish movement (q.v.). Jules Destrée before and during World War I (q.v.) and André Renard during and after World War II (q.v.) contributed most to the awakening of the autonomous Walloon identity. By the beginning of the 1970s, the wartime collaboration (q.v.) stigma of the Flemish federalist movement had faded and public sentiment had coalesced in favor of movement toward the federalization of Belgium. Wallonia could now gradually develop into an autonomous region. The French Cultural Council was officially installed by the law of 21 July 1971 in execution of the Constitutional Reform of 1970 (q.v.). The second and more important step was the creation of the Walloon Region with its council and government by the Constitutional Reform laws of 1980 (q.v.). The Walloon Regional Council (q.v.) meets at Namur. (q.v.)

Economically, Wallonia was the industrial center of the kingdom of Belgium in the 19th and first part of the 20th century. On the strength of its coal mines, steel and heavy industry were developed around the Sambre and Meuse basins. In the Ardennes, agriculture (qq.v.) and forestry flourished. With the exhaustion of the coal mines and the worldwide competition in the steel industry, the development of Wallonia stagnated after World War II.

American investments in light industry and petrochemicals after World War II favored the Flemish region, making use of its coastal ports and new infrastructure that helped to minimize transportation costs in international trading. The major industrial complexes in Wallonia were closed in the 1960s and the 1970s. At the beginning of the 1980s, Walloon entrepreneurs reacted by setting up new light and service industries on a competitive footing.

In its easternmost part around Eupen (q.v.) and St. Vith, the Walloon Region includes territory occupied by the Belgian German-speaking community. In economic matters, this community is linked to the Walloon Region and its council. *See also* WALLOON ASSOCIATION OF ENTERPRISES; WALLOON FLAG; WALLOON MOVEMENT; WALLOON UNION.

WALLOON ASSOCIATION OF ENTERPRISES. The Walloon Association of Enterprises (Union Wallonne des Entreprises, UWE) is the regional employers' organization of Wallonia (q.v.).

WALLOON FLAG. The symbol on the flag is a red rooster on a yellow field. It was designed by Pierre Paulus in 1913. The cock expresses the connection with France, though its shape differs from its French counterpart.

WALLOON MOVEMENT. The movement has its origins in a reaction against the Flemish movement (q.v.). Like its Flemish counterpart, it started as a linguistic movement. The Walloon movement first defended the rights of the French speakers in Flanders (q.v.), whose monopoly position and privileges in the administration were seriously threatened. Consequently, the first Walloon organizations were founded in Flanders and Brussels (q.v.). Paradoxically, they were in fact more defenders of the French language (q.v.), and less of the Walloon "dialect." Both Flemish and Walloon were thought to be inferior to the cultivated French language.

The Belgicist background of the Walloon movement has been strengthened by the alliance with the French-speaking elite of Brussels and has given it a dualist character. In 1883, a Walloon organization named La Ruche Wallonne (The Walloon Beehive) functioned under the motto "Wallon suis, Belge avant tout"

(I'm a Walloon, but a Belgian first). Another Walloon organization had been active in Uccle (near Brussels) in 1877. In 1888, the movement started its activities in Wallonia (q.v.). In Liège (q.v.), the Walloon Federation (Fédération Wallonne) was founded, and in Charleroi, The Walloon League (La League Wallonne et anti-flamingante). From the official Walloon perspective, this is the real starting point of the Walloon movement. In the four subsequent years from 1890, Walloon congresses took place in Brussels, Namur, Liège and Mons. This illustrates the suddenly intense activity of the movement. Support for the Belgian state and defense of the French interests in Belgium still prevailed in the idea of Walloon autonomy.

In 1905, in the context of the World Exhibition in Liège, the next Walloon Congress took place. For the first time, politicians were seated at the conference table. The Belgicist attitude remained and the main problem addressed was defense of the right to speak French in Flanders. On the eve of World War I (q.v.), Jules Destrée (q.v.) radicalized the Walloon movement. In 1912, he wrote to King Albert I (q.v.) his famous letter, exclaiming "Majesty, there are no Belgians." In 1913, Destrée acted as secretary of a Walloon parliament. This organ chose a flag, a weapon, a motto and a national holiday, all symbols of an independent Wallonia. Now, the Walloon movement was equipped for complete federalization. However, it would take more than half a century before the process of federalization really took off, as Belgium was twice invaded by the Germans and patriotic national ideas prevailed.

After World War I, every reference to the idea of federalization was suspect. Only after World War II (q.v.) would a new more federalist friendly attitude mature. In 1945, the National Walloon Congress (Congrès National Wallon) was held. All important Walloon politicians participated. A vote was organized on four options: the maintenance of the unitarian structure of Belgium, federalism, an independent Wallonia, or a union with France. In a first round, almost half of the participants chose the last solution. In a second round between only two remaining alternatives—union with France or federalism—the majority preferred complete federalism. However, the first postwar generation of Walloon politicians, who favored federalism, could not take immediate action. The federal idea had been compromised by the collaboration (q.v.) of the Flemish movement with the Germans during the war.

During the royal controversy (q.v.), the majority of Walloons voted against the return of the king, but a majority of Flemings did not. In Wallonia, acts of violence and strikes broke out. Four workers were shot down near Liège. Walloon politicians decided to form an illegal Walloon government. Some unconfirmed sources claimed that the French consul had expressed sympathy for such action and promised the military support of two regiments. The king resigned during the night of 31 July to 1 August and the conflict ended without further Walloon action.

Two main figures determined the future development of the Walloon movement: André Renard and José Happart (q.v.). In the period of 1960-1961, André Renard organized the biggest strike in postwar Belgian history. The strike was directed against the Unity Law proposal of the Flemish prime minister Gaston Eyskens (q.v.). On 21 November 1960, 50,000 workers demonstrated and the strike spread rapidly. The workers asked for structural reforms of industry and for Walloon independence. However, the strike failed and the Unity Law was approved in Parliament.

The next confrontation between the Flemish and Walloon movements took place in Voeren (Les Fourons) (q.v.). The battle on the linguistic frontier shifted the focus of contention from socio-economic to linguistic issues. After long debates, the region of Voeren was administratively transferred from the Walloon province of Liège to the Flemish province of Limburg. José Happart took a leading role in the Walloon protest movement. The problem of Voeren was the cause of enduring trouble between the linguistic communities and even provoked the fall of the national government. The problem could only be tackled in the broader context of the Constitutional Reforms of 1970, 1980, 1990 and 1993 (qq.v.). They put into place gradually a federal structure for the country that had constituted a long current in the Walloon movement.

Of course, some problems remain. With the economic decline of Wallonia, the enthusiasm for radical federalism has waned. Bonds of solidarity with Flanders in the form of a national social security system are now defended. Flemish support for further federalization is now countered with the threat of alignment or union with France. There is also much talk of new defensive strategies within the French-speaking community. The problem of Brussels, which is located on the border of the linguistic communities and regions is another contentious issue.

WALLOON POPULAR MOVEMENT. The Walloon Popular Movement (Mouvement Populaire Wallon, MPW) was founded in 1961 by André Renard (q.v.). It intended to be a broad movement for the achievement of a progressive and autonomous Wallonia (q.v.).

WALLOON REGIONAL COUNCIL. The Walloon Regional Council (Conseil Régional de Wallonie, CRW) is the central authority of the Walloon Region. It played a major role in the federalization of Belgium. Together with its Flemish counterpart, the Flemish Economic Council (q.v.), it promoted decentralization of political decision-making.

WALLOON UNION. The Walloon Union (Rassemblement Wallon, RW) was created in 1968 as a party with the merger of earlier Walloon organizations. It obtained immediate significant electoral success in 1968 with 10.8 percent of the vote, and in 1971 it secured 21.2 percent and 14 seats in Parliament (making it the second largest Walloon party). In 1974 it garnered 18.8 percent of the votes. It joined the coalition in the Tindemans (q.v.) II government (1974-1977). This caused a split in the party and a disastrous result in the 1977 elections. The party fell back to 9.1 percent and further decreased to 5.5 percent in 1981 (only two seats in Parliament). Later on, the economic crisis distracted the public from the community question.

The RW displayed a leftist, federalist and Walloon profile. Its heterogenous public resulted in continuous splitting. The more outspoken federalistic and Walloon positioning of the Socialist Party (Parti Socialiste, PS) (q.v.) has eroded the electorial position of the RW.

WALSCHAP, GERARD (1898-1989). Flemish modernist writer. He was a gifted story teller, creating a very unconventional universe, given the traditional Catholic way of life in Flanders (q.v.). His style was sober and devoid of the earlier romanticizing of Flemish traditional writers.

WATERLOO, BATTLE OF. In the Battle of Waterloo of 18 June 1815, Napoleon Bonaparte was defeated by the allied forces of the British and Prussian armies under command of Arthur Wellesley, the duke of Wellington and Gebhard Lebrecht von Blucher. As a consequence, the Low Countries (q.v.) were united into the Kingdom of the Netherlands under King William I of Orange (q.v.).

WHITE MARCH (WITTE MARS). Reacting to a growing list of perceived abuses by public officials, including attacks and murders by paramilitary forces, the corruption in the Agusta case (q.v.) and the abdication of Willy Claes (q.v.), the murder affair regarding the Socialist politician André Cools (q.v.) and others, public protest exploded in the middle of 1996 on the occasion of the Dutroux case (q.v.). Dutroux set up a network of pedophilia that was thought to be frequented by persons from high circles of the political and judicial system. The investigations were ostensibly neglected or hindered. Some kidnapped girls were not only abused, but also murdered. The impartiality of one investigator, Jean-Marc Connerote, who offered a break through in the case and that led to saving the lives of two victims, was challenged by the defenders of Dutroux as he was seen at a solidarity meeting for supporters of the victims, eating spaghetti.

Compelled to resign from the investigation in the interest of judicial objectivity, public indignation exploded. The parents of the victims organized a big meeting, the White March. More than one million people and especially pupils demonstrated in the streets of Brussels (q.v.). From then on, politicians tried to assuage the movement and a reform of the political and judicial system was announced. In fact, some minor but important steps were taken in these reforms. But one major protagonist remained unsatisfied, Paul Marchal, a father of missing children, who founded his Party for New Politics (Partij voor Nieuwe Politiek, PNP) at the beginning of 1998. *See also* REFORM OF THE JUDICIARY SYSTEM; REFORM OF THE POLITICAL SYSTEM.

WILLEMS, JAN FRANS (1793-1846). He was an early leader of the Flemish movement (q.v.). Willems was an Antwerp local government official and philologist. He defended Dutch as a national language in the Belgian state. He wrote patriotic poems and plays and published a history of literature in the southern Netherlands. Later generations identified him as the "Father of the Flemish Movement." *See also* WILLEMS FOUNDATION.

WILLEMS FOUNDATION (WILLEMSFONDS). Flemish nationalist cultural foundation of Liberal tendency. It is named in honor of the Flemish leader Jan Frans Willems (q.v.). *See also* FLEMISH MOVEMENT.

WILLIAM I OF ORANGE, KING OF THE NETHERLANDS (1772-1840). The Kingdom of the Netherlands was created by the European Powers by the Protocol of London in 1814. The Congress of Vienna (q.v.) recognized the new state. William I of Orange was appointed king of the new kingdom. He had some objections to the Constitution to which he had to take an oath. He led a very active industrialization policy and launched major infrastructure works. He stimulated the foundation of the Société Générale des Pays-Bas, later the Société Générale de Belgique. William I encountered considerable resistance in his reforms of the church and educational system and his language policy. In the south, the fact that the capital and centers of authority were located in Holland was much resented. Some autocratic tendencies in his policy eventually led to the revolt of the Belgian bourgeoisie.

In 1830, William I underestimated the force of the Belgian revolution (q.v.) and the international recognition it would acquire. It was not until 1839 that he finally recognized the secession of the southern provinces and the existence of the new state.

WORLD EXHIBITIONS. The world exhibitions in Belgium gave an incentive to promoting Belgian economic and technological development. The most important exhibitions took place at Liège (q.v.) in 1905, in Antwerp (q.v.) in 1930 and Brussels (q.v.) in 1958.

WORLD WAR I. Since its creation in 1830, the great powers had guaranteed the independence and neutrality of the Kingdom of

Belgium. At the beginning of World War I, Germany invaded the Grand Duchy of Luxembourg (q.v.) on 2 August 1914 and sent an ultimatum to Belgium, demanding free passage for its troops. Belgium refused this demand and the German forces invaded the country on 4 August 1914. Within three weeks, Liège, Namur and Brussels (qq.v.) were conquered. Antwerp (q.v.) fell on 6 October. Belgium was not prepared nor equipped to resist the well-armed and disciplined German troops.

The Belgian army then withdrew further to the west and entrenched itself along the banks of the IJzer River in the westernmost corner of Flanders (q.v.). The area was partly flooded. The front line in Belgium near Ypres (q.v.) remained deadlocked blocked for the rest of the war. Several offensives by both sides, sometimes accompanied by the use of poison gas by the Germans, had only minor effects on the front positions. King Albert I (q.v.) stayed with his troops at the front, while the government operated in exile at Le Havre in northern France. During almost four years, the soldiers lived in inhuman conditions and many died of exhaustion and disease.

At the front, members of the Flemish movement (q.v.) held cultural demonstrations and contributed to the Flemish awakening. A small number of Flemings, the Activists, collaborated with the Germans and advocated that the Flemish provinces should separate from Belgium. In 1917, the Activists tried to establish a seperate government in Ghent (q.v.), the Council of Flanders. In 1918, the Germans divided Belgium into two administrative units with headquarters at Brussels and Namur. When the German collapse began in the summer of 1918, the Activists fled to Holland or Germany.

Belgium was liberated by an Allied offensive in September 1918. The British entered Mons, the French and Americans liberated the region between the Sambre and Meuse Rivers and the Belgians themselves took Ghent. On 11 November 1918, the armistice was signed. The "knight-king" entered his capital Brussels in triumph.

After the war, universal (male) suffrage was announced and applied in the elections of 1919. The king returned to a restored Belgium as a war hero. The Treaty of Versailles (1919) ended Belgium's neutrality and transferred the German districts of Eupen and Malmedy to Belgium. Belgium also received a mandate over the former German colonies of Ruanda and Burundi (q.v.) in central Africa that Belgian forces had occupied during the war.

WORLD WAR II. On 3 September 1939, France and Great Britain declared war on Germany after its invasion of Poland. Belgium reaffirmed its neutrality, but began the mobilization of its army of 650,000 men. On 10 May 1940, the Germans invaded Belgium. After an 18-day campaign, King Leopold III (q.v.) capitulated. The king was commander in chief of the Belgian armed forces, but according to the interpretation of Parliament, his position as head of the country superseded his duty as commander in chief. The Belgian government first fled to France and then to London, where a government-in-exile was established.

With the aid of the British allies, an incipient resistance (q.v.) movement grew steadily. Meanwhile, within Belgium, a collaboration (q.v.) movement with the Germans had been successfully established in Flanders (q.v.). Along with collaborating political parties, groups of Flemish SS were formed, who wished to detach the Flemish provinces from the rest of the country. Nevertheless, the majority of the population remained politically indifferent about such issues and worried more about deteriorating living conditions. It suffered from food rationing, forced labor and even deportation to Germany to work in war industries. Of course, the most severe German repression was directed at the Jewish population. Especially the Antwerp (q.v.) community was harshly treated and many never returned from the concentration camps. Of Belgium's Jewish population of about 80,000, only 1,500 were said to have survived the war. Many resistance fighters were caught as well and emprisoned or executed by the German oppressor in places such as Fort Breendonk.

In Brussels (q.v.), the king tried to negotiate the fate of Belgium and, in doing so, sought to pursue positions perceived by some as preserving the status quo and by others as collaborating passively with the enemy. In the course of the war, the initially rather mild German occupation forces evolved toward a more and more oppressive regime. This contributed to the growing sympathy for the resistance forces, especially in the Walloon part of the country.

The Allied forces reached Belgium on 3 September 1944. General Bernard Montgomery's troops crossed the Belgian frontier near Tournai (q.v.) and a few hours later, the British army liberated Brussels (q.v.). The underground resistance army was able to protect the port of Antwerp, a strategic provisioning position for the Allies. It was liberated on 4 September by British and Canadian forces. Otherwise, the Resistance was not able to undertake major independent actions, which would have helped to build a strong power base from which to operate for those who sought radical changes in postwar Belgian political and social life. After liberation, the Resistance did play a major role in identifying and exacting punishment on collaborators. Meanwhile, the Americans entered southeast Belgium, capturing the fortresses of Liège and Namur (qq.v.). Within a week, the country had been liberated.

However, in a last attack, the Germans bombed Antwerp and Liège in the winter of 1944. They heavily damaged the infrastructure of both towns. Moreover, the Germans once more made a quick breakthrough in the Ardennes (q.v.). The Americans countered the Germans in the mountain roads near Bastogne (q.v.). Two months later the battle of the Ardennes was over, having inflicted heavy losses on both the Americans and Germans. Fighting in Belgium now ceased until the official end of the war on 8 May 1945.

Earlier, on 19 September 1944, the government had returned from exile in London. It managed to restore order in the country by setting up a broad coalition of all political parties and forces that had not openly collaborated. Along with the economic recovery of the country, the main political problem faced was the so-called royal controversy (q.v.). In the absence of the king, who had been deported by the Germans before the end of the war, Parliament (q.v.) appointed the brother of the king, Prince Charles (q.v.), as regent.

## - Y -

YPRES. Small town in West Flanders (q.v.). In the Middle Ages, it was an important textile center. It conserves a Gothic cloth market from the 13th century. It was on the battle line in World War I (q.v.). A British advance was achieved here during the battle of Passchendaele in 1917 at a cost of 400,000 lives.

YSAYE, EUGENE (1858-1931). Violinist and composer. He organized the country's musical life. One competition that carried his name grew into the Queen Elizabeth Contest, a world-renowned musical competition.

## - Z -

ZAIRE. *See* CONGO, BELGIAN.

ZAVENTEM. National airport of Belgium. It lies near the capital Brussels (q.v.). The national air company of Belgium (SABENA) and other airlines serve most international destinations from here.

ZIMMERTOREN. Tower built by a technician called Zimmer, full of clocks. It is the major attraction of the small town of Lier.

ZWARTE ZONDAG. *See* BLACK SUNDAY.

# APPENDIXES

## APPENDIX 1. Kings of Belgium (1831- )

| Monarch | Period of reign |
|---|---|
| Leopold I | 1831-1865 |
| Leopold II | 1865-1909 |
| Albert I | 1909-1934 |
| Leopold III | 1934-1951 |
| Baldwin | 1951-1993 |
| Albert II | 1993- |

## APPENDIX 2. Belgian Governments since World War II (1944- )

| Prime Minister | Period of office |
|---|---|
| 1. Pierlot | 1944-1945 |
| 2. Van Acker I | 1945 (Feb.-Aug.) |
| 3. Van Acker II | 1945-1946 |
| 4. Spaak II | 1946 (Mar.) |
| 5. Van Acker III | 1946 (Mar.-Jul.) |
| 6. Huysmans I | 1946-1947 |
| 7. Spaak III | 1947-1949 |
| 8. Eyskens I | 1949-1950 |
| 9. Duvieusart | 1950 (June-Aug.) |
| 10. Pholien | 1950-1952 |
| 11. Van Houtte | 1952-1954 |
| 12. Van Acker III | 1954-1958 |
| 13. Eyskens II | 1958 (June-Aug.) |
| 14. Eyskens III | 1958-1960 |
| 15. Eyskens IV | 1960-1961 |
| 16. Lefèvre | 1961-1965 |
| 17. Harmel | 1965-1966 |
| 18. Vanden Boeynants I | 1966-1968 |
| 19. Eyskens IV | 1968-1971 |
| 20. Eyskens V | 1972 (Jan.-Nov.) |
| 21. Leburton I | 1973 (Jan.-Oct.) |
| 22. Leburton II | 1973-1974 |
| 23. Tindemans I | 1974 (Apr.-June) |
| 24. Tindemans II | 1974-1977 |
| 25. Tindemans III | 1977-1978 |
| 26. Vanden Boeynants II | 1978-1979 |
| 27. Martens I | 1979-1980 |
| 28. Martens II | 1980 (Jan.-Apr.) |

| | |
|---|---|
| 29. Martens III | 1980 (May-Oct.) |
| 30. Martens IV | 1980-1981 |
| 31. Eyskens VI | 1981 (Apr.-Nov.) |
| 32. Martens V | 1981 (Dec.-1985) |
| 33. Martens VI | 1985 |
| 34. Martens VII | 1985-1987 |
| 35. Martens VIII | 1988-1991 |
| 36. Martens IX | 1991-1992 |
| 37. Dehaene I | 1992-1995 |
| 38. Dehaene II | 1995- |

## APPENDIX 3. Some Main Indicators of the Belgian Economy

-Gross National Product (1994): 7,626 billion BEF
-Population (1995): 10,137,000
-GNP per capita (1994): 754,000 BEF
-Real GDP growth (1995): 1.9 %
-Labour Force Population rate (1995): 63.4
-Unemployment rate (1995): 9.4 %
-General Government Deficit (1995): 4.1 % of GDP
-General Government Debt (1995): 133.7 % of GDP
-Current-account balance (1995): 5.2 % of GNP
-Imports (1996): 4,994 billion BEF
-Exports (1996): 5,274 billion BEF

Source: *Statistisch Zakjaarboek 1996* (NIS), p. 1; *Statistisch Tijdschrift* (NIS), 1997, 12, p. 46; *Country Profile Belgium 1996-97* (Economist Intelligence Unit), pp. 12, 14.

APPENDIX 4. Gross Value Added by Sectors, 1996, in current prices (billions of BEF)

| | |
|---|---|
| 1. Agriculture, forestry and fishing | 101.9 |
| 2. Mining | 20.6 |
| 3. Manufacturing | 1,761.9 |
| 4. Construction | 391.7 |
| 5. Electricity, gas and water | 204.3 |
| 6. Distribution, finance and insurance | 2.213.0 |
| 7. Transport and communications | 634.5 |
| 8. Services | 2,612.6 |
| Total (Corrections included) | 8,428.2 |

Source: *Statistisch Tijdschrift van de Nationale Bank van België,* 1997, 2, p. 20.

APPENDIX 5. Sectoral Structure of Gross Value Added, 1995, in percentages

| | |
|---|---|
| Agriculture, forestry and fishing | 1.5 |
| Manufacturing | 23.9 |
| Construction | 5.4 |
| Electricity, gas and water | 2.7 |
| Distribution | 13.2 |
| Finance and insurance | 6.2 |
| Transport and communications | 8.4 |
| Public administration and defence | 7.8 |
| Education and health | 8.9 |
| Other Services | 16.8 |
| Total (Included others) | 100.0 |

Source: *Country Report. Belgium. 1st quarter 1997* (Economist Intelligence Unit), p. 6.

APPENDIX 6. Imports to and Exports from Belgium, 1996, (in billions of BEF)

| | Imports | Exports |
|---|---|---|
| Total | 4994 | 5274 |
| Europe | 4020 | 4297 |
| European Union | 3795 | 3976 |
| Germany | 998 | 1081 |
| Netherlands | 936 | 710 |
| France | 771 | 948 |
| United Kingdom | 454 | 482 |
| Italy | 212 | 288 |
| Sweden | 132 | 75 |
| Spain | 93 | 160 |
| Americas | 409 | 313 |
| USA | 301 | 230 |
| Asia | 370 | 503 |
| Africa | 174 | 113 |
| Oceania | 20 | 24 |

Source: *Statistisch Tijdschrift* (NIS), 1997, 12, p. 46.

# BIBLIOGRAPHY

## CONTENTS

## *INTRODUCTION*

The purpose of this introduction is to give the English-reading public a few keys for a first discovery of Belgian history and life. Some guidelines concerning the use of the bibliography and a note for further study are added.

### *Bibliography and General Information*

All books published in Belgium are compiled in the *Belgische Bibliografie/Bibliographie de Belgique*, a periodical issued monthly by the Belgian National Library. A Belgian Bibliography from 1974 on can also be found on CD-ROM (CDBB : Bibliographie de Belgique: 1974-1995/Belgische Bibliographie, 1974-1995. Dilbeek: ODIS, 1995). A good selection of the Flemish production displayed in an annual book exhibition is listed in an accompanying guide. It also contains information on publishers and bookshops.

In the past decade the Belgian authorities began to deploy a more systematic information policy. They established the Federal Information and Documentation Service, INBEL. (Federale Voorlichtingsdienst. Informatiecentrum, Regentlaan 54, 1000 Brussels, tel 02/514.08.00, fax 02/612.51.25, http://belgium.fgov.be.). Among others, it issues *Feiten* (Facts), a weekly publication about the decisions of the Ministerial Council and an annual catalog of materials available to the public. It also produced the CD *Discover Belgium*. (Brussels: Federale Voorlichtingsdienst, 1996).

The regional authorities have begun an extended information campaign. For example, the Flemish authorities annually present a volume with studies available to the interested public, *Publikaties van de Vlaamse Overheid* (Brussels: Ministerie van de Vlaamse Gemeenschap. Department Coördinatie. Administratie Kanselarij en Voorlichting. Afdeling Communicatie en Ontvangst. Bibliotheek, 1997). There exists a functional regional databank: Functionele regionale databank or FRED. (Brussels, Ministerie van de Vlaamse Gemeenschap. Departement Algemene Zaken en Financiën. Administratie Planning en Statistiek, Boudewijnlaan 30, 1000 Brussels,tel 02/553.58.03, fax 02/ 553.58.08). The same service publishes five times a year *Stativaria* and quaterly *Conjunctuurnota*. One of the more popular publications edited by the Flemish government and dedicated to the English reader is the tri-monthly *Flanders*. It contains short articles on contemporary Flemish art, economy and society.

*Statistical Information*

The National Institute of Statistics (Nationaal Instituut voor de Statistiek, Leuvenseweg 44, 1000 Brussels, tel 02/548.62.11, fax 2/548.63.67) provides federal statistics about Belgium. It issues yearbooks, a monthly statistical review, a weekly information bulletin, specific studies and specialized statistical publications on demographic, sociological, economic, financial, juridical and other aspects.

*Economics*

The international institutions such as the OECD regularly publish economic reviews on the status of the Belgian economy. (Organisation for Economic Cooperation and Development. *Economic Survey of Belgium,* annual)

An excellent and up-to-date source on the evolution of Belgium's political life and its economy are the *Quarterly Country Reports* of the Economist Intelligence Unit (London) and its annual *Country Profile.*

The National Bank of Belgium publishes an annual report and monthly bulletins with financial information and statistics.

The Kredietbank has published for many years a *Monthly Bulletin* on the performance of the Belgium economy. In 1998, the Gemeentekrediet published an issue with statistical material of the national census of 1991. The census itself is organized every tenth year.

*Belgian Society and Art*

Four more general publications provide an excellent resource in deepening the reader's knowledge of Belgian society.

First, an instructive earlier bibliography on Belgium was published by R. C. Riley in the ABC-Clio World Bibliographical Series 104. (*Belgium.* Oxford; Santa Barbara: Clio Press, 1989).

Second, a very good introductory work in English on most aspects of Belgian society by specialized scholars was edited by Marina Boudart and René Bryssinck and entitled *Modern Belgium.* (Palo Alto, California: The Society for the Promotion of Science and Scholarship, 1990.) Though almost 10 years old, the synthetic reviews still provide the reader with much valuable insight into the functioning of present-day Belgium.

An excellent monograph in English on the Belgian political system written by John Fitzmaurice is *The Politics of Belgium. A Unique Federalism* (London: Hurst, 1996).

Finally, from a cultural point of view, invaluable for the English reader is the annual publication *The Low Countries. Arts and Society in Flanders and the Netherlands,* edited by the foundation Ons Erfdeel (Rekkem). Thematically very diverse, the many short contributions introduce the reader to all aspects of cultural life, both historical and contemporary. The book also contains an index of Flemish and Dutch books translated into English during the previous year. The yearbook is richly illustrated as well. Very useful as a first introduction are other publications in English from the same foundation. They include booklets on the Flemish language, literature, modern painting and the history of the Low Countries.

### *Journals*

The only weekly journal in English edited in Belgium and about daily life in Belgium is *The Bulletin*, published since 21 September 1962. It now has a half-yearly supplement, *The Newcomer,* providing interesting information for new immigrants and visitors to Belgium. *The Bulletin* presently has more than 11,500 subscribers and an estimated reading public of five times this figure or about 90 percent of English-reading foreigners residing in Belgium.

### *History*

In the historiographic field, most useful is a recent bibliographic guide by J. Ulens: *Geschiedenis van de Nederlanden. Historisch-bibliografische wegwijzer (Boek 3.* Leuven: Garant, 1993). Each year a scholarly review of the current Belgian historiographic production is published in the *Revue Belge de Philologie et d'Histoire* by Van Eeno et al.

For English-language readers with limited time who want to read just one or a few fine books on a historical subject, recommendations include—along with *The Low Countries. Arts and Society in Flanders and the Netherlands* and the historical booklet of the foundation Ons Erfdeel (J.A. Kossman-Putto and E.H. Kossman. *The Low Countries. History of the Northern and Southern Netherlands.* Rekkem: Ons Erfdeel, 1996) cited above—one of the following books: the broad and almost lyrical history of Flanders by Patricia Carson, *The Fair Face of Flanders* (Ghent, Story-Scientia, 1978), Flanders' interesting medieval history by David Nicholas, *Medieval Flanders* (London, New York: Longman, 1992), or the Low countries under the Burgundians by Walter Prevenier and Willem Pieter Blockmans, *The Burgundian Netherlands* (Cambridge: Cambridge University Press, 1986). Of course, there are also many art history books to be consulted, such as those magnificently edited and illustrated by the Mercator Fund.

*Recent Publications*

To find the most recent publications which because of the publication gap may not yet be incorporated in this dictionary, we refer the reader to the following databases.

*Historical Abstracts.* It gives a short description and evaluation of publications on history. A quick search using the index "Belgium" and a marker for the desired time period provides much valuable information.
*Humanities Index.* It has items mainly on history, archaeology, culture, literature, religion and art.
*Econlit.* It describes the main economic literature.
*Sociofile Database.* It contains references to sociological journals and dissertations.
*Social Sciences Citation Index.* It has an interesting system of cross-references.
*Scad* from Eurobases. This is a database of the Commission of the European Union with proposals, decisions and official publications of the Council and the European Parliament. It also contains references to other related documents.

*Internet*

Most Belgian institutions have a site on the Internet. Some can be easily found using www.name.be. Among the many interesting sites, one of them is the official Belgian Institute for Documentation (INBEL), *(http://Belgium.fgov.be),* another that of the Flemish government and yet another the Belgian church.

*Using This Bibliography*

It is self-evident that this bibliography does not aim at completeness. It serves as a good first guide to recent and easily obtainable sources. As has been indicated above, readers can update their queries by consulting databases and the Internet.

A last remark concerns the classification scheme of this bibliography. History is perceived here as a global process. So, the reader will find references to political and nationality problems under the heading "Historical." Only items about the most recent period will be found under a separate label "Political." Moreover, it was judged useful to group explicit references to the Belgian regions, such as "Flanders, Wallonia, Brussels." For the reader, it will be useful to consult more than one section. The same of course is valid for identifying books covering more than one historical period. The periodization of the historical section closely follows foreign occupations of the country. Books covering more than two periods have mostly, but not always, been transferred to the "General" section. In principle, with a few exceptions for bibliographic items, each reference appears only once.

# I. GENERAL

## 1. Bibliographies

Addison, Bland, Jr. "The bibliographie Liégeoise: From Jansénism to sans-culottism in the book industry of eighteenth-century Liège. *Primary Sources & Original Works,* 1(1991), 1-2, pp. 117-136.

*Belgische bibliografie. Belgische muziektijdschriften 1833-1985/Bibliographie de Belgique. Périodiques musicaux belges 1833-1985.* Brussels: Koninklijke Bibliotheek Albert I, 1987.

*Belgische Bibliografie: Maandelijkse lijst van belgische werken/Bibliographie de Belgique : Liste mensuelle des publications belges.* Brussels: Koninklijke Bibliotheek. (Monthly)

*Catalogus 1996-1997.* Brussels: Federale Voorlichtingsdienst, 1996.

Debae, Marguerite. *De Librije van Margareta van Oostenrijk. Catalogus.* Brussels: Koninklijke Bibliotheek Albert I and Europalia 87 Osterreich, 1987.

De Belder, J. and J. Hannes. *Bibliografie van de geschiedenis van België - Bibliographie de l'histoire de Belgique 1865-1914.* Leuven-Brussels, Nauwelaerts, 1965. Interuniversitair Centrum voor Hedendaagse Geschiedenis. Bijdragen 38.

DeHerdt, René. "Bibliografie van de Geschiedenis van Gent, 1983-1984." *Handelingen der Maatschappij voor Geschiedenis en Oudheidkunde te Gent,* 1984, 38, pp. 189-223.

Demoulin, Robert. "Le centre interuniversitaire d'histoire contemporaine: cent cahiers." *Cahiers de Clio,* 90-91(1987), pp. 27-33.

De Waele, M. *Bibliografie van de Belgische buitenlandse betrekkingen 1830-1980.* Ghent: RUG. Seminarie voor Hedendaagse Ontwikkeling van de Binnen- en Buitenlandse Politiek, 1980.

*Fondscatalogus 1996. Catalogue des publications disponibles.* Brussels: Algemeen Rijksarchief/Archives Générales du Royaume and Archives de l'Etat dans les Provinces, 1996.

Gaus, H. and R. Van Eeno. *Beknopte bibliografie van de politieke en sociaal-ekonomische evolutie van België 1945-1992.* Leuven-Apeldoorn, Garant, 1992.

Gaus, H., R. Van Eeno and M. De Waele. *Beknopte bibliografie van de politieke en sociaal-ekonomische evolutie van België 1918-1988.* Ghent: Centrum voor Politiek-Wetenschapelijk Onderzoek, 1988.

Gerin, P. *Bibliografie van de geschiedenis van België - Bibliographie de l'histoire de Belgique 1789-21 juillet 1831.* Leuven-Brussels, Nauwelaerts, 1960. Interuniversitair Centrum voor Hedendaagse Geschiedenis. Bijdragen 15.

*Gids van de overheidspublicaties.* Brussels, Federale Voorlichtingsdienst. (Bi-annually)

Heyse, M. and R. Van Eeno. *Bibliografie van de geschiedenis van België - Bibliographie de l'histoire de Belgique 1914-1940.* Leuven-Brussels: Nauwelaerts, 1986. Interuniversitair Centrum voor Hedendaagse Geschiedenis. Bijdragen 90.

*Het boek in Vlaanderen (1997-1998).* Antwerp: Vereniging ter Bevordering van het Vlaamse Boekwezen, 1997. (Annual)

Huys, Bernard. *Catalogue des partitions musicales éditées en Belgique et acquises par la Bibliothèque royale Albert Ier, 1966-1975/Catalogus van de muziekpartituren in België uitgegeven en verworven door de Koninklijke Bibliotheek Albert I, 1966-1975.* Brussels: Bibliothèque royale Albert Ier/Koninklijke Bibliotheek Albert I, 1976. 1976. Bibliographie de Belgique: fasc. spécial; *5.

Krewson, Margrit B. *The Netherlands and Northern Belgium: a Selective Bibliography of Reference Works.* Washington, D.C.: Library of Congress, 1989.

Lefevre, P. et J. Lorette (ed.). *La Belgique et la Première Guerre Mondiale. Bibliographie. België en de Eerste Wereldoorlog. Bibliografie.* Brussels: Koninklijk Legermuseum, 1987. Centrum voor Militaire Geschiedenis. Bijdragen 21.

Meyers, Willem C. M. "België in de Tweede Wereldoorlog. Een poging tot kritische selectie van de voornaamste werken gepubliceerd sinds 1970." *Bijdragen en mededelingen betreffende de geschiedenis der Nederlanden,* 105(1990), 2, pp. 280-294.

———"Bibliografie van de in 1988 en 1989 verschenen publikaties betreffende België tijdens de Tweede Wereldoorlog." *Cahiers/ Bijdragen,* 13(1980), pp. 235-276.

———"Bibliografie van de in 1982, 1983 en 1984 verschenen publikaties betreffende België tijdens de Tweede Wereldoorlog." *Cahiers/ Bijdragen,* 9(1985), pp. 375-439.

*Publikaties van de Vlaamse Overheid.* Brussels: Ministerie van de Vlaamse Gemeenschap. Department Coördinatie. Administratie Kanselarij en Voorlichting. Afdeling Communicatie en Ontvangst. Bibliotheek, 1995, 1996, 1997.

Riley, R.C. *Belgium.* Oxford, Santa Barbara: Clio Press, 1989. ABC-Clio World Bibliographical Series 104.

Ulens, J. *Geschiedenis van de Nederlanden. Historisch-bibliografische wegwijzer. Boek 3.* Leuven: Garant, 1993.

Van Den Berghe, Gie. *Getuigen: een case-study over ego-documenten: bibliografie van ego-documenten over de nationaal-socialistische kampen en gevangenissen, geschreven of getekend door 'Belgische' (ex-)gevangenen: Belgen, personen die in België gedomicilieerd waren of verbleven, en andere uit België gedeporteerde personen.* Brussels: Navorsings-en studiecentrum voor de geschiedenis van de tweede wereldoorlog, 1995.

Vandermeersch, Peter. "Revue des Travaux sur l'Humanisme dans les anciens Pays-Bas de 1969 à 1986." Bibliothèque d'Humanisme et Renaissance, 50(1988), 1, pp. 125-140.

Van Eenoo, R. (ed.). "Bibliographie de l'histoire de Belgique, 1990." *Revue Belge de Philologie et d'Histoire,* 70(1992), 2, pp. 420-546.

———"Bibliographie de l'histoire de Belgique, 1989." *Revue Belge de Philologie et d'Histoire,* 69(1991), 2, pp. 342-465.

———"Bibliographie de l'histoire de Belgique, 1988." *Revue Belge de Philologie et d'Histoire,* 68(1990), 2, pp. 352-463.

Van Eenoo, R. et al. "Bibliographie de l'histoire de Belgique, 1987." *Revue Belge de Philologie et d'Histoire,* 67(1989), 2, pp. 338-465.

———"Bibliographie de l'histoire de Belgique, 1986." *Revue Belge de Philologie et d'Histoire,* 66(1988), 2, pp. 329-430.

———"Bibliographie de l'histoire de Belgique, 1985." *Revue Belge de Philologie et d'Histoire,* 65(1987), 2, pp. 313-415.

———"Bibliographie de l'histoire de Belgique, 1984." *Revue Belge de Philologie et d'Histoire,* 63(1985), 4, pp. 795-880.

———"Bibliographie de l'histoire de Belgique, 1983." *Revue Belge de Philologie et d'Histoire,* 62(1984), 2, pp. 759-857.

———"Bibliographie de l'histoire de Belgique, 1982." *Revue Belge de Philologie et d'Histoire,* 61(1983), 4, pp. 895-1004.

———"Bibliographie de l'histoire de Belgique, 1981." *Revue Belge de Philologie et d'Histoire,* 60(1982), 4, pp. 898-1000.

———"Bibliographie de l'histoire de Belgique, 1980." *Revue Belge de Philologie et d'Histoire, 59*(1981), 4, pp. 883-993.

Verdoodt, A. "Dix ans de recherches bibliographiques sur les problèmes communautaires Belges." *Recherches Sociologiques,* 11(1980), 2, pp. 237-245.

Verhulst, Adriaan. "L'histoire rurale de la Belgique jusqu'à la fin de l'ancien régime (Aperçu bibliographique 1968-1983). *Revue Historique,* 271(1984), 2, pp. 419-437.

*Vervaeck, S. Bibliografie van de geschiedenis van België - Bibliographie de l'histoire de Belgique 1831-1865.* Leuven-Brussels, Nauwelaerts, 1965. Interuniversitair Centrum voor Hedendaagse Geschiedenis. Bijdragen 37.

## 2. *General Information and Libraries*

*Archives Générales du Royaume. Bruxelles.* Brussels: Archives Générales du Royaume, 1997.

*België 1492-1992.* Brussels: Federale Voorlichtingsdienst en Mercator, 1992.

*België, een Federale Staat.* Brussels: Federale Voorlichtingsdienst, 1993.

*België - Kunst en Handel.* Brussels: Federale Voorlichtingsdienst, 1987.

Boudart, Marina, Michel Boudart and René Bryssinck. *Modern Belgium.* Palo Alto, California: The Society for the Promotion of Science and Scholarship, 1990.

*De Belgen.* Brussels en Tielt: Federale Voorlichtingsdienst en Lannoo, 1992.

De Callataij, François. "De Koninklijke Bibliotheek gezien door buitenlandse reizigers in de eerste helft van de 19de eeuw." *Informatiebulletin Koninklijke Bibliotheek Albert I,* 40 (1996), 2, pp. 42-50.

*Federaal België, de staatshervorming in beeld.* Brussels: Federale Voorlichtingsdienst, 1995.

*Fondscatalogus 1996/Catalogue des publications disponibles.* Brussels: Algemeen Rijksarchief/Archives Générales du Royaume and Archives de l'Etat dans les Provinces, 1996.

*Frisse kijk op België.* Brussels: Federale Voorlichtingsdienst, 1987.

Mazur-Rzesos, Elisabeth. "Toekomstperspectieven voor on-line-catalogi op Internet." *Informatiebulletin Koninklijke Bibliotheek Albert I,* 39 (1995), pp. 24-27.

Nijhof, Kelly. *Explore Internet in Belgium.* Brussels: Best of Publishing, 1966.

*Twintig jaar wettelijk depot. Catalogus*. Brussels: Koninklijke Bibliotheek Albert I, 1986.

## 3. *Guides and Yearbooks*

*Beknopte Gids van de Vlaamse Overheid. Voorjaar 1977*. Brussels: Ministerie van de Vlaamse Gemeenschap. Departement Coördinatie. Administratie Kanselarij en Voorlichting, 1996.

*Gids van de Informatie- en Documentatiecentra van de administraties*. Brussels, Federale Voorlichtingsdienst. (Bi-annual)

*Jaarboek van de haven van Gent/ Annuaire du Port de Gand/ Ghent Port Annual*. Ghent: Vereniging Gentse Zeevaartbelangen, 1966.

*Répertoire des entreprises industrielles wallonnes exportatrices. Directory of the industrial exporting Walloon companies*. Namur: Ministère de la Région wallonne, 1987.

*Repertorium van de Voorlichting*. Brussels, Federale Voorlichtingsdienst (Annual)

*Samenstelling van de Ministeriële Kabinetten*. Brussels, Federale Voorlichtingsdienst. (Bi-annual)

Verleyen, Frans. *Vlaanderen Vandaag*. Tielt: Lannoo, 1985.

*Wegwijs in de federale administratie. Deel 1. De federale ministeries*. Brussels: Federale Voorlichtingsdienst. (Annual)

## 4. *Statistics*

*België in Cijfers*. Brussels, Federale Voorlichtingsdienst, 1997. (Annual)

*Catalogus van de produkten en diensten van het Nationaal Instituut voor de Statistiek. Toestand januari 1996*. Brussels: Ministerie van Economische Zaken, Nationaal Instituut voor de Statistiek, 1996.

*Cijfers 1997. Statistisch overzicht van België*. Brussels: Ministerie van Economische Zaken, Nationaal Instituut voor de Statistiek, 1997. (Annual)

Matthijs, Koen. *Statistisch zakboekje van België*. Brussels en Tielt: Federale Voorlichtigsdienst en Lannoo, 1994.

*Profiel Vlaanderen 1997*. Brussels: Ministerie van de Vlaamse Gemeenschap. Departement Algemene Zaken en Financiën. Administratie Planning en Statistiek, 1997.

*Trefpunt Economie. Macroeconomische gegevens.* Brussels: Ministerie van Economische Zaken. (Monthly).

*Vlaamse Regionale Indicatoren 1996.* Brussels: Ministerie van de Vlaamse Gemeenschap. Departement Algemene Zaken en Financiën. Administratie Planning en Statistiek, 1996.

*Vlaanderen in cijfers.* Brussels: Administratie Planning en Statistiek. Departement Algemene Zaken en Financiën. Ministerie van de Vlaamse Gemeenschap, 1997.

## 5. *Travel and Description*

Abicht, Ludo. "Antwerp, World Port and Provincial City." *The Low Countries. Arts and Society in Flanders and the Netherlands. A Yearbook. 1997-98.* Rekkem: Ons Erfdeel, 1997, pp. 12-20.

Adriaens-Pannier, A. et al. *Museum voor Moderne Kunst.* Brussels: Ludion, 1996. Musea Nostra 36.

*Antwerpen.* Ghent: Snoeck, Ducaju & Zoon, 1992.

*Ardenne. Provence de Namur. Guide Touristique/Toeristische Gids. Attractions-Loisirs/Attracties en Recreatie.* Naninne: Fédération du Tourisme de la Province de Namur, 1997.

*Ardennen. Provincie Namen. Land van Valleien.* Naninne: Fédération du Tourisme de la Province de Namur, 1997.

Baes, Walter et al. *De Praalstoet van de Gouden Boom/Les fastes de l'Arbre d'Or./Der Fustung des goldenen Baumes./The Pageant of the Golden Tree.* Bruges: Herrebout, 1985.

Bachrach, Fred G.H. "The Low Countries through British Eyes in Ages Past." *The Low Countries. Arts and Society in Flanders and the Netherlands. A Yearbook. 1997-98.* Rekkem: Ons Erfdeel, 1997 pp. 61-72.

*Belgium.* Ghent: Snoeck, Ducaju & Zoon, 1994.

Blyth, Derek. *Flemish cities explored. Bruges, Ghent, Antwerp, Mechelen and Brussels.* London: The Bodley Head, 1990.

Briels, Jo. *Belgium/La Belgique/Belgien/België.* Wijnegem: Illustra, 1986.

*Brugge Ondersteboven. De Beste adressen.* Antwerp: New Promotion, 1994.

*Brussels, Capital of Europe.* Ghent: Snoeck, Ducaju & Zoon, 1994.

"Brussels. Belgium." In Bryson, Bill, *Neither Here Nor There. Travels in Europe.* London: Minerva, 1992, pp. 42-50.

"Brussels. Capital with a Difference." *Newcomer. An Introduction to Life in Belgium.* September 1997, 20, pp. 10-14.

Carson, P. *The Fair Face of Flanders.* Ghent: Story-Scientia, 1978.

Carson, Patricia and Gaby Danhieux. *Ghent. Een stad van alle tijden.* Tielt: Lannoo, 1992.

———*Ghent: A Town for All Seasons.* Ghent: Story, 1981.

Clark, Sydney. *All the Best in Belgium and Luxembourg.* New York: Dodd, Mead and Company, 1956.

Claus, Helmut and Rosinne De Dijn. *A Taste of Belgium.* Tielt: Lannoo, 1989.

Costello, Dudley. *A Tour through the Valley of the Meuse with the Legends of the Walloon Country and the Ardennes.* London: Chapman & Hall: 1846.

Decavele, Johan. *Gent: historisch hart van Vlaanderen.* Ghent: Snoeck-Ducaju, 1985.

Decavele, Johan (ed.). *Ghent: in Defence of a Rebellious City: History, Art, Culture.* Translated by Ted Alkins et al. Antwerp: Mercatorfonds, 1989.

De Moor, Paul and Jan Decreton. *Buitengewoon België.* Tielt: Lannoo, 1966.

De Smet, Gaston. *Gent/Gand/Ghent/Gent. Tekeningen/Dessins/Drawings/Zeichnungen.* Ghent: Snoeck-Ducaju & Zoon, 1988.

De Vos, Dirk. *Groeningemuseum Brugge.* Brussels: Ludion, 1996. Musea Nostra 37.

De Wolf, Koenraad. *Architectuurgids Zuid-Oost-Vlaanderen.* Zottegem: Marnixring Sotteghem, 1996.

*Dinant. Fille de Meuse. Guide pratique. Praktische Gids.* Dinant: Syndicat d'Initiative/V.V.V, 1997.

Dorian, Donna. "Antwerp: The cultural capital of 1993, for music, literature, architecture and Rubens." *Art and Antiques,* 15 (1993), May, pp. 52-4.

Dumont, Georges-Henri. *Belgique. Un pays pour toutes les saisons. België. Land van alle getijden. Belgium. A country for all seasons. Belgien. Ein Land für alle Jahreszeiten.* Brussels: Editions Paul Merckx, 1993.

*Fietsen en wandelen in West-Vlaanderen.* St.-Michiels Brugge: Westtoerisme, 1996.

*Flemish Brabant. The Surroundings of Louvain and Brussels*. Leuven: Toeristische Federatie van de Provincie Vlaams-Brabant, 1996.

Fromont, D. *Belgique. België. Belgium. Belgien*. Brussels: Meddens, 1976.

Geerts, Paul. "Loppem castle. Triumph of the Neo Gothic." *Flanders*, September 1977, 35, pp. 35-37.

*Geïllustreerde toeristische gids voor België en het Groothertogdom Luxemburg*. Tielt: Lannoo, 1994.

*Gent*. Ghent: Snoeck, Ducaju & Zoon, 1985.

*Gids toeristische attracties en musea van België 1997*. Brussels: Toerisme Vlaanderen and Office de Promotion du Toerisme Wallonie-Bruxelles, 1997.

Grimme, Ernst Günther. *België. De Kunstschatten van Brussels, Antwerpen, Gent, Brugge, Luik en andere Steden*. De Bilt: Cantecleer, 1975.

*Henegouwen. De groene Provincie*. Mons: Province de Hainaut, 1966.

Herrebout, Jempie et al. *Brugge Binnenste Buiten*. Bruges: Herrebout, 1986.

Klok, R. H. J and F. Brenders. *Reisboek voor Romeins Nederland en België*. Haarlem/Antwerp: Fibula-Van Dishoeck/Standaard Uitgeverij, 1981.

Lemaire, Guy. *Ontdek de Ardennen en andere streken in Wallonië*. Tielt: Lannoo, 1988.

*Limburggids '97*. Hasselt: Toerisme Limburg, 1997.

*Luxembourg belge. General information*. La Roche-en-Ardenne; Fédération Tourististque du Luxembourg Belge, 1997.

*Luxembourg belge. Welkom*. La Roche-en-Ardenne: Fédération Tourististque du Luxembourg Belge, 1997.

Lyon, Margot. *Belgium*. London: Thames and Hudson, 1971.

Marinus, Marie Juliette. "St Anna's Chapel in Antwerp." *The Low Countries. Arts and Society in Flanders and the Netherlands. A Yearbook. 1997-1998*. Rekkem: Ons Erfdeel, 1997, pp. 277-278.

Mason, Anthony. *Brussels. Bruges. Ghent. Antwerp*. London: Globe Pecquot Press, 1995. Cadogan City Guides.

———*The Xenophobe's Guide to the Belgians*. Horsham, West Sussex: Ravette Publishing, 1995.

*Memling in Brugge/à Bruges/in Bruges/in Brügge*. Bruges: Stichting Kunstboek, 1994.

Merckx, Paul. *België-Belgique-Belgium-Belgiën.* Brussels: Federale Voorlichtingsdienst, 1994.

———*Brugge-Bruges-Bruges-Brügge.* Brussels: Federale Voorlichtingsdienst, 1993.

———*Brussel-Bruxelles-Brussels-Brussel.* Brussels: Federale Voorlichtingsdienst, 1994.

———*Kastelen in België.* Brussels: Federale Voorlichtingsdienst, 1994.

———*Steden in België.* Brussels: Federale Voorlichtingsdienst, 1994.

———*Vlaanderen-La Flandre-Flanders-Flandern.* Brussels: Federale Voorlichtingsdienst, 1994.

"On the Waterfront. Ostend: Past, Present, Ships, Shops." *The Bulletin. The Newsweekly of the Capital of Europe,* 1997, 13, pp. 22-31.

Polet, D. *La Wallonie/Wallonië/Wallonia/Walloniën/Valonia.* Brussels: Meddens, 1978.

Pudles, Lynne. "Fernand Khnopff, George Rodenbach, and Bruges, the dead city." *The Art Bulletin,* 74 (1992), December, pp. 637-54.

Robberechts, Wim. *Belgium. A view from the sky.* Bruges: Van de Wiele, 1997.

"The Belgians: the Openminded Opportunists." In: Richard Hill. *We Europeans.* Brussels: Europublications, 1992, pp. 121-131.

*Toeren door België.* Groot-Bijgaarden: Selectief, 1996.

*Tours et promenades en Belgique.* Brussels: Le Soir et Lannoo, 1996.

Van Alsenoy, Jan et al. *A Guided Tour of the City of Antwerp and its Harbour.* Antwerp: Royal Belgian Geographical Society and Publitra, 1996.

Van Den Berg, Bernard and Hanneke. *Reis-handboek voor de Ardennen.* Rijswijk: Elmar, 1993.

Van den Bremt, F. *Sites de Belgique/België's mooiste plekjes/Belgiëns Schönste Flehchen/Belgian finest sites/Parajes de Belgica.* Brussels: Meddens, 1994.

Van Overstraeten, Jozef. *De Nederlanden in Frankrijk. Beknopte Encyclopedie.* Antwerp: Vlaamse Toeristenbond, 1969.

Van Remoortere, J. *De Lesse van bron tot monding. 85,5 km wandelen van Ochamps naar Anseremme. 18 wandelingen langs zijrivieren van de Lesse.* Roeselare/Baarn: Globe/De Fontein, 1996.

———*Gent-Gand-Ghent-Gante.* Brussels: Meddens, 1982.

Van Remoortere, J. *Stadswandelingen door Wallonië. Waver, Couvin, Chimay, La Roche en Ardenne, Nijvel, Bouillon, Saint-Hubert, Malmédy, Virton, Binche, Dinant, Hoei, Luik, Doornik, Durbuy, Namen, Bergen, Eupen, Stavelot, Aarlen.* Soest/Deurne: Uitgeverij Publiboek/Baart, 1985.

Van den Berghe, Stephane. *Gruuthuse Museum Brugge.* Bruges: Die Keure, 1984.

*Vlaanderen.* Ghent: Snoeck, Ducaju & Zoon, 1990.

*Vlaanderen-La Flandre-Flanders-Flandern.* Brussels: Federale Voorlichtingsdienst, 1996.

*Walloon Brabant. Land of Charm and Beauty.* Brussels: Fédération Touristique de la Province de Brabant, 1992.

## *II. CULTURAL*

### *1. General*

Ashworth, G.J. "Language Society and the State in Belgium." *Journal of Area Studies,* 1980, 1, pp. 28-33.

Balthasar, Herman and Jean Stengers (ed.). *Dynastie en Cultuur in België.* Antwerp: Mercatorfonds, 1990.

Boenders, Frans. *Het boek van België. Een controversieel portret van cultureel België.* Hasselt: Heideland-Orbis, 1980.

Bostock, William W. "Recent Developments in Dutch Language Nationalism." *Canadian Review of Studies in Nationalism,* 18 (1991), 1-2, pp. 25-31.

Carson, Patricia. *Flanders in Creative Contrasts.* Leuven and Tielt: Davidsfonds and Lannoo, 1990.

*De bloesems van mijn schaduw. Brieven over cultuur en identiteit.* Antwerp: Epo, 1966.

*De Franse Nederlanden/Les Pays-Bas Français.* Rekkem: Stichting Ons Erfdeel, 1977.

De Jong, Martien J. C. *Vaderland en moederland. Over het Nederlands in de Lage Landen en Europa.* Leuven: Davidsfonds/Clauwaert, 1996.

Deleu, J. *The Low Countries. Arts and Society in Flanders and the Netherlands. A Yearbook, 1993-1994.* Rekkem: Ons Erfdeel, 1993.

———The Low Countries. Arts and Society in Flanders and the Netherlands. A Yearbook, 1994-1995. Rekkem: Ons Erfdeel, 1994.

———*The Low Countries. Arts and Society in Flanders and the Netherlands. A Yearbook, 1996-1997.* Rekkem: Ons Erfdeel, 1996.

Duytschaever, Joris. "Belgium and the Outsider's Perspective." *The Low Countries. Arts and Society in Flanders and the Netherlands. A Yearbook. 1995-96*, Rekkem: Ons Erfdeel, 1994, pp. 301-302.

Eemans, M. *L'art moderne en Belgique.* Brussels: Editions Meddens, 1974.

———*L'art vivant en Belgique.* Brussels: Editions Meddens, 1972.

Fontaine, J. *Culture Wallonne: à la censure répondons 'Résistance'.* Quenast: Le Coq Hardi, 1991.

Fox, René C. *In the Belgian Château. The spirit and Culture of a European Society in an Age of Change.* Chicago: Ivan R. Dee, 1994.

Gipman, S.P.A. *Honderd jaar Nobelprijs voor de literatuur in namen, feiten en cijfers.* Amsterdam: Meulenhoff, 1995.

Lanotte, Jacques. *L'avenir culturel de la communauté française.* Brussels: Editions Jules Destrée, 1979.

Liebaers, Herman et al. (eds.). *Vlaamse kunst van de oorsprong tot heden.* Antwerp: Mercatorfonds, 1985.

Liebaers, Herman and Philippe Jones (eds.) "Culture." In Marina Boudart, Michel Boudart and René Bryssinck, *Modern Belgium.* Palo Alto, California: The Society for the Promotion of Science and Scholarship, 1990, pp. 459-532.

Matthijs, Filip. "A New Encyclopedia of Dutch Art." *The Low Countries. Arts and Society in Flanders and the Netherlands. A Yearbook, 1997-1998.* Rekkem: Ons Erfdeel, 1997, pp. 311.

———"Seventy-five Years of Dutch Studies in London." *The Low Countries. Arts and Society in Flanders and the Netherlands. A Yearbook, 1995-1996.* Rekkem: Ons Erfdeel 1975, pp. 271-272.

Muller, Sheila D. *Dutch Art: An Encyclopedia.* New York/London: Garland Publishing, 1997.

Stiennon, J., J.P. Duchesne and Y. Randaxhe. *De Roger de la Pasture à Paul Delvaux. Cinq siècles de peinture en Wallonie.* Brussels: Lefebvre et Gillet, 1988.

Van Assche, Dirk. "The Dutch Language Union." *The Low Countries. Arts and Society in Flanders and the Netherlands. A Yearbook, 1995-96,* pp. 267-268.

———"The Promotion of Translation in the Netherlands and Flanders." *The Low Countries. Arts and Society in Flanders and the Netherlands. A Yearbook, 1995-96,* pp. 269-270.

Van Dam, Denise. "Wallonië weerspiegeld in zijn musea." *Kultuurleven,* 1991, December.

Van der Horst, J. M. "Brief History of the Dutch language." *The Low Countries. Arts and Society in Flanders and the Netherlands. A Yearbook, 1996-1997,* pp. 163-172.

Van Dijck, Leen. "A Paper Memory. The Archive and Museum of Flemish Culture." *The Low Countries. Arts and Society in Flanders and the Netherlands. A Yearbook, 1995-1996,* pp. 291-292.

Van Hauwermeiren, Paul and Femke Simonis. *Waar Nederlands de voertaal is. Nederland en Vlaanderenkunde.* Brussels: Van In, 1993.

Vermeersch, V. Brugge. *Duizend jaar kunst. Van Karolingisch tot neogotisch 875-1875.* Antwerp: Mercatorfonds, 1981.

Willemyns, R. "The northern connection: Towards the treaty on the Dutch Language Union." *Plural Societies,* 17 (1987), 3, pp. 40-51.

## 2. *Literature*

### *a. Manuscripts and Old Sources*

De Haan, Corrie and Johan Oosterman. *Is Brugge groot?* Amsterdam: Querido, 1996. Griffioen-reeks.

Glorieux-De Gand, Thérèse. *Cisterciënzer Handschriften van de Koninklijke Bibliotheek van België.* Brussels: Koninklijke Bibliotheek van België, 1990.

Nash, Ray. *Calligraphy and Printing in the Sixteenth Century: Dialogue attributed to Christopher Plantin in French and Flemish Facsimile. With English Translation and Notes by Ray Nash.* Foreword by Stanley Morison. Antwerp: The Plantin-Moretus Museum, 1964.

### *b. Literary Translations and Anthologies*

#### *From Flemish*

Aercke, Kristiaan. *Women Writing in Dutch.* New York: Garland,

1994.

Barnouw, Adriaan J. *Coming After: An Anthology of Poetry from the Low Countries*. New Brunswick, N.J.: Rutgers University Press, 1948.

Barnouw, Adriaan J. and E. Colledge. *Reynard the Fox and other Mediaeval Netherlands Secular Literature*. London: Heineman, 1967.

Beekman, E.M. "Modern Dutch Literature." *Shantih*, 2(1973), no. 4.

Boon, Louis Paul. *Chapel Road*. Translated by Adrienne Dixon. New York: Hypocrene, 1991.

Bousset, Hugo and Theo Hermans. "New Flemish Fiction." *The Review of Contemporary Fiction,* 14 (1994), 2, pp. 1-240.

Brems, Hugo. "Seven Woman Poets from the Low Countries. Poems by Miriam van Hee, Elma van Haren, Anneke Brassinga, Anna Enquist, Christine D'Haen, Eva Gerlach and Marieke Jonkman." *The Low Countries. Arts and Society in Flanders and the Netherlands. A Yearbook. 1993-1994*. Rekkem: Ons Erfdeel, 1993, p. 17-24.

Brems, Hugo and Ad Zuiderent. *Contemporary Poetry of the Low Countries*. Rekkem: Ons Erfdeel, 1995.

Brown, Paul and Peter Nijmeijer (eds.). "Modern Dutch Writing" *Chapman*, 2(1974), no. 5-6.

Claus, Hugo. "Back Home" and "The Life and Works of Leopold II." Translated by David Willinger and Luk Truyts. In David Willinger (ed.), *An Anthology of Contemporary Belgian Plays 1970-82*. New York: Troy, 1984.

———"The Lieutenant." Translated by J. S. Holmes and Hans van Marle. *Delta*, 6 (1964), pp. 63-72.

———*Four Works for the Theatre*. Translated by David Willinger, Luk Truyts and Luc Deneulin. New York: CASTA, 1990. CASTA plays in translation. Belgian Series.

———*Friday*. Translated by David Willinger and Lucas Truyts. Amsterdam: International Theatre and Film Books, 1993. Theatre in Translation.

———'In a harbour.' Translated by Jane Fenoulhet et al. *Dutch Crossing,* 14, July 1981, pp. 36-48.

———*The Sign of the Hamster*. Translated by Paul Claus et al. Leuven: Leuvense Schrijversaktie Kessel-Lo, 1986. European series. Louvain cahiers 65.

———*The Sorrow of Belgium*. Translated by Arnold J. Pomerans. Harmondsworth: Penguin, 1990.

———*The Sorrow of Belgium*. London: Viking, 1990; New York, Pantheon: 1990.

———*The Swordfish*. Translated and introduced by Ruth Levitt. London/Paris: Owen/Unesco Publications, 1996.

Colledge, E. (ed.). *Reynard the Fox and Other Secular Literature*. London: Heineman, 1967.

Decorte, Bert et al. (eds.). *A Bouquet of 50 Dutch Poems*. Bruges: Orion, 1975.

*Dedalus Books of Dutch Fantasy*. Translated by Richard Huijing. Sawtry: Dedalus, 1993.

De Ke, Andre. *A Safe Place*. Translated by Leon Meersseman and Arnold Strobbe. Roseville-Detroit: Belgian, 1993.

Elsschot, Willem. *Villa des roses*. Translated by P. Vincent. London: Penguin Books, 1992.

Fokkema, R. L. K. (ed.). *Writing in Holland and Flanders*. Amsterdam: Foundation of the Promotion of the Translation of Dutch Literary Work, s.d.

Gilliams, Maurice. *Elias or the Struggle with the Nightingales*. Translated by André Lefevere. Los Angeles: Sun and Moon Press, 1995.

Goedegebuure, Jaap and Anne Marie Musschoot. *Contemporary Fiction of the Low Countries*. Rekkem: Ons Erfdeel, 1995.

Hopkins, Konrad and Ronald van Roekel. *Quartet. An Anthology of Dutch and Flemish Poetry*. Judith Herzberg, Arie van den Berg, Patricia Lasoen, Eddy Van Vliet. Paisley (Scotland): Wilfion Books, 1978. The Genius of the Low Countries. Vol 1.

Joris, Lieve. *Back to Congo*. Translated by S. Knecht. London: Macmillan, 1992.

———*The Gates from Damascus*. Translated by Sam Garrett. Melbourne: Lonely Planet, 1996.

Korteweg, Anton and Frits Niessen. "Fresh Food. Ten young Poets from Flanders and the Netherlands. Poems by Henk van der Waal, Marc Reugebrink, Peter van Lier, René Huigen, Peter Verhelst, Bernard Dewulf, Rogi Wieg, Peter Ghyssaert, Jo Gevaerts and Mustafa Stitou." *The Low Countries. Arts and Society in Flanders and the Netherlands. A Yearbook, 1997-1998*. Rekkem: Ons Erfdeel, 1997, pp. 103-107.

———"Hardy Perennials of Dutch and Flemish Poetry. Poems by Karel van de Woestijne, Richard Minne, Paul van Ostaijen, Willem Elsschot et al." *The Low Countries. Arts and Society in Flanders and the Netherlands. A Yearbook, 1995-96.* Rekkem: Ons Erfdeel, 1995, pp. 68-75.

Kuin, R. (ed.). "Dutch Poetry Supplement." *Carcanet*, 1963.

*Mariken van Nieumeghen: a Bilingual Edition.* Translated by Therese Decker and Martin W. Walsh. Columbia, S.C.: Camden House, 1994.

McKinnell, John (ed.). *Mary of Nemmegem.* S.l.: Medieval English Theatre, 1993.

Meijer, R. P and P. Nijmeijer (eds.). *Postwar Dutch and Flemish Poetry.* Poetry Australia, 1974, 52.

Michiels, Ivo. *Book Alpha and Ochis Militaris.* Translated by Adrienne Dixon. Boston, Mass.,1979.

Nijmejer, Peter (ed.). *Four Flemish Poets.* London: Transgravity Press, 1976.

Peleman, Bert (ed.). *Vuurwerk voor Vlaanderen.* Deurne-Antwerp: MIM, 1980. Flandria Aeterna.

Snoek, Paul. *In the Sleep Trap.* New Malden: Tangent Books, 1977.

Snoek, Paul, Willem M. Roggeman and Eugène van Itterbeek (eds.). *A Quarter Century of Poetry from Belgium (Een kwarteeuw poëzie uit Belgie).* Brussels/The Hague: Manteau, 1970.

Stillman, Clark. *The Flemish Poet Karel van de Woestijne.* Boston: Poet Lore, 1941.

Stillman, Clark and Frances. *Lyra Belgica. Vol. 1. Guido Gezelle. Karel van de Woestijne. Vol. 2. Emile Verhaeren. Charles van Lerberghe. Maurice Maeterlinck. Max Elskamp.* New York: Belgian Government Information Center, 1950. Art, life and science in Belgium, 18.

Swepstone, Maude. *Guido Gezelle (1830-1899): Selections from his Poems.* Translated into English from the Flemish by Maude Swepstone; with a short account of his life. Bristol: Burleigh Press, 1937.

Van de Kamp, Peter and Frank van Meurs. *Turning Tides: Modern Dutch and Flemish Verse in English Verses by Irish Poets.* Introduction by Theo D'haen. Bownsville Ore: Story Line Press, 1994.

Van Ostaijen, Paul. *Feasts of Fear and Agony.* Translated by Hilde van Ameyen van Duym. New York/Toronto: New York Directions, 1976.

———*Homage to Singer and Other Poems.* London: Transgravity Press, 1976.

———*Patriotism and Other Tales.* Translated by E.M. Beekman. Amherst, 1971.

———*The First Book of Schmoll. Selected Poems, 1920-1928.* Translated by Theo Hermans, James S. Holmes and Paul Vincent. Amsterdam, 1982.

Van Ruusbroec, Jan. *Adornment of a Spiritual Marriage; Sparkling Stone: the Book of Supreme Truth.* Translated by C.A. Wynschenk. S.l.: Llanerch Publishers, 1994.

———*Flowers of a Mystic Garden.* Translated by C.E.S. Felinfach. S.l.: Llanerch Publishers, 1994.

Van Vliet, Eddy. *Farewell and Fall.* Translated by Matthew Blake et al. Dublin: Dedalus Press, 1994.

Weisbort, David (ed.). "Dutch." *Modern Poetry in Translation,* 1976, no. 27-28.

Willinger, David (ed.). *An Anthology of Contemporary Belgian Plays 1970-82.* New York: Troy, 1984.

Wolf, Manfred. *Ten Flemish Poems.* Berkeley, California: Twowindows Press, 1972.

———*The Shape of Houses: Women's Voices from Holland and Flanders.* Berkeley, California: Twowindows Press, 1976.

Wolf, Manfred (ed.). *Change of Scene: Contemporary Dutch and Flemish Poems in English Translation.* Berkeley, California: Twowindows Press, 1969.

*From French*

Bourgeois, Pierre and Fernand Verhesen. *A Quarter Century of Poetry from Belgium in the Original Text and with the English Translation (Un quart de siècle de poésie française de Belgique).* Brussels: Published for the Manteau and the Maison internationale de la Poésie, 1970.

*c. Literary Criticism*

*Dutch*

Beekman, E.M. *Homeopathy of the Absurd: The Grotesque in Paul van Ostaijen's Creative Prose.* The Hague, 1970.

Borré, Jos. "Looking for the Other Self. The Work of Kristien Hemmerechts. Extract from 'Back' by Kristien Hemmerechts." *The Low Countries. Arts and Society in Flanders and the Netherlands. A Yearbook, 1995-96*. Rekkem: Ons Erfdeel, 1995, pp. 208-216.

Brems, Hugo. "Ah, the Comfort of a Comparison. The Poetry of Herman the Coninck. Five Poems by Herman de Coninck." *The Low Countries. Arts and Society in Flanders and the Netherlands. A Yearbook, 1995-96*. Rekkem: Ons Erfdeel, 1995, pp. 212-219.

———"'Good and Bad have been Reduced to the Same Thing'. The Poetry of Charles Ducal. Four Poems by Charles Ducal." *The Low Countries. Arts and Society in Flanders and the Netherlands. A Yearbook, 1995-96*. Rekkem: Ons Erfdeel, 1995, pp. 143-147.

Burger, P. Jacob van Maerlant. *Het boek der Natuur*. Amsterdam: Querido, 1989.

Buyck, Jean F. "Paul van Ostaijen (1896-1928) in an International Context." *Flanders*, 1996, 31, pp. 4-9.

Claes, Paul. "Claus the Chameleon. 'I'd like to sing you a song' by Hugo Claus." *The Low Countries. Arts and Society in Flanders and the Netherlands. A Yearbook, 1993-1994*. Rekkem, Ons Erfdeel, 1993, pp. 17-24.

Couttenier, Piet. "'O, this is a place!' Aspects of the English World of Guido Gezelle. 'The Evening and the Rose' by Guido Gezelle." *The Low Countries. Arts and Society in Flanders and the Netherlands. A Yearbook, 1993-1994*. Rekkem: Ons Erfdeel, 1993, pp. 137-143.

De Ceulaer, José. "Bibliografie der werken van Felix Timmermans," *Dietsche Warande & Belfort,* 1947, 5, pp. 306-309.

Dirkx, Paul. "La presse littéraire Parisienne et 'les amis Belges,' (1944-60)." *Actes de la Recherche en Sciences Sociales,* 1996, 111-112, pp. 110-121.

Duytschaever, Joris. "Willem Elsschot. Villa des Roses." *The Low Countries. Arts and Society in Flanders and the Netherlands. A Yearbook, 1993-1994*. Rekkem, Ons Erfdeel, 1993, pp. 286-288.

Geys, Rita. "Een ten onrechte al te zeer vergeten man. Jos Joosten over 'Tijd en Mens en de vernieuwende rol van Jan Walravens.'" *Standaard der Letteren,* 26 December, 1996, pp. 11-12.

Guest, Tanis M. *Some aspects of Hadewijch's Poetic Form in the 'Strofische Gedichten.'* The Hague: Nijhoff, 1975.

Gysseling, M. *Corpus van Middelnederlandse teksten, reeks 2: literaire handschriften, dl. 3, De Rijmbijbel.* The Hague: Nijhoff,

1983, pp. 149-159.

Hadermann, Paul. "From the Message to the Medium. The poetic evolution of Paul van Ostaijen." *The Low Countries. Arts and Society in Flanders and the Netherlands. Yearbook, 1993-1994.* Rekkem: Ons Erfdeel, 1993, pp. 254-262.

Hogenelst, D. and F. Van Oostrom. *Handgeschreven wereld. Nederlandse literatuur en cultuur in de Middeleeuwen.* Amsterdam: Prometheus, 1995.

Jacob van Maerlant. *Spiegel Historiael.* Leuven; Davidsfonds/Clauwaert, 1977.

Joosten, Jos. *Feit en tussenkomst. Geschiedenis en opvattingen van Tijd en Mens (1949-1955).* Nijmegen: Vantilt, 1996.

———*Tom Lanoye. De onbereikendheid van het abstracte.* Nijmegen en Antwerp: Sun en Kritak, 1996.

"Klemmen voor Koorddanser. Henri-Floris Jespers over gaston Bursens." *Revolver*, 24 (1997), 2, Oktober.

Lovelock, Yann. "Total Writing. An Anthology of New Flemish Fiction." *The Low Countries. Arts and Society in Flanders and the Netherlands. A Yearbook, 1995-1996.* Rekkem: Ons Erfdeel, 1995, pp. 286-287.

Martens, J. "Lucifer en het wereldbeeld van Vondel." *Nova et Vetera,* 71 (1994), 5, pp. 356-374.

Meijer, Reinder P. *Literature of the Low Countries.* Assen: Van Gorcum and Co., 1971.

Mertens, Anthony. "Postmodern Elements in Postwar Dutch Fiction." In: D'Haen, Theo and Hans Bertens. *Postmodern Fiction in Europe and the America's.* Amsterdam/Antwerp: s.e, 1988.

Musschoot, Anne Marie. "In Search of Self. New Prose Writing in Dutch after 1985. Extracts by Connie Palmen, Arnon Grunberg, Eric de Kuyper, Stefan Hertmans and Adriaan van Dis." *The Low Countries. Arts and Society in Flanders and the Netherlands. A Yearbook, 1997-1998.* Rekkem: Ons Erfdeel, 1977, pp. 90-102.

———"Postmodernism in the Literature of the Low Countries." *The Low Countries. Arts and Society in Flanders and the Netherlands. A Yearbook, 1993-1994.* Rekkem: Ons Erfdeel, 1993, pp. 69-74

———"The Challenge of Postmodernism." *Dutch Crossing,* 41, Summer 1990, pp. 3-15.

Peeters, L. "Hinrek van Alckmer and Medieval Tradition. The Reynardian Interpretation of a Man and his World." *Marche Romans*, 29 (1978), pp. 89-110.

Pleij, Herman. "Reynard the Fox. The Triumph of the Individual in a Beast Epic. Extract from 'Reynard the Fox.'" *The Low Countries. Arts and Society in Flanders and the Netherlands. A Yearbook, 1995-96.* Rekkem: Ons Erfdeel, 1995, pp. 233-239.

Reynebeau, Marc. "The King is Dead. Long Live the King. The Uses of Reality in the Prose of Walter van den Broeck. Extract from 'Letter to Baudouin' by Walter van den Broeck." *The Low Countries. Arts and Society in Flanders and the Netherlands. A Yearbook, 1997-98.* Rekkem: Ons Erfdeel, 1997, pp. 84-89.

Seymour-Smith, Martin. *Guide to Modern World Literature.* Vol 2. London: Hodder and Stoughton, 1975.

Struyker Boudier, C. E. M. "Cirkelen om de Wereld...Uitzichten, inzichten, Doorzichten in Actuele Literatuur in België en Nederland." *Tijdschrift voor Filosofie,* 59 (1995), 3, pp. 553-569.

Van Elslander, A. "Literature." In Johan Decavele. *Ghent. In Defence of a Rebellious City. History, Art, Culture.* Antwerp: Mercatorfonds, 1989, pp. 397-417.

Van Oostrom, Frits Pieter. *Maerlants Wereld.* Amsterdam: Prometheus, 1996.

———*Court and Culture: Dutch Literatue 1350-1450.* Translated by Arnold J. Pomerans, with a foreword by James H. Marrow. Berkeley, Los Angeles/Oxford: University of California Press, 1992.

Wackers, P. "The Use of Fables in Reynaerts Historie." *Niederdeutsche Studien,* 30 (1991), pp. 461-484.

Weisberger, Jean. "Dutch-Language Literature." In Marina Boudart, Michel Boudart and René Bryssinck. *Modern Belgium.* Palo Alto, California: The Society for the Promotion of Science and Scholarship, 1990, pp. 478-486.

Wolf, Manfred. "The Rustling of Clothes. The Poetry of Eddy van Vliet." *The Low Countries. Arts and Society in Flanders and the Netherlands. A Yearbook, 1995-1996.* Rekkem: Ons Erfdeel, 1995 pp. 288-289.

*French*

Andrianne, René. *Ecrire en Belgique.* Brussels: Editions Labor, 1983.

Detemmerman, Jacques and Jean Lacroix. *Trois-quarts de siècle de lettres françaises en Belgique.* Brussels: Bibliothèque royale Albert

Ier, 1995.
Gothot-Mersch, Claudine. *Lire Simenon.* Brussels: Editions Labor, 1981.
Linkhorn, Renée (ed.). *La Belgique telle qu'elle s'écrit. Perspectives sur les lettres belges de langue française.* New York: Peter Lang, 1996. Belgian Francophone Library 4.
"Littératures contemporaires. Spécial Belgique." *Prétexte (Paris),* 1996, 10.
Sion, Georges. "French-Language Literature." In: Marina Boudart, Michel Boudart and René Bryssinck. *Modern Belgium.* Palo Alto, California: The Society for the Promotion of Science and Scholarship, 1990, pp. 463-477.
Wouters, Liliane. *Alphabet des lettres belges de langue française.* Brussels: Association pour la promotion des Lettres belges de langue française, 1982.

*Walloon*

Bal, W. *Maquet, Albert, Littérature dialectale de Wallonie.* Liège: Société de langue et de littérature Wallonnes, 1986.
Piron, Maurice. *Anthologie de la littérature wallonne.* Liège: Editions Pierre Mardaga, 1979.

*3. Linguistics*

*a. Old Flemish*

Van Kerckvoorde, Colette M. *An Introduction to Middle Dutch.* Berlin/New York: De Gruyter, 1993.

*b. Modern Dutch*

Aarts, F. G. A. M. *Contrastive Grammar of English and Dutch.* Leiden: Nijhoff, 1987.
Aarts, Flor and Eric Kellerman. *Translations: A Parallel-text Practice Book for Dutch Students of English.* Utrecht: Bohn, Scheltema en Holkema, 1983.

Aarts, Flor and Theo van Els (eds.). *Contemporary Dutch Linguistics* Washington, D. C.: Georgetown University Press, 1990.

Aarts, F. G. A. M and H. Chr. Wekker. *A Contrastive Grammar of English and Dutch/Contrastieve grammatica Engels - Nederlands.* Groningen: Nijhoff, 1993.

Brachin, P. *The Dutch Language. A Survey.* Leiden: Brill, 1985.

Collins, Beverley and Inger Mees. *Articulatory Setting in English, Danish and Dutch and the Implications for Second Language Acquisition.* Leiden: Rijksuniversiteit te Leiden, Vakgroep Engels, 1993. Dutch working papers in English language and linguistics, 29.

———*The Sounds of English and Dutch.* Leiden: Leiden University Press, 1984.

———*Working with the Sounds of English and Dutch.* Leiden: Brill, 1982.

De Schutter, G. and P. Van Hauwermeiren. *De structuur van het Nederlands. Taalbeschouwelijke grammatica.* Malle: De Sikkel, 1983.

Donaldson, B.C. *Dutch: A Linguistic History of Holland and Belgium.* Leiden: Nijhoff, 1983.

Donaldson, Bruce C. *Dutch Reference Grammar.* Leiden: Nijhoff, 1987.

Hermans, Theo. "Studying 'Single Dutch'? What next?! Dutch Studies in the Anglophone World." *The Low Countries. Arts and Society in Flanders and the Netherlands. A Yearbook, 1993-1994.* Rekkem: Ons Erfdeel, 1995, pp. 204-211.

Klep, Hanneke and Dick Rietveld. *Concise Dutch Grammar.* Groningen: Wolters-Noordhoff, 1992.

König, Ekkehard and Johan Van Der Auwera (eds.). *The Germanic Languages.* London/New York: Routledge, 1994.

Kooper-Erik (ed.). *This Noble Craft. . . : Proceedings of the Xth Research Symposium of the Dutch and Belgian University Teachers of Old and Middle English and Historical Linguistics.* Utrecht, 19-20 January, 1989. Amsterdam: Atlanta, 1991.

Kruyt, J.G. "Language databases for Dutch." *The Low Countries. Arts and Society in Flanders and the Netherlands. A Yearbook, 1996-1997.* Rekkem: Ons Erfdeel, 1996, pp. 279-280.

Lernout, Jo. "Multilingual Speech Technology from West Flanders." *The Low Countries. Arts and Society in Flanders and the Netherlands. A Yearbook, 1995-1996.* Rekkem: Ons Erfdeel, 1995, pp.

283-284.

Putseys, Y. "On duration measuring in Dutch and Flemish." *Foundations of Language,* 11 (1974), pp. 273-280.

Van Soest, Annette. *One Language, Many Voices. Literature from Flanders and the Netherlands, Guest at the '1997 Gotherberg Book Fair' from October 30th to November 2nd.* Flanders, September 1997, 35, pp. 20-21.

Vandeputte, O., P. Vincent and T. Hermans. *Dutch. The language of Twenty Million Dutch and Flemish people.* Rekkem: Ons Erfdeel, 1996.

Wekker, H. Chr., F. G. A. M. Aarts and H. W. A. J. Verhulst. *A Contrastive Grammar of English and Dutch: Workbook.* Groningen: Nijhoff, 1993.

Westerweel, Bart and Theo D'haen (eds.). *Something Understood: Studies in Anglo-Dutch Literary Translation.* Amsterdam/Atlanta: Rodopi, 1990. Dutch Quarterly Review Studies in Literature 5.

*c. Dutch Dictionaries*

Donaldson, Bruce C. *Beyond the Dictionary in Dutch: A Guide to Correct Word Usage for the English-speaking Student.* Muiderberg: Coutinho, 1990.

Van Der Sijs, Nicoline. *Leenwoordenboek. De invloed van andere talen op het Nederlands.* Den Haag, SDU uitgevers, 1996.

*4. Theater, Film, Music, Dance and Folk Arts*

*Belgische bibliografie. Belgische muziektijdschriften 1833-1985/Bibliographie de Belgique. Périodiques musicaux belges 1833-1985.* Brussels: Koninklijke Bibliotheek Albert I, 1987.

Bobkova, Hana. "'Big Black Holes with the Glittering of Diamonds.' Theatre According to Ivo van Hove." *The Low Countries. Arts and Society in Flanders and the Netherlands. A Yearbook, 1997-1998. Rekkem: Ons Erfdeel, 1997,* pp. 276-277.

Bossuyt, Ignace. *De Vlaamse polyfonie.* Leuven: Davidsfonds, 1994.

———"The Art of Give and Take. Musical Relations Between England and Flanders from the 15th to the 17th Centuries." *The Low Countries. Arts and Society in Flanders and the Netherlands. A*

*Yearbook, 1993-1994.* Rekkem: Ons Erfdeel, 1993, pp. 39-50.

Briers, Jan. "The Flanders Festival International." *Flanders*, September 1977, 35, pp. 31-33.

De Decker, Jacques. "Theater, Dance and Cinema." In Marina Boudart, Marina, Michel Boudart and René Bryssinck. *Modern Belgium.* Palo Alto, California: The Society for the Promotion of Science and Scholarship, 1990, pp. 508-513.

*De Koningin Elisabeth wedstrijd.* Brussels: Federale Voorlichtingsdienst, 1988.

Delaere, M. "Goeyvaerts, Karel, a Belgian Pioneer of Serial, Electronic and Minimal Music." *Tempo,* 195 (January 1996), pp. 2-5.

Demets, Paul. "A General of Beauty. The work of Jan Fabre." *The Low Countries. Arts and Society in Flanders and the Netherlands. A Yearbook, 1995-96.* Rekkem: Ons Erfdeel, 1995, pp. 117-125.

Devoldere, Luc. "The Royal Carillon School in Mechelen. Chimes from Flanders." *The Low Countries. Arts and Society in Flanders and the Netherlands. A Yearbook, 1997-1998.* Rekkem: Ons Erfdeel, 1997, p. 292.

Head, Anne. *A True Love for Cinema: Jacques Ledoux: Curator of the Royal Film Archive and Film Museum of Belgium, 1948-1988.* Rotterdam: Universitaire Pers Rotterdam, 1988.

Huys, Bernard. *Catalogue des partitions musicales éditées en Belgique et acquises par la Bibliothèque royale Albert Ier, 1966-1975/ Catalogus van de muziekpartituren in België uitgegeven en verworven door de Koninklijke Bibliotheek Albert I, 1966-1975.* Brussels: Bibliothèque royale Albert Ier/Koninklijke Bibliotheek Albert I, 1976. Bibliographie de Belgique : fasc. spécial; *5.

———"Music in Flanders." In Marina Boudart, Michel Boudart and René Bryssinck. *Modern Belgium.* Palo Alto, California: The Society for the Promotion of Science and Scholarship, 1990, pp. 514-520.

Knockaert, Yves. "New Music in Flanders." *Flanders*, 1996, 32, pp. 8-12.

*Koninklijke Muntschouwburg.* Brussels: Federale Voorlichtingsdienst, 1988.

Korteweg, Ariejan. "The Great Leap Forward. Dance in the Low Countries: The Advantage of a Lack of Tradition." *The Low Countries. Arts and Society in Flanders and the Netherlands. A Yearbook, 1993-1994.* Rekkem: Ons Erfdeel, 1993, pp. 111-117.

Lenoir, Yves. *Grétry Documenten in de verzamelingen van de*

*Koninklijke Bibliotheek Albert I.* Brussels: Koninklijke Bibliotheek Albert I, 1989.

Marshall, Kimberly. *Iconographical Evidence for the Late-Medieval Organ in French, Flemish, and English Manuscripts.* New York/ London: Garland, 1989. Outstanding dissertations in music from British Universities 2.

*Muziekgids van Vlaanderen/Guide musical de la Flandre/Musikfuhrer für Flandern/Musical guide of Flanders. 1986.* Brussels: Stuurgroep van de Vlaamse Gemeenschap voor het Europese Jaar van de Muziek, 1986.

Ruyters, Marc. "Dominique Deruddere, a Flemish Anglophile." The *Low Countries. Arts and Society in Flanders and the Netherlands. A Yearbook, 1995-96.* Rekkem: Ons Erfdeel, 1995, pp. 276-278.

Sion-Georges. *La malle de Pamela: comédie en cinq actes.* English adaptation by John L. Brown. *Key to my heart.* Brussels: Perrin, 1956. The Belgian theatre 2.

Swaen, Michiel de. *La botte couronnée: farce flamande du XVIIe siècle/The boot beneath the crown: 17th century Flemish farce/ Adaptation française de Charles Mahieu et Charles Desbonnets. English adaptation by Robert Vetter.* Brussels: Le Cabestan, 1960. Le théâtre belge 5.

Van Assche, Dirk. "Dance in Flanders." *The Low Countries. Arts and Society in Flanders and the Netherlands. A Yearbook, 1997-1998.* Rekkem: Ons Erfdeel, 1997, p. 275.

Van Keymeulen, Karel. "Jazz. Alive and Swinging in Flanders Too." *Flanders*, 1977, 33, pp. 21-25.

Vantyghem, Peter. "Rock in Flanders. An Ongoing Story." *Flanders*, September 1997, 35, pp. 22-25.

Verstockt, Katie. "Wim Vandekeybus and the Answer of Body Language." *The Low Countries. Arts and Society in Flanders and the Netherlands. A Yearbook, 1995-96.* Rekkem: Ons Erfdeel, 1995, pp. 274-275.

Wangermée, Robert. "Music in Wallonia and Brussels." In Marina Boudart, Michel Boudart and René Bryssinck. *Modern Belgium.* Palo Alto, California: The Society for the Promotion of Science and Scholarship, 1990, pp. 521-526.

Wangermée, Robert and P. Mercier (ed.). *La Musique en Wallonie et à Bruxelles.* Brussels: La renaissance du Livre, 1980-1982.

Willaert, Hendrik. "The Splendour of Flemish Polyphony." *The Low Countries. Arts and Society in Flanders and the Netherlands. A*

*Yearbook, 1995-96.* Rekkem: Ons Erfdeel, 1955, pp. 293-294.

*5. Architecture*

Acerboni, Francesca. "Le Corbusier: Maison Guiette. Antwerp." *Abitare*, April 1995, 339, pp. 144-52.

Aubry, Françoise. *Horta*. Aalst: Ludion, 1996.

———*Victor Horta in Brussel.* Tielt: Lannoo, 1966.

Bekaert, Geert. "Bob van Reeth and the Demands of Architecture." *The Low Countries. Arts and Society in Flanders and the Netherlands. A Yearbook, 1995-96.* Rekkem: Ons Erfdeel, 1995, pp. 148-152.

———"Henry van de Velde, a European Artist." *The Low Countries. Arts and Society in Flanders and the Netherlands. A Yearbook, 1993-94.* Rekkem: Ons Erfdeel, 1993, pp. 265-266.

———*Sea Trade Center Zeebrugge. Rem Koolhaes, Fuhimiko Maki, Aldo Rossi, Charles Vandenhove, Bob van Reeth.* Antwerp: Standaard Uitgeverij, 1990.

———"The Cathedral of Our Lady in Antwerp." *The Low Countries. Arts and Society in Flanders and the Netherlands. A Yearbook, 1993-94.* Rekkem: Ons Erfdeel, 1993, pp. 266-267.

Bekaert, Geert and Marc Dubois. *Architetti (della Fiandra)/ Architects (from Flanders).* Brussels: Ministerie van de Vlaamse Gemeenschap & Stichting Architectuurmuseum, 1991.

Demey, Anthony and Nico Van Campenhout. *Architectuur te Lokeren tussen 1890 en 1914.* Ghent: Provinciebestuur Oost-Vlaanderen, 1992.

De Meyer, Ronny, Frank Adriaensen and Jef Vanreusel. *Omtrent het Antwerpse Zuid.* Brussels: Koning Boudewijnstichting en Gemeentekrediet, 1993 (with English summary).

*De Stad in Woorden. De Gebouwen.* Brussels: Archives d'Architecture Moderne, 1997.

*De Stad in Woorden. Straten en Buurten.* Brussels: Archives d'Architecture Moderne, 1997.

Dierkens-Aubry, Françoise and Jos Vandenbreeden. *Art Nouveau in Belgium: Architecture & Interior Design.* English translation by Helen Swallow. Paris/ Tielt: Duculot/Lanno, 1991.

Doutriaux, Emmanuel. "La nouvelle generation: La maison seule, tableau de la jeune architecture flamande." *L'Architecture-d'Au-*

*jourd'hui*. April 1994, 292, pp. 78-85.
"Flandre: 10 article special section." *L'Architecture-d'Aujourd'hui*. April, 1994, 292, pp. 78-115.
Foucart, Bruno et al. *Prix Européen de la Reconstruction de la ville/ European Award for the Reconstruction of the City*. Brussels: Foundation pour l'Architecture, 1992.
Gaillemin, Jean-Louis. "Une sobre modernité: Latest building by M. Corbiau, Antwerp, Belgium." *Connaissance des Arts,* December 1994, 512, pp. 62-69.
Geerts, Paul. "Loppem Castle. Triumph of the Neo Gothic." *Flanders*, September 1997, 35, pp. 34-37.
Genicot, L.F. and H. Van Liefferinge. "De romaanse bouwkunst in het Zuiden, 1000-1150." In *Algemene Geschiedenis der Nederlanden*. Utrecht: Fibula-Van Dishoeck, 1982, pp. 277-288.
Goedleven, Edgard. *Het Martelaarsplein te Brussel*. Tielt: Lannoo, 1996.
*Jaarboek Architectuur Vlaanderen 1990-1993/ Yearbook Architecture Flanders 1990-1993. Annuaire Architecture Flandre 1990-1993*. Brussels: Ministerie van de Vlaamse Gemeenschap/ Ministry of the Flemish Community/ Ministère de la Communauté flamande, 1994.
Liebaut, Eugeen. "Art center." *L'Architecture-d'Aujourd'hui*. April 1994, 292, pp. 86-89.
Loze, Pierre, Dominique Vautier and Marina Festre. *Guide de Bruxelles/ XIXième Art Nouveau*. Brussels: Eifel Editions & C.F.C Editions, 1990.
Loze, Pierre and Marc Detiffe. *AUSIA/Michel Benoit & Thierry Verbist/Architectures*. Brussels: Didier Hatier, 1990.
Loyer, François. *Dix ans d'Art Nouveau - Ten years of Art Nouveau/ Paul Hankar*. Brussels, CFC & Archives d'Architecture Moderne, 1991.
Mari, Bartomeu. "Personal gardens of two Belgian landscape architects." *Domus*, July/August 1994, 762 pp. 70-74.
Mertens, Joseph. "The Church of Saint Donatian at Bruges." In Galbert of Bruges, *The Murder of Charles the Good, Count of Flanders*. Translated by James Bruce Ross. New York: Harper and Row, 1967, pp. 318-320.
Paysages. *Vision contemporaire/ Landschappen. Hedendaagse visie*. Brussels: Gemeentekrediet, 1991.
Peleman, Bert (red.). *Kastelen in Vlaanderen/ Chateaux en Flandre/ Schlösser in Flandern/ Castles in Flanders. Deel I.* Antwerp:

Buschmann, 1971. Flandria Illustrata 3.
Powel, Kenneth. *Sir Norman Foster and Partners/ Recente stedebouwkundige ontwerpen.* Antwerp: Desingel, 1993.
Simons, Walter et al. *Het Pand/Acht eeuwen geschiedenis van het oud Dominicanenklooster te Gent.* Tielt: Lanno, 1990.
Strauwen, Francis. *Jos. Bascourt 1863-1927/ Art Nouveau in Antwerpen/à Anvers/ in Antwerp.* Brussels: Archives d'Architecture Moderne en Ministerie van de Vlaamse Gemeenschap, 1993.
Tsinlias, George. "Victor Horta: The Maison Tassel: The Sources of its Development." *Canadian Journal of Netherlandic Studies,* 6 (1985), 2, pp. 28-59.
Uytterhoeven, Rik. *Het Begijnhof van Leuven.* Leuven: Davidsfonds, 1996.
Van Cleven, Jean. "The Gothic Revival in Britain and Belgium." *The Low Countries. Arts and Society in Flanders and the Netherlands. A Yearbook, 1995-1996. Rekkem: Ons Erfdeel, 1995,* pp. 268-270.
Van Hee, José. "Shop and Apartment." *L'Architecture d'Aujourd'-hui,* April 1994, 292, pp. 100-103.
"Van Reeth and Groupe AWG." *L'Architecture-d'Aujourd'hui,* April 1994, 292, pp. 110-11.
Van Remoortere, Julien. "Belfries in Flanders." *Flanders*, 1997, 36, pp. 33-37.
Welsh, John. "Glass Walls: A New Flemish School? A Villa near Antwerp." *RIBA-Journal,* September 1993, 100, pp. 58-63.

6. *Sculpture, Painting, Photography and Comic Strips*

*Jaarboek 1996 van het Koninklijk Museum voor Schone Kunsten te Antwerpen.* Antwerp: Koninklijk Museum voor Schone Kunsten, 1996.
*A. W. Finch 1854-1930.* Brussels: Gemeentekrediet, 1992.
Andries, Pool. "The Provincial Museum of Photography in Antwerpen. A Place for Photography." *Flanders*, 1997, 36, pp. 28-32.
Arnould, Alain and Jean-Michel Massing. *Splendours of Flanders. Late Medieval Art in Cambridge.* Cambridge and Brussels: Cambridge University Press and Gemeentekrediet, 1993.
Assouline, Pierre. *Hergé.* Paris: Plon, 1995.
———*Hergé. Biografie.* Amsterdam/Leuven: Meulenhoff/Kritak, 1996.

Bekkers, Ludo and Elly Steveman. *Contemporary Paintings of the Low Countries*. Rekkem: Ons Erfdeel, 1995.

Block, Jane. *Les XX and Belgian Avant-Gardism, 1868-1894.* Ann Arbor: UMI Research, 1984.

Boyens, Piet. *Flemish Art: Symbolism to Expressionism.* Tielt: Lannoo/Art Book Company, 1992.

Bracke, Eric. "Domestic Bliss and Excruciating Pain. The Life and Art of Rik Wouters." *The Low Countries. Arts and Society in Flanders and the Netherlands. A Yearbook, 1995-1996.* Rekkem: Ons Erfdeel, 1995, pp. 96-104.

Brakman, Willem. *Het groen van Delvaux.* Amsterdam: Querido, 1996.

Carrier, David. "Naturalism and Allegory in Flemish Painting." *Journal of Aesthetics and Art Criticism."* 45 (Spring 1987), pp. 237-249.

Châtelet, André. *Robert Campin, De Meester van Flémalle.* Antwerp: Mercatorfonds, 1996.

Cleary, Fritz. "Manneken Pis." *Sculpture Review,* 36 (1987), 3, p. 13.

D'Allones, Revault. "L'enseignement et la recherche en esthétique dans le monde." *Revue d'esthétique,* 25 (1992), pp. 1-244.

Dacos, Nicole. "Le retable de l'église Saint-Denis à Liège: Lambert Suavius, et non Lambert Lombard." *Oud-Holland,* 106 (1992), 3, pp. 103-116.

Daulte, Francois. "Chefs-d'oeuvre des Musées de Liège à Lausanne: un siecle d'art occidental, 1860-1960. Fondation de l'Hermitage." *L'Oeil,* November 1988, 400, pp. 58-65.

De Backer, L. *Kunst in Vlaanderen, Nu. Een keuze uit tien jaar aankopen van de Vlaamse Gemeenschap/L'art en Flandre, Aujoud'hui. Une sélection des achats de la Communauté Flamande des dix dernières années/Art in Flanders, Now. A selection out of ten years of purchases by the Flemish Community/ Kunst im jetzigen Flandern. Eine Wahl aus 10 Jahren von Ankäufen durch die flämische Gemeinschaft.* Brussels/Antwerp: Ministerie van de Vlaamse Gemeenschap and Museum van Hedendaagse Kunst Antwerpen, 1992.

*De beveiliging van het Lams Gods.* Brussels: Ministerie van de Vlaamse Gemeenschap—Arol, 1987.

De Cock, M. et al. *Artisti (Della Fiandra). Palazzo Sagredo Estate 1990/Artists (From Flanders). Palazzo Sagredo Summer 1990.*

Brussels: Ministerie van de Vlaamse Gemeenschap and Krediet-bank, 1990.

De Geest, Joost. "Panamarenko. 30 Years of Thinking about Space." *Arts and Society in Flanders and the Netherlands. A Yearbook, 1993-1994*. Rekkem: Ons Erfdeel, 1993, pp. 307-308.

———"Splendours of Flanders. Flemish Art in Cambridge." *The Low Countries. Arts and Society in Flanders and the Netherlands. A Yearbook, 1993-1994*. Rekkem: Ons Erfdeel, 1993, pp. 312-313.

De Nayer, Christine. *Willy Kessels*. Charlerloi: Musée de la Photographie, 1996.

De Poorter, Wim. "Daens, or Flanders in the Year 1900." *The Low Countries. Arts and Society in Flanders and the Netherlands. A Yearbook, 1993-1994*. Rekkem: Ons Erfdeel, 1993, pp. 275-276.

———"From 'Y manana?' to 'Manneken Pis.' Thirty Years of Flemish Filmmaking." *The Low Countries. Arts and Society in Flanders and the Netherlands. A Yearbook, 1997-98*. Rekkem: Ons Erfdeel, 1997, pp. 130-142.

———"In Motion. Animated Film in Flanders." *The Low Countries. Arts and Society in Flanders and the Netherlands. A Yearbook, 1995-96*. Rekkem: Ons Erfdeel, 1993, pp. 53-61.

De Saeger, Kris. "The Comic in Flanders. From Popular Illustrated Pamphlet to Worldwide Success Story." *Flanders*, 1996, 31, pp. 31-37.

De Vos, Dirk. *Hans Memling: The Complete Works*. Translated by Ted Alkins. London: Thames and Hudson, 1994.

———*Groeningemuseum Brugge. De volledige verzameling*. Bruges: Die Keure, 1984.

D'Haenens, E. "Ghent Painting and Sculture." In Johan Decavele. *Ghent. In Defence of a Rebellious City. History, Art, Culture*. Antwerp: Mercatorfonds, 1989, p. 202 ff.

Dony, Frans L.M. (ed.). *Meesters der Schilderkunst. Alle tot nu toe bekende werken van Van Eyck*. Rotterdam: Lekturama, 1976. Meesters der Schilderkunst.

Dubois, Marc. "Contemporary Furniture Design in Flanders." *Flanders*, 1997, 36, pp. 5-9.

Duchesne, Albert. "Jean Portaels, portraitiste de la famille royale de Belgique." *Revue Belge d'Archéologie et d'Histoire de l'Art*, 54 (1985), pp. 59-70.

Duron, Michel et al. *Beauvoorde, Cultuurdorp*. Brussels: Gemeente-krediet, 1989.

Duverger, Erik. "Flemish Tapestry." *The Low Countries. Arts and Society in Flanders and the Netherlands. A Yearbook, 1993-1994.* Rekkem: Ons Erfdeel, 1993, pp. 177-185.

Eemans, M. *Peinture flamande 15e-16e-17e s./Vlaamse Schilderkunst 15de-16de-17de e./Flämische Malerei 15.-16.-17. Jh./Flemish Painting 15th-16th-17th c./Pintura flamenca s. 15-16-17.* Brussels: Meddens, 1985.

Eisenman, Stephen F. "Allegory and Anarchism in James Ensor's Apparition: Vision Preceding Futurism." *Record of the Art Museum (Princeton-University),* 46 (1987), 1, pp. 2-17.

Filice, Eugenio. "A Retable from Brabant in the Royal Ontario Museum." *Canadian Journal of Netherlandic* Studies, 14 (1993), 1, pp. 10-17.

Filipczak, Zirka Zaremba and David Carrier. "Picturing Art in Antwerp, 1550-1700." *Arts-Magazine,* 63 (November 1988), pp. 119-120.

*Flemish Paintings in America.* Selected by Guy C. Bauman and Walter Liedke. Antwerp: Mercatorfonds, 1992.

Francastel, Pierre. *Bruegel.* Paris: Hazan, 1997.

Fromentin, Eugène. *The Masters of Past Time. Dutch and Flemish Painting from Van Eyck to Rembrandt.* Ithaca: Cornell University Press, 1948.

*Geschiedenis van de Schilderkunst in België.* Brussels: La Renaissance du Livre and Federale Voorlichtingsdienst, 1995.

Gibson, Walter. *Hieronymus Bosch.* London: Thames and Hudson, 1973.

Grauman, Brigid. "Brussels: Art Underground. In the Subway Stations." *Art News,* 86 (May 1987), pp. 69-70.

Grimme, Ernst Gunther. *België. De kunstschatten van Brussel, Antwerpen, Gent, Brugge, Luik en andere steden.* De Bildt: Cantecleer, 1979.

Gyselen, Gaby. "Old Masters from the Low Countries in American Collections." *The Low Countries. Arts and Society in Flanders and the Netherlands. A Yearbook, 1993-1994.* Rekkem: Ons Erfdeel, 1993, pp. 310-311.

Harris, Lynda. *The Secret Heresy of Hieronymus Bosch.* Edinburgh: Floris Books, 1995.

Horn, Hendrik J. "The Allegory on the Abdication of the Emperor Charles V by Frans Francken II: Some Observations on the Iconography of Antwerp's Plight in the Early Seventeenth Century."

*RACAR, Revue d'Art Canadienne, Canadian Art Review,* 13 (1986), 1, pp. 23-30.

Huys, Paul. "Flemish Art. Symbolism to Expressionism." *The Low Countries. Arts and Society in Flanders and the Netherlands. A Yearbook, 1993-1994.* Rekkem: Ons Erfdeel, 1993, pp. 309-310.

Janssens, Jozef and Martine Meuwese. *Jacob van Maerlant. Spiegel historiael. De miniaturen uit het handschrift Den Haag, Koninkl. Bibl., KA XX.* Leuven: Davidsfonds/De Clauwaert, 1997.

Jooris, Roland. "The Painter and His Surroundings. The Work of Roger Raveel." *The Low Countries. Arts and Society in Flanders and the Netherlands. A Yearbook, 1993-1994.* Rekkem: Ons Erfdeel, 1993, pp. 64-68.

*La Collection/de Verzameling/Die Sammlung/The Collection.* Brussels: Gemeentekrediet van België, 1988.

Lafontaine-Dosogne, Jacqueline. "Le cycle de Sainte Marguerite d'Antioche à la cathedrale de Tournai et sa place dans la tradition romane et byzantine." *Revue Belge d'Archeologie et d'Histoire de l'Art,* 61 (1992), pp. 87-125.

Lambrecht, Jef. "A Rehabilitation of Belgian Art." *The Low Countries. Arts and Society in Flanders and the Netherlands. A Yearbook, 1995-96.* Rekkem: Ons Erfdeel, 1995, pp. 307-309.

Lauwaert, Dirk and Helke Lauwaert. "Surrealisme in Belgische Collecties." *Openbaar Kunstbezit in Vlaanderen,* 1977, 1, pp. 1-43.

Leclercq-Marx, Jacqueline. "Tournai, deux fresques médiévales oubliées: L'entrée du Christ à Jerusalem (XIVe siecle) et un fragment d'annonciation de Robert Campin." *Revue Belge d'Archéologie et d'Histoire de l'Art,* 61 (1992), pp. 230-234.

Lefevre, Pascal. "Fifty Years of Bob and Bobette." *The Low Countries. Arts and Society in Flanders and the Netherlands. A Yearbook, 1995-1996.* Rekkem: Ons Erfdeel, 1995, pp. 46-52.

———"Flemish Comic Strips Today." *The Low Countries. Arts and Society in Flanders and the Netherlands. A Yearbook, 1997-1998.* Rekkem: Ons Erfdeel, 1997, pp. 247-252.

Legrand, Francine-Claire. "Architecture, Painting and Sculpture." In Marina Boudart, Michel Boudart and René Bryssinck. *Modern Belgium.* Palo Alto, California: The Society for the Promotion of Science and Scholarship, 1990, pp. 487-507.

Marijnissen, Roger-Henri. *Bosch.* Tielt: Lannoo, 1996.

Marijnissen, Roger-Henri et al. *Bruegel. Het volledige oeuvre.* Antwerp: Mercatorfonds, 1988.

McFadden, Sarah. "Paul Delvaux. In a World of His Own." *The Bulletin. The Newsweekly of the Capital of Europe,* 35 (1997), 12, pp. 24-32.

McGrath, Elizabeth. *Rubens: Subject from History (I and II).* London: Harvey Miller Publishers, 1996. Corpus Rubenianum Ludwig Buchard XIII.

Meewis, Wim. "Geometric-Abstract and Constructivist Art in Flanders." *Flanders*, 1997, 36, pp. 15-19.

Miedema, Hessel (ed.). *Karel van Mander. The Lives of the Illustriuous Nederlandisch and German Painters, from the First Edition of the 'Schilderboeck' (1603-1604). Preceded by The Lineage, Circumstances and Place of Birth, Live and Works of Karel van Mander, Painter and Poet and likewise his Death and Burial, from the Second Edition of the 'Schilderboeck' (1616-1618).* Translated by Mechael Hoyle, Jacqueline Pennial-Boer and Charles Ford. Doornspijk: Davaco Publishers, 1994.

Milne, Louise S. "Money and Excrement. The Psychology and the Marketplace in Pieter Bruegel the Elder's 'Dulle Griet'." *The Low Countries. Arts and Society in Flanders and the Netherlands. A Yearbook, 1997-1998,* Rekkem: Ons Erfdeel, 1997, pp. 21-30.

"Modernism in Painting, a Decade's Painting in Flanders. Provinciaal Museum voor Moderne Kunst, Oostende, Belgium." *Kunst and Museumjournaal,* 3 (1992), 6, p. 61-62.

Morand, Kathleen and David Finn. *Claus Sluter. Artist at the Court of Burgundy.* London: Harvey Miller Publishers, 1991.

Mundy, E. James. *Painting in Bruges, 1470-1550: an Annotated Bibliography.* Boston: G. K. Hall, 1985.

*Museum voor fotografie Charleroi.* Brussels: Gemeentekrediet, 1997. Musea Nostra 35.

*Museumgids van Oostende tot Maaseik.* Brussels: Museumfonds, Ministerie van de Vlaamse Gemeenschap, 1986.

*Nationaal Museum Brussel.* Bruges: Die Keure, 1984.

Palmer, Michael. *From Ensor to Magritte. Belgian Art 1880-1940.* Brussels/Tielt: Racine and Lannoo, 1994.

*Pieter Bruegel.* Zwolle: Waanders, 1997. Nederlands Kunsthistorisch Jaarboek, deel 47. (With two Dutch, one German and six English contributions).

Porteman, Karel. "From First Sight to Insight. The Emblem in the Low Countries." *The Low Countries. Arts and Society in Flanders and the Netherlands. A Yearbook, 1993-1994.* Rekkem: Ons Erfdeel, 1993, pp. 212-222.

Renoy, Georges. *Brussel onder Leopold I. 25 jaar porseleinkaarten 1840-1865*. Brussels: Gemeentekrediet, 1979.

Revelard, Michel. *Internationaal Museum van het Carnaval en het Masker. Binche*. Brussels: Gemeentekrediet, 1991. Musea Nostra 22.

Roberts-Jones, Philippe and Françoise. *Bruegel*. Ghent: Snoeck-Ducaju en Pandora, 1997.

*Rogier Van der Weyden/Rogier de la Pasture. Official Painter to the City of Brussels. Portait Painter of the Burgundian Court*. Brussels: Gemeentekrediet van België, 1979.

*Rubens and the Baroque*. Antwerp: Mercatorfonds, 1994.

Schneede, Uwe M. *René Magritte: Life and Work*. New York: Barron's, 1983.

Schoonbaert, Lydia M.A. "James Ensor. Pioneer of Modern European Art." *The Low Countries. Arts and Society in Flanders and the Netherlands. A Yearbook, 1994-1995*, Rekkem: Ons Erfdeel, 1994, pp. 156-167.

Scott, John Beldon. "The Meaning of Perseus and Andromeda in the Farnese Gallery and on the Rubens House." *Journal of the Warburg and Courtauld Institutes*, 51 (1988), pp. 250-260.

"Sculpture/sculpture: Video Installations and Photographic Work. Museum van Hedendaagse Kunst, Ghent, Belgium." *Kunst and Museumjournaal*, 5 (1994), 4, pp. 56.

Simmins, Geoffrey. "Fernand Khnopf and Ver Sacrum." *Canadian Journal of Netherlandic Studies*, 1988-89, 9(2)-10(1), pp. 33-51.

Smeyers, Maurits. "Flemish Miniatures for England." *The Low Countries. Arts and Society in Flanders and the Netherlands. A Yearbook, 1995-1996*. Rekkem: Ons Erfdeel, 1995, pp. 240-250.

Smeyers, M. and Jan Van der Stock (eds.). *Flemish Illuminated Manuscripts 1475-1550*. Ghent: Ludion Press, 1996.

Stallaerts, Rik and Robbe de Hert. *Binnenkort in deze zaal. Kroniek van de Belgische filmaffiche*. Ghent: Ludion, 1955.

Stroo, Cyriel and Pascale Syfer-D'Olne. *The Flemish Primitives I, The Master of Flémalle Rogier Van der Weyden*. Brussels: Royal Museum of Fine Arts of Belgium and Brepols, 1996.

Sullivan, Margaret A. *Bruegel's Peasants*. Cambridge: Cambridge University Press, 1997.

Theys, Hans. *Panamarenko*. Tervuren: Exhibitions International, 1992.

Timmermans, Felix. *Adriaan Brouwer.* Leuven: Davidsfonds, 1991.
*Tintin, Hergé et la Belgité.* Rimini: Clueb, 1995.
Todts, Herwig. "Piecing the Scraps Together. Roel D'Haese and his Sculptures." *The Low Countries. Arts and Society in Flanders and the Netherlands. A Yearbook, 1995-96.* Rekkem: Ons Erfdeel, 1995, pp. 258-263.
Tricot, Xavier. *James Ensor. Catalogue raisonné of the paintings.* Deurne: Continental publishing, 1996.
Todts, H. *Exhibition Catalogue James Ensor.* Utrecht: Central Museum Utrecht, 1993.
Vagianos, Andrea."The Sculpture of George Minne." *Canadian Journal of Netherlandic Studies,* 1988-1989, 9(2)-10(1), pp. 52-64.
Valcke, Johan. "Contemporary Jewellery in Flanders." *Flanders,* September 1977, 35, pp. 27-30.
Van de Perre, Harold. *Van Eyck. Het lam gods.* Tielt: Lannoo, 1996.
Van den Abbeele, Andries. *Brugge mort.* Antwerp-Baarn: Hadewych, 1990.
Van den Bussche, Willy. "A Master of Everyday Life. The Work of Constant Permeke. *The Low Countries. Arts and Society in Flanders and the Netherlands. A Yearbook, 1997-1998.* Rekkem: Ons Erfdeel, 1997, pp. 194-206.
Van den Kerkhove, A. and J. Baldewijns. *Museum voor Stenen Voorwerpen (Ruïnes van de Sint-Baafsabdij). Gids voor de bezoeker. Gent:* Stad Gent, 1993 (with English summary: The Lapidary Museum in Ghent).
Van der Velden, Hugo. "Cambyses Reconsidered: Gerard David's Exemplum iustitiae for Bruges Town Hall." *Simiolus,* 23 (1995), 1, pp. 40-62.
Van Parijs, Joris. *Frans Masereel. Een Biografie.* Antwerp: Houtekiet, 1995.
———*Masereel. 100 houtsneden.* Antwerp: Houtekiet, 1995.
Van Vaeck, Marc. "'Who described the Art of Painting in so Edifying and Instructive a Manner." *The Low Countries. Arts and Society in Flanders and the Netherlands. A Yearbook, 1995-96.* Rekkem: Ons Erfdeel, 1995, pp. 304-305.
Vanden Berghe, Stéphane. *Gruuthusemuseum Brugge: een overzicht.* Bruges: Die Keure, 1984.
Vergeer, Koen. *Dossier Delvaux.* Amsterdam/Antwerp: Atlas, 1996.
Vermeersch, Valentin. *The Museums of Brugge.* Translated by Ted

Alkins. Brussels: Crédit Communal, 1992. Musea Nostra 25.

Verplaetse, André. "L'Architecture en Flandre entre 900 et 1200, d'après les sources narratives contemporaires." *Cahiers de civilisation médiévale* 7 (1965), pp. 25-42.

White, Christopher. "Through Foreign Eyes. Painters from the Low Countries in the Seventeenth-Century England." *The Low Countries. Arts and Society in Flanders and the Netherlands. A Yearbook, 1995-1996.* Rekkem: Ons Erfdeel, 1995, pp. 190-197.

Williamson, Paul. "Late Gothic Sculpture. Meesterwerken van de gotische beeldhouwkunst; Laatgotische beeldhouwkunst in de Bourgondische Nederlanden: Museum voor Schone Kunsten, Ghent, Belgium." *The Burlington Magazine,* 136 (December 1994), pp. 861-862.

———"Late Gothic Sculpture from Limburg. Provinciaal Museum voor Religieuze Kunst, Sint-Truiden, Belgium." *The Burlington Magazine,* 132 (December 1990), pp. 893-894.

Wilson, Jean C. "Workshop Patterns and the Production of Paintings in Sixteenth-Century Bruges." *The Burlington Magazine,* 132 (December 1990), pp. 523-527.

Wright, Christopher. "The 'Vanitas' Piece in Dutch and Flemish Seventeenth-Century Painting." *The Low Countries. Arts and Society in Flanders and the Netherlands. A Yearbook, 1997-1998.* Rekkem: Ons Erfdeel, 1997, pp. 164-171.

### 7. *Philosophy and Ethics*

Cole, George D. H. *Socialist Thought and Anarchism (1850-1890).* London: Macmillan, 1954.

Commers, Ronald. "Wijsbegeerte in Vlaanderen." *Algemeen Nederlands Tijdschrift voor Wijsbegeerte,* 79 (1987), pp. 247-259.

Diels, Dirk. *Ondergesneeuwde Sporen. Een andere visie op arbeid en burgerschap.* Leuven: Acco, 1997.

Foriers, Paul. "L'état des recherches de logique juridique en Belgique." *Logique et Analyse,* 10, pp. 23-42.

Jonkers, Peter, "Metafysica in Leuven," *Tijdschrift voor Filosofie,* 57 (1995), 2, pp. 331-343.

Kerkhofs, Jan. *De Europeanen en hun waarden. Wat wij denken en voelen.* Leuven: Davidsfonds, 1997.

Kortooms, A. and C. Struyker Boudier. "Een bijdrage tot de Ge-

schiedenis van de Husserl-receptie in België en Nederland." *Algemeen Nederlands Tijdschrift voor Wijsbegeerte,* 81 (1987), January, pp. 1-20, April, pp. 79-101.
Pleij, Herman. *Dromen van Cocagne. Middeleeuwse fantasieën over het volmaakte leven.* Amsterdam: Prometheus, 1977.
Rosseel, Eric. *Ethisch Socialisme in Vlaanderen. De 20ste eeuw overbrugd.* Brussels: VUB-Press, 1996.
Taels, J. *De Vis heeft geen Weet van het Water. Ethiek tussen Berekening en Zorg.* Kapellen: Pelckmans, 1995.
Triest, Monika. "Afbraak en Opbouw." *Vlaams Marxistisch Tijdschrift,* 31 (1997), 4, pp. 93-94.
Vanlandschoot, Jaak en Koen Raes. *Afbraak en opbouw. Dialogen met Leo Apostel.* Brussels: VUBPRESS, 1997 (1986).
Van Parijs, Philippe. *Solidariteit voor de 21e eeuw.* Leuven: Garant, 1966.
Visker, Rudi. *Michel Foucault: genealogy as critique.* Translated by Chris Turner. London: Verso, 1995.
Voyé, L. et al. *Belges, heureux et satisfaits. Les valeurs des belges dans les années 90.* Brussels: Université Libre de Bruxelles and De Boeck, 1992.
Wenin, Christian. "Cinquante ans de philosophie en Belgique francophone." *Revue Philosophique de Louvain,* 86 (1988), pp. 87-104.

### *8. Religion*

Backhouse, Marcel. "De Engelse archivaria en de geschiedenis van de Vlaamse en Waalse vluchtelingenkerk in Sandwich in de 16de en 17de eeuw. Deel 1." *Bulletin de la Commission Royale d'Histoire,* 155 (1989), 3-4, pp. 245-262.
Baeten, Walter. "Patronaten in Vlaanderen en Nederland (1850-1941)." *Trajecta,* 3 (1994), 1, pp. 34-60.
Danneels, Godfried. *Christ or Aquarius. Exploring the New Age Movement.* Translated by Elena French. Dublin: Veritas, 1990.
Dantoing, Alain. *La "Collaboration" du Cardinal. L'Eglise de Belgique dans la Guerre 40.* Brussels: De Boeck, 1991.
De Boer, Eefje. "Een volksparochie te Antwerpen: gelovigen en priesters van Sint Andries (1865-1914)." *Trajecta,* 1 (1992), 3, pp. 262-278.

De Borchgrave, Christian. "Volksmissie in Vlaanderen (1918-1940): Minderbroeders en Jezuïeten op zoek naar een moderne pastorale strategie." *Trajecta*, 2 (1993), 3, pp. 260-272.

Decavele, Johan. "Historiografie van het zestiende-eeuws protestantisme in België." *Nederlands Archief voor Kerkgeschiedenis,* 62 (1982), 1, pp. 1-27.

De Grauwe, Jan. *Histoire de la Chartreuse Sheen Anglorum au Continent: Bruges, Louvain, Malines, Nieuport (1559-1783)*. Salzburg: Universität Salzburg, Institut für Anglistik und Amerikanistik, 1984. Analecta Cartusiana 48.

De Moreau, E. *Histoire de l'église en Belgique*. Brussels: Universelle, 1945-1952.

Devillé, Rik. *Het Werk. Een Katholieke sekte?* Leuven: Van Halewyck, 1996.

*Een eeuw vrijmetselarij in onze gewesten 1740-1840*. Brussels: ASLK, 1983.

Gevers, Lieve. "Vaticanum II en de Lage Landen: bronnen en historiografie." *Trajecta*, 1 (1992), 2, pp. 187-205.

Gilmont, Jean-François. "L'église de Wallonie entre la Belgique et la Flandre." *Etudes*, 1987, 366, 5, pp. 675-685.

Hasquin, H. (ed.). *Visages de la franc-maçonnerie belge du XVIIIe au XXe siècle*. Brussels: Université de Bruxelles, 1983.

Hillyer, Philip. *On the Threshold of the Third Millennium: International Congress for Theology in Honour of the 25th Anniversary of Concilium at the University of Leuven, Belgium*. London: The Foundation, 1990. Concilium 1990/1.

Humblet, J.E. *Eglise-Wallonie*. Brussels: Vie Ouvrière, 1983-84.

Kerkhofs, Jan. "Between Christendom and Christianity. The Church in Flanders." *The Low Countries. Arts and Society in Flanders and the Netherlands. A Yearbook, 1995-1996*. Rekkem: Ons Erfdeel, 1995, pp. 225-232.

Mertens, Herman Emiel. "Max Wildiers, Theologian and Cultural Philosopher." *The Low Countries. Arts and Society in Flanders and the Netherlands. A Yearbook, 1997-1998,* Rekkem: Ons Erfdeel, 1997, p. 295.

Nauta, D. et al. *Biografisch lexicon voor de geschiedenis van het Nedelandse protestantisme*. Kampen: Kok, 1983.

Pirotte, J. "Les catholiques wallons depuis 1830. Pistes de recherche." In: J. E. Humblet. *Jalons pour une histoire religieuse de la Wallonnie*. Brussels: Vie Ouvrière, 1984. Eglise-Wallonie 2.

Plavsic, Wladimir. *Monseigneur Charue. Evêque de Namur.* Louvain-la-Neuve, 1996.

Rémy, J. "Le catholicisme en Belgique, similitude et différence entre la Flandre et la Wallonie." In *Diagnostics.* Louvain-la-Neuve: Ecole de Sociologie de Louvain, Ciaco, 1989.

Reszohazy, Rudolf, Jacques de Groote and Daniel Pyle. "Religion, Secularism, and Politics." In Marina Boudart, Michel Boudart and René Bryssinck. *Modern Belgium.* Palo Alto, California: The Society for the Promotion of Science and Scholarship, 1990, pp. 41-53.

Rion, Pierre. "Pastorale et propagande: à propos d'un texte du Cardinal Mercier." *Revue d'Histoire Ecclésiastique,* 77 (1982), pp. 1-2, pp. 95-99.

Sauvage, P. *La Cité Chrétienne, une revue autour de Jacques Leclercq.* Brussels: Duculot, 1987.

———*Jacques Leclercq, les catholiques et la question wallonne.* Charleroi: Institut Jules Destrée, 1988.

Schillebeeckx, Edward and Catharina J.M. Halkes. *Mary: Yesterday, Today, Tomorrow.* Translated by J. Bowden. London: SCMP, 1993.

Shelley, Thomas J. "Belgian Bishops and Papal Diplomats, 1831-1846." *American Benedictine Review,* 43 (1992), 1, pp. 12-28.

———"Mutual Independence: Church and State in Belgium: 1825-1846." *Journal of Church and State,* 32 (1990), 1, pp. 49-63.

"The Church in Belgium." *Pro Mundi Viata Dossiers,* 1982, No. 18.

Tollebeek, Jo and Tom Verschaffel. "De Jezuïeten en de Zuidnederlandse kerkgeschiedschrijving (1542-1796). *Trajecta,* 1 (1992), 4, pp. 313-331.

Torfs, Rik. *A Healthy Rivalry. Rights in the Church.* Leuven: Peeters, 1995. Louvain theological and pastoral monographs 20.

Tyssens, Jeffrey and Els Witte. *De vrijzinnige traditie in België: van getolereerde tegencultuur tot erkende levensbeschouwing.* Brussels: Balans/VUB-Press, 1997.

Van den Abbeele, A. *De kinderen van Hiram. Vrijmetselaars en vrijmetselarij.* Brussels: Roularta Books, 1981.

Van Isacker, Karel. *Herderlijke brieven over politiek 1830-1960.* Antwerp: De Nederlandsche Boekhandel, 1969.

Van Straaten, Werenfried. *They call me the Bacon Priest: The Story of the World-wide Pastoral Relief Organisation founded by the Author.* San Francisco: Ignatius Press, 1991.

Voyé, L. "Kerkelijkheid en Christendom in Wallonië." *Kultuurleven,* 1991, December.

White, Robert. "Fifteen Years of Calvin Studies in French (1965-1980)." *Journal of Religious History,* 12 (1982), 2, pp. 140-161.

## 9. *Press*

Burgelman, J. C. "The Impact of Politics on the Structure and Development of Belgian Broadcasting and Broadcast-News Policies, 1945-1960." *Historical Journal of Film, Radio and Television,* 7 (1987), 1, pp. 35-46.

De Bens, Els. *De Pers in België. Het verhaal van de Belgische dagbladpers. Gisteren, vandaag en morgen.* Tielt: Lannoo, 1997.

Deltour, Pol. *Man bijt hond. Over pers, politiek en gerecht.* Antwerp: Icarus, 1996.

Durnez, Gaston. *De Standaard. Het levensverhaal van een Vlaamse krant.* Tielt/Weesp: Lannoo, 1985.

Gaus, Helmut. *Pers, kerk en geschreven fictie. Groeiproblemen en conflicten in een democratiseringsproces (Gent 1836-1860).* Bruges: De Tempel, 1975.

Selleslach, Geert. "Het nieuwe mediadecreet." *Samenleving en Politiek,* 4 (1997), 9, pp. 4-8.

Stéphany, Pierre. *Histoire d'un Journal Libre. La Libre Belgique 1884-1996.* Louvain-la-Neuve: Duculot, 1996.

Tolleneer, Jan. "Gymnastics and Religion in Belgium, 1892-1914." *International Journal of the History of Sport,* 7 (1990), 3, pp. 335-347.

Veestraeten, Jan. *Afscheid van een krant. Blijft Gazet van Antwerpen op Linkeroever?* Antwerp: Icarus, 1997.

## *III. ECONOMIC*

### *1. General*


Bastian, Jens. "From Work Sharing to Temporal Flexibility: Working Time Policy in Belgium 1975-1990." *Res Publica,* 34 (1992), 1, pp. 35-51.

———"Modern Times: Institutional Dynamics in Belgian and French Labour Market Policies." *West European Politics,* 17 (1994), 1, pp. 98-122.

*Belgium. Country Profile.* London: Economist Intelligence Unit, 1997.

*Belgium. Country Report.* London: Economist Intelligence Unit, 1997.

Boekestijn, Arend Jan. "Economic Integration and the Preservation of Post-war Consensus in the Benelux Countries." *Economic and Social History in the Netherlands,* 5 (1993), pp. 179-212.

Brockmans, Hans. *200 jaar filiaal. De Franse greep op de Vlaamse economie.* Leuven: Davidsfonds, 1995.

Bughin, J. "Union-Firm Efficient Bargaining and Test of Oligopolistic Conduct". *Review of Economics and Statistics,* 75 (3), August 1993, pp. 563-567.

Capron, H. et al. "Modele Wallonie: Conception theorique et modele de simulation. (With English summary.)" *Cahiers Economiques de Bruxelles,* 129 (1991), First Trimester, pp. 27-49.

"Company profits in 1995." *Kredietbank. Monthly Bulletin,* October 1996, pp. 1-7.

Compston, Hugh. "Union Participation in Economic Policy Making on Austria, Switzerland, the Netherlands, Belgium and Ireland, 1970-1992." *West European Politics,* 17 (1994), 1, pp. 123-145.

DeBrabander, Guido L. "Regional Differentiation of Economic Growth in Belgium, 1846-1977." *Historical Social Research,* 33 (1985), pp. 42-59.

Demeyere, Karel. "VDAB on Line." *Flanders*, 1997, 36, pp. 25-27.

De Roover, R. *Money, Banking and Credit in Mediaeval Bruges. Italian Merchant-Bankers, Lombards and Money Changers. A Study in the Origins of Banking*. Cambridge, Mass.: Mediaeval Academy of America, 1948.

Deschamps, C. *Overheidsopdrachten voor aanneming van werken, leveringen en diensten.* Heule: UGA, 1979-1993. (Losbl.)

De Wilde, Bart. *Witte boorden, blauwe kielen. Patroons en arbeiders in de Belgische textielnijverheid in de 19de en 20ste eeuw.* Ghent: Ludion, 1997.

*European Employment and Industrial Relations Glossaries. Belgium.* Luxembourg: Office for Official Publications of the European Communities, 1991.

Gaus, H. en R. Van Eeno. *Beknopte bibliografie van de politieke en sociaal-ekonomische evolutie van België 1945-1992.* Leuven-Apeldoorn: Garant, 1992.

Gaus, H., R. Van Eeno en M. De Waele. *Beknopte bibliografie van de politieke en sociaal-ekonomische evolutie van België 1918-1988.* Ghent: Centrum voor Politiek-Wetenschapelijk Onderzoek, 1988.

Gevers, Louis and Marie Eve Hoet-Mulquin. *Public Expenditures and Welfare Policy: A Study of Local Decisions in the Walloon Region.* Namur: Facultés universitaires Notre-Dame de la Paix. Faculté des sciences économiques et sociales, 1988.

Hatry, Paul. "Energy." In Marina Boudart, Michel Boudart and René Bryssinck. *Modern Belgium.* Palo Alto, California: The Society for the Promotion of Science and Scholarship, 1990, pp. 272-279.

Hendricks, Danny et al. *Vademecum of the Belgian Industry. Japan Project.* Leuven: Vlaamse Technische Kring, 1988.

Hogg, Robin L. *Structural Rigidities and Policy Inertia in Inter-war Belgium.* Brussels: Brepols, 1986. Paleis der Academiën. Verhandelingen, Klasse der Letteren: 118.

Janssens, V. "Natievorming in België en het Geldstelsel." *Tijdschrift voor Geschiedenis* 95(1982), 4, pp. 507-512.

Kestens, Paul. "General Trends." In Marina Boudart, Michel Boudart and René Bryssinck. *Modern Belgium.* Palo Alto, California: The Society for the Promotion of Science and Scholarship, 1990, pp. 225-232.

L'âge d'homme. *Energium 2000.* Brussels: Ministry of the Walloon Region, 1985.

*La Belgique Industrielle en 1850.* Deurne: Continental Publishing, 1996.

Lesage, A. and Chr. de la Rochefordière. *Industrial Impact of the European Single Market: The Case of the Walloon Region.* Louvain-la-Neuve: UCL. IRES, 1988. Bulletin de l'IRES 124.

Luyten, Dirk. *Sociaal-economisch overleg in België sedert 1918.* Brussels: Balans en VUB-Press, 1995.

Moden, J. and J. De Sloover. *Le Patronat Belge.* Brussels: CRISP, 1991.

Mokyr, J. *Industrialization in the Low Countries, 1795-1850.* New Haven-London: Yale University Press, 1976.

Mommen, A. *The Belgian Economy in the Twentieth Century.* London: Routledge, 1995.

*Nijver België.* Deurne: Continental Publishing, 1996.

*Région Wallonne: au coeur du marché Européen: la Wallonie, un technopole ouvert sur le monde/The Walloon Region: in the heart of the European market place: Wallonia, a high tech centre open to the world.* Brussels: Ministère de la Région Wallonne de Belgique. Direction Génerale des Relations Extérieures, 1990. Extrait de la revue Regions d'Europe 2/1990/Extract from the magazine Regions of Europe 2/1990.

Riley, Raymond C. et al. *Benelux: An Economic Geography of Belgium, The Netherlands, and Luxemburg.* London: Chatto & Windus, 1975.

Seghers, Hendrik. *De Nieuwe Collaboratie. Een ondernemer in het verzet.* Leuven: Davidsfonds, 1997.

Sneessens, Henri R. and Jacques H. Dreze. "A Discussion of Belgian Unemployment, Combining Traditional Concepts and Disequilibrium Econometrics." *Economica*, 53 (1986), 210, Supplement, pp. 89-119.

*Sociaal Economische Atlas ván Vlaanderen. Editie 1977.* Brussels: Sociaal-Economische Raad van Vlaanderen, 1996.

Thomas, Peter. "Belgium's North-South Divide and the Walloon Regional Problem." *Geography*, 75 (1990), 1, pp. 36-50.

Van der Wee, H. (ed.). *The Rise and Decline of Urban Industries in Italy and in the Low Countries (Late Middle Ages - Early Modern Times).* Leuven: University Press, 1988.

Van Driessche, Hugo. *Economisch Zakboekje 1977/1.* Diegem: Samsom, 1997.

Vanthemsche, Guy. *Les paradoxes de l'Etat, L'Etat face à l'économie de marché XIX & XXe siècles.* Brussels: Labor, 1997.

"Volledige werkgelegenheid en arbeidsduurvermindering. De 35 uren week ook in België? *VMT*, 31 (1977), 4, pp. 76-83.

Wauters, Luc and Jan Huyghebaert (eds.). "The Economy." In Marina Boudart, Michel Boudart and René Bryssinck. *Modern Bel-*

*gium.* Palo Alto, California: The Society for the Promotion of Science and Scholarship, 1990, pp. 221-299.

Witlox, H. J. M. *Schets van de ontwikkeling van welvaart en bedrijvigheid in het Verenigd Koninkrijk der Nederlanden. Benelux 1815-1830.* Nijmegen, Centrale drukkerij, 1956.

## 2. *Agriculture*

Aerts, Erik and Delbeke, Jos. "Problemen bij de sociaal-economische geschiedenis van het Vlaamse platteland, 1700-1850." *Bijdragen en Mededelingen betreffende de Geschiedenis der Nederlanden,* 98-(1983), 4, pp. 583-596.

Belgian Bioindustries Association. Minister of Technology Development of the Walloon Region. *Directory of Biotechnology: Wallonia-Brussels.* Brussels: Belgian bioindustries association. Minister of Technology Development of the Walloon Region, 1992.

Belgique. Région wallonne. Ministère des technologies nouvelles. *Europe of the Biopoles, Liège, March 23-24-25, 1987 : Detailed Programme, Abstracts of Papers / Belgique. Région Wallonne. Ministère des Technologies Nouvelles.* Brussels: Walloon Ministry for New Technologies and External Relations of Belgium, 1987.

*Biotechnology in the Walloon Region: Directory of Academic and Industrial Laboratories 1987.* Brussels: Biosurvey, 1986.

Blomme, Jan. "Produktie, produktiefactoren en produktiviteit: De Belgische Landbouw 1846-1910." *Belgisch Tijdschrift voor Nieuwste Geschiedenis,* 24 (1993), 1-2, pp. 275-293.

Cohen, Yolande and Dungen, Pierre Van Den. "A l'origine des cercles de fermières: étude comparée Belgique-Quebec." *Revue d'Histoire de l'Amérique Française,* 48 (1994), 1, pp. 29-56.

Hinnekens, Jan. "Agriculture." In Marina Boudart, Michel Boudart and René Bryssinck. *Modern Belgium.* Palo Alto, California: The Society for the Promotion of Science and Scholarship, 1990, pp. 233-237.

*Wit goud uit België (Witloof).* Brussels: Federale Voorlichtingsdienst, 1987.

### *3. Finance, Credit and Banking*


Beauvois, Roland. "Government Finance." In Marina Boudart, Michel Boudart and René Bryssinck. *Modern Belgium.* Palo Alto, California: The Society for the Promotion of Science and Scholarship, 1990, pp. 294-299.

Beauvois, Roland. "Monetary Policy and Organization." In Marina Boudart, Michel Boudart and René Bryssinck. *Modern Belgium.* Palo Alto, California: The Society for the Promotion of Science and Scholarship, 1990, pp. 280-293.

Collaerts, Karel. "Gedeeltelijke regionalisering van de overheidsschuld. Zijn pro en contra verenigbaar?" *Vlaanderen Morgen,* 1997, 6, pp. 15-24.

Decoster, André. "A Microsimulation Model for Belgian Indirect Taxes with a Carbon/Energy tax Illustration for Belgium." *Tijdschrift voor economie en management,* 40 (1995), 2, p. 133-156.

Janssens, Valéry. *De beheerders van ons geld.* Tielt: Lannoo, 1997.

Lefebvre, Christian and John Flower. *Belgium.* London/New York: Routledge, 1994. European Financial Reports.

Siaens, Alain. "Financial Services and Markets." In Marina Boudart, Michel Boudart and René Bryssinck. *Modern Belgium.* Palo Alto, California: The Society for the Promotion of Science and Scholarship, 1990, pp. 253-260.

"The Monetary Situation in Belgium." *Kredietbank. Monthly Bulletin,* October 1996, p. 8.

Van den Nieuwenhof, Jozef. "Banking IT in Belgium.—'The Road ahead'." *Revue de la Banque/Bank- en Financiewezen,* 60 (1996), 3, pp. 115-117.

*Wat U moet weten over de bankcommissie.* Brussels: INBEL-Belgisch Instituut voor Voorlichting en Documentatie, 1985.

Wilms, Wilfried, Jan Leers and Diego De Vos. *New Belgian banking law.* Chichester: Wiley, 1994. AEDBF-Belgium Yearbook 1994.


### *4. Foreign Aid, Trade and Investment*


*Belgium. Country Report. A Special Study on the Conditions for Foreign Investment.* Stratford: Century House Information, 1993.

Beuning, Marijke. "Belgium's Foreign Assistance: Decision Maker Rhetoric and Policy Behavior." *Res Publica*, 26 (1994), 1, pp. 1-21.

Fayat, Hendrik. "Benelux: An Aspect of Belgium's Dynamic Foreign Politcy." In Marina Boudart, Michel Boudart and René Bryssinck. *Modern Belgium.* Palo Alto, California: The Society for the Promotion of Science and Scholarship, 1990, pp. 108-111.

Godeaux, Jean. "International Monetary Arrangements." In Marina Boudart, Michel Boudart and René Bryssinck. *Modern Belgium.* Palo Alto, California: The Society for the Promotion of Science and Scholarship, 1990, pp. 142-151.

Peeters, Theo. "Foreign Trade." In Marina Boudart, Michel Boudart and René Bryssinck. *Modern Belgium.* Palo Alto, California: The Society for the Promotion of Science and Scholarship, 1990, pp. 267-271.

Sleuwaegen, Leo. "Multinationals, the European Community and Belgium: the Small Country Case." *Journal of Common Market Studies,* 26 (1987), 2, pp. 255-272.

### 5. *Mining, Industry, Commerce and Communication*

*Antwerp, Monograph of a World Port.* Antwerp: Publitra, 1995.

*Antwerp, the New Spring.* Deurne: Continental Publishing, 1996.

*Antwerpen, Een Haven/ Anvers Un Port/Antwerp. A Port/ Antwerpen/ Ein Hafen.* Deurne: Continental publishing, 1996.

*België is een ster. De historische rol van België in de communicatiewereld.* Brussels: Federale Voorlichtingsdienst, 1987.

Bernard, P. et al. *Delocalisatie.* Brussels: Planbureau, 1994.

Bouveroux, Jos. "Flanders Greenlights Mobility." *Flanders*, 1996, 32, pp. 29-31.

Brockmans, Hans. "Colruyt. Making a Bundle from Small Margins" *Flanders*, 1997, 36, pp. 20-24.

———"Corona-Lotus takes the Biscuit." *Flanders*, 1996, 32, pp. 17-21.

———"Barco. From Ugly Duckling to Graceful Swan." *Flanders*, 1996, 31, pp. 20-24.

*The Brilliant Story of Antwerp Diamonds.* Deurne: Continental Publishing, 1996.

Davies, W.J.K. *100 years of the Belgian Vicinal: SNCV-NMVB 1885-1985: A Century of Secondary Rail Transport in Belgium.* London: Light Rail Transit London, 1985.

De Groote, Patrick and Christophe de Rynck. "Toerisme in Ieper en het Heuvelland. Een economische analyse." *Kultuurleven*, 1997, Juli, pp. 100-103.

"De-industrialization in Belgium." *Monthly Bulletin. Kredietbank,* 52 (1997), April, pp. 1-8.

Donckels, Rik. "Small and Medium-Sized Enterprises." In Marina Boudart, Michel Boudart and René Bryssinck. *Modern Belgium.* Palo Alto, California: The Society for the Promotion of Science and Scholarship, 1990, pp. 247-252.

Evans, I. M. "Economic Crisis. Belgium. Luxembourg. Steel crisis in Europe, with particular reference to Belgium and Luxembourg." *Geographical Journal,* 146 (1980), 3, pp. 396-407.

Laffut, Michel. "Le bilan du role des chemins de fer dans le développement de la Belgique du XIXe Siècle." *Histoire, Economie et Société,* 11 (1992), 1, pp. 81-90.

Luystermans, Patrick. "Telenet puts Flanders in Pole Position in the Race on the Information Highway." *Flanders*, 1997, 36, pp. 11-14.

*Mercator*. Deurne: Continental Publishing, 1996.

Neef, Arthur, Christopher Kask and Christopher Sparks. "International Comparisons of Manufacturing Unit Labor Costs." *Monthly Labor Review,* 116 (1993), 12, pp. 47-58.

*Petrofina, un groupe international et la gestion de l'incertitude. Tome I: 1920-1979.* Leuven: Peeters, 1997. Recueil d'Histoire et de Philologie, Septième Série 4.

Pulinckx, Raymond. "Manufacturing and Construction Industry." In Marina Boudart, Michel Boudart and René Bryssinck. *Modern Belgium.* Palo Alto, California: The Society for the Promotion of Science and Scholarship, 1990, pp. 238-246.

Samuel, Adam and Marie-Françoise Currat. *Jurisdictional problems in international commercial arbitration: a study of Belgian, Dutch, English, French, Swedish, Swiss, US and West German law.* Zurich: Schulthess polygraphischer Verlag, 1989. Veröffentlichungen des Schweizerischen Instituts für Rechtsvergleichung 11.

Sill, Michael. "National Responses to the Energy Crises of the 1970s: Belgium and Denmark." *Geography*, 71 (1986), 1, pp. 65-67.

Sluyterman, Keetie E. "From Licensor to Multinational Enterprise: The small Dutch Firm OCE-Van Der Grinten in the International World, 1920-1966." *Business History*, 34 (1992), 2, pp. 28-49.

Suykens, F. et al. *Antwerp. A Port for All Seasons*. Antwerp: MIM, 1986.

Van der Wee, H. *The Growth of the Antwerp Market and the European Economy (Fourteenth-Sixteenth Centuries)*. Leuven: Bureau du Recueil, 1963.

*Vlaanderen, knooppunt in de wereldhandel.* Brussels: Federale Voorlichtingsdienst, 1993.

## *IV. HISTORIC*

### *1. General*

Abicht, Ludo. "The Jerusalem of the West. Jews and Goyim in Antwerp." *The Low Countries. Arts and Society in Flanders and the Netherlands. A Yearbook, 1995-96,* Rekkem: Ons Erfdeel, 1995, pp. 21-26.

*Algemene Geschiedenis der Nederlanden.* Utrecht: Fibula-Van Dishoeck, 1982.

Berben, Henri. "Henri Pirenne, notre professeur." *Cahiers de Clio,* 86 (1986), pp. 131-134.

Boulangé, B., R. Cavenaille and M. Colle-Michel. *La Belgique: Des origines à l'Etat Fédéral.* Namur: Editions Erasme, 1990.

*Brugge méér dan een kunststad.* Brussels: Cygnus, 1997.

"Bulletin d'histoire de Belgique, 1983-84." *Revue du Nord,* 67 (1985), 267, pp. 1025-1109.

Carette, Hendrik. "Onze Lage Landen als slagveld van Europa." *Vlaanderen Morgen*, 96, 3, pp. 55-58.

Carson, P. *The Fair Face of Flanders*. Ghent: Story-Scientia, 1978.

Dankers, J. en J. Verheul (eds.). *Lexicon historische figuren van de Lage Landen.* Utrecht-Antwerp: Het Spectrum, 1985. Prisma pocket 2525.

Decavele, Johan (ed.). Ghent. In Defence of a Rebellious City. History, Art, Culture. Antwerp: Mercatorfonds, 1989.

*De Gouden Delta der Lage Landen. Twintig eeuwen beschaving tussen Seine en Rijn.* Antwerp: Mercatorfonds Paribas, 1996.

De Meeüs, Adrien. *History of the Belgians*. Translated by G. Gordon. New York: Frederick A. Praeger, 1962.

De Schrijver, Reginald. "Belgium until World War I." In Marina Boudart, Michel Boudart and René Bryssinck. *Modern Belgium.* Palo Alto, California: The Society for the Promotion of Science and Scholarship, 1990, pp. 54-85.

De Vos, Luc. *Veldslagen der Lage Landen.* Leuven: Davidsfonds, 1995.

Dorchy, H. *Histoire des Belges. Des origines à 1991.* Bruxelles: De Boeck, 1993.

Dumoulin, M. "Historiens étrangers et historiographie de l'expansion belge aux XIXe et XXe Siècles." *Bijdragen en Mededelingen betreffende de Geschiedenis der Nederlanden,* 100 (1985), 4, pp. 685-699.

Duncker, D.R. and H. Weiss. *Het hertogdom Brabant in kaart en prent. Zijn vier kwartieren: Leuven-Brussel-Antwerpen-'s Hertogenbosch.* Tielt/Bussum: Lannoo/Fibula-Van Dishoeck, 1983.

Félix-André, A. et al. "Bulletin d'histoire de Belgique, 1982-83." *Revue du Nord,* 66 (1984), 263, pp. 1097-1203.

Genicot, Léopold. "Vingt ans de recherche historique en Belgique, 1969-1988." Académie Royale de Belgique. *Bulletin de la Classe des Lettres et des Sciences Morales et Politiques,* 2 (1991), 1-2, pp. 11-14.

Gérin, Paul. "La condition de l'historien et l'histoire nationale en Belgique à la fin du 19e et au début du 20e siècle." *Storia della Storiografia,* 11 (1987), pp. 64-103.

Kossman-Putto, J. A. and E. H. Kossman. *The Low Countries. History of the Northern and Southern Netherlands.* Rekkem: Ons Erfdeel, 1996.

Laermans, Jacques. "Brugge beschreven en herschreven." *Kultuurleven,* 1997, July, pp. 92-97.

Lamarcq, Danny en Marc Rogge (red.) *De taalgrens. Van de oude tot de nieuwe Belgen.* Leuven: Davidsfonds, 1997.

Luykx, Théo. *Politieke Geschiedenis van België.* Amsterdam/Brussels: Elsevier, 1977.

Morelli, Anne (ed.). *Les Grandes Mythes de l'histoire de Belgique, de Flandre et de Wallonie.* Brussels: Vie Ouvrière, 1995.

Perin, F. *Histoire d'une nation introuvable.* Brussels: Legrain, 1988.

Pirenne, Henri. *Histoire de Belgique, I: Des Origines au commencement du XIVe siècle.* Brussels: Maurice Lamertin, 1929 (5 ed.). *II. Du Commencement du XIVe siècle à la mort de Charles le Téméraire.* Brussels: Maurice Lamertin, 1922 (3 ed.).

Platel, Marc. *Het nieuwe België. Andere Belgen. Het Sint-Michiels-akkoord*. Knokke-Heist: Creart, 1993.

Prevenier, Walter. "La Commission Royale d'Histoire pendant les vingt-cinq dernières années, 1959-1984." *Bulletin de la Commission Royale d'Histoire,* 1984, 150, pp. 41-71.

Reynebeau, Marc. *Het Klauwen van de Leeuw. De Vlaamse identiteit van de 12e tot de 21ste eeuw*. Leuven: Van Halewyck, 1995.

Stengers, Jean. "Belgian National Sentiment." In Marina Boudart, Michel Boudart and René Bryssinck. *Modern Belgium*. Palo Alto, California: The Society for the Promotion of Science and Scholarship, 1990, pp. 86-97.

———*De Koningen der Belgen. Macht en invloed. Van 1831 tot nu*. Leuven: Davidsfonds, 1992.

———*La formation de la frontière linguistique en Belgique ou de la légitimité de l'hypothèse historique*. Brussels: Latomus, 1959.

———"Le mythe des dominations étrangères dans l'historiographie belge." *Revue Belge de Philologie et d'Historire,* 59 (1981), pp. 382-401.

*The Drama of the Low Countries. Twenty Centuries of Civilization between Seine and Rhine*. Antwerp: Fonds Mercator - Paribas, 1996.

Tollebeek, Jo. "An Overview and a Remembering. A New History of the Low Countries." *The Low Countries. Arts and Society in Flanders and the Netherlands. A Yearbook, 1997-98*. Rekkem: Ons Erfdeel, 1997, pp. 281-282.

———*De ijkmeesters. Opstellen over geschiedschrijving in Nederland en België*. Amsterdam: Bert Bakker, 1994.

———*De ekster en de kooi, nieuwe opstellen over geschiedschrijving*. Amsterdam: Bert Bakker, 1996.

Ulens, J. *Geschiedenis van de Nederlanden. Historisch-biliografisch wegwijzer-Boek 3*. Leuven: Garant, 1993.

*Une autre histoire des Belges*. Brussels: De Boeck and Le Soir, 1997.

Vandermeersch, Peter. "Revue des Travaux sur l'Humanisme dans les anciens Pays-Bas de 1969 à 1986." Bibliothèque d'Humanisme et Renaissance, 50 (1988), 1, pp. 125-140.

Van Eenoo, R. (ed.). "Bibliographie de l'histoire de Belgique, 1990." *Revue Belge de Philologie et d'Histoire,* 70 (1992), 2, pp. 420-546.

———"Bibliographie de l'histoire de Belgique, 1989." *Revue Belge de Philologie et d'Histoire,* 69 (1991), 2, pp. 342-465.

———"Bibliographie de l'histoire de Belgique, 1988." *Revue Belge de Philologie et d'Histoire,* 68 (1990), 2, pp. 352-463.

Van Eenoo, R. et al. "Bibliographie de l'histoire de Belgique, 1987." *Revue Belge de Philologie et d'Histoire,* 67 (1989), 2, pp. 338-465.

———"Bibliographie de l'histoire de Belgique, 1986." *Revue Belge de Philologie et d'Histoire,* 66 (1988), 2, pp. 329-430.

———"Bibliographie de l'histoire de Belgique, 1985." *Revue Belge de Philologie et d'Histoire,* 65 (1987), 2, pp. 313-415.

———"Bibliographie de l'histoire de Belgique, 1984." *Revue Belge de Philologie et d'Histoire,* 63 (1985), 4, pp. 795-880.

———"Bibliographie de l'histoire de Belgique, 1983." *Revue Belge de Philologie et d'Histoire,* 62 (1984), 2, pp. 759-857.

———"Bibliographie de l'histoire de Belgique, 1982." *Revue Belge de Philologie et d'Histoire,* 61 (1983), 4, pp. 895-1004.

———"Bibliographie de l'histoire de Belgique, 1981." *Revue Belge de Philologie et d'Histoire,* 60 (1982), 4, pp. 898-1000.

———"Bibliographie de l'histoire de Belgique, 1980." *Revue Belge de Philologie et d'Histoire,* 59 (1981), 4, pp. 883-993.

Van Ermen, E. et al. *Limburg in kaart en prent. Historisch cartografisch overzicht van Belgisch en Nederlands Limburg*. Tielt/Bussum: Lannoo/Fibula-Van Dishoeck, 1985.

Verhulst, Adriaan. "L'historiographie concernant l'origine des villes dans les anciens Pays-Bas depuis la mort de Henri Pirenne (1935)." *Cahiers de Clio,* 1986, 86, 107-116.

Verschaffel, T. *Beeld en Geschiedenis. Het Belgische en Vlaamse Verleden in de romantische boekillustraties*. Turnhout: Brepols, 1987.

Volmuller, H. W. J. (ed.). *Nijhoffs geschiedenislexicon Nederland en België*. The Hague/Antwerp: Nijhoff, 1981.

Waar is de Tijd. Gent. *1350 jaar Gentenaars en hun rijke verleden*. Deurne: Waanders/Diogenes, 1997.

Watelet, M. *Luxembourg en cartes et plans. Cartographie historique de l'espace luxemburgeois XVe-XIXe siècle*. Tielt: Lannoo, 1989.

Witte, Els (red.). *Geschiedenis van Vlaanderen van de oorsprong tot heden/Histoire de Flandres des origines à nos jours*. Brussels: Historische getuigen/La renaissance du livre, 1983.

Wils, Lode. "De Grootnederlandse geschiedbeschrijving." *Revue Belge de Philologie et d'Histoire/Belgisch Tijdschrift voor Filologie en Geschiedenis*, 61(1983), pp. 322-366.

———*Vlaanderen, België, Groot-Nederland. Mythe en Geschiedenis.* Leuven: Davidsfonds, 1994.

———*Van Clovis tot Happart. De lange weg van de naties in de lage landen.* Leuven: Garant, 1992.

## 2. *Archaeology*

Bloemers, J. H. F. en Van Dorp, T. *Pre- & Protohistorie van de lage landen.* Houten: Open Universiteit en Unieboek, 1991.

Cahen, D. et P. Haesaerts (ed.). *Peuples chasseurs de la Belgique préhistorique dans leur cadre naturel.* Brussels: Patrimoine de l'Institut Royal des Sciences Naturelles en Belgique, 1984.

Cahen-Delhaye, Anne. *Tombelles celtiques de la région de Bovigny.* Brussels: Service National des Fouilles, 1970. Archaeologia Belgica 122.

Caspar, Jean-Paul and Marc De Bie. "Preparing for the Hunt in the late Paleolithic Camp at Rekem, Belgium." *Journal of Field Archaeology*, 23 (1966), 4, pp. 437-460.

De Laet, S. J. *La Belgique d'avant les Romains.* Wetteren: Universa, 1982.

Lefebvre, Louis. *L'église Saint-Pierre à Bastogne.* Bastogne: Schmitz 1972.

Nijhof, Erik and Peter Scholliers (eds.). *Het tijdperk van de machine. Industriecultuuur in België en Nederland.* Brussels: VUB Press, 1996.

Van den Kerkhove, A and J. Baldewijns. *Museum voor Stenen voorwerpen (Ruïnes van de Sint-Baafsabdij). Gids voor de bezoeker.* Ghent: Stad Gent, 1993.

Viaene, Patrick and René De Herdt. *Industriële Archeologie in België.* Ghent: Stichting Mens en Kultuur, 1990.

*3. Historical Periods*

*a. Roman Period (57 B.C. - 402 A.D.)*

Amand, M. and H. Lambert. "Ensemble funéraire à Antoing: les fouilles de 1954 à 1978." *Conspectus*, 1978-79, pp. 88-92. Archaeologia Belgica, 213.

Amand M. and R. Nouwen. *Gallo-Romeinse tumuli in de Civitas ungrorum.* Hasselt: Provinciebestuur Limburg, 1989. Publikaties van het Provinciaal Gallo-Romeins Museum te Tongeren, 40.

Berckmans, Frits. *Romeins Tongeren binnen de Wallen. Compendium.* Antwerp: Vereniging Vlaamse Leerkrachten, 1996.

Bertrang, A. *Histoire d'Arlon.* Arlon: Everling, 1953.

Breuer, J. "Les ramparts romains de Tongres." *Parcs Nationaux,* 15 (1960), pp. 97-107.

Brou, Willy and Marcel Brou. *Routes romaines et vertes chaussées en Gaule Belgique.* Brussels: Editions Techniques et Scientifiques, 1981.

Brulet, R. *Liberchies gallo-romains*. Gembloux: Duculot, 1975.

Cahen-Delhaye, A. and H. Gratia. "Sauvetage dans le vicus romain de Saint-Mard." *Conspectus*, 1979-80, pp. 46-50. Archaeologica Belgica 223.

———"La fortification du Château Renaud à Virton." *Conspectus*, 1979-1980, pp. 67-71. Archaeologica Belgica, 223.

Cave, Roy C. and Herbert H. Coulson (eds.). *A Source Book for Medieval Economic History*. New York: Biblo and Tanner, 1965.

De Laet, S. J. "Note sur les thermes romains de Furfooz." *Helenium*, 7 (1967), pp. 144-149.

De Loë, Baron. *Belgique ancienne. Catalogue descriptif et raisonnée, III, La période romaine.* Brussels: Vroman, 1928-1937.

———"Exploration des tumulus de Tirlemont." *Annales de la Société d'Archéologie de Bruxelles*, 9 (1895), pp. 419-453.

Dubois, Charles. *Vieux-Virton Romain.* Gembloux: Duculot, 1970.

Fouss, M. *La vie romaine en Wallonie.* Gembloux: Duculot, 1974.

Geirnaert, Noel. "Classical Texts in Bruges around 1473: Cooperation of Italian Scribes, Bruges Parchment Rulers, Illuminators and Bookbinders for Johannes Crabbe, Abbot of Les Dunes Abbey." *Transactions of the Cambridge Bibliographical Society,* 10 (1992), 2, pp. 173-181.

Hunik, Vincent. "Caesar en de Gallische Goden." *Streven,* 64 (1997), 4, pp. 313-324.

Klok, R. H. J en F. Brenders. *Reisboek voor Romeins Nederland en België.* Haarlem/Antwerp: Fibula-Van Dishoeck/Standaard Uitgeverij, 1981.

Lefebvre, L. *Les sculptures gallo-romaines du Musée d'Arlon.* Arlon: Service Nationale des Fouilles, 1975.

Mariën, M.E. *Belgica Antiqua, de Stempel van Rome.* Antwerp: Mercatorfonds, 1980.

Mertens, Jozef. "Een Romeins tempelcomplex te Tongeren." *Kolner Jahrbuch für Vor- und Frühgeschichte,* 9 (1967-1968), pp. 101-106.

———"Enkele beschouwingen over Limburg in de Romeinse tijd. Brussels: Service Nationale des Fouilles, 1964. Archaeologia Belgica, 75.

———*Le castellum du bas-empire romain de Brunehaut-Liberchies.* Brussels: Service Nationale des Fouilles, 1974.

——— "Le refuge antique de Montauban-sous-Buzenol. Brussels: Service Nationale des Fouilles, 1954. Archaeologia Belgica, 16.

———"Le refuge protohistorique de Montauban-sous-Buzenol. Brussels: Service Nationale des Fouilles, 1962. Archaeologia Belgica, 63.

———*Le relais romain de chamelaux.* Brussels: Service Nationale des Fouilles, 1968.

———*Les routes romaines de la Belgique.* Brussels, Service Nationale des Fouilles, 1957. Archaeologia Belgica 33.

Mertens, Jozef and A. Cahen-Delhaye. *Saint Mard, Fouilles dans le vicus romain de Vertunum (1961-1969).* Brussels: Service Nationale des Fouilles, 1970. Archaeologia Belgica, 119.

Mertens, Jozef en A. Despy-Meyer. *België in het Romeins Tijdvak.* Brussels: Nationale Dienst voor Opgravingen, 1968. Archaeologische Kaarten van België, 1-2.

Meyers, W. *L'administration de la province romaine de Belgique.* Bruges: De Tempel, 1964.

Nenquin, J. *La nécropole de Furfooz.* Bruges: De Tempel, 1953.

Nouwen, Robert. *Tongeren, en het land van de Tungri (31 v. Chr - 284 n. Chr).* Leeuwarden/Mechelen: Elsma, 1997.

Rober, A. *Site du bas empire à Matagne-la-Grande.* Brussels: Service Nationale des Fouilles, 1980. Archaeologia Belgica 223.

Rogge, M. "Kerkhove." *Hermeneus,* 52 (1980), pp. 114-116.

Van Doorselaer, A. "De Romeinen in de Nederlanden." In *Algemene Geschiedenis der Nederlanden 1*. Utrecht: Fibula-Van Dishoeck, 1982, pp. 22-98.

Vanvinckenroye, W. *Tongeren, Romeinse stad*. Tielt: Lannoo, 1985.

Wankenne, A. *La Belgique au temps de Rome. Des tribus celtiques au royaume franc*. Namur: Presses Universitaires de Namur, 1979.

*b. Merovingians and Carolingians (406-862)*

*Carolingian Chronicles. Frankish Royal Annals and Nithard's Histories*. Translated by Bernard Walter Scholz with Barbara Rogers. Ann Arbor: University of Michigan Press, 1970.

"Charles the Bald: Court and Kingdom." *British Archaeological Reports*, 1981, International Series 101.

D'Haenens, A. *Les invasions normandes en Belgique au IXe siècle. Le phénomène et sa répercussion dans l'historiographie médiévale*. Leuven: Bureaux du Recueil. Bibliothèque de l'Université de Louvain, 1967.

Dierkens, A. *Le moyen age dans l'art et la littérature belges du 19e siècle*. Liège: Université de Liège. Faculté Ouverte, 1987.

Faider-Feytmans, G. *La Belgique à l'époque mérovingienne*. Brussels: La Renaissance du Livre, 1964.

Ganshof, F. L. *La Belgique carolingienne*. Brussels: La Renaissance du Livre, 1974. Notre Passé.

———"Le domaine Gantois de l'abbaye de Saint-Pierre-au-Mont-Blandin à l'époque carolingienne." *Revue Belge de Philologie et d'Histoire*, 26 (1948), pp. 1021-1041.

Ganshof, F. L. and D. P. Blok. "De staatsinstellingen in de Merowingische tijd." In *Algemene Geschiedenis der Nederlanden*. Utrecht: Fibula-Van Dishoeck, 1982, pp. 232-40.

Ganshof, F. L. and G. Berings. "De staatsinstellingen in de Karolingische tijd." *Algemene Geschiedenis der Nederlanden*. Utrecht: Fibula-Van Dishoeck, 1982, pp. 243-63.

Joris, A. *Du Ve au milieu du VIIIe siècle: à la lisière de deux mondes*. Brussels: Fondation Charles Plisnier, 1967.

McKitterick, Rosamond. *The Frankish Kingdoms under the Carolingians, 751-987*. London: Longman, 1983.

Mestdagh, M. *De Vikingen bij ons. Het Grote Leger (879-892) in België en Frankrijk*. Ghent: Stichting Mens en Kultuur, 1989.

Van der Gucht, Katrien. "Semmerzake (Gavere, Oost Vlaanderen): Merovingische Nederzettingsceramiek." *Handelingen der Maatschappij voor Geschiedenis en Oudheidkunde te Gent, 35 (1981).*

Van Doorselaer, A. (ed.). *De Merovingische beschaving in de Scheldevallei. Handelingen van het internationaal colloquium Kortrijk, 28-30 oktober 1980.* Kortrijk: Vereniging voor Oudheidkundig Bodemonderzoek in West-Vlaanderen, 1981.

*c. The Middle Ages (862-1363)*

*Annales Gandenses. Annals of Ghent.* Translated from the Latin by Hilda Johnstone. London: Thomas Nelson and Sons, 1951.

Baerten, J. *Het graafschap Loon (11de-14de eeuw). Ontstaan—politiek—instellingen.* Assen: Van Gorcum, 1989.

Baldwin, J. W. *The Government of Philip Augustus. Foundations of French Royal Power in the Middle Ages.* Berkeley/Los Angeles: University of California Press, 1986.

Bauer, R. et al. *Brabant in de twaalfde eeuw: een renaissance?* Brussels: Centrum Brabantse Geschiedenis UFSAL, 1987.

Blockmans, F. and W. P. "Devaluation, Coinage and Seignorage under Louis de Nevers and Louis de Male, Counts of Flanders, 1330-84." in N. J. Mayhew. *Coinage in the Low Countries (880-1500). The Third Oxford Symposium on Coinage and Monetary History.* Oxford: BAR, 1979, pp. 69-94.

Blockmans, W. P. "A Typology of Representative Institutions in Late Medieval Europe." *Journal of Medieval History,* 4 (1978), pp. 189-215.

———*Een middeleeuwse vendetta. Gent 1300.* Houten: De Haan, 1987.

Bovesse, J. "Le Comte de Namur Jean Ier et les événements du comte de Flandre en 1325-26." *Bulletin de la Commission Royale d'Histoire,* 131 (1965), pp. 385-454.

Brown, A.D. "Medieval Flanders, by D. Nicholas." *English Historical Review,* 110 (1995), Iss. 439, pp. 1239-1240.

Brugmans, H. "Digging into Bruges's Past." *The Low Countries. Arts and Society in Flanders and the Netherlands. A Yearbook, 1993-94.* Rekkem: Ons Erfdeel, 1993, pp. 277-279.

Carson, P. *James van Artevelde. The man from Ghent.* Ghent: Story-Scientia, 1980.

Chorley, P. "The Cloth Exports of Flanders and Northern France during the Thierteenth Century: A Luxury Trade?", *Economic History Review,* 40 (1987), pp. 349-379.

Courtenay, W. J. "Token Coinage and the Administration of Poor Relief during the Late Middle Ages." *Journal of Interdisciplinary History,* 3 (1972-73), pp. 275-95.

Degryse, Louis M. "Some obervations on the Origin of the Flemish Bailiff (Bailli): The Reign of Philip of Alsace." *Viator,* 7 (1976), pp. 243-294.

De Hemptinne, T. "Vlaanderen en Henegouwen onder de erfgenamen van de Boudewijns 1070-1214." In *Algemene Geschiedenis der Nederlanden.* Utrecht, 1982.

D'Haenens, Albert. *Les Invasions normandes au Belgique au IXe siècle.* Louvain: Publications Universitaires de Louvain, 1967.

Dhondt, J. *Les Origines de la Flandre et de l'Artois.* Arras: Centre d'Etudes Régionales du Pas-de-Calais, 1944.

Duby, Georges. *The Early Growth of the European Economy.* Ithaca, Cornell University Press, 1974.

Dunbabin, J. *France in the Making, 843-1180.* Oxford: Oxford University Press, 1985.

Fryde, E. B. "The financial Resources of Edward III in the Netherlands." *Revue Belge de Philologie et d'Histoire,* 45(1967).

Galbert of Bruges. *The Murder of Charles the Good, Count of Flanders.* Translated by James Bruce Ross. New York: Harper and Row, 1967.

Ganshof, F. L. "La Flandre." In Ferdinand Lot and Robert Fawtier (eds.). *Histoire des institutions françaises au Moyen Age.* Paris: Presses Universitaires de France, 1957, pp. 343-426.

George, R. H. "The contribution of Flanders to the Conquest of England, 1065-1086." *Revue Belge de Philologie et d'Histoire,* 5 (1926), pp. 81-99.

Goossens, Jean. "Een rondreis door onze middeleeuwse steden." *Kultuurleven,* 1997, 2, pp. 92-95.

Grierson, Philip. "The relations between England and Flanders before the Norman Conquest." *Transactions of the Royal Historical Society,* Series 4 (1941).

Hodges, Richard and David Whitehouse. *Mohammed, Charlemagne, and the Origins of Europe: Archaeology and the Pirenne Thesis.* Ithaca: Cornell University Press, 1983.

Huizinga, Johan. *The Autumn of the Middle Ages.* Translated by Rodney L. Payton and Ulrich Mammitzsch. Chicago: University of Chicago Press, 1996.

Koch, A. C. F. "De ambtenaren I. De Middeleeuwen." *Flandria Nostra,* 5 (1960), pp. 319-342.

———*De rechterlijke Organisatie van het graafschap Vlaanderen tot in de 13e eeuw.* Antwerp/Amsterdam: Standaard Boekhandel, n.d.

Koziol, C.G. "Monks, Feuds, and the Making of Peace in Eleventh-Century Flanders." *Historical Reflections,* 14 (1987), pp. 531-549.

Kunzel, Rudi. *Beelden en zelfbeelden van middeleeuwse mensen. Historisch-antropologische studies over groepsculturen in de Nederlanden, 7de-13de eeuw.* Nijmegen: SUN, 1997.

Lejeune, L. *Liège et son pays. Naissance d'une patrie, XIIIe-XIVe siècles.* Liège: Université de Liège. Faculté de Philosophie et Lettres, 1948.

Mayhew, N.J. "The Circulation and Imitation of Sterlings in the Low Countries. In N. J. Mayhew. *Coinage in the Low Countries (880-1500). The Third Oxford Symposium on Coinage and Monetary History.* Oxford: BAR, 1979, pp. 54-68.

McDonnell, E. *Beguines and Beghards in Medieval Culture, with Special Emphasis on the Belgian Scene.* New Brunswick: Rutgers University Press, 1954.

Nicholas, David. *Medieval Flanders.* London/New York: Longman, 1992.

———"Medieval Urban Origins in Northern Continental Europe: State and Research and some Tentative Conclusions." *Studies in Medieval and Renaissance History,* 6 (1969), p. 96 ff.

———"Of Poverty and Primacy: Demand, Liquidity, and the Flemish Economic Miracle, 1050-1200." *American Historical Review,* 96 (1991).

———*The Arteveldes of Ghent. The Varieties of Vendetta and the Hero in History.* Leiden: Brill, 1988.

Nicholas, David. *Town and Countryside: Social, Economic, and Political Tensions in Fourteenth-Century Flanders.* Bruges: De Tempel, 1971. University of Ghent: Publications of the Arts Faculty, no. 152.

Pirenne, Henri (ed.). *Le soulèvement de la Flandre maritime en 1323-1328.* Brussels: Commission Royale d'Histoire, 1900.

Rottier, Honoré. *Rondreis door middeleeuws Vlaanderen.* Leuven: Davidsfonds, 1996.

Searle, Eleanor. *Predatory Kinship and the Creation of Norman Power, 840-1066.* Berkeley: University of California Press, 1988.

Sumberg, L. A. M. "The 'Tafurs' and the First Crusade." *Medieval Studies* 21 (1959), pp. 225 ff.

Thorndike, Lynn. *University Records and Life in the Middle Ages.* New York: Columbia University Press, 1944.

Van Acker, K. G. "De 'libertas castrensis operis' van Antwerpen en de Ottogracht te Gent." *Handelingen der Maatschappij voor Geschiedenis en Oudheidkunde te Gent,* 41 (1987), pp. 1-9.

Van Caeneghem, R.C. "Criminal Law in England and Flanders under King Henry II and Count Philip of Alsace." *Actes du congrès de Naples (1980) de la Société de l'Histoire du Droit,* pp. 231-254.

——— "Notes on Canon Law Books in Medieval Belgian Book-Lists." *Studia Gratiana,* 12(1967), pp. 265-92.

Van Goethem, H. "De Annales Gandenses. Auteur en Kroniek. Enkele nieuwe elementen." *Handelingen der Maatschappij voor Geschiedenis en Oudheidkunde te Gent,* 35 (1982), pp. 49-59.

Van Houtte, J. A. *An Economic History of the Low Countries 800-1800.* New York: St. Martin's Press, 1977.

Van Wanseele, Annie. *Flemish Weavers in England.* Brussels: UFSAL. Department of English Linguistics, 1986. Contacts between Flanders and England, 2.

Van Werveke, H. "Currency Manipulation in the Middle Ages: The Case of Louis de Male, Count of Flanders." *Transactions of the Royal Historical Society,* Series 4, 31 (1949), pp. 115-127.

———*Een Vlaamse Graaf van Europees formaat: Flips van de Elzas.* Haarlem: Fibula-Van Dishoeck, 1976.

———"La contribution de la Flandre et du Hainaut à la troisième croisade." *Le Moyen Age,* 78 (1972), pp. 55-90.

Van Werveke, H. and A. Verhulst. "Castrum en Oudburg te Gent." *Handelingen der Maatschappij voor Geschiedenis en Oudheidkunde te Gent,* 14 (1960), pp. 56-57.

Verberckmoes, Johan. "Flemish Tenants in Chief in Domesday England." *Revue Belge de Philologie et d'Histoire,* 66 (1988), p. 726 ff.

Vercauteren, F. (ed.). *Actes des comtes de Flandre, 1071-1128.* Brussels: Palais des Académies, 1938.

Verhulst, Adriaan. "The Origins of Towns in the Low Countries and the Pirenne Thesis." *Past and Present,* 122 (1989), pp. 3-35.

Verlinden, C. *Robert Ier le Frison, comte de Flandre. Etude d'histoire politique.* Antwerp: De Sikkel, 1935.

Vermeersch, Valentin. *Bruges and Europe.* Antwerp: Mercatorfonds, 1993.

Wolff, R. L. "Baldwin of Flanders and Hainault, First Latin Emperor of Constantinople: His Life, Death, and Resurrection, 1172-1225." *Speculum* 27 (1952), pp. 281-322.

*d. The Burgundian Period (1363-1482)*

Ainsworth, Peter. *Jean Froissart and the Fabric of History: Truth, Myth and Fiction in the Chroniques.* Oxford: Clarendon Press, 1990.

Armstrong, C. A. J. *England, France and Burgundy in the Fifteenth Century.* London: Hambledon Press, 1983.

———"Had the Burgundian Government a Policy for the Nobility?" In J.S. Bromley and E.H. Kossman. *Britain and the Netherlands, II: Papers Delivered to the Anglo-Dutch Conference,* 1962. Groningen: J.B. Wolters, 1964, pp. 9-32.

Arnould, M. A. "Les lendemains de Nancy dans les 'Pays de par deça' (janvier-avril 1477)." In: Wim P. Blockmans (ed.). *Le Privilège Général et les Privilèges Régionaux de Marie de Bourgogne pour les Pays-Bas. 1477./Het Algemene en de Gewestelijke Privilegiën van Maria van Bourgondië voor de Nederlanden.* Kortijk-Heule: UGA, 1985. Anciens pays et assemblées d'états. LXXX. Standen en Landen, pp. 1-95.

Avonds, P. *Brabant tijdens de regering van hertog Jan III (1312-1356). De grote politieke crisissen.* Brussels: Koninklijke Academie voor Wetenschappen, Letteren en Schone Kunsten van België, 1984.

Blockmans, Wim P. "Breuk of continuïteit? De Vlaamse Privilegieën van 1477 in het licht van het staatsvormingsproces." In Wim P. Blockmans (ed.). *Le Privilège Général et les Privilèges Régionaux de Marie de Bourgogne pour les Pays-Bas. 1477./Het Algemene en de Gewestelijke Privilegiën van Maria van Bourgondië voor de*

*Nederlanden.* Kortrijk-Heule: UGA, 1985. Anciens pays et assemblées d'états. LXXX. Standen en Landen, pp. 96-84.

———"La signification 'constitutionelle' des Privilèges de Marie de Bourgogne (1477)." In Wim P. Blockmans (ed.). *Le Privilège Général et les Privilèges Régionaux de Marie de Bourgogne pour les Pays-Bas. 1477./Het Algemene en de Gewestelijke Privilegiën van Maria van Bourgondië voor de Nederlanden.* Kortrijk-Heule: UGA, 1985. Anciens pays et assemblées d'états. LXXX. Standen en Landen, pp. 495-516.

———"The Social and Economic Effects of Plague in the Low Countries 1349-1500." *Revue Belge de Philologie et d'Histoire* 60 (1982), pp. 833-63.

Blockmans, Wim P. (ed.). *Le Privilège Général et les Privilèges Régionaux de Marie de Bourgogne pour les Pays-Bas. 1477./Het Algemene en de Gewestelijke Privilegiën van Maria van Bourgondië voor de Nederlanden.* Kortrijk-Heule: UGA, 1985. Anciens pays et assemblées d'états. LXXX. Standen en Landen.

Blockmans, Wim P. and Walter Prevenier. *In de ban van Bourgondië.* Houten: Fibula, 1988.

———"Poverty in Flanders and Brabant from the Fourteenth to the Mid-Sixteenth Century: Sources and Problems." *Acta Historiae Neerlandicae,* 10 (1978), pp. 20-57.

Boone, Marc. *Gent en de Bourgondische hertogen ca. 1384 - ca. 1453. Een sociaal-politieke studie van een staatsvormingsproces.* Brussels: Paleis der Academiën, 1990. Verhandelingen van de Koninklijke Academie voor Wetenschappen, Letteren en Schone Kunsten van België, Klasse der Letteren.

Boone, Marc and Maarten Prak. "Rulers, Patricians and Burghers: the Great and the Little Traditions of Urban Revolt in the Low Countries." In Karel Davids and Jan Lucassen (eds.). *A Miracle Mirrored. The Dutch Republic in European Perspective.* Cambridge: Cambridge University Press, 1995.

Bouldin, Wood. "Renaissance libraries, publications and the 'textual condition'." *Sixteenth Century Journal,* 26 (1995), 2, pp. 379-384.

Bromley, J. S. and E. H. Kossman. *Britain and the Netherlands, II: Papers Delivered to the Anglo-Dutch Conference,* 1962. Groningen: Wolters, 1964.

Carlier, Philippe. "Contribution à l'étude de l'unification bourguignonne dans l'historiographie nationale belge de 1830 à 1914." *Bel-*

*gisch Tijdschrift voor Nieuwste Geschiedenis,* 16 (1985), 1-2, pp. 1-24.

Compère, Gaston. *Ondergetekende, Karel de Stoute, Hertog van Bourgondië.* Antwerp: Manteau, 1987. Translated from *Je soussigné, Charles le Téméraire, duc de Bourgogne.* Paris: Belfond, 1985.

Danneel, M. "Orphanhood and Marriage in Fifteenth-Century Ghent." In W. Prevenier (ed.). *Marriage and Social Mobility in the Late Middle Ages.* Handelingen van het colloquium gehouden te Gent op 18 april 1988. Ghent: Rijksuniversiteit te Gent, 1989, pp. 99-111.

Day, J. *The Medieval Market Economy.* Oxford: Basil Blackwell, 1987.

De Belder, J. and J. Hannes. *Bibliografie van de geschiedenis van België—Bibliographie de l'histoire de Belgique 1865-1914.* Leuven-Brussels: Nauwelaerts, 1965. Interuniversitair Centrum voor Hedendaagse Geschiedenis. Bijdragen 38.

Denoo, Joris. *Repelsteel in Bourgondië. Annalen, stylen, mensen. Een leesboek.* Leuven: De Clauwaert, 1986.

Dupont, Guy. *Maagdenverleidsters, hoeren en speculanten. Prostitutie in Brugge tijdens de Bourgondische periode (1385-1515).* Bruges: Genootschap voor Geschiedenis/Marc Van de Wiele, 1997.

Froissart, Jean. *Chronique de Flandre.* Lille: Desclée De Brouwer, s.d.

Froissart, Jehan. *Les Chroniques.* De Witt-Guizot, Henriette (ed.). Paris: Hachette, 1881.

Gerlo, Aloïs and Rudolf de Smet. *Marnixi Epistulae. De briefwisseling van Marnix van Sint Aldegonde. Een kritische uitgave. Pars III (1579-1581).* Brussels: University Press, 1996.

Haegeman, M. *De Anglofilie in het graafschap Vlaanderen tussen 1379 en 1435. Politieke en economische Aspecten.* Kortrijk-Heule: UGA, 1988. Standen en Landen 90.

Hugenholtz, F. W. N. "The 1977 Crisis in the Burgundian Duke's Dominions." In J.S. Bromley and E.H. Kossmann. *Britain and the Netherlands, II,* Groningen: Wolters, 1964, pp. 40-41.

Hughes, Muriel J. "The Library of Philip the Bold and Margaret of Flanders, First Valois Duke and Duchess of Burgundy." *Journal of Medieval History,* 4 (1978), pp. 145-188.

Huizinga, Johan. *The Waning of the Middle Ages. A Study of the Forms of Life, Thought, and Art and the Netherlands in the XIVth and XVth Centuries*. New York: Doubleday, 1956.

Janssonius, Mart. *Isabella van Portugal. Moeder van Karel de Stoute*. Zutphen: Thieme, 1985.

———*Maria van Bourgondië. Bruid van Europa. 1457-1482*. Zutphen: Thieme, 1980.

Kallendorf-Carol, Imme. *Crime and Society in Medieval Flanders: the Oudburg of Ghent 1302-1401*. Ann Arbor, Mich.: University microfilms international, 1985.

Lecat, Jean-Philippe. *De Bourgondische uitdaging: bewogen leven in de late middeleeuwen*. Amsterdam/Brussels: Elsevier, 1985.

Lyon, B. "Fact and Fiction in English and Belgian Constitutional Law." In: *Medievalia et Humanistica,* 10 (1956), pp. 82-101.

Martens, M. *L'Administration du domaine ducal en Brabant au bas moyen âge 1250-1406*. Brussels: Palais des Académies, 1954.

Morand, Kathleen and David Finn. *Claus Sluter: Artist at the Court of Burgundy*. London: Harvey Miller, 1991.

Morren, Paul. *Van de dood van Karel de Stoute tot de troonsbestijding van aartshertog Karel (1477-1515)*. Brussels: Algemeen Rijksarchief, 1997. De Geschiedenis van België in Documenten.

Munro, J. H. *Wool, Cloth and Gold. The Struggle for Bullion in Anglo-Burgundian Trade 1340-1478*. Brussels: Université de Bruxelles, 1973.

Murray, John J. *Flanders and England. A Cultural Bridge. The Influence of the Low Countries on Tudor-Stuart England*. Antwerp: Fonds Mercator, 1985.

Pirenne, Henri. *Early Democracies in the Low Countries: Urban Society and Political Conflict in the Middle Ages and the Renaissance*. New York: Harper and Row, 1963.

Pirenne, Henri (ed.). *Chronique rimée des troubles de Flandre 1379-1380*. Gand: A. Siffer, 1902.

Prevenier, Walter. "Chivalric and Urban Culture in the Low Countries during the Late Middle Ages." *The Low Countries. Arts and Society in Flanders and the Netherlands. A Yearbook, 1997-1998*. Rekkem: Ons Erfdeel, 1997, pp. 278-280.

———"Briefwisseling tussen de vier Leden van Vlaanderen en Filips de Stoute, hertog van Bourgondië, en diens echtgenote Margareta van Male, over de inbreuken op de Vlaamse privileges door vorstelijke ambtenaren en instellingen (1398-1402)." *Bulletin de la Commission Royale d'Histoire,* 150 (1984), pp. 506-22.

Prevenier, Walter. (ed.). *Marriage and Social Mobility in the Late Middle Ages.* Handelingen van het colloquium gehouden te Gent op 18 april 1988. Ghent: Rijksuniversiteit te Gent, 1989.

Prevenier, Walter and Willem Pieter Blockmans. *The Burgundian Netherlands.* Cambridge: Cambridge University Press, 1986.

Prevenier, Walter and Wim Blockmans. *De Bourgondische Nederlanden.* Antwerp: Mercatorfonds, 1983.

Schelle, K. *Karel de Stoute. Leven en dood van een Boergondische hertog.* Nijmegen/Bruges: Gottmer/Orion, 1978.

Sivery, Gerard. *Structures agraires et vie rurale dans le Hainaut à la fin du moyen âge.* Lille: Université de Lille III, Villeneuve d'Ascq, 1977.

Tabri, Edward A. "The Funeral of Duke Philippe the Good." *Essays in History,* 1990-91, 33, pp. 2-17.

Unterkircher, F. *Getijdenboek voor Maria van Bourgondië.* Antwerp/Utrecht: Het Spectrum, 1974.

Uyttebrouck, A. *Le gouvernement du duché de Brabant au bas moyen âge (1335-1430).* Brussels: Université Libre de Bruxelles, 1975.

Van Uytven, R. and W. Blockmans. "Constitutions and their Application in the Netherlands during the Middle Ages." *Belgisch Tijdschrift voor Filologie en Geschiedenis* 38 (1969), pp. 399-424.

Vaughan, R. *De Bourgondiërs.* Bussum: Fibula-Van Dishoeck, 1976.

———*Charles the Bold: The Last Valois Duke of Burgundy* London: Longman, 1973.

———*John the Fearless: The Growth of Burgundian Power.* London: Longman, 1979.

———*Philip the Bold: The Formation of the Burgundian State.* London/New York: Longman, 1979.

———*Philip the Good. The Apogee of the Burgundian State.* London: Longman, 1970.

———*Valois Burgundy.* London: Lane, 1975.

Walsh, R. "The Coming of Humanism to the Low Countries. Some Italian Influences at the Court of Charles the Bold." *Humanistica Lovaniensia,* 25 (1976), pp. 146-197.

*e. The Low Countries under the Habsburgs (1482-1506)*

Brulez, W. "Bruges and Antwerp in the 15th and 16th Centuries: An Antithesis?" *Acta Historiae Neerlandicae,* 6 (1973), p. 1-26.

Craig, E. Harline (ed.). *The Rhyme and Reason of Politics in Early Modern Europe.* Dordrecht: Kluwer Academic Publishers, 1992.

Roegiers, Jan and Bart Van der Herten (eds.). *Eenheid op papier. De Nederlanden in kaart van Keizer Karel tot Willem I.* Leuven: Davidsfonds, 1994.

*f. The Spanish Period (1506-1713)*

Alsop, J. D. "British Intelligence for the North Atlantic Theatre of the War of Spanish Succession." *Mariner's Mirror,* 77 (1991), 2, pp. 113-118.

Beemon, F. E. "Calvinist Conscience and Rebellion: Marnix of Saint Aldegonde's Justification of the Dutch Revolt." *Fides et Historia,* 24 (1993), 3, pp. 91-99.

———"The Myth of the Spanish Inquisition and the Preconditions of the Dutch Revolt." *Archiv für Reformationsgeschichte,* 85 (1994), pp. 246-264.

Boer, Harm den. "Was Uriel Da Costa's Examen seized by the Spanish Inquisition? The Spanish Index Librorum Prohibitorum as a Bibliographical Source." *Studia Rosenthaliana,* 23 (1989), 1, pp. 3-7.

Boogman, J. C. "The Union of Utrecht: Its Genesis and Consequences." *Czasopismo Prawno-Historyczne,* 32 (1980), 1, pp. 77-108.

Coppens, Christian. "A Monomachia against Alciato: A Hitherto Unkown Pacifist Tract dedicated to Cardinal Granvelle and printed by Gillis Coppens of Diest, Antwerp, 1563." *Gutenberg-Jahrbuch,* 65 (1990), pp. 143-161.

Craeybeeckx, Jan et al. (ed.). *1585: Op gescheiden Wegen.* Leuven: Peeters, 1988. Colloquia Europalia 6.

Decavele, Johan (ed.). *Het eind van een rebelse droom. Opstellen over het calvinistisch bewind te Gent (1577-1584) en de terugkeer van de stad onder de gehoorzaamheid van de koning van Spanje (17 september 1584).* Ghent: Stadsbestuur, 1984.

De Grauwe, Jan. *Histoire de la Chartreuse Sheen Anglorum au Continent: Bruges, Louvain, Malines, Nieuport (1559-1783).* Salzburg:

Universität Salzburg, Institut für Anglistik und Amerikanistik, 1984. Analecta Cartusiana 48.

De Landtshaar, Jeannine. "Justus Lipsius herdacht. Een Vlaams humanist met Europese uitstraling." *Kultuurleven*, 1997, 5, pp. 102-107.

Dieterich, D. Henry. "Confraternities and Lay-leadership in Sixteenth-Century Liège." *Renaissance and Reformation,* 13 (1989), 1, pp. 15-34.

Duke, Alastair. "From King and Country or Country? Loyalty and Treason in the Revolt of the Netherlands." *Transactions of the Royal Historical Society,* 32 (1982), pp. 113-135.

Geyl, P. *History of the Low Countries: Episodes and Problems.* London: s.e, 1964.

Grever, John H. "The French Invasion of the Spanish Netherlands and the Provincial Assemblies in the Dutch Republic 1667-1668." *Parliaments, Estates & Representation,* 4 (1984), 1, pp. 25-35.

Israel, Jonathan. "Lopo Ramirez (David Curiel) and the Attempt to Establish a Sephardi Community in Antwerp in 1653-1654." *Studia Rosenthaliana,* 28 (1994), 1, pp. 99-119.

Israel, Jonathan I. "The Politics of International Trade Rivalry During the Thirty Years War: Gabriel de Roy and Olivares' Mercantilist Projects, 1621-1645." *International History Review,* 8 (1986), 4, pp. 517-549.

Koenigsberger, H. G. "Orange, Granvelle and Philip II." *Bijdragen en Mededelingen betreffende de Geschiedenis der Nederlanden,* 99 (1984), 4, pp. 573-595.

Lees, Lynn Hollen and Paul M. Hohenberg. "Urban Decline and Regional Economies: Brabant, Castile and Lombardy, 1550-1750." *Comparative Studies in Society and History,* 31 (1989), 3, pp. 439-461.

Lovett, Albert. "The General Settlement of 1577: An Aspect of Spanish Finance in the Early Modern Period." *Historical Journal*, 25 (1982), 1, pp. 1-22.

Marneff, Guido. *Antwerpen in de tijd van de reformatie: ondergronds protestantisme in een handelsmetropool 1550-1577.* Amsterdam/ Leuven: Meulenhoff/Kritak, 1996.

Parker, Geoffrey. "July 26th, 1581: The Dutch 'Declaration of Independence.'" *History Today*, 31 (July 1981), pp. 3-6.

———"New Light on an Old Theme: Spain and the Netherlands 1550-1650." *European Studies Quarterly,* 15 (1985), 2, pp. 219-236.

Rooden, P. T. van and J.W. Wesselius. "The Early Enlightment and Judaism: The 'Civil Dispute' between Philippus van Limborch and Isaac Orobio De Castro (1687)." *Studia Rosenthaliana*, 21 (1987), 2, pp. 140-153.

Schokkaert, E. and H. Van der Wee. "A Quantitative Study of Food Consumption in the Low Countries during the Sixteenth Century." *Journal of European Economic History,* 17 (1988), 1, pp. 131-158.

Steen, Charlie R. and William Beik (commentary). "The modernization of Pasquier de le Barre, Historian and magistrate of sixteenth-century Tournai." *Proceedings of the Annual Meeting of the Western Society for French History,* 14 (1987), pp. 12-19.

Stols, Eddy. "Flemish and Dutch Brazil. The Story of a Missed Opportunity." *The Low Countries. Arts and Society in Flanders and the Netherlands. A Yearbook, 1995-96.* Rekkem: Ons Erfdeel, 1995, pp. 163-171.

Strien, C. D. van. "Recusant Houses in the Southern Netherlands as seen by British Tourists, c. 1650-1720." *Recusant History,* 20 (1991), 4, pp. 495-511.

Sutherland, N. M. "The Origins of the Thirty Years War and the Structure of European Politics." *English Historical Review,* 107 (1992), 424, pp. 587-625.

Tracy, James D. "With and Without the Counter-Reformation: The Catholic Church in the Spanish Netherlands and the Dutch Republic, 1580-1650. A Review of the Literature since 1945." *Catholic Historical Review* 71 (1985), 4, pp. 547-575.

Van Peteghem, Paul. "De Pacificatie van Gent; triomf van de herwonnen eenheid?" In *Opstand en pacificatie in de Lage Landen. Bijdrage tot de studie van de Pacificatie van Gent.* Ghent/The Hague: Snoeck-Ducaju/Nijgh en Van Ditmar, 1976, pp. 99-121.

———"Politieke ideologie in de Apologie." *In Apologie van Willem van Oranje. Hertaling en evaluatie na vierhonderd jaar 1580-1980.* Tielt/Amsterdam: Lannoo, 1980, p. 43 ff.

*g. The Austrian Low Countries (1713-1795)*

Black, Jeremy. "From Pillnitz to Valmy: British Foreign Policy and Revolutionary France 1791-1792." *Francia*, 21 (1994), 2, pp. 129-146.

Devleeshouwer, Robert. "Albert Soboul et la Belgique." *Annales Historiques de la Révolution Française*, 54( 1982), 4, pp. 572-574.

Gerin, P. *Bibliografie van de geschiedenis van België—Bibliographie de l'histoire de Belgique 1789-21 juillet 1831*. Leuven-Brussels: Nauwelaerts, 1960. Interuniversitair Centrum voor Hedendaagse Geschiedenis. Bijdragen 15.

Howe, Patricia and Michael J. Sydenham (commentary). "Belgian Influence on French Policy, 1789-1793." *Consortium on Revolutionnary Europe 1750-1850. Proceedings 16 (1986)*, pp. 213-222.

Kossmann, E.H. *De Lage Landen 1780-1980. Twee eeuwen Nederland en België*. Amsterdam/Brussels: Elsevier, 1986.

———*The Low Countries 1780-1940*. Oxford: s.e., 1978.

Leboutte, René. "La condition ouvrière en Wallonie aux XVIIIe-XIXe Siècles." *Cahiers de Clio*, 92 (1987), pp. 5-41.

Lenders, Piet. *S.J. Vilain*. Leuven: Davidsfonds, 1995.

Mielants, Eric. "De publieke opinie ten tijde van de Brabantse Omwenteling. Een comparatief onderzoek tussen Brabant en Vlaanderen." *Belgisch Tijdschrift voor de Nieuwste Geschiedenis/ Revue Belge d'Histoire contemporaine*, 26 (1996), 1-2, 5-32.

Polasky, Janet. "Revolution, Industrialization and the Brussels Commercial Bourgeoisie, 1780-1793." *Belgisch Tijdschrift voor Nieuwste Geschiedenis*, 11 (1980), pp. 205-239.

Polasky, Janet. "The Success of a Counter-revolution in Revolutionary Europe: The Brabant Revolution of 1789." *Tijdschrift voor Geschiedenis*, 102 (1989), 3-4, pp. 413-421.

Proud, Judith K. "Essence and Impartiality: French-Language Periodical Digests of the Literary Press in the Eighteenth Century." *Studies in Newspaper and Periodical History*, 1993, pp. 53-65.

Rauch, Margarete. "De Betrekkingen tussen Oostenrijk en België." In *Geschenken aan het Keizerlijk Hof van Oostenrijk*. Brussels: Gemeentekrediet, 1987, pp. 12-23.

Raxhon, Philippe. "Henri Pirenne et la Révolution Liégeoise de 1789: contribution à l'histoire des révolutions." *History of European Ideas*, 13 (1991), 5, pp. 571-590.

———*La Révolution Liégoise de 1789. Vue par les Historiens Belges (de 1805 à Nos Jours).* Brussels: Université de Bruxelles, 1989.

Verhulst, Adriaan. "L'histoire rurale de la Belgique jusqu'à la fin de l'ancien régime (Aperçu bibliographique 1968-1983)." *Revue Historique,* 1984, 271 (2), pp. 419-437.

### *h. The French Period (1795-1815)*

Addison, Bland. "Secularization in the Monde Livresque and Literate Mentality at the end of the Ancien Regime." *Consortium on Revolutionary Europe 1750-1850: Proceedings,* 19 (1989), pp. 15-31.

———"The Bibliographie Liegeoise: From Jansenism to Sans-culottism in the Book Industry of Eightteenth-Century Liège." *Primary Sources & Original Works,* 1 (1991), 1-2, pp. 117-136.

Addison, Bland and Bud Burkhard (commentary). "Secularization and Revolution in the Bishop-Principality of Liège." *Proceedings of the Annual Meeting of the Western Society for French History,* 16 (1989), pp. 155-165.

Addison, Bland and Anne C. Meyering (commentary). "Historical Consciousness and Revolutionary Consciousness in Liège at the end of the Ancien Régime." *Consortium on Revolutionary Europe 1750-1850: Proceedings,* 23 (1994), pp. 332-340.

Destatte, Ph. "Elans révolutionnaires et réalisme d'Etat: les Wallons et la France (1789-1815)." In *De la déclaration des droits de l'homme au droit des peuples à disposer d'eux-mêmes.* Paris: Dixième conférence des Communautés de Langue française, 1995.

Gerard, J. et F. T'Sas. *Quand la Belgique était française.* Brussels: Legrain, s.d.

Howe, Patricia and Bland Addison (commentary). "The Revolutionary Press: Pierre Lebrun and le Journal General de l'Europe, 1785-1789." *Consortium on Revolutionary Europe 1750-1850: Proceedings,* 21 (1992), pp. 121-130.

Howe, Patricia and Michael J. Sydenham (commentary). "Belgian Influence on French Policy, 1789-1793." *Consortium on Revolutionary Europe 1750-1850: Proceedings* 16 (1986), pp. 213-222.

Lis, Catharina. *Social Change and the Labouring Poor: Antwerp, 1770-1860.* New Haven, Conn.: Yale University Press, 1986.

Maras, Raymond J. and June Burton (commentary). "Napoléon and Levies on the Art and Sciences." *Consortium on Revolutionary Europe 1750-1850: Proceedings,* 1987, 17, pp. 433-446.

Polasky, Janet L. and Sydenham, Michael J. (commentary). "The French Revolution: A Belgian Perspective." *Consortium on Revolutionary Europe 1750-1850: Proceedings,* 16 (1986), pp. 203-212.

Soltow, Lee. "The Distribution of Wealth in Belgium in 1814-1815." *Journal of European Economic History,* 10 (1981), 2, pp. 401-413.

Van Daele, Henri. *Van Bastille tot Boerenkrijg.* Tielt, Lannoo, 1997.

Van de Voorde, Hugo et al. *Bastille, Boerenkrijg en tricolore. De Franse revolutie in de Zuidelijke Nederlanden.* Leuven: Davidsfonds, 1989.

### *i. The Holland Period (1815-1830)*

Gerard, J. *Quand la Belgique était hollandaise.* Brussels: Legrain, s.d.

Laureyssens, Julienne M. "Growth of Central Banking: The Société Générale and its Impact on the Development of Belgium's Monetary System during the United Kingdom of the Netherlands (1815-1830). *Journal of European Economic History,* 15 (1986), 3, pp. 599-616.

Veve, Thomas D. and Donald D. Horward, (commentary). "The Barrier Fortresses in the Low Countries: Guaranteeing the Peace?" *Consortium on Revolutionary Europe 1750-1850: Proceedings,* 1992, 21, pp. 56-63.

### *j. The Kingdom of Belgium in the 19th Century (1830-1914)*

Bekaert, Geert. "Caloric Consumption in Industrializing Belgium." *Journal of Economic History,* 51 (1991), 3, pp. 633-655.

Clark, Samuel. "Nobility, Bourgeoisie and the Industrial Revolution in Belgium." *Past & Present,* 105 (1984), pp. 140-175.

De Beelde, I. "Interpreting Historical Financial Accounting Data. Examples from the Belgian Coal-mining Industry." *Belgisch Tijdschrift voor Nieuwste Geschiedenis/Revue Belge D'Histoire Contemporaine,* 24 (1993), 1-2, pp. 57-106.

Delbeke, Jos. "Glissements structuraux et sectoriaux dans l'économie flamande de 1850 à 1940." *Cahiers de Clio,* 66 (1981), pp. 23-38.

Delfosse, Pascale. "La petite bourgeoisie en crise et l'état: Le cas belge (1890-1914). *Mouvement Social,* 1981, 114, pp. 85-103.

———"La terre contre l'état? Pouvoir d'état et résistances traditionnelles en Belgique (1851-1929). *Mouvement Social,* 1994, pp. 53-90.

Deneckere, Gita. *Geuzengeweld. De invloed van antiklerikaal straatrumoer in de politieke geschiedenis van België (1831-1914).* Brussels: VUB-press, 1997.

———"The Transforming Impact of Collective Action: Belgium, 1886." *International Review of Social History,* 38(1993), 3, pp. 345-367.

De Wilde, Bart. *Witte Boorden, blauwe kielen. Patroons en arbeiders in de Belgische textielnijverheid in de 19de en 20ste eeuw.* Ghent: Ludion, 1997.

Eeckhout, Patricia van den. "Family Income of Ghent Working-Class Families ca. 1900." *Journal of Family History,* 18 (1993), 2, pp. 87-110.

Fishman, J. S. *Diplomacy and Revolution: The London Conference of 1830 and the Belgian Revolt.* Amsterdam: CHEV, 1988.

Fremdling, Rainer. "The Puddler. A Craftman's Skill and the Spread of a new Technology in Belgium, France and Germany. *Journal of European Economic History,* 20 (1991), pp. 529-567.

Gerard, J. *Albert I et la Belgique de 1900 à 1930.* Brussels: Legrain, s.d.

———*Chronique de la régence 1944-1950.* Bruxelles: Collet, 1983.

Gubin, Eliane. "Home, sweet home: l'image de la femme au foyer en Belgique et au Canada avant 1914." *Belgisch Tijdschrift voor Nieuwste Geschiedenis,* 22 (1991), 3-4, pp. 521-568.

Hasquin, Hervé. "Quelle Révolution en 1830?" *Revue de l'Université de Bruxelles,* 1989, 3-4, pp. 35-39.

Hilden, Patricia J. "The Rhetoric and Iconography of Reform: Women Coal Miners in Belgium, 1840-1914." *Historical Journal,* 34 (1991), 2, pp. 411-436.

Horgan, John C. and John W. Rooney (commentary). "The British Press and the Belgian Revolution." *Consortium on Revolutionary Europe, 1750-1850: Proceedings,* 1989, 19, part 2, pp. 408-424.

Jadoulle, Jean-Louis. *La Pensée de l'Abbé Pottier (1849-1923): Contribution à l'Histoire de la Démocratie Chrétienne en Belgique.* Louvain-la-Neuve: Collège Erasme, 1991.

Kalb, Don. "Moral Production, Class Capacities and Communal Commotion: an Illustration from Central Brabant Shoemaking (c. 1900-20)." *Social History,* 16 (1991), 3, pp. 279-298.

Krysiek, James S. and John W. Rooney Jr. (commentary). "White-hall and the Belgian Revolt." *Consortium on Revolutionary Europe, 1750-1850: Proceedings,* 1989, 19, part 2, pp. 380-392.

Laureyssens, Julie M. "Financial Innovation and Regulation. The Société Générale and the Belgian State after Independence (1830-1850)." *Belgisch Tijdschrift voor Nieuwste Geschiedenis,* 20 (1989), 1-2, pp. 223-250.

———"Financial Innovation and Regulation. The Société Générale and the Belgian State after Independence (1830-1850). Part 2." *Belgisch Tijdschrift voor Nieuwste Geschiedenis/ Revue Belge D'Histoire Contemporaine,* 23 (1992), 1-2, pp. 61-89.

Lebrun, Pierre. "Histoire quantitative et développement de la Belgique au XIXe siècle: Etat des Recherches, Règles méthodologiques, choix épistémologiques. *Cahiers de Clio,* 64(1980), pp. 35-58.

Lefevre, Patrick. "Le mouvement libéral flamand at Bruges-(1872-1940)." *Revue Belge de Philologie et d'Histoire,* 58 (1980), 2, pp. 382-392.

Legros, H. "Les structures de la cooperation socialiste, 1900-1940." *Belgisch Tijdschrift voor Nieuwste Geschiedenis,* 22 (1991), 1-2, pp. 73-127.

Lintsen, Harry and Rik Steenaard. "Steam and Polders: Belgium and the Netherlands: 1790-1850." *Tractrix*, 1991, 3, pp. 121-147.

Mabille, Xavier. *Histoire politique de la Belgique.* Brussels: CRISP, 1986.

Moulaert, Jan. *De vervloekte staat. Anarchisme in Frankrijk, Nederland en België 1880-1914.* Berchem: Epo, 1981.

———*Rood en Zwart. De anarchistische beweging in België 1880-1914.* Leuven: Davidsfonds, 1995.

Musin, Linda and Robert Flagothier. "De la coopération locale à la société multirégionale: l'union coopérative de Liège (1914-1940)." *Belgisch Tijdschrift voor Nieuwste Geschiedenis,* 22 (1991), 1-2, pp. 281-309.

Nijhof, Erik and Peter Scholliers (ed.). *Het tijdperk van de machine. Industriecultuur in België en Nederland.* Brussels: VUB-Press, 1997.

Noiret, Serge. "Political Parties and the Political System in Belgium before Federalism, 1830-1980." *European History Quarterly,* 24 (1994), 1, pp. 85-122.

Polasky, Janet L. "Traditionalists, Democrats and Jacobins in Revolutionary Brussels." *Journal of Modern History,* 56 (1984), 2, pp. 227-262.

———"Women in Revolutionary Belgium: From Stone Throwers to Hearth Tenders." *History Workshop Journal,* 21(1986), pp. 87-104.

Rooney, John. *Revolt in the Netherlands: Brussels 1830.* Lawrence, Kans.: Coronado Press, 1982.

Schmidt, Daniel P. and John W. Rooney, Jr. (commentary). "France, Great Britain and Belgian Independence." *Consortium on Revolutionary Europe 1750-1850: Proceedings,* 1989, 19 part 2, pp. 393-407.

Scholliers, Peter. "From the 'Crisis of Flanders' to Belgium's 'Social Question': Nutritional Landmarks of Transition in Industrializing Europe (1840-1890)." *Food and Foodways,* 5 (1992), 2, pp. 151--175.

Strikwerda, Carl. "Interest-group Politics and the International Economy: Mass Politics and Big Business Corporations in the Liège Coal Bassin, 1870-1914." *Journal of Social History,* 2 (1991), pp. 277-307.

———"The Divided Class: Catholics versus Socialists in Belgium, 1880-1914." *Comparative Studies in Society and History,* 30 (1988), 2, pp. 333-359.

———*A House Divided: Catholics, Socialists, and Flemish Nationalists in Nineteenth-Century Belgium.* Lanham, Md.: Rowman & Littlefield Publishers, 1997.

Thomas, Daniel H. *The Guarantee of Belgian Independence and Neutrality in European Diplomacy, 1830's-1930's.* Kingston, R.I.: D. H. Thomas, 1984.

Trausch, Gilbert. "Historiens, publicistes et nationalistes belges face à la question du Luxembourg à la veille de la première guerre mondiale." *Revue de l'Université de Bruxelles,* 1981, 1-2, pp. 37-60.

Vanhaute, Eric. "Processes of Peripheralization in a Core Region: The Campine Area of Antwerp in the 'Long' Nineteenth Century." *Review (Fernand Braudel Center),* 16(1993), 1, pp. 57-81.

Vervaeck, S. *Bibliografie van de geschiedenis van België—Bibliographie de l'histoire de Belgique 1831-1865.* Leuven-Brussels: Nauwelaerts, 1965. Interuniversitair Centrum voor Hedendaagse Geschiedenis. Bijdragen 37.

Vlerick, A. J. "Flanders' Socio-Economic Emancipation since the Industrial Revolution." *Plural Societies,* 17 (1987), 3, pp. 9-16.

Witte, Els. "The Formation of a Centre in Belgium: The Role of Brussels in the Formative Stage of the Belgian State (1830-40)." *European History Quarterly,* 19 (1989), 4, pp. 435-468.

Witte, Els et al. *Politieke geschiedenis van België van 1830 tot heden.* Antwerp: Standaard, 1990.

*k. World War I (1914-1919)*

Brants, Chrisje and Kees. *Velden van weleer. Reisgids naar de Eerste Wereldoorlog.* Amsterdam/Antwerp: Nijgh & Van Ditmar/Dedalus, 1994.

Catoire, Philippe. "Un hiver à Veurne. Le témoignage d'un officier belge attaché au GQG (Octobre 1914-Janvier 1915)." *Revue Belge d'Histoire Militaire,* 29 (1992), 6, pp. 423-448, 7, pp. 489-510.

Chielens, Piet and Wim. *De Troost van Schoonheid. De literaire Salient. (Ieper 1914-1918).* Groot-Bijgaarden: Globe, 1996.

*De IJzertoren. Vlaams memoriaal in een Europees en mondiaal vredesdomein.* Diksmuide: Ijzerbedevaartsecretariaat, 1997.

De Schaepdrijver, Sophie. *De Groote Oorlog. Het koninkrijk België tijdens de Eerste Wereldoorlog.* Amsterdam: Atlas, 1997.

De Vos, Luc. *De Eerste Wereldoorlog.* Leuven: Davidsfonds, 1996.

De Weerdt, Denise. *De Vrouwen van de Eerste Wereldoorlog.* Ghent: Stichting Mens en Kultuur, s.d. (English Summary on p. 303).

Geldof, Wim. *Camille Huysmans. De Man van Stockholm.* Antwerp: Contact, 1996.

Helaers, Michel. "De Albertijnse mythe voor de soldaat aan de IJzer: een beeldvorming door de 'legerbode' (1914-1918), *Revue Belge d'Histoire Militaire,* 28 (1990), 6, pp. 441-466.

Heyse, M. and R. Van Eeno. *Bibliografie van de geschiedenis van België—Bibliographie de l'histoire de Belgique 1914-1940.* Leuven-

Brussels: Nauwelaerts, 1986. Interuniversitair Centrum voor Hedendaagse Geschiedenis. Bijdragen 90.

Johansson, Rune. *Small State in Boundary Conflict: Belgium and the Belgian-German Border, 1914-1919.* Lund: Lund University Press, 1988.

Lefevre, P. and J. Lorette (eds.). *La Belgique et la Première Guerre Mondiale. Bibliographie. België en de Eerste Wereldoorlog. Bibliografie.* Brussels: Koninklijk Legermuseum, 1987. Centrum voor Militaire Geschiedenis. Bijdragen 21.

Macdonald, Lyn. *They Called it Passchendaele: The Story of the Third Battle of Ypres and of the Men Who Fought in It.* London: Michael Joseph, 1984.

Marks, Sally. *Innocent Abroad: Belgium at the Paris Peace Conference of 1919.* Chapel Hill: University of North Carolina Press, 1981.

Marks, Sally and John C. Cairns (commentary). "Sacred Egoism: France and Belgian Aims in World War I." *Proceedings of the Annual Meeting of the Western Society for French History* 10 (1982), pp. 472-481.

Palo, Michael F. "Belgium's Response to the Peace Initiative of December 1916: An Exercise in Diplomatic Self-Determination. *Historian*, 42 (1980), 4, pp. 583-597.

Schepens, Luc. *14-18. Een oorlog in Vlaanderen.* Tielt/Weesp: Lannoo, 1984. Perspectief.

Schuursma, R. I. et al. *14-18. De Eerste Wereldoorlog.* Amsterdam: Amsterdam Boek, 1975.

Smart, Judith. "'Poor Little Belgium' and Australian Popular Support for War 1914-1915." *War & Society,* 12 (1994), 1, pp. 27-46.

Sorgeloos, C. and Veirman, G. "La guerre du silence ou le journal de la comtesse D'Outremont (1914-1918)." *Revue Belge d'Histoire Militaire* 29 (1991), 2, pp. 123-144, 3, pp. 209-228.

Stevenson, D. "Belgium, Luxemburg, and the Defence of Western Europe, 1914-1920." *International History Review,* 4 (1982), 4, pp. 504-523.

Vanschoenbeek, Guy. "Titanenwerk in de schaduw van Huysmans." *Vlaanderen Morgen,* 1996, 6, November-December, pp. 7-21.

Verschaeve, Cyriel. *Oorlogsindrukken (1914-1917).* Ingeleid door Daniël Vanacker. Brussels: Selectief, 1966.

Wiest, Andrew. "Haig's Abortive Amphibious Assault on Belgium, 1917." *Historian*, 54 (1992), 4, pp. 669-682.

*l. The Interbellum Period (1919-1940)*

Balthazar, Herman. "Belgium Since World War I." In Marina Boudart, Michel Boudart and René Bryssinck. *Modern Belgium.* Palo Alto, California: The Society for the Promotion of Science and Scholarship, 1990, pp. 73-85.

Brustein, William. "The Political Geography of Rexism. The Case of Rexism." *American Sociological Review,* 53 (1988), 1, pp. 69-80.

Bussière, Eric. *La France, la Belgique et l'Organisation Economique de l'Europe, 1918-1935.* Paris: Comité pour l'Histoire Economique et Financière de la France, 1992.

Debrouwere, Jan. "Jef Van Extergem en zijn tijd." *Vlaams Marxistisch Tijdschrift,* 31 (1997), 4, pp. 69-75.

Enssle, Manfred J. *Stresemann's Territorial Revisionism: Germany, Belgium, and the Eupen-Malmédy Question, 1919-1929.* Wiesbaden: Steiner, 1980.

Gobijn, Ronny and Winston Spriet. *De jaren '30 in België. De massa in verleiding.* Brussels: ASLK en Ludion, 1994.

Hogg, Robin L. *Structural Rigidities and Policy Inertia in Inter-war Belgium.* Brussels: Paleis der Academiën, 1986. Verhandelingen: Klasse der Letteren 118.

LeBéguec, Gilles. "Prélude à un syndicalisme bourgeois: l'association de défense des classes moyennes (1907-1939)." *Vingtième Siècle,* 37 (1993), pp. 93-104.

Luyten, Dirk. "Politiek corporatisme en de crisis van de liberale ideologie (1920-1944): Deel 2." *Belgisch Tijdschrift voor Nieuwste Geschiedenis,* 24 (1993), 1-2, pp. 107-184.

Marks, Sally. "Ménage à Trois: The Negotiations for an Anglo-French-Belgian Alliance in 1922." *International History Review,* 4 (1982), 4, pp. 524-552.

Pels, Dick. "The Dark Side of Socialism: Hendrik De Man and the Fascist Temptation." *History of the Human Sciences,* 6 (1993), 2, pp. 75-95.

Scholliers, Peter. "Index-linked Wages, Purchasing Power and Social Conflict between the Wars: the Belgian Approach (Internationally compared)." *Journal of European Economic History,* 20 (1991), 2, pp. 407-439.

———"Regionale verschillen tussen consumptiepatronen tijdens het interbellum: een methodologische verkenning." *Revue Belge de Philologie et d'Histoire,* 60 (1982), 2, pp. 312-338.

Van Causenbroeck, Bernard. Herman Vos. *Van Vlaams-nationalisme naar socialisme.* Antwerp/Ghent: Hadewijch/Amsab, 1997.

*Wies Moens, Memoires. Bezorgd door Olaf Moens en Yves T'Sjoen.* Amsterdam/Antwerp: Meulenhof/Kritak, 1997.

### *m. World War II (1940-1945)*

Binion, Rudolph. "Repeat Performance: A Psychohistorical Study of Leopold III and Belgian Neutrality." *History and Theory,* 8 (1969), pp. 213-259.

Couttenier, Jean-Pierre. "Collaboratie of cultuur?" *Kultuurleven,* 1997, July, pp. 188-191.

De Decker, Cynrik and Jean Louis Roba. *Luchtgevechten boven België 1941-1942: de Luftwaffejagers tegen de Britse en Amerikaanse luchtmacht.* Erpe: De Krijger, 1994. België in oorlog 5.

De Geest, Dirk et al. *Collaboratie of Cultuur? Een Vlaams tijdschrift in bezettingstijd (1941-1944).* Antwerp: Kritak/Meulenfhoff/ SOM-A, 1997.

Delaunois, J.M. "From Spiritual Exaltation to Political Action—Streel, José or the Tragic Fate of a Belgian Collaborator." *Revue du Nord,* 77 (1995), Iss. 311, pp. 599-611.

De Wever, Bruno. *Greep naar de macht. Vlaams-nationalisme en Nieuwe Orde. Het VNV 1933-1945.* Tielt/Ghent: Lannoo/ Perspectief, 1994.

D'Ydewalle, Pierre. *Mijn oorlogsjaren.* Tielt: Lannoo, 1997.

Fagnoul, Kurt. "Aspects de la seconde guerre mondiale au pays de Saint Vyth." *Cahiers d'Histoire de la Seconde Guerre Mondiale,* 7 (1982), pp. 185-211.

Flam, Leopold and Hubert Dethier. *Naar de dageraad. Kroniek en getuigenis van de orlogsjaren 1943-45.* Brussels: VUBPRESS, 1996.

Gérard, Jo. *La Belgique 1940-1944 sous l'Occupation.* Meddens: Bruxelles, 1974.

Huysse, Luc and Steven Dhondt. *Onverwerkt verleden.* Leuven: Kritak, 1991.

Luyten, Dirk. *Burgers boven elke verdenking? Vervolging van de economische collaboratie in België na de Tweede Wereldoorlog.* Brussels: VUB-press, 1996.

———"Het Katholieke patronaat en het korporatisme in de jaren dertig en tijdens de bezetting." *Cahiers/Bijdragen,* 13 (1990), pp. 91-148.

———*Ideologie en praktijk van het corporatisme tijdens de Tweede Wereldoorlog*. Brussels: VUB-press, 1997.

Matanle, Ivor. *De Tweede Wereldoorlog.* Lisso: Rebro Productions, 1989.

Meyers, Willem C. M. "België in de Tweede Wereldoorlog. Een poging tot kritische selectie van de voornaamste werken gepubliceerd sinds 1970." *Bijdragen en mededelingen betreffende de geschiedenis der Nederlanden,* 105 (1990), 2, pp. 280-294.

———"Bibliografie van de in 1982, 1983 en 1984 verschenen publikaties betreffende België tijdens de Tweede Werelddoorlog. *Cahiers/Bijdragen,* 9 (1985), pp. 375-439.

———"Bibliografie van de in 1985 verschenen publikaties betreffende België tijdens de Tweede Wereldoorlog. *Cahiers/Bijdragen,* 10 (1986), pp. 223-246.

———"België in de Tweede Wereldorlog. Een poging tot kritische selectie van de voornaamste werken gepubliceerd sinds 1970." *Bijdragen en Mededelingen betreffende de Geschiedenis der Nederlanden,* 105 (1990), 2, pp. 280-294.

Moens, Olaf and Yves T'Soen (eds.). *Moens, Wies. Memoires.* Amsterdam/Antwerp: Meulenhoff/Kritak, 1996.

Pauwels, Wilfried. *De bevrijdingsdagen van 1944. De geheime rapporten van François Louis Ganshof.* Antwerp: De Nederlanden, 1994.

Raskin, Evrard. *Gerard Romsée. Een ongewone man, een ongewoon leven.* Antwerp/Baarn: Hadewych, 1995.

Rémy. *The Eighteenth Day: The Tragedy of King Leopold III of Belgium.* Translated by Stanley R. Rader. New York: Everest House, 1978.

Scholliers, Peter. "Naar de dageraad." *Vlaams Marxistisch Tijdschrift,* 31(1997), 4, pp. 96-98.

Steinberg, M. *1942: les cent jours de la déportation des juifs de Belgique.* Brussels: Vie Ouvrière, 1984.

———*La question juive. 1942-1944*. Brussels: Vie Ouvrière, 1986.

Van den Berghe, Gie. "De Geschiedenis is nooit voorbij." *Bijdragen tot de Eigentijdse Geschiedenis* (Studiecentrum Oorlog en Hedendaagse Maatschappij) 1,1.

———"De rekenkunde van het leed. Hou jij je mond maar, ik was in Auschwitz." *Belgisch Tijdschrift voor Nieuwste Geschiedenis,* 26 (1996), 3-4, pp. 241-267.

———*De zot van Rekem & Gott mit uns.* Antwerp/ Baarn: Hadewych, 1995.

———*Getuigen: een case-study over ego-documenten: bibliografie van ego-documenten over de nationaal-socialistische kampen en gevangenissen, geschreven of getekend door 'Belgische' (ex-)gevangenen: Belgen, personen die in België gedomicilieerd waren of verbleven, en andere uit België gedeporteerde personen.* Brussels: Navorsings-en studiecentrum voor de geschiedenis van de tweede wereldoorlog, 1995.

Van den Wijngaert, Mark. *Nood breekt wet. Economische collaboratie of accomodatie: het beleid van Alexandre Galopin, gouverneur van de Société Générale tijdens de Duitse bezetting (1940-1944).* Lannoo: Tielt, 1990.

Vanwelkenhuyzen, J. and J. Dumont. *1940. Le grand exode.* Paris/Gembloux: Duculot, 1983.

Verhoeyen, Etienne. "Boven elke verdenking. Dirk Luyten licht voor het eerst de bestraffing van economische collaboratie door." *De Morgen,* 9.1.1996, p. 27.

———"Résistances et résistants en Belgique occupée, 1940-1944." *Revue Belge de Philologie et d'Histoire,* 70 (1992), 2, pp. 381-398.

———"Un groupe de résistants du nord Hainaut: La phalange blanche." *Cahiers/Bijdragen,* 12 (1989), pp. 163-205.

Willequet, J. *La Belgique sous la botte. Résistances et collaborations 1940-1945.* Paris: Editions Universitaires, 1986.

*n. After World War II (1945-)*

*i. Belgium*

*Albert II en Paola, Koning en Koningin der Belgen.* Brussels: Federale Voorlichtingsdienst, 1996.

Beaufays, Jean. "Belgium: A Dualist Political System?" *Publius*, 18 (1988), 2, pp. 63-73.

*Boudewijn, het levén van een Vorst 1930-1993.* Brussels: Federale Voorlichtingsdienst, 1993.

Boulangé, B., R. Cavenaille and M. Colle-Michel. *La Belgique: Des origines à l'Etat Fédéral.* Namur: Editions Erasme, 1990.

Brassine, J. "Les Nouvelles Institutions Politiques de la Belgique." *Dossiers du CRISP,* 1989, no. 30.

Covell, Maureen. "Belgium's New Regional Institutions." *Canadian Journal of Netherlandic Studies,* 1983, 4 (2) - 5 (1), pp. 82-88.

———"Regionalization and Economic Crisis in Belgium: The variable Origins of Centrifugal and Centripetal Forces." *Canadian Journal of Political Science,* 19 (1986), 2, pp. 261-281.

De Clercq, Bertrand J. "Een Vlaams pleidooi voor België", *Kultuurleven*, 1997, January, pp. 78-81.

Dujardin, Vincent. *Gaston Eyskens tussen koning en regent. België 1949-1950: een sleuteljaar.* Vertaald door Karin Kustermans. Leuven/Amsterdam: Kritak/Meulenhoff, 1996.

Fitzmaurice, J. *The Politics of Belgium. Crisis and Compromise in a Plural Society.* London: Hurst, 1983.

———*The Politics of Belgium. A Unique Federalism.* London: Hurst, 1996.

Groep Coudenberg. *Naar een ander België? Groep Coudenberg.* Tielt: Lannoo, 1987.

Hooghe, Liesbet. *A Leap in the Dark: National Conflict and Federal Reform in Belgium.* New York: Ithaca, 1991.

Huyse, Luc en Kris Hoflack (eds.). *De democratie heruitgevonden. Oud en nieuw in politiek België. 1944-1950.* Leuven: Van Halewyck, 1995.

Huyse, Luc and Steven Dhondt. *La Répression des Collaborations, 1942-1952: Un Passé Toujours Présent.* Brussels: Centre de Recherche et d'Information Socio-Politiques, 1991.

Jacquemin, Nico, Mark van den Wijngaert and Martine Goossens. *O dierbaar België: ontstaan en structuur van de federale staat. Met de*

*tekst van de nieuwe grondwet.* Antwerp: Hadewych, 1996.
*Koninklijk Paleis 1996-1997.* Brussels: Federale Voorlichtingsdienst, 1997. Jaarboek.
Linden, H. Van der. *Belgium. The Making of a Nation.* Oxford: Clarendon Press, 1920.
Platel, Marc. *Het nieuwe België. Andere Belgen. 1930—het Sint-Michielsakkoord.* Knokke-Heist: Creart, 1993.
"Redactioneel: De beproeving van de Federalisten." *Vlaanderen Morgen,* 1997, 6, pp. 3-5.
Rochtus, D. "België als 'bewuste keuze'? Zeven stellingen omtrent de Vlaamse identiteit binnen een tweetalig land." *De Gids op Maatschappelijk Gebied,* 1996, 11, pp. 955-959.
Schepers, Stefan. "The Third Revision of the Belgian Constitution." *Indiana Social Studies Quarterly,* 37 (1984-85), 3, pp. 5-17.
Séguy, Philippe and Antoine Michelland. *Fabiola. Koningin in het Wit.* Antwerp/Baarn: Hadewijch/Fontein, 1996.
Stengers, Jean. *De koningen der Belgen.* Leuven: Davidsfonds, 1997.
Van Daele, Henri. *Zes koninginnen.* Tielt: Lannoo, 1996.
Van Lobkowicz, Prins. *Boudewijn, biografie.* Eigenbrakel: Collet, 1995.
Velímsky, Vítezlav. "Belgium of the Eighties: Unitary, Bi-cultural or Made up of Three Regions?" *Euopa Ethnica,* 40 (1983), 1, pp. 1-14.
Verhofstadt, Guy. *De Belgische ziekte. Diagnose en remedies.* Antwerp/Baarn: Hadewijch, 1997.
Wegwijs in de Federale Administratie. Deel 1: Federale Ministeries. Deel 2. Federale Overheidsinstellingen. Brussels: Federale Voorlichtingsdienst, 1997.
Witte, Els. "Belgian Federalism: Towards Complexity and Asymmetry." *West European Politics,* 15 (1992), 4, pp. 95-117.
Wyvekens, Pierre. *De monarchie in België.* Brussels: Federale Voorlichtingsdienst, 1992.
*Zes Koningen.* Brussels: Federale Voorlichtingsdienst, 1995.

### *ii. Brussels*

Corijn, Eric. "Brussel scheef bekeken." *Vlaams Marxistisch Tijdschrift,* 31 (1997), 4, pp. 6-8.
De Ridder, Martine and Luis Ricardo Fraga. "The Brussels issue in

Belgian politics." *West European Politics,* 9 (1986), 3, 376-392.

De Ridder, Paul. *Brussel. Geschiedenis van een Brabantse Stad.* Ghent: Mens en Kultuur, 1997.

Gatz, Sven en Johan Basiliades. "De rechten van de minderheden in Brussel." *Vlaanderen Morgen,* 1997, 6, pp. 7-14.

Govaert, S. Le Conseil de Région Bruxelles Capitale. *Courrier Hebdomadaire du CRISP,* 1351/2.

Groothaert, Jacques. "Brussels." In Marina Boudart, Michel Boudart and René Bryssinck. *Modern Belgium.* Palo Alto, California: The Society for the Promotion of Science and Scholarship, 1990, pp. 25-27.

Hasquin, Hervé. "Les Wallons, la Belgique et Bruxelles: une histoire de frustations." *Revue de l'Université de Bruxelles,* 1989, 3-4, pp. 41-58.

Monteyne, A. "Brussels, the Central Problem." *Plural Societies,* 17 (1987), 3, pp. 31-39.

Pashley, Wilfried. *Brussel. De hoofdstad van Vlaanderen en de Staatshervorming.* Brussels: Vlaamse Gemeenschap, Departement Coördinatie. Administratie Kanselarij en Voorlichting, 1996. Tweede bijgewerkte druk.

Smolar-Meynaert, A en J. Stengers (ed.). *Het gewest Brussel. Van de oude dorpen tot de stad nu.* Brussels: Gemeentekrediet, 1989.

Stengers, J. Brussel. *Groei van een hoofdstad.* Antwerp: Mercatorfonds, 1979.

Tastenhoye, Guido. *Vlaams Brabant ingelijfd bij Brussel.* Leuven: Davidsfonds, 1997.

Teirlinck, H. *Brussel 1900.* Antwerp/Amsterdam: Elsevier/Manteau, 1981.

Van Alboom, R. *De verbeulemansing van Brussel.* Brussels: BRT, 1990.

Van den Brande, Luc and Anne Van Asbroeck. *Beleidsplan Brussel van de Vlaamse regering. Goedgekeurd op 11 maart 1997.* Brussels: Ministerie van de Vlaamse Gemeenschap, Administratie Kanselarij en Voorlichting, 1997.

Van Istendael, Geert. "Brussels, City of the Coming Century." *The Low Countries. Arts and Society in Flanders and the Netherlands. A yearbook, 1994-95.* Rekkem: Ons Erfdeel, 1994, pp. 10-17.

*1989-1992; drie jaar beslissingen in het Brussels hoofdstedelijk gewest.* Brussels: Iris, 1992.

Witte, E. *Le bilinguisme en Belgique. Le cas de Bruxelles.* Brussels:

Editions de l'Université de Bruxelles, 1984.
Witte, E. et al. *Het probleem Brussel sinds Hertoginnedal (1963). Acta van het colloquium VUB-CRISP van 20 en 21 oktober 1988/ Le problème Bruxelles depuis Val Duchesse (1963). Actes du colloque VUB-CRISP du 20 et 21 octobre* 1988. Brussels: VUB-Press, 1989.

### *iii. Flemish Movement and Flemish Government*

Abicht, Ludo. *De herinnering is een vorm van hoop. Vlaanderen in de postmoderniteit.* Brussels: Wij, 1997.
Baert, Frans. "Proeve van een grondwet voor Vlaanderen." *Vlaanderen Morgen,* 1996, 5, pp. 33-46.
Baeten, Jean. *Harde Vlaamse koppen. De boeren van Voeren.* Sint-Genesius-Rode: Eigen Beheer, 1995.
Balthazar, Herman. *De weg naar vernederlandsing van de RUG.* Ghent: Rijksuniversiteit Gent, 1985.
Becker, Jean-Jacques. "La guerre de 1914, La Belgique et la question Flamande." *Histoire,* 71 (1984), pp. 87-89.
Becuwe, Frank and de Lentdecker, Louis. *Van IJzerfront tot Zelfbestuur.* Diksmuide: VZW Bedevaart naar de Graven aan de IJzer, 1993.
Boeva, L. *Pour les flamands la même chose.* Ghent: Provinciebestuur, Oost-Vlaanderen.
Boudens, Robrecht. "Een rapport van hoofdaloezenier J. Marinis aan kardinaal Mercier over de Vlaamse Beweging aan het front tijdens de Eerste Wereldoorlog." *Wetenschappelijke Tijdingen,* 1995, 54, pp. 72 ff.
Cammaerts, Emile. *The Flemish Movement.* London: New Europe, 1918.
Clough, Shepard B. *A History of the Flemish Movement in Belgium: A Study in Nationalism.* New York: Smith, 1930.
Coppens, E. C. *Paul Fredericq.* Ghent: Liberaal Archief, 1990; Verhandelingen 5.
Coppieters, Maurice. *Het jaar van de klaproos.* Bruges: Kruispunt, 1987-1993.
Defoort, Eric. *Al mijn illusies bloeien.* Antwerp/Baarn: Hautekiet, 1991.
———*Het klauwen van de historicus.* Antwerp: Hautekiet, 1996.

De Geest, Wim. "De leeuwenjager schiet tekort. Over de sociolinguistische bijziendheid van Marc Reynebeau." *Vlaanderen Morgen,* 1996, 5, pp. 7-19.

Demeurie, Dirk (ed.). *De IJzertoren. Vlaams memoriaal in een Europees en mondiaal vredesdomein.* Diksmuide: Ijzerbedevaartssecretariaat, 1997.

Deprez, A. (ed.). *F.A. Snellaert en J.A. Alberdink Thijm. Briefwisseling 1843-1872.* Ghent: Koninklijke Vlaamse Academie voor Taal- en Letterkunde, 1972. Moderne Letteren, 22.

———*Kroniek van F.A. Snellaert (1909-1972).* Bruges: Orion, 1972.

Deprez, K. "Le flamand? Non, le néerlandais ou la Flandre minoritaire de néerlandophonie." *Toudi,* 2 (1988), pp. 209-224.

De Vroede, Maurits. *The Flemish Movement in Belgium.* Antwerp: Kultuurraad voor Vlaanderen, 1975.

De Wachter, F. "Wie is mijn volk? De verleiding van het zachte nationalisme." In R. Detrez and J. Blommaert (red.), *Nationalisme.: Kritische opstellen.* Berchem: EPO, 1994, pp. 71-91.

De Wever, Bruno. *Greep naar de macht. Vlaams-Nationalisme en Nieuwe Orde. Het VNV 1933-1945.* Tielt/Ghent: Lannoo/Perspectief, 1994. (obb dest.935.4)

Durnez, Gaston. *Zeg mij waar de bloemen zijn. Vlaanderen 1914-1918.* Leuven: Davidsfonds, 1988.

Dutoit, Christian. *Jef van Extergem en de Vlaamse beweging.* Antwerp: Soethoudt, 1983.

*Eén regering voor de Vlamingen. De Executieve van de Nederlandse Gemeenschap en het Vlaamse Gewest in de onmiddellijke fase van de staatshervorming.* Brussels: Executieve van de Nederlandse Gemeenschap en het Vlaamse Gewest, 1979.

Elias, H. J. *Geschiedenis van de Vlaamse gedachte.* Antwerp: De Nederlandsche Boekhandel, 1970-1971.

———*Vijfentwintig jaar Vlaamse beweging 1914-1939.* Antwerp/ Utrecht: De Nederlandsche Boekhandel, 1971.

*Encyclopedie van de Vlaamse Beweging (3 delen).* Tielt: Lannoo, 1998.

Gerard, Emmanuel. "Vlaanderen—België—Groot-Nederland. De visie van Lode Wils." *Ons Erfdeel,* 38 (1995), 5, p. 643-651.

Goossens, Martine. "The Flemish Parliament." *The Low Countries. Arts and Society in Flanders and the Netherlands. A yearbook, 1996-1997,* Rekkem: Ons Erfdeel, 1996, pp. 297-299.

Goossens, Martine. *Ontstaan en groei van het Vlaams parlement: 1970-1995.* Kapellen: Pelckmans, 1996.

Gubin, Eliane. "D'une histoire nationale à l'autre: à propos de l'historiographie du mouvement Flamand en Belgique." *Revue de l'Université de Bruxelles,* 1981, 1-2, pp. 125-146.

Hermans, Théo, Lode Wils and Louis Vos (eds.) *The Flemish Movement. A Documentary History 1780-1990.* London: Athlone Press, 1992.

*Hersens op z'n Vlaams. Bekende Vlamingen over het Vlaanderen van morgen.* Antwerp: Icarus, 1995.

"Het klauwen van de leeuw. Een debat met Eric Defoort, Marc Reynebeau en Harry Van Velthoven." *VMT*, 1966, 2, p. 79-89.

*Het Vlaams Parlement - een glazen Huis in het Hart van Brussel.* Tielt: Lannoo, 1996.

"Het Vlaamse debat nu." *Vlaanderen Morgen,* 1996, 5, pp. 3-7.

Huysmans, Camille. *The Flemish Question.* S.l: Royal Institute of International Affairs, 1930.

Lesage, Dieter. *Onzuivere Gedachten. Over het Vlaanderen van de Minister-President.* Antwerp: Daedalus, 1996.

Luyten, Walter. "Uit de nood der tijden geboren. Het aktivistisch avontuur." In Van Haegendoren, Maurits (ed.). *Geel en zwart van de driekleur. Van oude en andere Belgen tot 1980.* Leuven: Davidsfonds, 1980.

Passelecq, Fernand. *Belgian Unity and the Flemish Movement.* London, Spottiswoode: Ballantine, 1916.

Peeters, Jaak. *Waarde landgenoten. Brief van een Vlaams nationalist aan de nieuwe Vlamingen.* Antwerp: Icarus/Standaard Uitgeverij, 1997.

Peeters, Jaak. "Wat is er van het Vlaams nationalisme?" *VMT,* 29 (1995), 3, p. 75-86.

Platel, Marc. "Lettre ouverte à ma Flandre aimée." *Vlaanderen Morgen,* 1997, 6, pp. 25-32.

Reynebeau, Marc. *Het klauwen van de leeuw. De Vlaamse identiteit van de 12de tot de 21ste eeuw.* Leuven: Van Halewyck, 1995.

Ruys, Manu. "Flemish Nationalism, a Rainbow Phenomenon." *The Low Countries. Arts and Society in Flanders and the Netherlands. A Yearbook, 1996-1997.* Rekkem: Ons Erfdeel, 1996, pp. 173-181.

Sonders, W. *The Flemish Movement in Belgium.* Antwerp: Kultuurraad Vlaanderen, 1975.

Todts, Herman. *Federalisme het einde?* Leuven: Davidsfonds, 1996.

Tollebeek, Jo. "Het treurige verhaal van een nationale conventie." *Ons Erfdeel,* 39 (1996), 1, p. 141-142.

Van Causenbroeck, Bernard. *Herman Vos. Van Vlaams-nationalisme naar socialisme.* Antwerp/Ghent: Hadewijch/Amsab, 1997.

Vandenbroeke, Chris. *De toekomst van het Vlaamse volk. Geschiedenis en futurologie.* Leuven: Kritak, 1985.

Van den Driessche, Pol and Verlinde, Rik. *Zestig keer op Bedevaart naar de IJzer.* Diksmuide: IJzerbedevaartcomité, 1988.

Van Doorslaer, Rudi. *Herfsttij van de 20ste eeuw. Extreem-rechts in Vlaanderen 1920-1990.* Leuven: Kritak, 1992.

Van Haegendoren, Maurits. *The Flemish Movement in Belgium.* Antwerp: Flemish Cultural Council, 1965.

———"De Volksunie ziet het zo." *Vlaams Nationale Standpunten,* 1980, 6/7, pp. 8-10.

Van Haegendoren, Maurits (ed.). *Geel en zwart van de driekleur. Van oude en andere Belgen tot 1980.* Leuven: Davidsfonds, 1980.

Van Hees, Pieter. "The Flemish Movement." *The Low Countries. Arts and Society in Flanders and the Netherlands. A Yearbook, 1995-96.* Rekkem: Ons Erfdeel, 1995, pp. 276-277.

Van Hees, Pieter and Hugo de Schepper. *Tussen cultuur en politiek. Het Algemeen-Nederlands Verbond 1895-1995.* Putte: ANV, 1995.

Van Hoorick, Bert. *In tegenstroom. Herinneringen 1919-1956.* Ghent: Masereelfonds, 1982.

Van Isacker, Karel. *Mijn land in de Kering 1830-1980.* Antwerp/Amsterdam: De Nederlandsche Boekhandel, 1983.

Van Velthoven, Harry. "De Vlaamse kwestie voor de Eerste Wereldoorlog." *Spiegel Historiael,* 16 (1981), 1, pp. 13-18.

———*De Vlaamse kwestie 1830-1914. Macht en onmacht van de Vlaamsgezind(hed)en.* Heule: UGA, 1982. Standen en Landen 82.

———*E. de Laveleye en de Vlaamse kwestie.* Gent: Liberaal Archief, 1992. Verhandelingen 8.

Velaers, Jan. "La communauté et la région Flamandes: Leurs institutions, territoire et capitale. Pourquoi La Flandre?" *Revue de l'Université de Bruxelles,* 1989, 3-4, pp. 69-93.

*Verder met Vlaanderen. Informatie van en over de Vlaamse overheid.* Brussels: Ministerie van de Vlaamse Gemeenschap. Departement Coördinatie. Administratie kanselarij en Voorlichting. Afdeling Communicatie en Ontvangst, 1995. (With supplement 1997).

Verdoodt, F-J. "De Actualiteit van het IJzertestament." *Vlaanderen Morgen,* 1995, Sept-Oct, pp. 54-57.

Verhoeyen, Etienne en Frank Uytterhaegen. *De kreeft met de zwarte scharen. 50 jaar rechts en uiterst rechts in België.* Ghent: Masereelfonds, 1981.

Verhulst, Adriaan. "Van Clovis tot Happart." *Wetenschappelijke Tijdingen,* 1993, pp. 65-66.

Verlooy, Jan Baptist Crysostomus. *Verhandeling op d'onacht der moederlyke tael in de Nederlanden (1788). Ingeleid en toegelicht door J. Smeyers en J. Van Den Broeck.* The Hague/Noordijn: Martinus Nijhoff/Tjeenk Willink, 1979.

Vermeersch, Etienne. "Cultuur en nationalisme." *Ons Erfdeel,* 37 (1994), 1, pp. 73-82.

Vermeylen, August. "Vlaamsche en Europeesche Beweging." *Van Nu en Straks,* 1900, pp. 302-304.

*The Vlaams Blok: Facts and Objectives.* Brussels: Vlaams Blok, 1995.

*Vlaanderen Europa 2002: Een Project van de Vlaamse Regering.* Tielt: Lannoo, 1993.

Vos, Louis. "Die onkende Vlaamse Kwestie. Het aandeel van Buitenlandse historici in de geschiedschrijving van de Vlaamse Beweging." *Bijdragen en Mededelingen betreffende de Geschiedenis der Nederlanden,* 100 (1985), 4, pp. 700-721.

———"De rechts-radicale traditie in het Vlaams-Nationalisme." *Wetenschappelijke Tijdingen,* 52, 1993, pp. 129-149.

Westerlinck, Albert. *Wie was Hendrik Conscience?* Leuven/Amersfoort: Acco, 1993.

Wils, Lode. "Alleen maar Vlaming zijn? Over de waarden die de Vlaamse Beweging verdedigd heeft." *Wetenschappelijke Tijdingen* 59 (1990), 3, p. 164-170.

———*A brief History of the Flemish Movement.* Leuven: KUL - Departement Geschiedenis, 1992. (Reprint of The Flemish Movement: a documentary history, pp. 1-39). Historica Lovaniensa, 246.

———"De Grootnederlandse Geschiedschrijving." *Revue Belge de Philologie et d'Histoire,* 61 (1983), 2, pp. 322-366.

———*De Vlaamse Beweging in het kader van de nationale bewegingen.* Leuven: Acco, 1977.

———"Elias of het gevecht met de geschiedenis." *Wetenschappelijke Tijdingen,* 1992, p. 193-209.

———*Honderd jaar Vlaamse Beweging. Deel 1 : Geschiedenis van het Davidsfonds tot 1914. Deel 2 : Geschiedenis van het Da-*

*vidsfonds 1914-1936*. Leuven: Davidsfonds, 1977.

*iv. Walloon Movement and Walloon Government*

"Beslissingen van de Waalse regering." *Anderzijds. Nieuwsbrief van de Waalse Regering*, December 1993, pp. 9-10.
Bologne, M. *Notre passé wallon. Esquisse d'une histoire des événements politiques des origines à 1940*. Charleroi: Institut Jules Destrée, 1973.
Courtois, L. "La Wallonie a-t-elle une culture?" *Subjectif*, 1993, 10-11, pp. 8-13.
Courtois, L. and J. Pirotte. *L' imaginaire wallon*. Louvain-La-Neuve: Foundation wallonne P. M. and J. F. Humblet, 1994.
Destatte, Ph. *L'identité wallonne, aperçu historique*. Namur: Exécutive du Région Wallonne, 1990.
Destatte, Ph. et al. *Nationalisme et post-nationalisme*. Namur: PUN, 1995.
Dhondt, J. "Essai sur l'origine de la frontière linguistique." *L'Antiquité classique*, 16 (1948), pp. 261-286.
———"Note sur l'origine de la frontière linguistique." *L'Antiquité classique*, 21 (1952), pp. 107-122.
Dubois, J. "Des intellectuels en Wallonie, la Wallonnie et ses intellectuels," *Cahiers Marxistes* 1993, 187, *Toudi*, 7 (1993), pp.11-17.
Fonteine, J. "Fourons/Happart: Pomme de discorde et fruit défendu." In: *Toudi, culture et société*. Quenast: Centre d'Etudes Wallonnes, 1987.
Fonteyn, Guido. *Wallonië*. Amsterdam: Atlas, 1994.
Fonteyn, Guido et al. *Wallonië. De andere Belgen*. Brussels: BRT-Open school, 1984.
Génicot, L. *Racines d'espérance. Nouvelle histoire de Wallonie par les textes, les images et les cartes*. Brussels: Hatier, 1986.
Génicot, L. (ed.). *Histoire de la Wallonie. Univers de la France et des pays francophones*. Toulouse: Privat, 1973.
Ghuer, H., P. Kervyn and P. Husson. *Namur selon les Namurois*. Namur: Centre de Développement du Namurois, 1991.
Hasquin, Hervé. "Le mouvement Wallon: une histoire qui reste à écrire." *Revue de l'Université de Bruxelles*, 1981, 1-2, pp. 147-155.
Jongen, François. "Communauté Française et Région Wallonne:

Wallonie-Bruxelles, même combat?" *Revue de l'Université de Bruxelles,* 1989, 3-4, pp. 95-103.

Kesteloot, Ch. and A. Gavroy. *Françoise Bovesse, pour la défense intégrale de la Wallonie.* Mont-sur-Marchienne: Institut Jules Destrée, 1990.

Mougenot, Catherine. "Les populations rurales: évolutions et perceptions en Wallonie." *Espace, Populations, Sociétés,* 1986, 3, pp. 11-18.

Quévit, Michel. *Les causes du déclin wallon.* Brussels: Vie Ouvrière, 1978.

Swennen, René. "Oui à la séparation." *Le Monde des Débats,* January 1993, p.10.

Thomas, Peter. "Belgium's North-South Divide and the Walloon Regional Problem." *Geography*, 75 (1990), 1, pp. 36-50.

Urbain, Benoit. *Wallonie. Le dynamisme d'une région./Wallonia. A region on the move.* Brussels: Encres Couleurs, 1994.

Van Dam, Denise. *Blijven we buren in België? Vlamingen en Walen over Vlamingen en Walen.* Leuven: Van Halewyck, 1996.

———"Culturele en politieke beeldvorming bij de Vlaamse en Waalse leidinggevende klasse. Een vergelijkend onderzoek." *Tijdschrift voor Sociologie,* 17 (1996), 1, pp. 51-82.

———"L'affirmation d'une identité culturelle." *La Revue Nouvelle,* 3 (1991), pp. 21-25.

———*Weet je, in Wallonië.* Leuven: Davidsfonds, 1992.

Verlinden, Ch. *La frontière linguistique en Belgique.* Brussels: Notre Passé, 1955.

*Wallonie/Bruxelles.* Brussels: French Community of Belgium and the Walloon Region, 1989.

Zolberg, A. "The making of Flemings and Walloons," *The Journal of Interdisciplinary History*, 5 (1974), 2, pp. 179-237.

### *v. Belgian Congo and Rwanda*

Brown, Stephen D. "Destination Stanleyville." *Military Review*, 71 (1991), 3, pp. 38-50.

De Meulder, Bruno. *De kampen van Kongo.* Amsterdam/Antwerp: Meulenhoff/Kritak, 1996.

De Witte, Ludo. *De rol van de Verenigde Naties, de regering-Eyskens en het koningshuis in de omverwerping van Lumumba en de opkomst van Mobutu*. Leuven: Van Halewijck, 1996.

Dickerman, Carol and Northrup, David. "Africanist Archival Research in Brussels." *History in Africa,* 1982, 9, pp. 359-365.

Duarte, Mary T. "Education in Ruanda-Urundi, 1946-61." *Historian* 57 (1995), 2, pp. 275-284.

Ganshof van der Meersch, W. J. *Fin de la souverainité belge au Congo*. Brussels: IRRI, 1963.

Gérard, Jo. *La Monarchie belge abandonnera-t-elle le Congo?* Brussels: Editions Euro-Afrique, 1960.

Gibbs, David N. "Dag Hammarskjold, the United Nations, and the Congo crisis of 1960-1: A Reinterpretation." *Journal of Modern African Studies,* 31 (1993), 1, pp. 163-174.

Gleijeses, Piero. "'Flee! The White Giants are Coming!' The United States, the Mercenaries, and the Congo, 1964-65." *Diplomatic History,* 18 (1994), 2, pp. 207-237.

Helmreich, J.E. "United States Foreign Policy and the Belgian Congo in the 1950s." *Historian*, 58 (1996), 2, pp 315-328.

Higginson, John. *A Working Class in the Making: Belgian Colonial Labor Policy, Private Enterprise, and the African Mineworker, 1907-1951*. Madison: University of Wisconsin Press, 1989.

Hunt, Nancy Rose. "Domesticity and Colonization in Belgian Africa: Usumbura's Foyer Social, 1946-1960." *Signs*, 15 (1990), 3, pp. 447-474.

Lumumba-Kasongo, Tukumbi. "Zaire's Ties to Belgium: Persistence and Future Prospects in Political Economy." *Africa Today*, 39 (1992), 3, pp. 23-48.

Lyman, Stanford M. "Robert E. Park's Congo Papers: A Gothic Perspective on Capitalism and Imperialism." *International Journal of Politics, Culture, and Society,* 4 (1991), 4, pp. 501-516.

Morel, E.D. *King Leopold's Rule in Africa*. London, s.e., 1904.

Rouvez, Alain, Michael Coco and Jean-Paul Paddack. *Disconsolate Empires: French, British and Belgian Military Involvement in Post-Colonial Sub-Saharan Africa*. Lanham, Md.: University Press of America, 1994.

Thomson, Robert Stanley. *Fondation de l'Etat Indépendent du Congo*. Brussels: Office de Publicité, 1933.

Van Bellinghem, Jean-Paul. "Belgium and Africa." In Marina Boudart, Michel Boudart and René Bryssinck. *Modern Belgium*. Palo Alto, California: The Society for the Promotion of Science and Scholarship, 1990, pp. 152-166.

Vinck, Honoré. "Les papiers de Ryck: Documents pour l'étude de l'époque coloniale au Zaire." *History in Africa,* 21 (1994), pp. 441-446.

Winters, Christopher. "Urban morphogenesis in Francophone Black Africa." *Geographical Review,* 72 (1982), 2, pp. 139-154.

## *V. JURIDICAL*

Alen, André. *Handboek van het Belgisch Staatsrecht.* Deurne: Kluwer, 1995.

Alen, André (ed.). *Treatise on Belgian Constitutional Law.* Deventer/Boston: Kluwer, 1992.

Alen, A. et al. "Het federale België in de gecoördineerde Grondwet van 17 februari 1994." *Rechtskundig Weekblad,* 1993-1994, 1355, 35.

Baert, Frans. Proeve van Grondwet voor Vlaanderen. *Vlaanderen Morgen,* 1996, 5, pp. 33-46.

Blanpain, R. (ed.). *Staat, Gemeenschappen en Gewesten.* Bruges: Die Keure, 1988.

Blanpain, Roger and Alain Boyaert. *Glossaire du droit de travail et des relations du travail en Belgique/Glossarium van het arbeidsrecht en de arbeidsverhoudingen in België.* Brussels: Bruylant and Fondation Européenne pour l'amélioration des conditions de vie et de travail, 1995.

Clement, Jan et al. *Proeve van Grondwet voor Vlaanderen.* Bruges: Die Keure, 1996.

*Code Civil Belge/Belgisch Burgerlijk Wetboek.* Verviers: Marabout, 1973.

"Corruption. Two Judges Face Fraud Rap." *The Bulletin. The Newsweekly of the Capital of Europe,* 1997, 12, p. 22-23.

Delpérée, I. *La constitution fédérale de 1993.* Brussels: Bruylant, 1993.

Eliaerts, Chris (ed.). *Kritische reflecties omtrent de zaak Dutroux. Ouders, justitie, nieuwe burger, media.* Brussels: VUBPRESS, 1997.

Huyse, Luc en Hilde Sabbe. *De mensen van het recht.* Leuven: Van Halewyck, 1997.

Keunings, Luc. "The Secret Police in Nineteenth-Century Brussels." *Intelligence and National Security,* 4 (1989), 1, pp. 59-85.

"La Révision de la Constitution: Juillet 1988." *Courrier Hebdomadaire,* 1988, no. 1207.

Mast, A. et al. *Overzicht van het Belgisch Grondwettelijk Recht.* Deurne: Kluwer Rechtswetenschappen, 1996.

Parmentier, Stephan (ed.). *Mensenrechten tussen retoriek en realiteit.* Ghent: Mys en Breesch, 1994. Tegenspraakcahier 14.

Schepers, Stefan. "The Third Revision of the Belgian Constitution." *Indiana Social Studies Quarterly,* 37 (1984-85), 3, pp. 5-17.

Senelle, Robert. "The Current Constitutional System." In Marina Boudart, Michel Boudart and René Bryssinck. *Modern Belgium.* Palo Alto, California: The Society for the Promotion of Science and Scholarship, 1990, pp. 169-200.

Suetens, L. P. "De invloed van het Arbitragehof op het grondwettelijk recht." *Rechtskundig Weekblad,* 1993-1994, 1913 ff.

"The Dutroux Case. Commission's Report Fails to Name Names. Party Politics Hinder Progress: Parents Threaten New White March." *The Bulletin. The Newsweekly of the Capital of Europe,* 1997, 12, p. 22.

*The New Belgian Institutional Framework.* Brussels: Group Coudenberg, 1989.

Vande Lannotte, Johan. *Overzicht van het publiek recht.* Bruges: Die Keure, 1994.

Van Loon, F. and E. Langerwerf. "Socioeconomic Development and the Evolution of Litigation Rates of Civil Courts in Belgium, 1835-1980." *Law & Society Review,* 24 (1990), 2, pp. 283-298.

Van Outrive, Lode, Yves Catuyvels and Paul Ponsaers. *Sire, ik ben ongerust. Geschiedenis van de Belgische politie 1794-1991.* Leuven: Kritak, 1992.

Van Parijs, Daniël. *The Belgian Constitution and Constitutional Development: An Introduction to an Exhaustive Bibliography.* Brussels: Group Coudenberg, 1987.

Velu, F. *La dissolution du Parlement.* Bruxelles: Bruylant, 1966.

Verstraete, Mario. "SP-justitiespecialisten pleiten voor een drastische hervorming van het gerecht." *Doen. Magazine voor de leden van de SP,* 5 (1996), 43, pp. 16-18.

*Wat U moet weten over het Arbitragehof.* Brussels: Belgisch Instituut voor Voorlichting en Documentatie (INBEL), 1985.

Winckelmans, Wim. *De commissie Dutroux. Het rapport (met commentaar).* Leuven: Van Halewijck, 1997.

## *VI. POLITICAL*

### *1. Domestic*

Abs, R. *Histoire du Parti Socialiste Belge.* Brussels: Editions Fondation Louis de Brouckère, 1979, pp. 17-46.

Alen, A. and L.P. Suetens (eds.). *Het federale België na de vierde Staatshervorming. Een commentaar op de nieuwe grondwet en haar uitvoeringsbesluiten.* Bruges: Die Keure, 1993.

Alen, A. en P. van Speybroeck. *La Réforme de l'Etat belge de 1974 jusqu'au Pacte d'Egmont.* Brussels: CEPESS, 1987.

Anciaux, Bert. *Kinderen van de hoop. Uitnodiging aan de durvers.* Antwerp: Icarus, 1997.

Arcq, Etienne, Pierre Blaise and Evelyne Lentzen "Enjeux et compromis de la législature 1988-1991." *Courrier Hebdomadaire,* 1332-33, pp. 6-68.

Baeteman, Gustaaf. *De nieuwe staat. Aspecten van het Belgisch Federalisme.* Antwerp: Kluwer Rechtswetenschappen, 1994.

Beaufays, Jean. "Belgium: a Dualist Political System?" *Publius,* 18 (1988), 2, pp. 63-73.

"Belgium. A Continuing State of Compromise." *Newcomer. An Introduction to Life in Belgium,* September 1997, 20, p. 5.

Beni, Jos. "The Peace Movement in Belgium." *Journal of Area Studies,* 1984, 9, pp. 13-18.

Billiet, Jaak. "On Belgian Pillarization: Changing Perspectives. *Acta Politica,* 19 (1984), 1, pp. 117-128.

Billiet, Jaak. "Verzuiling en politiek: Theoretische beschouwing over België via 1945." *Belgisch Tijdschrift voor Nieuwste Geschiedenis,* 1982, p. 83-113.

Blyth, Derek. "The Dutroux Case. The Chronicle of a Failure Waiting to Happen. Leaked Report Reveals Appalling Conduct of Police and Magistrates." *The Bulletin. The Newsweekly of the Capital of Europe,* 1997, 15, pp. 18-19.

Boehm, Rudolf. "Wat heet nationalisme?" *VMT,* 29 (1995), 2, p. 35-41.

Bouveroux, Jos. *De partij van de burger: de verruiming van de Vlaamse liberalen.* Antwerp: Standaard Uitgeverij, 1992.

———*Het St. Michielsakkoord: Naar een Federaal België.* Antwerp: Standaard Uitgeverij, 1993.

———"Pandora's Box Political Culture in Belgium." *The Low Countries. Arts and Society in Flanders and the Netherlands. A Yearbook 1997-1998.* Rekkem: Ons Erfdeel, 1997, pp. 38-45.

———*Van Zwarte Zondag tot Zwarte Zondag.* Antwerp: Icarus, 1966.

Braes, G. *L'Affront National: le nouveau visage de l'extrême droite en Belgique.* Brussels: EPO, 1991.

Brassinne, J. "Les Nouvelles Institutions Politiques de la Belgique." *Dossier du CRISP,* 1989, no. 30.

Buelens, Jo and Kris Deschouwer (eds.). *De Dorpsstraat is de Wetstraat niet. Een onderzoek naar de plaatselijke woordvoerders van nationale partijen.* Brussels: VUBPRESS, 1996.

Busquin, Philippe. *Aujourd'hui le futur.* Ottignies: Quorum, 1997.

Clement, Jan et al. *Het Sint-Michielsaccoord en zijn achtergronden.* Antwerp/Apeldoorn: Maklu-uitgevers, 1993.

Covell, Maureen. "Agreeing to Disagree: Bargaining and the Revision of the Belgian Constitution." *Canadian Journal of Political Science,* 15 (1982), 3, pp. 451-469.

———"Ethnic Conflict and Elite Bargaining: the Case of Belgium." *West European Politics,* 4 (1981), 3, pp. 197-218.

De Clercq, Bertrand J. "De Waarden van de Belgen." *Kultuurleven,* 59 (1992), 5, p. 82-85.

Dehousse, F. "Apparences et réalités de la Réforme de l'Etat belge." *Courrier Hebdomadaire,* 1986, 1138.

Dejaegher, Peter. "Faciliteiten sinds ontstaan verschillend geïnterpreteerd," *De Standaard*, 29.10.1997, p. 3.

Delwit, Pascal and Jean-Michel de Waele. *Ecolo.* Brussels: De Boeck, 1996.

*De Provincieraad van West-Vlaanderen, deel 3 (1978-1995).* Bruges Sint-Andries: Westvlaams Provinciebestuur, 1997.

Deridder, Hugo. *Jean-Luc Dehaene.* Tielt: Lannoo, 1996.

———*Le cas Martens.* Paris: Duculot, 1991.

———*Sire, donnez-moi cent jours.* Paris: Duculot, 1990.

Deschouwer, Kris. "Patterns of participation and competition in Belgium. *West European Politics,* 12 (1989), 4, pp. 28-41.

Deschouwer, Kris. "The 1987 Belgian Election: The Voter Did Not Decide." *West European Politics*, 11 (1988), 3, pp. 141-145.

Desmet, Yves. Het Vervloekte Land. *Vlaanderen Morgen*, 1996, 5, pp. 47-48.

*De Staatshervorming*. Brussels: INBEL, 1993.

Detrez, Raymond and Jan Blommaert (eds.). *Nationalisme. Kritische opstellen*. Berchem, EPO, 1994.

De Wachter, Frans. "Wie is mijn volk? De verleidingen van het zachte nationalisme." In Raymond Detrez en Jan Blommaert. *Nationalisme. Kritische opstellen*. Berchem: EPO, 1994, pp. 71-91.

Dewachter, W. *Tussen staat en maatschappij. 1945-1995. Christendemocratie in België*. Tielt: Lannoo, 1995.

Dewachter, W. and E. Clijsters. "Belgium: Political Stability Despite Coalition Crises." In E. Browne and J. Dreijmanis (eds.). *Government Coalitions in Western Democracies*. New York: Longman, 1982, pp. 187-216.

Dierickx, Guido. *De logica van de politiek*. Leuven: Garant, 1996.

Dierickx, Guido and Philippe Majersdorf. *De politieke cultuur van ambtenaren en politici in België*. Bruges: Van den Broele, 1994.

*Documents Parlementaires*, Chambre 516-516 (SE 1988), p. 65 ff.

*Ecolo. Les Verts en Politique*. Brussels: De Boeck Université, 1966.

Elchardus, M. *Op de ruines van de waarheid. Lezingen over tijd, politiek en cultuur*. Leuven: Kritak, 1994.

Falter, Rolf. *Tweedracht maakt macht. Wegwijs in het Federale België*. Tielt: Lannoo, 1994.

Fitzmaurice, John. "Belgium." In F. Jacobs (ed.). *Western Political Parties*. London: Longman, 1989.

———"Belgium: Reluctant Federalism." *Parliamentary Affairs*, 37 (1984), 4, pp. 418-433.

———*Crisis and Compromise in a Plural Society*. With a foreword by Leo Tindemans. London: Hurst, 1983.

———"The Belgian Election of 1991." *Electoral Studies*, 11 (1992), 2, pp. 162-165.

———"The Extreme Right in Belgium: Recent Developments." *Parliamentary Affairs*, 1992, Summer.

———*The Politics of Belgium. A Unique Federalism*. With a foreword by Guy Spitaels. London: Hurst, 1996.

Fitzmaurice, John and Guido Vandenberghe. "The Belgian Election of 1985." *Electoral Studies*, 5 (1986), 1, pp. 73-76.

Gaus, Helmut. *Politiek biografisch lexicon van de Belgische ministers en staatssecretarissen (1960-1980).* Antwerp: s.d., p. 961-1012.

Gilissen, John. "Evolution des systèmes électoraux dans les pays du Benelux (1814-1921)." *Cahiers de Clio,* 62 (1980), pp. 26-48.

Goossens, Martine. *Ontstaan en groei van het Vlaams Parlement 1970-1995.* Brussels en Kapellen: Vlaams Parlement en Pelckmans, 1995.

Hemmerijckx, Rik. "The Belgian Communist Party and the Trade Unions, 1940-60." *Journal of Communist Studies,* 6 (1990), 4, pp. 124-142.

Hooghe, Marc. *Het Witte Ongenoegen. Hoop en Illusie van een uniek experiment.* Groot-Bijgaarden: Scoop, 1997.

Houbert, B. and P. Vandernoot. "La nouvelle loi des Réformes Institutionelles du 8 août 1988." *Administration publique,* 1988, 3, p. 213.

Huyse, Luc. *De lange weg naar Neufchâteau.* Leuven: Van Halewyck, 1996.

———*Passiviteit, Pacificatie en Verzuiling in de Belgische Politiek.* Antwerp: Standaard Uitgeverij, 1970.

———"Pillarization Reconsidered." *Acta Politica*, 19 (1984), 1, pp. 145-158.

Ilegems, D. and J. Willems. *De kroon ontbloot.* Leuven: Kritak, 1991.

Kalisz, Serge and Patrick Moriau. *Les cahiers d'un commissaire.* Brussels: Editions Luc Pire, 1997.

Kerkhofs, Jan et al. *De versnelde ommekeer. De waarden van Vlamingen, Walen en Brusselaars in de jaren negentig.* Tielt: Lannoo, 1992.

Kitschelt, Herbert. *The Logics of Party Formation: Ecological Politics in Belgium and West Germany.* Ithaca, N.Y.: Cornell University Press, 1989.

Kitschelt, H. and S. Hellemans. *Beyond the European Left: Ideology and Political Action in the Belgian Ecology Parties.* Durham, N.C.: Duke University Press, 1990.

"La Belqique fédérale." *Socialisme*, 1993, no. 239.

Lehoucq, Nicole and Tony Valcke. *De fonteienen van de Oranjeberg, deel 2.* Ghent: Stichting Mens en Cultuur, 1997.

*Les parties politiques en Belgique.* Brussels: CRISP, 1978. Dossier du CRISP, no. 10.

Loumoye, S. "Les nouvelles Institutions Bruxelloises." *Courrier Hebdomadaire,* 1989, 1232/3, pp. 32-53.

Mabille, Xavier. "Les débat politique d'avril 1990 sur la sanction et la promulgation de la loi." *Courrier Hebdomadaire,* 1990, 1275.

———"Political Decision-Making." In Marina Boudart, Michel Boudart and René Bryssinck. *Modern Belgium.* Palo Alto, California: The Society for the Promotion of Science and Scholarship, 1990, pp. 201-220.

Mabille, Xavier and J. Brasinne. "La formation du Gouvernement et des Exécutifs." *Courrier Hebdomadaire,* 1992, 1356/2.

Mabille, Xavier and Eveline Lentzen. "Les elections du 13 octobre 1985." *Courrier Hebdomadaire,* 1985, 1095/6.

Mabille, Xavier, Eveline Lentzen and Pierre Blaise. "Les elections du 24 novembre 1991." *Courrier Hebdomadaire,* 1991, 1335/6.

Maddens, Bart. "De Witte mars: twee keer een jaar later." *Vlaanderen Morgen,* 1997, 6, pp. 56-59.

Marchal, Paul. *Op zoek naar An en Eefje.* Antwerp: Hadewijch, 1997.

McCrae, Kenneth. D. *Conflict and Compromise in Multilingual Societies.* Vol 2: Belgium. Waterloo, Ont.: Wilfrid Laurier University Press, 1986.

*Mémento politique.* Antwerp: Kluwer, 1989.

Morlan, Robert L. "Local Government Reorganization: the Components of Success." *National Civic Review,* 70 (1981), 8, pp. 404-409.

Mormont, Marc. "The Emergence of Rural Struggles and their Ideological Effects." *International Journal of Urban and Regional Research,* 7 (1983), 4, pp. 559-575.

Mughan, A. "Accommodation or Defusion in the Management of Linguistic Conflict in Belgium?" *Political Studies,* 31 (1983), 3, pp. 434-451.

Mughan, Anthony. "The Belgian Election of 1981: The Primacy of the Economic." *West European Politics,* 5 (1982), 3, pp. 298-304.

Ollevier, van. *De laatste communisten. Hun passies, hun idealen.* Leuven: Van Halewyck, 1997.

*Opinion of the conseil d'état, Documents Parlementaires SE 1988,* no. 516, p. 32.

Platel, M. *Het altaar van de politiek.* Leuven: Davidsfonds, 1993.

Riesler, Frank. *Nieuwe politieke cultuur. Een terugblik 1996-2002.* Leuven, Van Halewijck, 1997.

Rogge, André. *Het riool van België, de waarheid achter de affaires.* Antwerp/Amsterdam: Kritak/Arena, 1996.

Rogiers, Filip. *Het orkest van de wetstraat.* Leuven: Van Halewijck, 1997.

Rose, Richard. "National Pride in Cross-national Perspective." *International Social Science Journal,* 37 (1985), 1, pp. 85-96.

Rudd, Chris. "Coalition Formation and Maintenance in Belgium: A Case Study of Elite Behaviour and Changing Cleavage Structure 1965-81." In G. Pridham (ed.). *Coalition Behaviour in Theory and Practice.* Cambridge: Cambridge University Press, 1986, pp. 117-144.

Rudolph, Joseph R., Jr. and Robert J. Thompson. "Ethnoterritorial Movements and the Policy Process: Accommodating Nationalist Demands in the Developed World." *Comparative Politics,* 17 (1985), 3, pp. 291-311.

Ruys, Manu. *Achter de maskerade. Over macht, schijnmacht en onmacht.* Kapellen: Pelckmans, 1996.

———"Belgian Federalisation." In *The Low Countries. Arts and Society in Flanders and the Netherlands. A Yearbook, 1993-1994.* Rekkem: Ons Erfdeel, 1993, pp. 118-124.

———*Op de korrel. Politieke meditaties.* Dilbeek: Cultura Fonds, 1997.

Samson, Chantal and Livio Serafini. *Eli di Rupo. De la Chrysalide au papillon.* Brussels: Editions Luc Pire, 1997.

Sauviller, Raf and Danny Ilegems. *Een Belgisch politicus.* Amsterdam/Antwerp: Atlas, 1997.

Senelle, Robert. "The Reform of the Belgian State. Memo from Belgium." *Views and Surveys* (Brussels: Ministry of Foreign Affairs), 5 (1990), no. 198.

Standaert, Felix. "Voeren: een status questionis." *Coudenberg. Tijdschrift voor Federalisme en Demokratie,* 1988, October.

Swyngedouw, Marc. *Kiezen is verliezen. Onderzoek naar de politieke opvattingen van Vlamingen.* Leuven-Amersfoort: Acco, 1993.

———*Waar voor je waarden. De opkomst van Vlaams Blok en Agalev in de jaren tachtig.* Leuven, Sociologisch Onderzoeksinstituut, ISPO-schrift 1992/1.

Timmerman, Georges. *De doofpotten. De sabotage van het Hoog Comité van Toezicht.* Antwerp/Baarn/Brussels: Hadewijch/De Morgen, 1997.

Vandenberghe, Guido. "Belgium." *Electoral Studies,* 3 (1984), 3, pp. 264-267.

Van Den Bulck, Jan. "Pillars and Politics: Neocorporatism and Policy Networks in Belgium." *West European Politics,* 15 (1992), 2, pp. 35-55.

Vandeputte, R. *Economische geschiedenis van België 1944-1984.* Tielt/Weesp: Lannoo, 1987.

———*Sociale geschiedenis van België 1944-1985.* Tielt: Lannoo, 1987.

*Volksunie: Identity, History and Programme.* Brussels: Volksunie, 1979.

Walgrave, Stefaan and Benoit Rihoux. *De Witte Mars. Een jaar later. Van emotie tot politieke commotie.* Leuven: Van Halewijck, 1997.

Wallach, H. G. Peter. "Dominant Parties, Economic Trends and Western European Election Behavior." *Journal of Political Science* 11 (1984), 2, pp. 111-127.

Weil, Gordon L. *The Benelux Nations: The Politics of Small Country Democracies.* New York: Holt, Rinehart, and Winston, 1970.

Wils, L. *Van Clovis tot Happart. De lange weg van de naties in de lage landen.* Leuven: Garant, 1992.

Winckelmans, Wim. *De Commissie Dutroux. Het rapport (met commentaar).* Leuven: Van Halewijck/Scoop, 1997.

Witte, Els. "Aperçu des Etudes consacrées aux partis belges." *Revue de l'Université de Bruxelles,* 1981, 1-2, pp. 97-124.

Ysebaert, Clair. *Decisionmakers. Politiek Zakboekje 1995.* Diegem: Kluwer Editoriaal, 1995.

———*Politicograaf. Politiek Zakboekje 1997.* Diegem: Kluwer Editorial, 1997 (16e ed.).

## *2. Foreign Relations*

Brierley, William. "Cruise Missiles and the Peace Movement: Some Background Information." *Journal of Area Studies,* 1984, 9, pp. 11-13.

Craenen, Godelieve. "België en het buitenland. De nieuwe regeling van de buitenlandse betrekkingen." In A. Alen and L.P. Suetens (ed.). *Het Federale België na de vierde Staatshervorming. Een*

*Commentaar op de nieuwe Grondwet en haar Uitvoeringsbesluiten.* Bruges: Die Keure, 1993.

Cremer, Pierre. "Military Policy." In Marina Boudart, Michel Boudart and René Bryssinck. *Modern Belgium.* Palo Alto, California: The Society for the Promotion of Science and Scholarship, 1990, pp. 99-166.

Davignon, Etienne, Hugo Paemen and Paul Noterdaeme. "Belgium and the European Communities." In Marina Boudart, Michel Boudart and René Bryssinck. *Modern Belgium.* Palo Alto, California: The Society for the Promotion of Science and Scholarship, 1990, pp. 122-129.

De Gordijnen van Maastricht. *Zestien beschouwingen over de Europese Unie.* Brussels: Masereelfonds, 1993.

Delcorde, Raoul. "Contribution of Belgium to Peace and Security." *Pakistan Horizon,* 41 (1988), 2, pp. 23-30.

Delpérée, F. and Lejeune, Y. (eds.). *La Collaboration de l'Etat des Communautés et des Régions dans le domaine de la Politique Extérieure.* Louvain-la-Neuve: Academia, 1988.

De Staercke, André (ed.). "International Policy." In: Marina Boudart, Michel Boudart and René Bryssinck. *Modern Belgium.* Palo Alto, California: The Society for the Promotion of Science and Scholarship, 1990, pp. 99-166.

Dever, Edmonde. "Belgium and the United Nations." In Marina Boudart, Michel Boudart and René Bryssinck. *Modern Belgium.* Palo Alto, California: The Society for the Promotion of Science and Scholarship, 1990, pp. 130-133.

De Waele, M. *Bibliografie van de Belgische buitenlandse betrekkingen 1830-1980.* Ghent: RUG. Seminarie voor Hedendaagse Ontwikkeling van de Binnen- en Buitenlandse Politiek, 1980.

Dumoulin, Michel. "Vingt ans d'historiographie des relations internationales de la Belgique (1964-1984). *Relations Internationales* 42 (1985), pp. 169-182.

Fitzmaurice, J. "Belgium and Luxembourg." In J. Lodge (ed.). *The 1989 Election of the European Parliament.* Basingstoke/London: Macmillan, 1990, pp. 37-47.

*Flanders: the golden passport to Europe.* Brussels: Ministerie van de Vlaamse Gemeenschap. Commissariaat-Generaal voor de Internationale Samenwerking, 1989

Helmreich, J. E. *Belgium and Europe. A study in small power diplomacy.* The Hague/Paris: Mouton, 1976.

Ingelaere, Frank. "The New Legislation on the International Relations of the Belgian Communities and Regions." *Studia Diplomatica,* 47 (1994), 1.

Keating, Thomas F. and Terence A. Keenleyside. "Voting Patterns as a Measure of Foreign Policy Independence." *International Perspectives,* May-June 1980, pp. 21-26.

Liénard, Albert. *Wallonia: the World in Mind.* Brussels: Ministry of the Walloon Region in Charge of External Relations, s.d.

Noiret, Serge. "Political Parties and the Political System in Belgium before Federalism, 1830-1980." *European History Quarterly,* 24 (1994), 1, pp. 85-122.

Nothomb, Charles-Ferdinand. "The Role of National Parliaments and the European Parliament in Building the European Nation." *The Brussels Review,* September/October 1994.

Standaert, Felix. *Buitenlandse Betrekkingen in de Federale Staat België. Analyse en kritiek.* Sint Lambrechts Woluwe: Eigen Beheer, 1995.

———*De Buitenlandse Betrekkingen in de Federale Staat België. Een rapport van de groep Coudenberg.* Brussels: Coudenberg Groep, 1990.

Tastenhoye, Guido. *Vlaams-Brabant ingelijfd bij Brussel?* Leuven: Davidsfonds, 1997.

Van Bellinghem, Jean-Paul. "Belgium and Africa." In Marina Boudart, Michel Boudart and René Bryssinck. *Modern Belgium.* Palo Alto, California: The Society for the Promotion of Science and Scholarship, 1990, pp. 152-166.

Van den Brande, Luc. *Policy Letter Concerning the Foreign Relations of Flanders/Submitted to the Flemish Parliament by Luc Van den Brande, Minister-President of the Government of Flanders, Brussels, April 28th, 1992.* Brussels: The Government of Flanders. The Minister-President, 1992.

———Flanders International. *Towards a pro-active foreign policy valorizing the assets of Flanders and the Flemings. Policy Priorities 1995-1999.* Brussels: Office of the Minister of the Government of Flanders for Foreign Policy, European Affairs and Technology, 1996.

Velímsky, Vítezlav. "Belgium of the Eighties: Unitary, Bi-cultural or Made up of the Three Regions?" *Europa Ethnica,* 40 (1983), 1, pp. 1-14.

Willequet, Jacques. "La politique étrangère: un bilan historiographique." *Revue de l'Université de Bruxelles,* 1981, 1-2, pp. 157-174.

## *VII. SCIENTIFIC*

### *1. Information Science and Communication*

Deltour, Pol. *Man bijt hond. Over pers, politiek en gerecht.* Antwerp: Icarus, 1996.
Nijhof, Kelly. *Explore Internet in België.* Brussels: The Best of Publishing, 1996.
Lips, Benoit. *Internet in België.* Brussels: The Best of Publishing, 1996.
Van den Brande, Luc and Flemish Institute for the Promotion of Scientific-Technological Research in Industry. *Biotechnology.* Preface by Luc Van den Brande. Brussels: Ministry of the Flemish Community. Coordination Department. Science Policy Programming Administration, 1993.

### *2. Environment*

Ashworth, Greg. "The International Planning of Frontier Regions: The Recent Experience of the Benelux Middengebied." *Journal of Area Studies,* 1982, 6, pp. 32-37.
Cotur, Peter. "Aquafin. Flanders gains recognition on the water purification front." *Flanders*, 1996, 31, pp. 10-14.
"Dioxines veroorzaken de 'Belgische ziekte'." *De Morgen,* 1.12.97, p. 6.
Du Champs, G. *De mooiste natuurreservaten van België.* Brussels: Reader's Digest, 1986.
*Ghent. Journey into the Historical and Industrial Past of Ghent.* Ghent: VIAT, 1985.
Leroy, Pieter. "The Low Countries do Smell of Manure, Don't They? Environmental Problems, Environmental Awareness and Environmental Policy in the Netherlands and Flanders." In: *The Low Countries. Arts and Society in Flanders and the Netherlands. A Yearbook, 1993-1994.* Rekkem: Ons Erfdeel, 1993, pp. 56-63.

Renard, Peter. *Wat kan ik voor U doen? Ruimtelijke wanorde in België: een hypotheek op onze toekomst.* Antwerp: Icarus, 1997.

Tack, G., P. Van den Bremt and M. Hermy. *Bossen van Vlaanderen—een historische ecologie.* Leuven: Davidsfonds, 1995.

Van de Kam, J. *Spectrum Atlas van Beschermde Natuurgebieden Nederland en België.* Utrecht/Antwerp: Het Spectrum, 1984.

Vandermotten, Christian. "Reflexions sur l'amenagement du territoire en Wallonie." *Revue de l'Institut de Sociologie,* 1984, 3-4, pp. 543-566.

Vanhecke, L., G. Charlier and L. Verelst. *Landschappen in Vlaanderen vroeger en nu.* Meise: Nationale Plantentuin van België, 1981.

Vissers, Partick. "Flemish Heritage Foundation." *Flanders*, 1996, 32, pp. 5-7.

Vlaams Gewest. "Ruimtelijke Ordening en Stedenbouw. Wetgeving en reglementering." Supplement to *Het Tijdschrift voor Ruimtelijke Ordening en Stedenbouw,* 1997.

Vandaele, Wilfried. "The Vlaamse Milieumaatschappij (Environmental company for Flanders). Working for an ever-cleaner environment." *Flanders*, September 1997, no. 35, pp. 4-8.

### *3. Geography*

*Administratieve kaart van België.* Brussels: Carto, 1995.

*Administratieve kaart van België na de fusies.* Brussels: Carto, 1979.

André, Robert. "Geography." In Marina Boudart, Michel Boudart and René Bryssinck. *Modern Belgium.* Palo Alto, California: The Society for the Promotion of Science and Scholarship, 1990, pp. 10-24.

Christians, Charles and H. Daels. *Belgium: A Geographical Introduction to its Regional Diversity and its Human Richness.* Liège: UL, Séminaire de Géographie de Liège, 1984.

*Dictionnaire des communes de Belgique/Woordenboek der Belgische gemeenten/Lexikon der Gemeinden Belgiens/Dictionary of the Municipalities of Belgium.* Brussels: Guyot, 1997.

*Geografie van België.* Brussels: Federale Voorlichtingsdienst, 1990.

*Gerard Mercator. Cartograaf 1512-1594.* Brussels: Gemeentekrediet 1994.

Hayt, Franz et al. *Atlas van de Algemene en Belgische Geschiedenis.* Lier: Van In, 1997.

Krogt, Peter van der. *Globi Neerlandici: The Production of Globes in the Low Countries.* Translated by Elizabeth Daverman. Utrecht: HES, 1993.

Pasleau, Suzy. "Cartographie et analyse factorielle: le bassin de Seraing entre 1866 et 1910." *Histoire & Mesure,* 5 (1990), 3-4, pp. 271-313.

*Polders en Wateringen.* Brussels: Federale Voorlichtingsdienst, 1989.

Purjahn, E. and Van den Bremt. *Les Ardennes belges/De Belgische Ardennen/Die Belgische Ardennen/The Belgian Ardennes/Las Ardenas belgas.* Brussels: Meddens, 1982.

Riley, R. C. and G. J. Ashworth. *Benelux: An Economic Geography of Belgium, the Netherlands and Luxembourg.* London: Chatto and Windus, 1975.

Roberts, Ann M. "The Landscape as Legal Document: Jan de Hervy's View of the Zwin." *The Burlington Magazine,* 133 (February 1991), pp. 82-86.

Sluyterman, K. et al. *Ancient Interiors in Belgium. With 100 Heliotype Plates from Photographs by G. Sigling.* London: Hutchinson, 1915.

*Sociaal Economische Atlas van Vlaanderen.* Kaartenboek. Brussels: Sociaal-Economische Raad van Vlaanderen, 1996.

Van Ermen, Eduard. "Maps for Eternity. Sixteenth and Seventeenth-Century Cartography in the Low Countries." *The Low Countries. Arts and Society in Flanders and the Netherlands. A Yearbook, 1997-1998.* Rekkem: Ons Erfdeel, 1997, pp. 73-82.

Van Ham, W.A. and L. Danckaert. *De wandkaart van het hertogdom Brabant, uitgegeven door Nicolaas Visscher en Zacharias Roman (1656).* Leuven: Canaletto en Universitaire Pers, 1997.

### *4. Natural History and Biology*

Bastin, Marjolein and Nico de Haan. *Kijk op vogels. In het duin.* Amsterdam: Sesam/Anthos, 1997.

Bury, Jo. VIB. "Flemish Biotechnology, a World Product." *Flanders,* 32, pp. 23-27.

Cerny, W. and K. Drchal. *Welke vogel is dat?* Zutphen: Thieme, 1973.

Daems, Wim. "Biotechnology in Flanders. Big in the Microcosm of Cells and Molecules." *The Low Countries. Arts and Society in Flanders and the Netherlands. A Yearbook, 1993-1994,* Rekkem: Ons Erfdeel, 1993, pp. 166-171.

Keith, Stuart and John Gooders. *Kosmos Vogelveldgids van Europa.* New York: Cantecleer Press, 1979.

Norman, David B. "On the History of the Discovery of Fossils at Bernissart in Belgium." *Archives of Natural History,* 14 (1987), 1, pp. 59-75.

Peterson, R. T., G. Mountfort and P.A.D. Hollom. *Vogelgids van alle in ons land en overig Europa voorkomende vogelsoorten.* Amsterdam/Brussels: Elsevier, 1965.

Van Gansen, Paulette (ed.). "Developmental Biology in Belgium. "*The International Journal of Developmental Biology,* 36 (1992), 1.

Vanpaemel, Geert H. W. "Transformationism and the Question of Species in Belgium before the Introduction of Darwinism." *Tractrix*, 1992, 4, pp. 13-37.

Vlaamse Avifaunacommissie. *Vogels in Vlaanderen. Voorkomen en verspreiding*. Bornem: I.M.P, 1989.

## *VIII. SOCIAL*

### *1. Anthropology and Ethnology*

*Geboorte en doopsel. Levensrituelen. Ten geleide door Leijssen, Lambert, Michel Cloet en Karel Dobbelaere.* Leuven: Kadoc en Universitaire Pers, 1996.

Newman, Saul. "Does Modernization Breed Ethnic Political Conflict?" *World Politics*, 43 (1991), 3, pp. 451-478.

Peeters, Yvo J. D. "Some Recent Reading on Belgium's Ethnopolitics (1973-1988). *Plural Societies,* 17(1987), 3, pp. 62-90.

Rudolph, Joseph R., Jr. and Robert J. Thompson. "Ethnoterritorial Movements and the Policy Process: Accommodating Nationalistic Demands in the Developed World." *Comparative Politics*, 17 (19j85), 3, pp. 291-311.

*Verliefd, verloofd, getrouwd. Huwelijksgebruiken in Vlaanderen en Wallonië, vroeger en nu.* Foreword by Renaat van der Linden. Sint Niklaas: Agora, 1988.

## 2. *Demography*

André, Robert. "Population." In Marina Boudart, Michel Boudart and René Bryssinck. *Modern Belgium.* Palo Alto, California: The Society for the Promotion of Science and Scholarship, 1990, pp. 28-40.

André, Robert and Guilmont, Pierre. "Analyse du vieillissement dans les aires d'influences urbaine en Wallonnie." *Espace, Populations, Sociétés,* 2 (1987), pp. 403-414.

Lesthaeghe, R. J. *The Decline of Belgian Fertility 1800-1970.* Princeton, New Yersey: Princeton University Press, 1977.

Mougenot, Catherine. "Les populations rurales: evolutions et perceptions en Wallonie." *Espace, Populations, Sociétés,* 1986, 3, pp. 11-18.

Pasleau, Suzy. "Une population dans le développement économique. La formation d'un prolétariat industriel. Séraing, 1846-1914." *Belgisch Tijdschrift voor Nieuwste Geschiedenis,* 20 (1989), 3-4, pp. 544-548.

Thomson, Claire. "Going Behind the Veil." *The Bulletin. The Newsweekly of the Capital of Europe,* 1997, 15, pp. 22-29.

Urdank, Albion M. "The Family and Demographic Behavior in Belgium, Germany, and Italy, 1700-1920: A Review Essay." *Historical Methods,* 24 (1991), 1, pp. 41-47.

## 3. *Education*

Art, Jan. "Colloque International, 'L'Histoire des Universités Européennes depuis la Deuxième Guerre Mondiale,' Ghent, 28-30 septembre 1992." *Paedagogica Historica,* 28 (1992), 3, pp. 679-682.

———"Les rapports triennaux sur l'état de l'enseignement supérieur: un arrière-fond pour des recherches ultérieures sur l'histoire des élites belges entre 1814 et 1914." *Belgisch Tijdschrift voor Nieuwste Geschiedenis,* 17 (1986), 1-2, pp. 187-224.

Bosmans-Hermans, An. "The Impact of the Catholic-Liberal Antithesis on Teacher Training Policy in Belgium, 1842-1844." *Journal of Educational Administration and History,* 14 (1982), 2, pp. 7-13.

Bruneau, William A. "The International Standing Conference on the History of Education (ISCHE): The Significance of the Meeting at Leuven/Louvain. Sepember 1979." *Paedagogica Historica,* 19 (1979), 1, pp. 238-241.

De Belder, Hein. "Education in Flanders. Democratic and of a High Standard." *Flanders,* 1977, 33, pp. 17-20.

De Clerck, K. "De Vernederlandsing van de Rijksuniversiteit te Gent." *Spiegel Historiael,* 15 (1980), 12, pp. 658-664.

De Keyser, Raf et al. *Geschiedenis in onderzoek, onderwijs en samenleving. Historisch-bibliografische wegwijzer/ Boek 1.* Leuven: Garant, 1997.

De Smedt, Kristel. "De herziening van de schoolboeken tijdens de bezetting (1940-1944)." *Cahiers/Bijdragen,* 1991, 14, pp. 177-201.

Despy-Meyer, Andrée. *Les Femmes et l'Enseignement Supérieur: l'Université Libre de Bruxelles de 1880 à 1914.* Brussels: Service des Archives de l'Université Libre de Bruxelles, 1980.

Deurinck, Gaston (ed.). "Education." In Marina Boudart, Michel Boudart and René Bryssinck. *Modern Belgium.* Palo Alto, California: The Society for the Promotion of Science and Scholarship, 1990, pp. 377-412.

Devroede, Maurice. "Primary Education and the Fight against Alcoholism in Belgium at the Turn of the Century." *History of Education Quarterly,* 25 (1985), 4, pp. 483-497.

Dierickx, G. "The Management of Subcultural Conflict: the Issue of Education in Belgium (1950-1975). *Acta Politica,* 19 (1984), 1, pp. 85-95.

Hirtt, Nico, Annemie Mels and Hugo van Droogenbroeck. *School onder schot: de democratisering van het onderwijs niet bestand tegen de crisis.* Berchem: EPO, 1997.

Leblon, Muriel. "La formation du personnel enseignant des écoles gardiennes en Belgique: le point de vue du législateur (1880-1914) et la création de la première école normale Frobel (1910). *Belgisch Tijdschrift voor Nieuwste Geschiedenis,* 22 (1991), 3-4, pp. 657-690.

Renson, Roland. "'Le corps académique': la génèse de l'éducation physique universitaire en Belgique." Stadion, 17(1991), 1, pp. 87-100.

Roucek, Joseph S. "Educational Sociology in France, Germany, Belgium and England." *Educational Theory,* 8 (1958), pp. 249-258.

Simon, Frank and Dirk van Damme. "Education and Moral Improvement in a Belgian Industrial Town (1860-90): François Laurent (1810-87) and the Working Classes in Ghent." *History of Education* 22 (1993), 1, pp. 63-84.

Thielemans, Marie-Rose. "Les Sociétés Scientifiques." *Revue de l'Université de Bruxelles,* 1981, 1-2, pp. 217-231.

Tolleneer, Jan. "Formation pour la vie and formation pour l'armée: La Fédération Nationale des sociétés catholiques de gymnastique et d'armes de Belgique (1892-1914)." *Stadion*, 17 (1991), 1, pp. 101-120.

Tyssens, Jeffrey. *De Schoolkwestie in de jaren vijftig. Van Conflict naar Pacificatie.* Brussels: VUB Press, 1977.

### 4. *Health and Medical Science*

Blondeau, Roger A. *Jan Palfijn. Een Vlaams heelmeester in de 17de en 18de eeuw.* Tielt: Lannoo, 1997. (895 bef)

Cotur, Peter. "Focus on the Visually Handicapped." *Flanders*, 1996, 32, pp. 13-16.

Elchardus, Mark, Guy Peeters and Ivan Van Der Meeren. "Ziek in verschillende bedjes? Over de institutionele inbedding van de gezondsheidszorg." *Samenleving en Politiek,* 4 (1977), 5, pp. 12-27.

Gutmann, Myron R. and Randy Wyrick "Adapting Methods to Needs: Studying Fertility and Nuptiality in Seventeenth- and Eighteenth-Century Belgium." *Historical Methods*, 14 (1981), 4, pp. 163-171.

Koninklijke Academie voor Geneeskunde van België. *Biografisch lexicon van de academieleden 1938-1988.* Brussels: Paleis der Academiën, 1988.

Leneman, Leah. "Medical Women at War, 1914-1918." *Medical History,* 38 (1994), 2, pp. 160-177.

Riley, James C. *Sickness, Recovery, and Death: A History and Forecast of Ill Health.* Iowa City: University of Iowa Press, 1989.

Schepers, R.M.J. "Towards Unity and Autonomy: the Belgian Medical Profession in the Nineteenth Century." *Medical History,* 38 (1994), 3, pp. 237-254.

Van Hee, R. *Heelkunde in Vlaanderen door de eeuwen heen. In de voetsporen van Yperman.* Brussels: Gemeentekrediet, 1990.

Vandenbroeke, C., F. Poppel, and A. M. van der Woude. "De zuigelingen-en kindersterfte in België en Nederland in seculair perspectief." *Tijdschrift voor Geschiedenis,* 94 (1981), 3, pp. 461-491.

## 5. *Psychology and Psychiatry*

D'Hoker, Mark. "Contribution de Maurice Rouvroy (1879-1954) aux soins en résidence de la jeunesse à problèmes psycho-sociaux pendant l'entre-deux-guerres." *Paedagogica Historica,* 26 (1990), 2, pp. 211-222.

Liégeois, Axel. "Historiography of Psychiatry in Belgium." *History of Psychiatry,* 2 (1991), 3, pp. 263-270.

Stevelynck, Carine. *Kleine martelaars. Een historisch document over misbruikte kinderen, Kindermishandeling, incest en prostitutie.* Antwerp: Icarus, 1997.

## 6. *Sociology*

Beaupain, T. et al. *50 jaar Arbeidsverhoudingen.* Bruges: Die Keure and Belgische Vereniging voor Arbeidsverhoudingen, 1989.

*Beirne, Piers. "Adolphe Quetelet and the Origins of Positivst Criminology." American Journal of Sociology,* 92 (1987), 5, pp. 1140-1169.

Beknopt overzicht van de sociale zekerheid in België. Brussels: Ministerie van Sociale Zaken, 1997.

Compston, Hugh. "Union Participation in Economc Policy-making in Austria, Switzerland, The Netherlands, Belgium and Ireland, 1970-1992." *West European Politics,* 17 (1994), 1, pp. 123-145.

Corver, C. J. M. and M. Elchardus (eds.). *Sociologisch en antropologisch jaarboek 1989.* Brussel: Tijdschrift voor Sociologie, 1989.

Cousineau, Paige. "The Support Function and Social Change—a Feminist Case History." *Women's Studies International Forum,* 8 (1985), 2, pp. 137-144.

De Bie, Pierre. "Les débuts de la sociologie en Belgique. III. Les sociétés belges de sociologie et le centre interuniversitaire." *Recherches Sociologiques,* 17 (1986), 2, pp. 193-230.

De Gordijnen van Maastricht. *Zestien beschouwingen over de Europese Unie.* Brussels: Masereelfonds, 1993.

De Mayer, Jan. *Arthur Verhaegen. De Rode Baron (1847-1917).* Leuven: Universitaire Pers, 1994. KADOC studies 18.

Deneckere, Gita. *Sire, het volk mort. Sociaal protest in België (1831-1918).* Ghent/Antwerp/Baarn: AMSAB & Hadewijch, 1997.

De Schaepdrijver, Sophie. "Regulated Prostitution in Brussels, 1844-1877: A Policy and its Implementation." *Historical Social Research,* 37 (1986), pp. 89-108.

De Weerdt, Denise. *De dochters van Marianne. 75 jaar SVV.* Ghent/Antwerp: Amsab/Hadewijch, 1997.

Dierickx, Guido (ed.). *Sociologie, politiek, beleid. Verslagboek.* Leuven: Vereniging voor Sociologie, 1988. Reeks van het Tijdschrift voor Sociologie.

Drenthe, Gusta. "The Dutch Women's Thesaurus: a Tool for Cooperation between Women's Collections in the Netherlands and Belgium." *Women's Studies International Forum,* 16 (1993), 4, pp. 437-444.

Dumoulin, André. "L'armée belge en mutation." *Défense Nationale,* 49 (1993), June, pp. 93-105.

Elchardus, Mark and Peter Heyvaert. *Soepel, flexibel en vagebonden. Een vergelijking van twee laat-moderne generaties.* Brussels: VUB-Press, 1990.

Elchardus, Mark et al. *Voorspelbaar ongeluk. Over letsels die werkloosheid nalaat bij mannen en hun kinderen.* Brussels: VUBPRESS, 1996.

Fox, Renée C. *In the Belgian Château. The Spirit and Culture of a European Society in an Age of Change.* Chicago: Ivan R. Dee, 1994.

———*Le Chateau des Belges. Un peuple se retrouve.* Brussels: Duculot, 1997.

Hancke, Bob. "The Crisis of National Unions: Belgian Labor in Decline." *Politics & Society,* 19 (1991), 4, pp. 463-487.

Kurzer, Paulette. "The Internalisation of Business and Domestic Class Compromises: a Four Country Study." *West European Politics,* 14 (1991), 4, pp. 1-24.

Lootens, Ilse and Erik van Hove. *Ruimte maken voor de stad.* Leuven: Garant, 1997.

Luyten, Dirk. *Sociaal-economisch overleg in België sedert 1914.* Brussels: VUBPRESS, 1995.

Luyten, Dirk and Guy Vanthemse (eds.). *Het sociaal pact van 1914. Oorsprong, betekenis en gevolgen.* Brussels: VUBPRESS, 1995.

Oris, Michel. "Contributions migratoires, structures démographiques et mouvements naturels dans les centres urbains traditionnels. L'expérience d'une ville wallonne, Huy, entre 1820 et 1910." *Revue du Nord,* 76(1994), pp. 53-89.

Pacolet, J. et al. *Sociale Zekerheid in een federaal België. Eindverslag van de leden van het Coördinatiecomité van de Vlaamse Onderzoeksgroep Sociale Zekerheid 2002.* Leuven/Amersfoort: ACCO, 1994.

Pieters, Danny. *Federalisme voor onze Sociale Zekerheid. Beleidsconclusies van de Voorzitter van de Vlaamse Onderzoeksgroep Sociale Zekerheid 2002.* Leuven en Amersfoort: ACCO, 1994.

Puissant, Jean. "L'historiographie de la coopération en Belgique." *Belgisch Tijdschrift voor Nieuwste Geschiedenis,* 22(1991), 1-2, pp. 13-30.

———"L'historiographie du mouvement ouvrier." *Revue de l'Université de Bruxelles,* 1981, 1-2, pp. 175-192.

Renson, Roland. "Sport Historiography in Belgium: Status and Perspectives. *Stadion*, 11 (1985), 1, pp. 1-19.

Robert, J. and Bawin-Legros, B. "Le partage des postes: une réelle alternative?" *Recherches Sociologiques,* 16(1985), 1, pp. 39-76.

Stallaerts, R. (ed.). *Financiële participatie.* Leuven: Garant, 1992.

Tulkens, Françoise. *Généalogie de la défense sociale en Belgique (1880-1914). Travaux du séminaire qui s'est tenu a l'Université Catholique de Louvain sous la direction de Michel Foucault.* Brussels: Story-Scientia, 1988.

Turney, High and Harry Holbert. *Chateau-Gérard: The Life and Times of a Walloon Village.* Columbia: University of South Carolina Press, 1953.

Van Hove, Erik and Stefan Nieuwinckel. *Het Bomboek. Het verhaal van de buurtontwikkelingsmaatschappij Noordoost-Antwerpen.* Brussels: Koning Boudewijnstichting, 1997.

Vandermotten, Christian. "Reflexions sur l'amenagement du territoire en Wallonie." *Revue de l'Institut de Sociologie,* 1984, 3-4, pp. 543-566.

*Wat zoudt gij zonder 't werkvolk zijn. Anderhalve eeuw arbeidersstrijd in België. Deel 1 : 1830-1966.* Leuven: Kritak, 1977.

*Wat zoudt gij zonder 't werkvolk zijn. Anderhalve eeuw arbeidersstrijd in België. Deel 2 : 1966-1980.* Leuven: Kritak, 1981.

### *7. Urbanization and Internal Migration*

Castles, Stephen. "The Guest-Worker in Western Europe: An Obituary." *International Migration Review,* 20 (1986), 4, pp. 761-778.

Govaerts, M.P. et al. *Urbanisation et aménagement rural dans le Brabant wallon: le cas de la commune de Grez-Doiceau.* Liège: Commission d'aménagement rural, 1983. Séminaire de Géographie de l'Université de Liège: Travaux de Terrain du 7 septembre 1983, 2.

Grimmeau, J.P. "Analysis of Migration by Age in Belgium 1971-1981." *Revue Belge de Géographie,* 13 (1989), no. 2.

Leboutte, René. "Les migrants en Wallonie, 1846-1930: approche statistique." *Belgisch Tijdschrift voor Nieuwste Geschiedenis,* 21 (1990), 3-4, pp. 303-349.

Morelli, Anne. "Histoire et immigrés ou un million de 'Belges' sans histoire." *Cahiers de Clio,* 70 (1982), pp. 39-46.

Moulaert, Frank. "Economic Crisis and the Employment of Foreign Workers in Belgium." *Studies in Comparative International Development,* 16 (1981), 2, pp. 47-66.

Moulaert, Frank and Philippe Deryckere. "The Employment of Migrant Workers in West-Germany and Belgium: A Comparative Illustration of the Life-cycle of Economic Migration (1960-1980)." *International Migration,* 22 (1984), 3, pp. 178-198.

Norro, Peter. "Accueil et répartition des candidats-réfugiés politiques en Belgique." *Espace, Populations, Sociétés,* 2 (1990), pp. 191-205.

Roosens, Eugeen. "Migrations and Cast Formation in Europe: The Belgian Case." *Ethnic and Racial Studies,* 11 (1988), 2, pp. 207-217.

———"Immigrants in Belgium: The Sociocultural Structure." *Kroeber Anthropological Society Papers,* 65-66 (1986), pp. 15-24.

Wagenaar, Michael. "Conquest of the Center or Flight to the Suburbs? Divergent Metropolitan Strategies in Europe, 1850-1914." *Journal of Urban History,* 19 (1992), 1, pp. 60-83.

*8. Emigration and Belgian Culture Abroad*

Anderson, Freda. "The Tournai Marble Sculptures of the Priory of St. Pancras at Lewes, East Sussex." *Revue Belge d'Archeologie et d'Histoire de l'Art,* 57 (1988), pp. 23-49.

Liedtke, Walter. *Flemish Paintings in America.* Antwerp: Mercatorfonds, 1992.

Magee, J. *The Belgians in Ontario. A History.* Toronto-Reading: Dundurn Press, 1987.

Peters, J. *A Family from Flanders.* London: Collins, 1985.

Stengers, Jean. "Emigration et immigration en Belgique aux XIXe et XXe Siècles." *Cahiers de Clio,* 71 (1982), pp. 7-17.

Vincentelli, M. "The Davies Family and Belgian Refugee Artists and Musicians in Wales." *National Library of Wales Journal,* 22 (1981), 2, pp. 226-233.

## ABOUT THE AUTHOR

Robert Stallaerts was born in Antwerp (Belgium) and had his primary and secondary education there. He took a university degree in moral science at the State University of Ghent (Belgium). At the same university, he defended his doctoral thesis in development economics. For eight years, he has been a researcher at the Center of Ethics of UFSIA (University of Antwerp) and worked in a team on a project called "Ethics and Economics." With contributions to the report on that project, he published a book on financial and other forms of participation in the Belgian economy (*Financiële participatie*. Garant, 1992).

Robert Stallaerts is now a member of the University and the Mercator Hogeschool at Ghent. His main research interests still include the interaction of economics and ethics in economic doctrines and the economics of self-management and participation. His principal contributions are articles on the economics and politics of the former Yugoslavia, e.g., in *Economic Analysis and Workers' Management* (Belgrade), and two books: *Afscheid van Joegoslavië. Achtergronden van de crisis* (Garant, 1992), and a *Historical Dictionary of the Republic of Croatia* (Scarecrow Press, 1995). He also published a collection of Dutch translations of poetry from the peoples of the former Yugoslavia (*Poëzie uit Ex-Joegoslavië*. Kreatief, 1997).